CRISIS LAWYERING

Crisis Lawyering

Effective Legal Advocacy in Emergency Situations

Edited by

Ray Brescia and Eric K. Stern

NEW YORK UNIVERSITY PRESS
New York

NEW YORK UNIVERSITY PRESS
New York
www.nyupress.org

References to Internet websites (URLs) were accurate at the time of writing. Neither the author nor New York University Press is responsible for URLs that may have expired or changed since the manuscript was prepared.

Library of Congress Cataloging-in-Publication Data
Names: Brescia, Ray, editor. | Stern, Eric K., editor.
Title: Crisis lawyering : effective legal advocacy in emergency situations /
edited by Ray Brescia and Eric K. Stern.
Description: New York : New York University Press, [2021] |
Includes bibliographical references and index.
Identifiers: LCCN 2020015045 (print) | LCCN 2020015046 (ebook) | ISBN 9781479801701 (cloth) | ISBN 9781479835218 (paperback) | ISBN 9781479801718 (ebook) | ISBN 9781479801725 (ebook)
Subjects: LCSH: Practice of law—United States. | Emergency management—Law and legislation—United States.
Classification: LCC KF300 .C75 2021 (print) | LCC KF300 (ebook) | DDC 344.7305/34—dc23
LC record available at https://lccn.loc.gov/2020015045
LC ebook record available at https://lccn.loc.gov/2020015046

New York University Press books are printed on acid-free paper, and their binding materials are chosen for strength and durability. We strive to use environmentally responsible suppliers and materials to the greatest extent possible in publishing our books.

Manufactured in the United States of America

10 9 8 7 6 5 4 3 2

Also available as an ebook

Ray Brescia dedicates this work to the late Michael Ratner, a true crisis lawyer, who was a friend and mentor to so many.

Eric K. Stern dedicates it to Cecilia, Adam, Elliott, Steve, and his late father, Harold, for their constant love and support.

CONTENTS

Introduction

Lawyers as Problem-Solvers in Crisis

RAY BRESCIA AND ERIC K. STERN

In the earliest days of Donald Trump's presidency, his administration issued an executive order banning travel to the United States from several predominantly Muslim countries. Almost instantaneously, a small army of lawyers and law students, from some of the nation's most distinguished law firms and most prestigious law schools, fanned out to airports across the United States to fight for individuals they had never met before who were being held nearly incommunicado behind literal, bureaucratic, and legal walls. But those were not the only lawyers active that night. There were also government lawyers in the US Department of Justice, the Department of Homeland Security, and other agencies, lawyers for the airlines, and the lawyer-judges who would rule on the legal challenges. They all had a role to play in crafting legal solutions to the many issues associated with the implementation of the policy, even when at least some, if not all, of them were blindsided by the events as they unfolded. The crisis surrounding the issuance of the travel ban, and the response to it, reveal something at the heart of most contemporary crises: the law and lawyers are often at their center, serving as leaders and advisers within crisis-response teams, addressing and helping to resolve conflict, interpreting the law, and advocating within it. The pervasiveness of law to all aspects of human conduct, reaching all corners of the globe, means that lawyers generally have significant roles to play in the day-to-day affairs of individuals, families, and communities throughout the world. When crises occur, whether it involves a threat to the rule of law, a dramatic and widespread deprivation of human and civil rights, or a global health pandemic, the need for lawyers to step in to assist in the resolution of those crises, and in the crafting of solutions to the problems those crises create, is particularly acute. In this book we explore this phenomenon and attempt to identify and define what it means to engage in the practice of law during crisis situations. It hopes not only to provide guidance to lawyers in such situations but also to help those who deal with crises understand those crises better, so that they may respond more effectively, efficiently, ethically, and creatively. This work strives to make crisis and emergency response better by shining a light on the role of the law and lawyers in helping to resolve crises. It offers insights into an emerging field of legal practice—what we call "crisis lawyering."

Journalist Tom Friedman calls the current period in history the "Age of Accelerations."[1] Crises today come in many shapes and sizes, but the frequency of crises and their intensity are only accelerating. Natural disasters, like hurricanes and tsunamis, seem to be occurring more frequently and their devastating power is increasing. Globalization and the internet have brought the world together, creating opportunities but also generating friction, fostering violence, and inviting cybersecurity breaches. The growing chasm between the wealthy and the poor, exacerbated by a global economy often perceived as increasingly skewed to benefit the rich, means tensions flare between the "haves" and the "have-nots," leading to political protests, a growing populist nativism across the world, and a willingness to retreat into social enclaves that minimize opportunities for communities to come together to solve shared problems, which only makes them worse. Finally, whereas only a few years ago a business leader, elected official, or candidate for office might speak privately to associates or even journalists with few ramifications, today, with the twenty-four-hour news cycle; a social-media environment that thrives on instantaneous, total access; and a mode of communication that enables those leaders and journalists to speak to millions with a tap on a cell phone, crises—some deliberately manufactured—can arise instantaneously and spread like wildfire.

While the frequency and intensity of crises have increased, the sophistication of crisis response has not necessarily grown apace, despite the emergence in recent decades of an interdisciplinary field of crisis management and communication (CMC) striving to enable governments, businesses, and communities to respond more effectively and legitimately to crises. At the same time, and to a certain extent, a vast patchwork of laws has emerged to provide those who engage in crisis response some degree of guidance for dealing with a crisis. Whether it is a multinational organization investigating a claim of sexual harassment against one of its leaders, or a rural town responding to a flash flood, a legal ecosystem for responding to crises has developed. Yet those who must respond to crises, and act within the legal constraints that bind them in such situations, need effective, useful, timely, and creative guidance in how to operate within (and sometimes test the bounds of) this legal ecosystem. Just as there is a growing field of crisis response generally, so too is there a need for guidance for how to operate within the legal ecosystem of crisis response, for both leaders and lawyers alike.

What follows in this volume of essays is an attempt to do just that: to create an understanding of the emerging field of crisis lawyering. It undertakes this task primarily through first-person accounts of lawyers dealing with crisis situations, from the effort to address the travel ban described earlier, to the role that lawyers play in dealing with crises in private practice settings, serving as lawyers within the government, reacting to acute emergency situations like natural disasters, addressing long-term crises like climate change, and working in public interest settings such as nonprofit legal services organizations. Each chapter in this collected volume provides a somewhat unique peek into what it means to serve as a lawyer in crisis situations, which requires significant technical legal capacities and professional judgment. But it also means that lawyers must have leadership skills, communicate effectively, coordinate legal and nonlegal professionals, negotiate with diverse parties with typically diverging interests, address acute humanitarian emergencies, and manage oneself and others through dangerous and sometimes life-threatening situations. This description of an emerging field in the law is what we mean by crisis lawyering, and it is our goal that this volume helps to map the contours and boundaries of this exciting and evolving field.

The nascent legal discipline of crisis lawyering has not received much sustained and focused attention to date but can learn from the multidisciplinary academic and applied fields of crisis management and communication mentioned earlier.[2] While the diversity of the CMC field precludes a simple telling of its history, it can be said that the modern sociological study of natural disasters dates back at least to Samuel Henry Prince's seminal work on the 1917 Halifax explosion *Catastrophe and Social Change*[3] and includes post–World War II political science/political psychological work on cold war foreign policy (e.g. Korea, Berlin, Cuba, and the Middle East in 1973) and other Great Power crises (e.g. July 1914);[4] post-1970s oil crisis work on domestic and international "all hazards crisis management";[5] post Three Mile Island work on risk and crisis communication;[6] post–September 11 work on "homeland security" and "consequence management";[7] behavioral and political economic work on economic crisis and financial turbulence following the financial crises of the 1990s and 2008;[8] management science work on corporate crisis management;[9] public health work on epidemics such as SARS, H1N1, Ebola, and COVID-19;[10] as well as the growing body of work on cybersecurity and crisis leadership generally.[11]

Note that much of this work has—in one way or another—been stimulated and driven by major historical events that tested the mettle of leaders (and their various formal and informal advisers—including, of course, their lawyers), as well as the effectiveness and legitimacy of public-, private-, and nonprofit-sector organizations, and posed substantial symbolic and material threats to citizens and elites alike. While crises (and closely related terminology such as "disaster," "emergency," "catastrophe," "major accident," "critical incident," etc.) are defined in different ways by different researchers and disciplines, scholars interested in crisis decision-making and crisis leadership have defined "crisis" as a situation in which decision makers (and often other actors and stakeholders) perceive threats to (as well as potential opportunities to advance) core values, time pressure, and uncertainty.[12] Such coincidences of these dimensions mean that crisis decision makers must make some of the most critical decisions under the most difficult conditions. This places extraordinary pressure and psychological stress on leaders and their advisers (including lawyers). Again, a robust general finding of the CMC literature is that processes and modes of professional activity that may be of high quality and good practice in normal "steady state" conditions may be highly vulnerable under crisis stress.

Let us look more closely at the literature on crisis leadership, as much of this work is relevant to the parallel and interrelated challenge of crisis lawyering.[13] Several decades of intensive empirical research on crisis management shows that leaders face recurring challenges when confronted with (the prospect of) community (or organizational/national/international) crises. These are: *preparing, sense-making, decision-making, meaning-making, terminating and accounting*, and *learning*. These tasks are as germane to military leaders as they are to their civilian counterparts and are central not only to effective crisis leadership in a particular incident but also to creating better preconditions for future incidents and resilient adaptation to extreme conditions over the longer term. Hannah et al. suggest that different forms of leadership may be needed in different phases of a disaster or crisis.[14] This conceptualization identifies crisis leadership tasks likely to arise across a variety of extreme events and contexts.

Preparing refers to the task of creating preconditions and dispositions that facilitate collaborative effort as well as effective and legitimate intervention when crises occur. Elements of preparing include activities such as organizing, planning, training, and exercising. This generally entails attempting to identify key players and roles likely to be required for effective response and making sure that each role player is capable of enacting that role skillfully and in a fashion conducive to not only particularistic but also collective success.

Sense-making in crisis refers to the challenging task of developing an adequate interpretation of what are often complex, dynamic, and ambiguous situations.[15] This entails developing not only a picture of what is happening but also an understanding of the implications of the situation from one's own vantage point and that of other important stakeholders. As Alberts and Hayes put it: "Sense-making is much more than sharing information and identifying patterns. It goes beyond what is happening and what may happen to what can be done about it."[16]

Decision-making refers to the fact that crises tend to be experienced by leaders (and those who follow them) as a series of "what do we do now" problems triggered by the flow of events. These "decision occasions" emerge simultaneously or in succession over the course of the crisis.[17] Protecting communities tends to require an interdependent series of crucial decisions, to be taken in a timely fashion, under very difficult conditions.

Meaning-making refers to the fact that leaders—civilian and military alike—must attend not only to the operational challenges associated with a contingency but also to the ways in which various stakeholders and constituencies perceive and understand it. Because of the emotional charge associated with disruptive events, followers look to leaders to help them to understand the meaning of what has happened and place it within a broader perspective.

Terminating and accounting refers to the nontrivial task of finding the appropriate timing and means to end the crisis, manage accountability processes, and return to normalcy. Furthermore, attempting to end a crisis prematurely can endanger or alienate constituencies who may still be in harm's way, traumatized, or otherwise emotionally invested in the crisis. Crises may be particularly difficult to terminate if the operational challenges lead to a "crisis after the crisis" in which serious recriminations—resulting in losses of trust and legitimacy—are launched against those who failed to prevent, respond to, or recover effectively from a negative event.

Learning requires an active, critical process that re-creates, analyzes, and evaluates key processes, tactics, techniques, and procedures in order to enhance performance, safety, capability, and the like. The learning process has just begun when a so-called lessons-learned document has been produced. In order to bring the learning process to fruition, change in management/implementation must take place in a fashion that leaves the organization with improved prospects for future success.[18]

CMC (including both crisis leadership and crisis lawyering) should be seen as an "extreme" activity requiring high levels of psychological, organizational, and professional preparedness. Though, as we will see, many legal subdisciplines involve aspects of crisis lawyering, this challenge has thus far not received much attention from legal scholars and practitioners.

Is there something unique about crisis lawyering that calls for particular skills and expertise? Is there a particular approach to a crisis situation that a lawyer should embrace? Is crisis lawyering different from traditional lawyering, and does it require a lawyer to approach his or her work differently, with different considerations in mind? Are all crises different, so there is no single way to approach this type of lawyering? This work attempts to address these and other questions as the contributors—experts in the field who are themselves handling crisis situations—help to define not only the qualities of crisis lawyering but also the strategies and tactics a lawyer can and should utilize when helping a client to navigate through a crisis situation. As we hope the contributions to this volume show, crisis lawyering is in fact different from traditional lawyering and often requires the lawyer to approach his or her work in ways that take into account a level of risk and complexity that often sets it apart from traditional lawyering. Such complexity and risk require not only a different approach but also a creative one that focuses on communication, informational awareness, interdisciplinary strategies, and effective decision-making.

The collection of chapters is organized into four parts that highlight similar themes and address similar questions. In Part I ("Beyond the Familiar and the Imperative of Creativity"), we see lawyers who were thrust into new territory and needed to bring creativity to their work in order to address the crisis at hand. Caroline Bettinger-López (chapter 1) explores what it is like when traditional legal avenues seem foreclosed and a legal advocate must work with her client to pursue new and creative channels for addressing a crisis. Baher Azmy (chapter 2) addresses the role that lawyers played in bringing law to an otherwise lawless place: the detention facility at Guantánamo Bay, Cuba. Christy E. Lopez (chapter 3) examines the role that the US Department of Justice played in addressing the policing crisis in Ferguson, Missouri. David McCraw (chapter 4) writes about his experience in the counsel's office at the *New York Times*, where hostage negotiations and other crises that would not seem to be the bailiwick of a lawyer nevertheless became his responsibilities. Similarly, Lee Wang (chapter 5) explores the role that lawyers played in making changes at the courthouse, where lawyers had to take frontline roles in addressing the crisis facing their clients, even engaging in creative acts of civil disobedience in furtherance of their clients' interests. In a similar vein, Sarah Rogerson (chapter 6) discusses the role that creativity plays in crisis lawyering; in defending her clients from deportation, they had few rights and seemingly few resources. In each of these situations, the contributors describe being put in situations where traditional lawyering practices and approaches did not seem sufficient to address the particular crisis at hand.

In Part II ("Crisis and Systemic Contexts"), we attempt to capture the fact that lawyers must deal with a range of somewhat similar crises, all of which required strategies to deal with systemic and broad issues that created the crisis situation. At the same time, the differing nature of each crisis situation led to different approaches and to lessons learned. John Travis Marshall (chapter 7) explores lawyering tactics used to address the fallout from natural disasters and the role lawyers play in long-term recovery efforts. Also dealing with environmental crises, Eleanor Stein (chapter 8) describes the state of New York's efforts to address one aspect of climate change, which she describes as the "long emergency." Another such emergency was the crisis of homelessness in New York City during the 1980s, and Richard Pinner (chapter 9) describes the legal strategies deployed to address that crisis. Around the theme of economic inequality, Carmen Huertas-Noble, Missy Risser-Lovings, and Christopher Adams (chapter 10) discuss their efforts in addressing economic and political inequality by helping their clients form a low-income, worker-owned cooperative. Unlike natural disasters, or slowly unfolding disasters like climate change or rising economic inequality, David Turetsky (chapter 11) describes his work as an election lawyer, when the lawyer knows precisely the day on which the "crisis" will occur.

Part III ("Beyond Borders and Silos") brings an international focus to this volume. Brian Wilson and Nora Johnson (chapter 12) explore the role of lawyers cooperating in international crises and set forth best practices and competencies for doing so. In a similar vein, volume coeditor Eric K. Stern, Brad Kieserman, Torkel Schlegel, Per-Åke Mårtensson, and Ella Carlberg (chapter 13) describe the lessons they learned training Swedish crisis-response lawyers and how their approach to crisis lawyering generally was similar to, and in some respects different from, the approach that has been developed in the context of domestic crisis response in disasters involving the Federal Emergency Management Agency in the United States.

Following on the theme of educating lawyers for crisis response, in Part IV ("Educating and Skill-Building") Muneer Ahmad and Michael J. Wishnie (chapter 14) describe their work training students at Yale Law School during several crises, including the emergency response to the Trump administration's travel ban. Similarly, Scott Westfahl (chapter 15) describes his work training lawyers to become leaders in crisis situations. Jay Sullivan (chapter 16), a lawyer and expert in crisis situations, also shares key lessons on how to communicate effectively in crisis situations.

In the conclusion we attempt to capture some of the key questions and cross-cutting themes of the essays. In the chapters throughout this volume, readers will see that several critical questions emerge in the field of crisis lawyering, including the following:

- How do lawyers define a crisis situation in their work, and does this vary depending on the context?

- Who is the client in crisis lawyering?
- What are the potential conflicts of interest that emerge during crisis lawyering that may not arise in traditional advocacy settings?
- Are the ethical rules governing lawyer conduct and standards of care (diligence) relaxed in crisis situations?
- How do lawyers ensure effective lines of communication in crisis situations?
- What expertise must a crisis lawyer possess in a given crisis situation?
- How do crisis lawyers interact with leaders and other constituencies in crisis situations?
- How do crisis lawyers interact with other professionals and disciplines in crisis situations?
- Are there common guiding principles for crisis lawyering that emerge from these contributions?
- Can anyone plan, prepare, and train for crisis lawyering?

While on its own each chapter addresses many, if not all, of these questions, the conclusion attempts to highlight and surface the ways that, taken together, the chapters help us to understand the contours of the emerging field of crisis lawyering, using these questions as the prompts that help us define this area of practice.

In the end, this book is aimed at two kinds of lawyers (and lawyers to be): those having or seeking highly specialized and crisis-prone practices who will see crises and near crises on a relatively frequent basis; and those who may see them rarely—if at all—during their careers. In either case, cultivating an understanding of the art and science of crisis lawyering will be helpful. In the former case, this volume will help provide a conceptual framework, vocabulary, good practices, and professional benchmarks for thinking about how to be a better crisis lawyer. In the latter case, reflection on the rigors and ethical challenges of crisis lawyering is a kind of insurance policy to be salted away in the memory palace for a future rainy day and offers a chance to explore contexts in which professional challenges and dilemmas arise in more traditional forms of lawyering in particularly dramatic and vivid form.

As was recognized long ago in ancient Chinese thought and reflected in Chinese characters, crises bring both dangers and opportunities. Minimizing the dangers (and damages) and capitalizing on the opportunities inherent in crisis situations require not only the effective enactment of professional roles and application of general knowledge and skills by lawyers and others but also a broader understanding of the nature of crises and the legal, ethical, and practical challenges associated with crisis management. They require both a professional and personal capacity to cope with the highly demanding, and often emotionally loaded, tasks and contexts associated with crisis lawyering. This volume and the stories of our contributors provide a rare, and perhaps at times even frightening, window into this world. As the proverb says: "Forewarned is forearmed."

NOTES

1 THOMAS FRIEDMAN, THANK YOU FOR BEING LATE: AN OPTIMIST'S GUIDE TO THRIVING IN THE AGE OF ACCELERATIONS 3–5 (2016).

2 Some recent research has begun to address some aspects of lawyering in disaster and crisis situations. *See, e.g.,* Peter Margulies, *Legal Dilemmas Facing White House Counsel in the Trump Administration: The Costs of Public Disclosure of FISA Requests,* 87 FORDHAM L. REV. 1913 (2019) (describing what author calls "lifeboat lawyering," which involves serving as a limited check on potentially illegal activity within an institution); *see also* a recent symposium on national security lawyering in crisis situations in volume 31 of the *Georgetown Journal of Legal Ethics* in 2018.

3 SAMUEL HENRY PRINCE, CATASTROPHE AND SOCIAL CHANGE, BASED ON A SOCIOLOGICAL STUDY OF THE HALIFAX DISASTER 212 (1920).

4 Charles F. Herman, *Some Consequences of Crisis Which Limit the Viability of Organizations,* 8 ADMIN. SCI. Q. 61, 61–82 (1963); Alexander L. George, *Avoiding War: Problems of Crisis Management* (Alexander L. George & Yaacov Bar-Siman-Tov eds., 1st ed. 1991).

5 COPING WITH CRISIS: THE MANAGEMENT OF DISASTERS, RIOTS AND TERRORISM (Uriel Rosenthal et al. eds., 1989); MANAGING CRISES: THREATS, DILEMMAS, OPPORTUNITIES 5–27 (Uriel Rosenthal et al. eds., 2001); MEGA-CRISES: UNDERSTANDING THE PROSPECTS, NATURE, CHARACTERISTICS, AND THE EFFECTS OF CATACLYSMIC EVENTS (Ira Helsloot et al. eds., 2012).

6 MICHAEL REGESTER & JUDY LARKIN, RISK ISSUES AND CRISIS MANAGEMENT IN PUBLIC RELATIONS: A CASEBOOK OF BEST PRACTICE (4th ed. 2008); ROBERT R. ULMER ET AL., EFFECTIVE CRISIS COMMUNICATION: MOVING FROM CRISES TO OPPORTUNITY (4th ed. 2017); Eva-Karin Olsson, *Crisis Communication in Public Organisations: Dimensions of Crisis Communication Revisited,* 22 J. OF CONTINGENCIES AND CRISIS MGMT. 113, 113–25 (2014).

7 DAVID KAMIEN, MCGRAW-HILL HOMELAND SECURITY HANDBOOK: THE DEFINITIVE GUIDE FOR LAW ENFORCEMENT, EMT, AND ALL OTHER SECURITY PROFESSIONALS (2nd ed. 2012); James M. Kendra and Tricia Wachtendorf, *Elements of Resilience in the World Trade Center Disaster: Reconstituting New York City's Emergency Operations Centre,* 27 DISASTERS 37, 37–53 (2003).

8 *See, e.g.,* ANDREW ROSS SORKIN, TOO BIG TO FAIL: THE INSIDE STORY OF HOW WALL STREET AND WASHINGTON FOUGHT TO SAVE THE FINANCIAL SYSTEM—AND THEMSELVES (2009).

9 IAN I. MITROFF & CHRISTINE M. PEARSON, CRISIS MANAGEMENT: A DIAGNOSTIC GUIDE FOR IMPROVING YOUR ORGANIZATION'S CRISIS-PREPAREDNESS (Jossey Bass Bus. and Mgmt. Ser. 1993).

10 *See, e.g.,* Eric K. Noji, *The Global Resurgence of Infectious Disease,* 9 J. OF CONTINGENCIES AND CRISIS MGMT. 223 no. 4 (2001); SARS FROM EAST TO WEST (Eva-Karin Olsson & Lan Xue eds., 2011); DONATO GRECO ET AL., STOCKHOLM: ECDC, REVIEW OF ECDC'S RESPONSE TO THE INFLUENZA PANDEMIC 2009–2010 (2011).

11 ARJEN BOIN ET AL., THE POLITICS OF CRISIS MANAGEMENT: PUBLIC LEADERSHIP UNDER PRESSURE (2nd ed. 2016); *see also* Leonard J. Marcus et al., *Meta-leadership and National Emergency Preparedness: A Model to Build Government Connectivity,* 4 BIOSECURITY AND BIOTERRORISM: BIODEFENSE, STRATEGY, PRACTICE, AND SCIENCE 128 (2006); Sean T. Hannah et al., *A Framework for Examining Leadership in Extreme Contexts,* 20 LEADERSHIP QUARTERLY 897 (2009).

12 COPING WITH CRISIS (Uriel Rosenthal et al. eds., 1989); BOIN ET AL., THE POLITICS OF CRISIS MANAGEMENT.

13 Eric Stern, *Preparing: The Sixth Task of Crisis Leadership,* 7 J. OF LEADERSHIP STUD. 51 (2013); Eric Stern, *Crisis, Leadership, and Extreme Contexts,* in LEADERSHIP IN EXTREME SITUATIONS 41 (M. Holenweger et al. eds., 2017).

14 Hannah et al., *A Framework,* 902; *see also* Marcus et al., *Meta-leadership* 128.

15 K. E. Weick, *Enacted Sensemaking in Crisis Situations,* 25 J. OF MGMT. STUD. 305 (1988); Eric Stern, *From Warning to Sense-Making: Understanding, Identifying and Responding to Strategic Crises,* in THE CHANGING FACE OF STRATEGIC CRISIS MANAGEMENT (Org. for Econ. Co-operation Dev. 2015).

16 DAVID S. ALBERTS & RICHARD E. HAYES, POWER TO THE EDGE: COMMAND AND CONTROL IN THE INFORMATION AGE 102 (Info. Age Transformation Ser. 2003).

17 ERIC STERN, STOCKHOLM UNIV., CRISIS DECISIONMAKING: A COGNITIVE-INSTITUTIONAL APPROACH (1999). Eric Stern et al., *Post-Modern Crisis Analysis: Dissecting the London Bombings of July 2005,* 1 J. OF ORGANIZATIONAL EFFECTIVENESS: PEOPLE AND PERFORMANCE 402 (2014).

18 BOIN ET AL., THE POLITICS OF CRISIS MANAGEMENT; Eric Stern, *Crisis and Learning: A Conceptual Balance Sheet,* 5 J. OF CONTINGENCIES AND CRISIS MGMT. 69 (1997).

PART I

Beyond the Familiar and the Imperative of Creativity

1

A Client's Crisis Becomes a Legal Crisis

A Domestic Violence Ruling Goes Global

CAROLINE BETTINGER-LÓPEZ

Crisis lawyering is often associated with legal advocacy in the face of a natural disaster or an abrupt change in circumstances from the status quo. This is a story of a different kind of crisis lawyering: the story of a domestic violence tragedy that culminated in a personal crisis for the individual victim and a legal crisis for the advocacy community that supported her and supported the cause that her case represented—a cause that had taken decades to build. It is also the story of how legal institutions have repeatedly failed to deal effectively with domestic violence, a societal crisis that is ubiquitous and yet often viewed as outside the purview of the state.

Introduction

In 2005, the United States Supreme Court issued a vexing decision in *Castle Rock v. Gonzales*,[1] finding that a domestic violence victim had no property interest in the enforcement of her restraining order and that the police therefore had no constitutional duty to enforce the order under the Fourteenth Amendment. The case involved a tragic set of facts: six years earlier, Jessica Gonzales's three daughters were killed after being abducted by their father, in violation of a domestic violence restraining order. Gonzales repeatedly called the police for help and showed them a restraining order against her estranged husband, but the police disregarded her entreaties and did virtually nothing. The Supreme Court's *Castle Rock* decision precipitated a legal crisis in the women's and anti–gender violence community. Advocates feared it would send a signal to police officers that restraining orders and mandatory arrest laws—which had been enacted in more than thirty states during the 1980s and 1990s specifically in response to police inaction in the domestic violence context—need not be enforced. The decision also precipitated a personal crisis for Jessica Gonzales, who stood in disbelief upon realizing that her country's legal system provided no avenue for relief or a remedy for the grave harms she and her daughters suffered.

Gonzales demanded that action be taken to reverse the effects of the Supreme Court's decision. She assembled a new legal team (which included myself) that, working closely alongside our client, decided to shift tactics and fora. We ultimately filed the first international human rights case against the US government on behalf of a domestic violence victim. In August 2011, the Inter-American Commission on Human Rights (IACHR) issued a landmark decision, *Lenahan v. United States*, which found that the US government was responsible for human rights violations against Jessica Gonzales (who subsequently remarried and changed her last name to Lenahan) and her three deceased children. The case made international headlines and has been cited in judicial decisions and legislation around the world.[2]

In this chapter, I explore the strategy decisions that went into pursuing the case at the IACHR and my assessment of the outcome/results from those decisions. I will also discuss a new project I have undertaken, the Community Oriented and United Responses to Address Gender Violence and Equality (COURAGE) in Policing Project, as an outgrowth of *Lenahan v. United States*. Finally, I will explore the ways in which these issues play out today as the election of President Donald Trump, coupled with the rise of the #MeToo movement, have put these crises in sharp relief, particularly for domestic violence survivors who are women of color, immigrant women, and LGBTQI individuals.

Jessica Lenahan (Gonzales)'s Personal Tragedy and Prolonged Legal Battle

The story starts in 1999, when Jessica Gonzales's three young daughters—Rebecca, Katheryn, and Leslie Gonzales—were abducted on June 22 in Castle Rock, Colorado, by her abusive estranged husband (and the girls' father), Simon Gonzales, in violation of the terms of a judicial restraining order that, as part of a divorce proceeding, strictly limited his access to them.[3] Colorado, like most states, had a "mandatory arrest" law in 1999 stating that "[a] peace officer shall use every reasonable means to enforce a restraining order" and attempt to arrest the restrained person upon finding probable cause of a violation. In the months leading up to the abduction, Jessica—a Latina and Native American woman who had worked as a janitor at, among other places, the Castle Rock Police Department (CRPD)—called the police repeatedly to report Simon breaking into her house and threatening her and the children. During this time period, Simon had at least seven run-ins with the police: among other things, he was ticketed for "road rage" while the girls were in the truck and for trespassing in a private section of the Castle Rock police station and then trying to flee after officers served him with the restraining order. The Castle Rock Police Department was certainly on notice of Simon Gonzales's erratic and threatening behavior.

On June 22, after she discovered the girls were missing, Jessica Gonzales repeatedly called the CRPD, reporting she feared for her daughters' safety. The police repeatedly told her to wait for the return of her daughters, to call back later, or to wait for further police action that never materialized. When she was able to identify their location at Elitch Gardens, an amusement park in Denver, the CRPD said that it was outside their jurisdiction and that there was nothing they could do. Later in the evening, the police dispatcher who took her call chided her for being "a little ridiculous," a sentiment subsequently echoed by the town's police chief during an interview on a *60 Minutes* television program. Jessica Gonzales was sent home when she showed up at the CRPD near midnight. At 3:30 A.M., nearly ten hours after the abduction, Simon Gonzales, armed with a semiautomatic handgun purchased that evening, drove his truck to the CRPD and, standing beside his truck, opened fire at the police station. The police shot him dead and subsequently discovered the bodies of the three deceased children inside his bullet-ridden truck. Colorado authorities investigated the CRPD's use of lethal force against Simon Gonzales but never conducted an investigation that squarely focused on the children's deaths, resulting in uncertainty to this day about when, where, and how the children died.[4] As described below, the state's failure to investigate precipitated an added personal crisis for Jessica Gonzales involving her fundamental right to know the truth about the circumstances surrounding her daughters' deaths.

The Gonzales tragedy made nationwide headlines, but most stories focused on the family dynamics, not the police department's response or responsibility. One local newspaper headline following the tragedy read: "Man Dies in Shootout; Daughters Found Dead; Family Was Troubled, Friends Say." As Jessica's legal team later argued, these headlines reflected profound institutional and societal biases against domestic violence victims, the vast majority of whom are women. Why not focus instead on the profound failure of the justice system to protect this family?

Jessica Gonzales scoured the Yellow Pages to find an attorney, but no one wanted to touch the police. Finally, she found a commercial litigator, with no civil rights background, who took her case on a contingency-fee basis. She filed a lawsuit in federal district court in Colorado against the town of Castle Rock and three of its police officers under the federal civil rights statute, 42 U.S.C. §1983, alleging violations of the Fourteenth Amendment's guarantee of due process of law. She argued that Castle Rock's duty to enforce the restraining order against her estranged husband created a property interest under Colorado law and that she was entitled, at the very least, to the town's reasoned consideration and an explanation for its inaction (i.e., a fair procedure) as a matter of *procedural due process* (PDP). She also argued that the police violated her and her children's *substantive due process* (SDP) rights when they failed to take reasonable steps to protect her children from the real and immediate risk posed by their father, whom the state itself had identified as a threat to them when it issued the restraining order.

On the government's motion, before even reaching the discovery phase of litigation, the district court dismissed both claims. On appeal, a panel of the Tenth Circuit Court of Appeals affirmed the district court's dismissal of the SDP claim but reversed the district court's ruling that Gonzales had failed to state a PDP claim.[5] On rehearing *en banc*, the Tenth Circuit reached the same conclusion but ruled that the individual police officers were entitled to a defense of qualified immunity.

In rejecting the SDP claim, the Tenth Circuit relied on *DeShaney v. Winnebago Cty Dep't of Soc. Serv.*, 489 U.S. 189 (1989), which holds that the substantive guarantees of the Fourteenth Amendment's Due Process Clause do not generally require the government to protect an individual from third-party acts of violence, absent the rare circumstances when state actors either created or exacerbated the danger faced by an individual. Castle Rock appealed, and the Supreme Court granted certiorari on the PDP claim.

The Supreme Court's decision to hear *Castle Rock* worried many women's and civil rights advocates in the United States. The Court rarely took on cases concerning private acts of violence—and when it did, it usually ruled against the victim. *DeShaney*, described above, involved the failure of child protective services to respond to calls from a mother expressing concern over potential abuse of her son Joshua by his father. Ultimately, the father inflicted grave injury upon Joshua. The Supreme Court found that "[w]hile the State may have been aware of the dangers that Joshua faced in the free world, it played no part in their creation, nor did it do anything to render him any more vulnerable to them" (*DeShaney*, 489 U.S. at 201). The Court found that the state of Wisconsin was immune from liability under the Due Process Clause because it had merely acquiesced in—but not contributed to—the victim's danger. Justice Blackmun issued a famous dissent:

> Poor Joshua! Victim of repeated attacks by an irresponsible, bullying, cowardly, and intemperate father, and abandoned by respondents who placed him in a dangerous predicament and who knew or learned what was going on, and yet did essentially nothing except, as the Court revealingly observes . . . "dutifully recorded these incidents in [their] files." It is a sad commentary upon American life, and constitutional principles–so full of late of patriotic fervor and

proud proclamations about "liberty and justice for all"–that this child, Joshua DeShaney, now is assigned to live out the remainder of his life profoundly re-tarded. Joshua and his mother, as petitioners here, deserve–but now are denied by this Court–the opportunity to have the facts of their case considered in the light of the constitutional protection that 42 U.S.C. § 1983 is meant to provide.

A decade later, in *United States v. Morrison*, 529 U.S. 598 (2000), the Court struck down as unconstitutional a private right of action for victims of gender-motivated crimes, such as domestic and sexual violence, against their abusers. Congress had created this private right of action under the 1994 Violence Against Women Act, in light of a massive effort in the 1990s to rec-ognize domestic violence as a civil rights violation that was of "national," and not merely "local," import.

Given this precedent, advocates worried that *Castle Rock* would become the third case in a trilogy of bad case law concerning private acts of violence impacting women and children. After a series of strategic planning calls with leading antiviolence, women's rights, children's rights, and civil/human rights organizations, among others, the ACLU Women's Rights Project (WRP) offered to coordinate an amicus brief effort and assist with developing a communica-tions strategy. As a young attorney at ACLU WRP, I coordinated this effort.

Ultimately, more than 110 organizations and individuals filed nine amicus briefs in support of Jessica Gonzales. These included briefs from domestic vio-lence advocacy organizations about the history of domestic violence restraining orders and mandatory arrest laws; a brief from policing organizations on good practices in police response to domestic violence; a brief from international law scholars offering a human rights analysis of the case; briefs focusing on the children's rights and elders' rights dimensions of the case; and briefs offering a deeper legal analysis of the constitutional issues raised in the case.[6]

The case made national headlines and was featured on *60 Minutes*, *Good Morning America*, *Nancy Grace*, and many other shows. To the shock of many, Castle Rock police chief Tony Lane pushed back on any notion of wrongdo-ing and, displaying a profound misunderstanding of the dynamics of family violence, remarked on *60 Minutes* that no one has a crystal ball and even asked "[W]hat safer place could children be than with one of their parents, the mother or the father?" While the American public easily understood and supported Jessica Gonzales's basic plea—that her "restraining order should be worth the piece of paper it's printed on"—her lawyer's efforts to persuade the Supreme Court proved far more daunting.

Castle Rock was one of the last decisions that the Supreme Court an-nounced during that term. As Justice Scalia began to read the opinion of the

Court on June 27, 2005, he quipped: "I thought Castle Rock was a 1920s dance but it is also a Town in Colorado."[7] The decision that Justice Scalia proceeded to read brought Jessica Gonzales's personal crisis to a distinctly new level—and precipitated the next legal crisis for our movement.

Writing for a 7-2 majority, Justice Scalia reversed the Tenth Circuit's *en banc* decision and held that Gonzales had no personal entitlement under the Due Process Clause to police enforcement of her restraining order.[8] Despite the Colorado legislature's repeated use of the word "shall" in the mandatory arrest law, the Court explained: "We do not believe that these protections of Colorado law truly made enforcement of restraining orders mandatory." It was also unclear, the Court thought, whether the preprinted notice on the back of the restraining order required the police to arrest Simon Gonzales or enforce the order—further evidence of police discretion over enforcement. The Court also challenged the presumption that the statute was intended to give victims "a personal entitlement to something as vague and novel as enforcement of restraining orders," rather than simply protect the public interest in punishing criminal behavior. Finally, the Court reasoned that, even assuming Jessica Gonzales had overcome these obstacles, "it is by no means clear that an individual entitlement to enforcement of a restraining order could constitute a 'property' interest for purposes of the Due Process Clause." The Court concluded that third-party benefits from having someone else arrested for a crime are a matter of state common-law or statutory tort claims—not the Fourteenth Amendment's Due Process Clause.

In dissent, Justice Stevens, joined by Justice Ginsburg, chided the majority for ignoring the clear language and intent of the Colorado statute, which, like other domestic violence mandatory arrest statutes nationwide, was passed in response to a persistent pattern of nonenforcement of domestic violence laws. The express language of the statute, they asserted, was "unmistakabl[y]" intended to remove police discretion over whether to arrest perpetrators. "[T]he crucial point," the dissent argued, "is that, under the statute, the police were required to provide enforcement; they lacked the discretion to do nothing." The statute's mandate, the dissent concluded, "undeniably create[d] an entitlement to police enforcement of restraining orders." The entitlement to have the restrained person arrested was clearly for the benefit of recipients of restraining orders—not for the benefit of the community at large as the majority had improperly concluded in its overly formalistic analysis. The entitlement to police protection, Justices Stevens and Ginsburg found, was akin to entitlements to other government services that constituted "concrete" and "valuable" property under the Due Process Clause, such as public education and utility services.

A Legal Crisis and a Personal Crisis

The Supreme Court's ruling precipitated a personal crisis for Jessica Lenahan. The Court's decision, which arose from a Fed. R. Civ. P. 12(b)(6) motion to dismiss, abruptly ended the case, denying Jessica (still going by her married name Gonzales) the opportunity to engage in a meaningful discovery process. She never had the opportunity to collect evidence from Castle Rock, depose witnesses, or present evidence at trial. And no state court avenues were available to her because of the impossibly high threshold for overcoming the blanket of immunity extended to governmental actors under Colorado law. Gonzales stood in disbelief that she had no legal means to hold the individual officers and the CRPD accountable for grave missteps that profoundly changed the course of her life. Adding to her crisis of confidence in the US legal system was her own personal financial crisis: in the wake of the tragedy, the primary source of family income and benefits (Simon Gonzales) was gone, and a woman who had offered Jessica Gonzales support ultimately swindled her savings and destroyed her credit.

Additionally, and crucially for Jessica Gonzales, the Court's ruling meant that she might never uncover information pertaining to the circumstances surrounding her daughters' deaths. Nearly everyone in the case—even Gonzales's attorney—had summarily concluded that the children had undoubtedly been killed by their father. Indeed, Simon Gonzales had purchased a gun that evening from a private seller, thereby sidestepping the federal background checks that should have prevented him from making such a purchase (due to the existence of the restraining order). Jessica Gonzales and her family, without challenging this conclusion, wanted definitive answers as to whether any of the police bullets that peppered Simon Gonzales's truck entered the girls' bodies. Despite extensive forensic analyses and autopsies of the girls that were performed, no definitive investigation ever matched the bullet holes in her daughters' bodies with a specific gun. These forensic questions haunt her to this day.

The Supreme Court's ruling in *Castle Rock* also precipitated a legal and policy crisis in the women's and anti–gender violence community. Legal experts expressed outrage that the Supreme Court would characterize a domestic violence victim's entitlement to enforcement of her restraining order as "vague and novel," considering the prevalence of legal protections for victims in the United States, and the express language of—and clear legislative history behind—mandatory arrest laws, including in Colorado. Advocates feared that, after decades of (often successful) efforts to get law enforcement to take domestic violence seriously, the *Castle Rock* decision would send a signal to the police that they need not enforce restraining orders and would nourish an all-too-prevalent US culture of impunity for lazy, rogue, or misguided officers.

Meetings were scheduled to discuss legislative, litigation, and public policy strategies, as well as plans for engagement with state and local officials about *Castle Rock*'s implications. It was a critical moment for advocates to discuss how to best respond to the unmistakable message that the general public might take away from the case: that domestic violence restraining orders were not worth the paper they were printed on.

However, advocates generally agreed that, legally speaking, *Castle Rock* marked the end of the line for Jessica Gonzales. After a Supreme Court decision rejecting her claims, what other remedy could she have? I remember calling Jessica Lenahan (formerly Gonzales—though I will hereinafter refer to her by her remarried name, Lenahan) and her mother, Tina Rivera, to discuss the Supreme Court's devastating decision. While expressing profound disappointment, they quickly shifted their gaze forward. "What's next?" they asked. I remember being shocked that this family, who had already been through the unimaginable, had the fortitude and resilience to even imagine a "next." I also had great anxiety about how I would break it to them that we had reached the end of the line in terms of legal recourse. When I began to say, with my US lawyer hat on, "There is no 'next'; we've exhausted all remedies," Lenahan responded, "Of course there is—everyone's got a boss! We can't just let this rest!"

Jessica Lenahan and Tina Rivera's persistence and vision ultimately spurred an inflection point in the case. They pushed me and the rest of the ACLU team (which at the time included the Human Rights Program's senior staff attorney, Steven Watt; and the Women's Rights Project's director, Lenora Lapidus, and deputy director, Emily Martin) to put our thinking caps on and, ultimately, to look to international human rights law as a potential site of justice. Although one amicus brief in the case had considered the chasm between international human rights law and US constitutional law, I had never seriously considered bringing this quintessentially constitutional civil rights case before the international community.

Below I further describe how and why our team brought Lenahan's case to the Inter-American Commission on Human Rights. I will briefly note here that doing so marked a profound moment for me as a young lawyer in two respects: first, *Lenahan v. United States of America* (the case we filed before the IACHR) represented a real-life example of how human rights strategies could be employed as a last resort when domestic legal systems fail—even in the United States. This was a cornerstone principle of the "Bringing Human Rights Home" (BHRH) movement that was largely incubated in Columbia

Law School's Human Rights Institute during my time as a law student there, and especially following September 11, 2001. The BHRH movement, supported by a network of more than 800 US lawyers (including legal aid, civil rights, and human rights attorneys), encourages US compliance with international human rights law and the development of strategies to use human rights law in federal courts and domestic policy-making and debate.

Second, the *Lenahan* case taught me one of the most important lessons in my life, a point I emphasize to law students and lawyers: listen to your clients. They generally know better than anyone what's best for themselves, and they can make critical contributions to legal or advocacy strategies and challenge lawyers to think outside the box. The innovative lawyering approach that my ACLU colleagues and I employed was available only because of our client's demands and the space we made available to her (through many long phone calls and email correspondence) to articulate them to us.

International Human Rights Law: A Potential Avenue for Relief?

In fact, a little-known but promising legal avenue was available to Jessica Lenahan. The Washington, DC–based Inter-American Commission on Human Rights is an autonomous organ of the Organization of American States (OAS) created in 1959 "to promote the observance and defense of human rights" in OAS Member States, which include all thirty-five countries in North, South, and Central America and the Caribbean. Composed of seven independent human rights experts, the Inter-American Commission, along with the Inter-American Court of Human Rights (a panel of seven judges based in San José, Costa Rica), considers claims of human rights violations and issues written decisions on state responsibility. The IACHR and the court, which together form the "Inter-American system" for human rights, are largely unfamiliar to US lawyers and advocates. In other parts of the Western Hemisphere, however, civil society and lawyers regularly use the system to hold governments accountable for corruption, abuse, negligence, and violence committed by state actors as well as private individuals. Having exhausted her domestic remedies, Lenahan could petition the IACHR for relief, claiming that the United States was responsible for human rights violations resulting from the CRPD's inaction and the Supreme Court's decision.

Because the US government has not ratified any Inter-American human rights treaties, human rights complaints against the United States are brought before the Commission under the American Declaration on the Rights and Duties of Man and the OAS Charter. Unlike contemporary human rights treaties, the American Declaration, drafted in 1948, does not contain a "general obligations" clause that requires states to respect, ensure, and promote guaranteed rights and freedoms through the adoption of appropriate or necessary measures. However, signatories to the OAS Charter (including the United States) are legally bound by the American Declaration's provisions, and the Commission has consistently applied "general obligations" principles when interpreting the wide spectrum of rights set forth in the American Declaration. Moreover, Inter-American jurisprudence directs governments to provide special protections to particularly vulnerable groups such as children, the mentally ill, undocumented migrant workers, indigenous communities, and domestic violence victims.

The IACHR is a victim-friendly forum that has produced groundbreaking human rights reports and recommendations and has made a significant impact in regard to on-the-ground change in many countries. When an aggrieved individual has exhausted her domestic legal remedies or has nowhere to turn for relief in her home country, she may submit a human rights petition to the IACHR. Ultimately, the Commission may hold hearings and issue a "merits decision" that analyzes the facts in light of international human rights law and include recommendations to the state. Although no enforcement mechanism exists to ensure state compliance with Commission decisions, these reports do carry significant moral and political weight and contribute to international standard-setting.

As I have discussed in my previous scholarship, *Castle Rock* had all the markings of a good IACHR test case: a horrific set of facts, a widely criticized US Supreme Court decision, an international human rights standard (described below) that directly conflicted with domestic precedent, a community of advocates and supporters asking "What can we do?," and a petitioner who would not rest until justice was done. Alongside our client, the legal team weighed the possibilities and limitations of the IACHR as a forum for providing Lenahan her day in court and for establishing international jurisprudence that directly contravened *DeShaney*.

But the Inter-American system had its drawbacks. The Commission is underfunded and prone to prolonged delays in its decision-making. The chances of getting a hearing at the IACHR are slim and unpredictable, and cases can drag on for years. Moreover, the US government, having declined to ratify the American Convention on Human Rights, routinely opposes IACHR cases brought against it on jurisdictional grounds. Although the Commission is an important institution in many parts of the Americas, its lack of recognition in the United States, coupled with enforcement limitations, make it a far less desirable avenue than a US court for pronouncing rights violations and providing remedies, in the eyes of many US advocates.

When Jessica Lenahan learned of the Inter-American human rights system, she was hopeful that framing her case as a human rights violation could give her a forum to seek redress for her personal tragedy and initiate important legislative and policy reforms in the United States. Yet she and her lawyers, including myself, were wary of a system that has weaker "teeth" and far less credibility in the United States compared to a federal court.

After I painstakingly presented these pros and cons to Lenahan, she chose to move forward. She was inspired by the transnational nature of the IACHR, thought it could shame the United States into doing right by her and future victims, and felt that no other viable options were available. In 2005, my ACLU colleagues and I filed *Lenahan v. United States* before the IACHR, alleging violations of the American Declaration by the CRPD and the US courts.[9] The petition shined a light on how out of touch the Supreme Court's decisions in *Castle Rock, DeShaney,* and *Morrison* were. We sought to reframe domestic violence from a "private matter"—as depicted by that newspaper headline—and instead frame it as a societal epidemic that demands responsiveness from government—local, state, and federal. We highlighted the gulf between *DeShaney* and the doctrine of affirmative obligations under international human rights law, which requires states to exercise "due diligence" and protect individuals known to be at risk from private or state-sponsored acts of violence.

Jessica Lenahan testified three times before the IACHR—an opportunity that was denied to her in the federal district court proceedings. She, her son Jessie, and her mother Tina submitted declarations that finally told the world their full version of their story.[10] More than seventy individuals and organizations submitted eight amicus briefs and two expert reports to the IACHR in support of Jessica Lenahan. Her case also caught the attention of other international human rights bodies, including the United Nations Human Rights Committee, the United Nations Committee on the Elimination of Racial Discrimination, and the United Nations Special Rapporteur on Violence Against Women.

In 2011, the IACHR issued a landmark decision, finding the United States responsible for human rights violations against Lenahan and her children, specifically the rights to life, nondiscrimination, due process, and special protections for children. The Commission found grave failures to protect the children's lives and underscored that, when the government fails to protect women from domestic violence, it is a form of sex discrimination because domestic violence disproportionately affects women.

The IACHR concluded its decision with several recommendations to the United States. On the individual front, the Commission recommended that

Jessica receive compensation and a thorough investigation into the policing failures in her case—a subject of recent heated conversations I have had with Colorado authorities. On the policy front, the Commission recommended that the US government improve its enforcement of restraining orders and "adopt public policies aimed at shattering stereotypes of domestic violence victims."[11]

Lenahan v. United States made history. It was the first time that an international tribunal found the United States responsible for human rights violations against a domestic violence victim. It created new channels for diplomatic and political pressure on the US State Department, and for dialogue with the US Department of Justice (DOJ) about implementing the Commission's recommendations. In the years since, the *Lenahan* case has been cited in international and domestic case law and legislation throughout the world. It left Jessica Lenahan with a profound sense of vindication and pride even though she simultaneously remained uncertain as to the tangible results she would get from it all.

How Human Rights Strategies Can Make a Difference

The legal and personal crises precipitated by the CRPD's inaction and the Supreme Court's decision prompted Lenahan's legal team to pursue a shift in tactics and forum. As described above, the Inter-American system was a promising, albeit limited, venue for Lenahan. However, not every case is the right fit for review by the IACHR. So, when is the "right time" to look to international human rights law as a tool to supplement domestic-facing social justice struggles—particularly those in the United States?

In my previous scholarship,[12] I have identified five factors to consider when evaluating the potential efficacy of any given human rights-based approach— that is, why and when we should invoke human rights in a social justice campaign. The first factor, *Survivor Dignity*, addresses whether a human rights case/campaign reaffirms a victim's dignity by providing a forum for the individual to mobilize change, feel empowered, and attain some closure in the wake of tragedy. The second factor, *Coalition and Movement Building*, probes whether the human rights approach provides a new space for synergies among groups who may operate in proverbial siloes, whose mandates may be narrow or locally focused, or whose grueling day-to-day work may impede big-picture aspirational thinking. The third factor, *Normative Developments and Accountability Mechanisms*, asks whether a given human rights case/campaign offers opportunities for normative developments that expand rights at the domestic or international levels, pushes beyond a cramped domestic legal framework, and/or holds rights violators accountable. The fourth factor, *Political Pressure*, examines whether a human rights campaign can generate political or diplomatic pressure on a country to fall in line with world opinion and practice. And the fifth factor, *Public Opinion*, concerns whether human rights messaging can influence public opinion and change hearts and minds, especially in areas—such as domestic violence—that have historically been understood, in law and in society, as "private matters."

These five factors are the guideposts—and guardrails—of my international human rights law practice. Ideally, all five factors should be affirmatively present in a given human rights case or campaign; if they are not, I tell my clients, I teach my students, and I argue in my scholarship, then any lawyer should tread carefully before entering into the human rights space. The negative and unanticipated consequences of an overenthusiastic embrace of international human rights without a well-informed and locally grounded strategy are potentially significant: following such a path could raise unrealistic expectations of affected individuals and communities about the tangible outcomes from a human rights case or campaign, rendering them even more vulnerable, and could have long-term consequences for future advocacy.

So how do these factors play out in the case of Jessica Lenahan, and in light of the personal and legal crises that her case precipitated?

FACTOR ONE: SURVIVOR DIGNITY—Lenahan describes the experience of bringing a case before the IACHR as having her proverbial day in court, and reclaiming her dignity, through the ability to testify publicly and having an authoritative international human rights body declare that what happened to her was both legally and morally wrong. Her son Jessie and mother Tina also told their stories through declarations submitted to the IACHR—finding their voice recognized in the legal process for the first time. Lenahan has become an internationally recognized human rights champion and takes great comfort in this global solidarity, despite her continuing disappointment at the intransigence of Castle Rock and Colorado authorities, who have repeatedly refused to conduct the investigation into her daughters' deaths that she continues to seek to this day. She recently completed a fellowship at Cornell Law School and is currently working as a spokesperson for the ERA Coalition to pass the Equal Rights Amendment, which is one state vote away from potential ratification.

FACTOR TWO: COALITION AND MOVEMENT BUILDING—Lenahan's voice has had special resonance in the United States, where advocates credit her for amplifying the importance of state accountability for fulfilling survivors' human rights. The domestic violence and women's rights advocacy communities galvanized around Lenahan's IACHR case, inspired by the notion that "freedom from domestic violence is a fundamental human right." This solidarity manifested itself through the significant number of US domestic violence and women's rights advocates who signed on as amici in support of Lenahan's case before the IACHR[13]—a forum previously unfamiliar to most of these advocates—as well as their support for HOME TRUTH, a documentary film about Lenahan's life and her case, which premiered at the Human Rights Watch Film Festival in 2017 and on PBS in 2018.[14] The film has been featured at conferences and screened at universities across the United States and around the world; Jessica, the filmmakers, and I have spoken before thousands of people at post-showing "talk-backs." A shorter, eight-minute video posted on YouTube titled "Domestic Violence & Human Rights: Lenahan v. USA" documents Jessica's case and the movement it represents.[15]

FACTOR THREE: NORMATIVE DEVELOPMENTS AND ACCOUNTABILITY MECHANISMS—Although the US government officially rejected the IACHR's decision on technical and jurisdictional grounds, the decision has had an undeniable effect on federal policy. Beginning in 2011, the US Department of Justice (DOJ) began stepping up its investigations into discriminatory law enforcement responses to domestic violence and sexual assault in several cities—the exact type of government action that the IACHR had called for.[16] Then, in 2015 (while I was working as White House Advisor on Violence Against Women), United States Attorney General Loretta Lynch released official guidance on Identifying and Preventing Gender Bias in Law Enforcement Response to Sexual Assault and Domestic Violence (hereinafter "DOJ Guidance")—a step originally proposed by myself and other advocates who supported Lenahan's lawsuit.[17] A year later, the DOJ gave nearly $10 million in grants to police departments and experts in gender violence and policing to implement the DOJ Guidance nationwide.[18]

From those grants, the International Association of Chiefs of Police developed a national demonstration site initiative to strengthen law enforcement response to domestic and sexual violence, involving six police departments across the United States[19]; additionally, the Police Executive Research Forum, the Battered Women's Justice Project, and other organizations have developed reports and training and technical assistance programs to address gender bias in policing and improve the law enforcement response to domestic violence and sexual assault.[20]

The Lenahan decision, as well as the increasing federal gaze on gender bias in institutional responses to domestic and sexual violence, have also had an effect at the local and state levels. Following the 2011 IACHR decision, more than thirty municipalities adopted resolutions and publications recognizing "freedom from domestic violence is a basic human right," many of them citing Lenahan's case.[21] These resolutions have been linked to concrete law and policy changes in Ithaca, New York; Austin, Texas; and Miami, Florida. In Illinois, the state legislature passed the Illinois Sexual Assault Incident Procedure Act, which addresses gender bias in law enforcement and medical responses to victims.

The *Lenahan* case has also had regional and global reverberations: it is taught in textbooks and law schools around the world, and it has been cited by a high court in Kenya,[22] the European Court of Human Rights,[23] and the International Criminal Court.[24] A representative from the IACHR recently told Lenahan at an open forum that her case created groundbreaking international jurisprudence and is invoked on a daily basis at the IACHR's Rapporteurship on Women.

FACTOR FOUR: POLITICAL PRESSURE—All of the above-described federal, state, and local policy developments undeniably emanated, at least in part, from the domestic outrage and international embarrassment created by the Supreme Court's *Castle Rock* decision. (It was also essential, of course, that the DOJ under President Barack Obama was attuned to bias issues and was open to expanding its antibias work to focus on gender bias in policing.) In a powerful scene in *HOME TRUTH*, a DOJ representative approaches Jessica Lenahan after an IACHR hearing with tears in her eyes and says that, although they were sitting on opposite sides of the table, they are really on the same team. State Department representatives told me privately over the years that *Castle Rock* created diplomatic obstacles in US foreign policy work as the United States sought to hold foreign governments to higher accountability standards for protecting domestic violence victims than the standards created by our own Supreme Court.

Even back in 2007, Representative Jerry Nadler of New York sponsored an amendment to the Violence Against Women Act, called the Jessica Gonzales Victim Assistance Act, to commit $5 million to placing special victim assistants to act as liaisons between local law enforcement agencies and victims of domestic violence, dating violence, sexual assault, and stalking in order to improve the enforcement of protection orders. This act, Nadler emphasized, was created to "restore[] some of the effectiveness of restraining orders that the Supreme Court took away with its [*Castle Rock*] ruling."[25] Prior to the IACHR decision, Nadler privately told Lenahan that he thought it would be an international embarrassment "for an international body to call the United States a violator of the rights of women and children."[26]

FACTOR FIVE: PUBLIC OPINION—As described above, Lenahan's voice and case have reverberated throughout law and society, in the United States and globally. In addition to the legal and policy developments described above, Lenahan's message has been captured through film (*HOME TRUTH*, described above), and the *Castle Rock* decision is spurned in the recent Broadway hit *What the Constitution Means to Me*. As described in a *New Yorker* article, the show's playwright and star, Heidi Schreck, "draws connections: between her mother's abusive childhood and *Castle Rock v. Gonzales*; between her great-great-grandmother's 'melancholia' and her own reproductive freedom, protected by *Roe v. Wade*." Schreck dedicated her June 20, 2019, show to Jessica Lenahan in commemoration of the twenty-year anniversary of Rebecca's, Katheryn's, and Leslie's deaths. Lenahan's friends, family, and supporters from around the country—even several generations of law students who worked on her case—attended the play and honored her afterward.[27] For Lenahan, these moments of public recognition and narrative change about domestic violence create a counterbalance to the ongoing impact of her personal crisis.

Ongoing Struggles and Looking Forward

None of this is easy or clean. Jessica Lenahan still struggles with her tragedy every day of her life—especially with the pain of still not knowing the circumstances surrounding her children's deaths. I sometimes struggle with a professional and ethical crisis of sorts, wondering whether I have effectively represented this survivor through my legal and nonlegal forms of advocacy and whether continuing to push for an investigation has antitherapeutic effects. In light of Colorado's recent "blue wave" in the 2018 elections, Lenahan felt strongly that we should try to make progress in our ongoing demands for an investigation into the children's deaths. After many phone calls and meetings, the town of Castle Rock committed in June 2019 to producing a report for Lenahan reviewing all evidence in their possession and providing an analysis of what is known regarding the circumstances of the girls' deaths in a report. But I constantly aim to manage my own and my client's expectations: this is an uphill battle. All statutes of limitations have passed, legislation that provides individual remedies is not permitted under the Colorado Constitution, and there are many powerful forces in Colorado who are adamantly opposed to reopening this case.

I have learned from fifteen years of work on Lenahan's case that one must measure success on multiple scales—and that crisis can be both protracted and prolonged. There is the ongoing journey for "justice for Jessica," and there is the ongoing effort to change law, policy, and hearts and minds on a broader scale. Recently, I have undertaken a new clinic project that builds directly on my experiences litigating the *Lenahan* case and working in the Obama

White House: the COURAGE (Community Oriented and United Responses to Address Gender Violence and Equality) in Policing Project, which aims to implement the 2015 DOJ Guidance by engaging marginalized community groups at the local, national, and global levels.[28] COURAGE works with community-based organizations, police departments, and national leaders on gender violence and policing to enhance law enforcement responses to domestic violence and sexual assault, with a particular focus on women of color, immigrant women, disabled women, indigenous women, LGBTQI individuals, and other underserved populations.

Through the COURAGE Project, we are gathering data on the local level to replicate national data concerning police response to domestic and sexual violence. For instance, a 2015 survey of victims who called the National Domestic Violence Hotline revealed a strong reluctance on the part of many victims to turn to law enforcement for help, as well as significant barriers that many victims encounter when they do seek law enforcement assistance. We are working with police departments to emphasize the importance of improving responses and recognizing and addressing bias. Indeed, while domestic and sexual violence calls represent the majority of 911 calls to many police departments, and are among the most dangerous assignments for responding officers, improving the response to gender violence is often not a law enforcement priority. Moreover, we are trying to change national conversations about bias in policing, which have tended to focus more on race and national origin than on sex or gender identity and often fail to address the intersection of these issues. These issues are especially important in the contemporary (Trumpian) crisis context for domestic violence survivors, especially women of color, immigrant women, and LGBTQI individuals.

I am also engaged on COURAGE themes in the international space. In 2018, the COURAGE team from the University of Miami School of Law Human Rights Clinic, joined by prominent national organizations focused on gender violence and policing, filed a third-party intervention brief before the European Court of Human Rights in a case concerning gender bias and officer-perpetrated domestic violence in the country Georgia. We argued for a heightened standard of state responsibility in cases of officer-perpetrated gender violence; if the European Court of Human Rights adopts this approach, it could set a new standard internationally and underscore the importance of creating cultures of accountability in the gender violence/law enforcement arena. As of November 2019, the case is still pending before the European Court.

* * *

As the author Joshua C. Wilson has emphasized, "at its core, cause lawyering is distinguished from traditional lawyering in that it is done in the service of a political or social cause that seeks to rearrange existing state or social power relations."[29] Lenahan's case is, in many ways, quintessential cause lawyering, in that it sought to address a gap in the law that reflected historic patriarchal views about family violence and women's place in society. Yet her case is also a case study in client-centered lawyering: without her vision, persistence, and support, her lawyers would never have arrived at the inflection point in the case, where we identified the Inter-American human rights system as a forum for seeking justice for Lenahan or transformative change for the cause her case represented. Lenahan's personal crisis and legal crisis crisscrossed in curious ways over the years, ultimately resulting in transformative change for Lenahan and for the advocates who supported and represented her. She has also changed hearts and minds and challenged our country—indeed, our world—to recognize the human rights and dignity of survivors in a whole new way.

NOTES

1 *Castle Rock v. Gonzales*, 545 U.S. 748 (2005).
2 The formal name of the case is *Jessica Lenahan (Gonzales) v. United States*, but I will refer to it as *Lenahan v. United States* for the sake of simplicity.
3 The facts presented in this chapter reflect the factual findings of the Inter-American Commission on Human Rights in *Lenahan v. United States*, Case 12.626, Inter-Am. Comm'n. H.R., Report No. 80/11 (2011).
4 Caroline Bettinger-López, *Human Rights at Home: Domestic Violence as a Human Rights Violation*, 40 COLUM. HUM. RTS. L. REV. 19 (2008).
5 *Gonzales v. City of Castle Rock*, 366 F.3d 1093, 1117 (10th Cir. 2004) (*en banc*).
6 *See* the following amicus curiae briefs filed in support of Jessica Gonzales: Brief of International Law Scholars et al.; Brief of the National Ass'n of Women Lawyers and the National Crime Victims Bar Ass'n; Brief of the American Civil Liberties Union et al.; Brief of National Black Police Ass'n et al.; Brief of National Network to End Domestic Violence et al.; Brief of AARP; Brief of the Family Violence Prevention Fund et al.; Brief of Peggy Kerns, Former Member of the House of Representatives of the State of Colorado, and the Texas Domestic Violence Direct Service Providers; Brief of National Coalition Against Domestic Violence and National Center for Victims of Crime.
7 Opinion Announcement, *Castle Rock v. Gonzales*, 545 U.S. 748 (2005) (No. 04-278), www.oyez.org.
8 *Castle Rock v. Gonzales*, 545 U.S. 748, 768 (2005).
9 *Lenahan v. United States*, Case 12.626, Inter-Am. Comm'n. H.R., Report No. 80/11 (2011).

10 *See* Declarations of Jessica Lenahan (2006), Jessie Rivera (2008), and Tina Rivera (2008), *available at* www.law.columbia.edu and www.aclu.org.

11 *Lenahan v. United States*, Case 12.626, Inter-Am. Comm'n. H.R., Report No. 80/11 (2011).

12 Bettinger-López, *Human Rights at Home.*

13 The amicus briefs filed before the IACHR can be found at www.law.columbia.edu.

14 For more information about *Home Truth, see* www.hometruthfilm.com.

15 See the video "Domestic Violence & Human Rights: Lenahan v. USA," www.youtube.com/watch?v=UvPtMCrl4J4.

16 The DOJ initiated investigations into gender bias in police response to domestic violence and/or sexual assault in New Orleans, Puerto Rico, Missoula, Maricopa County, Newark, and Baltimore. *See Identifying and Preventing Gender Bias in Law Enforcement Response to Sexual Assault and Domestic Violence, Resource Guide*, www.justice.gov.

17 *Identifying and Preventing Gender Bias in Law Enforcement Response to Sexual Assault and Domestic Violence*, U.S. Dep't of Justice (Dec. 2015).

18 *Department of Justice Awards $9.85 Million to Identify and Prevent Gender Bias in Policing*, U.S. Dep't of Justice (Oct. 5, 2016).

19 *See Identifying and Preventing Gender Bias*, Int'l Ass'n of Chiefs of Police.

20 *See, e.g.,* www.ncdsv.org.

21 *See Freedom from Domestic Violence as a Fundamental Human Right Resolutions, Presidential Proclamations, and Other Statements of Principle*, Cornell Law School.

22 *C.K. (A Child) & 11 Others v. Commissioner of Police/Inspector General of the National Police Service & 3 Others*, Petition 8 of 2012, High Court of Meru (2013).

23 *Valiulienė v. Lithuania*, Application no. 33234/07, European Court of Human Rights, Mar. 26, 2013.

24 *The Prosecutor v. Jean-Pierre Bemba Gombo (re Situation in the Central African Republic)*, Int'l Criminal Court, Oct. 17, 2016.

25 *Floor Statement on the Jessica Gonzales Victim Assistance Program*, Congressman Jerry Nadler (July 25, 2007).

26 *See* Bettinger-López, *Human Rights at Home*, 64.

27 Michael Schulman, *Heidi Schreck Takes the Constitution to Broadway*, THE NEW YORKER (Feb. 11, 2019)

28 For more information on the COURAGE Project, *see* www.law.miami.edu.

29 Joshua C. Wilson, *It Takes All Kinds: Observations From an Event-Centered Approach to Cause Lawyering*, 50 STUD. LAW, POL., & SOC'Y 169, 170 (2009).

2

Crisis Lawyering in a Lawless Space

Reflections on Nearly Two Decades of Representing Guantánamo Detainees

BAHER AZMY

I first saw my client on a TV screen.

As the third civilian lawyer entering the inner sanctum of Camp Echo in October 2004, inside the notorious military prison in Guantánamo, Cuba, guards showed me the surveillance they would use during my meeting with my client, Murat. He appeared on a video screen, seated, waiting for me. The image was dark, blurry, and unsettling, like the feed from a grainy store security camera—I could make out a man with a beard and hair befitting a prehistoric warrior. The military told me Murat would be chained to the floor, and should he "attack" me all I needed to do was jump backward. In less than fifteen minutes, the military had cast him in monstrous terms—Hannibal Lecter who prays five times a day. To my surprise, an impossibly young guard told me Murat didn't want the German-speaking translator who had accompanied me. "What?" I retorted, incredulously, "he speaks English now?" He was a Turkish national, born and raised in Germany—and his mother had told me that when he left home three years earlier, he spoke only those two tongues. "Yes, sir, he appears to speak it."

I sent away the German translator and braced to meet him alone. When the door to our meeting room in Camp Echo opened, he was seated, squinting at the incoming sunlight. Dressed in a tan shirt and cotton pants, with a flowing beard and a red-brown mane of hair, Murat looked like a castaway on a desert island—which in a sense he was. He shook my hand and motioned for me to sit on a flimsy plastic chair, as if he were welcoming me to tea in his home. Despite my suit, tie, and dress shoes, the dissonance of this legal meeting was accented by the sound of practice machine-gun fire outside. I tried to sound confident, like a lawyer. "Murat, my name is Baher Azmy," I told him. "I am a lawyer. I do not work for the US government. Your family asked me to help you."

I handed him a handwritten note from his worried mother to help convince him I was on his side. For three years he had not talked to anyone who was not a military guard or interrogator and was surely not predisposed to trust this stranger. The simple honesty and loving reassurance of her message still moves me: "My dear son Murat, You will be visited by an American lawyer whom you can trust. His name is Baher Azmy. Murat, your brothers go to school and we have been for vacation in Turkey. We were shopping with [your wife] and she is loving you." As I watched his pained expression while reading his first message from home—his first taste of humanity in three years—I felt as though I was delivering bread to Robinson Crusoe.

I explained that his mother had been fighting for him for years and that, following a big decision four months prior from the United States Supreme Court, I had filed a case for him in court in an attempt to challenge the legality of his indefinite detention. He had never been charged with any crime, let alone put on trial. Indeed, because he had been held incommunicado for almost three years, he had no idea anyone even knew of Guantánamo's existence—or his own. I told him I was a Muslim born in Egypt and a law professor with faith in the American legal system—albeit a faith that I have considerably muted since our first 2004 meeting. "You have sued President Bush?" he asked. "Yes, you and I have sued him together. And, I will do everything I can to help you," I answered. To my relief, he said in his German accent, "This is goot."

How I got to this place at this time—one of the strangest legal, geopolitical, and moral spaces I have ever encountered—requires some background.

* * *

Soon after the September 11, 2001, attacks, George W. Bush's administration proclaimed a "Global War on Terror" and sought to consolidate unquestioned executive power by braiding together two narratives: First, the necessity of deferring to presidential decision-making during (conventional) wars; and second, the specter of a shadowy, fanatical, global enemy threatening the American way of life. These narratives undergirded a wide series of brutal and extraconstitutional practices, many of which my organization, the Center for Constitutional Rights (CCR), challenged—including the CIA's secret detention and torture of terrorist suspects;[1] the extraordinary rendition of individuals for torture in third countries;[2] and the dragnet roundup and the registration, detention, and deportation of Muslim men without any connections to terrorism.[3]

At the heart of these now discredited practices was the Bush administration's crown jewel in its so-called war on terror: Guantánamo. For human rights advocates and zealots of muscular executive power, Guantánamo remains a central flashpoint for purposes of understanding questions of legality and democratic legitimacy. Guantánamo poses a fundamental question: In a constitutional republic, can there be a prison outside the law? In the years since 9/11, a fundamental recognition has played out before our eyes: bad things happen in dark places.

In this chapter I tell a truncated story of the initial, bold—dare I say heroic—legal intervention led by CCR and several other seasoned human rights lawyers to challenge the Bush administration's actions only months after the 9/11 attacks and in the midst of a bellicose, nationalistic fever. The first phase of the legal intervention commenced in early 2002 with a seemingly hopeless petition for habeas corpus on behalf of demonized suspected terrorists, which resulted in a seismic United States Supreme Court victory, two and a half years later, authorizing detainees to challenge the legality of their imprisonment in Guantánamo. The second phase of the litigation, following the Court's authorization of legal representation for detainees, saw CCR coordinate a mass mobilization of lawyers, activists, and human rights institutions to surface stories of innocence, bureaucratic incompetence, and torture. In doing so, these lawyers would dramatically reverse the administration's muscular Guantánamo narrative. The impact of these mutually reinforcing interventions was nothing short of dramatic. When CCR filed the first challenge to detentions in Guantánamo in February 2002, it was vilified for daring to question the president's efforts to protect national security. Then, after six years of litigation and advocacy, including multiple Supreme Court victories and the mass mobilization of lawyers and advocates, CCR's coalition produced a judicial and political consensus that Guantánamo was illegitimate and should be closed.

This leads us to the third and most complex phase, representing a tension we currently inhabit. Despite the courage, creativity, and exhaustive efforts of emergency lawyering, the legal architecture in Guantánamo, like all forms of government power, is resilient. The ultimate takeaway from this work is conflicted. On the one hand, lawyering and advocacy resulted in the release of 730 men, discredited Guantánamo as an anomalous experiment, and powerfully reaffirmed first principles regarding the rule of law and the dangers of unchecked executive power. On the other, the prison facility at Guantánamo remains open to this day, the current detentions of forty men are largely sanctioned by the courts, and not one Bush administration official has been held accountable for any of the egregious human rights abuses they perpetrated.

These three phases offer a set of modestly generalizable lessons from the Guantánamo experience: (1) that radical, decisive, courageous lawyers with political grounding in how the state dehumanizes subjects are necessary to articulate and leverage a principled vision of law as a force for dignity and rights and to challenge the state's deployment of law as a weapon of control and violence; (2) that a mass mobilization of lawyers, activists, and international human rights entities is necessary to elevate stories of individuals facing injustice, as well as to create an alternative, in mutually reinforcing ways, to the reductive narrative of national security; and (3) that in the darkest of places, lawyers can sometimes offer what all repressive systems seek to deny their subjects: hope and recognition. Ultimately, there may rarely be clear or durable victories when the state leverages emergency power against marginalized individuals, but there are always compelling reasons for lawyers to boldly stand up against it.

Phase 1 Crisis Lawyering: Radical Lawyers' Challenge to the Emergency Executive Action

Guantánamo's Authoritarian Logic

On November 13, 2001, President George W. Bush issued Military Order No. 1, "Detention, Treatment, and Trial of Certain Non-Citizens in the War Against Terrorism,"[4] which authorized the Secretary of Defense[5] to try noncitizens in military tribunals and to carry out executions without the possibility of judicial review. Appreciating the emergency legal intervention undertaken by the first group of radical lawyers and the subsequent legal strategies deployed by the hundreds of lawyers that arrived later on the scene in this effort requires some understanding of the interlocking political and narrative scaffolding erected by the Bush administration to sustain its cruel, extraconstitutional experiment. To begin with, the administration did not seek to leverage Guantánamo's claimed operational advantages in order to *try* captured enemies for war crimes. Trial—or any other imagined adjudication of guilt or innocence—was at best an afterthought. Guantánamo predominantly functioned as the largest piece in a broad policy that contemplated the indefinite, secret detention of suspected terrorists or sympathizers in the service of the U.S. military's global interrogation operation.[6] The Bush administration pursued this strategy by developing a legal narrative that sought to displace rights with power. It created a novel legal category—the "enemy combatant"—and proclaimed that such persons were not entitled to any rights whatsoever, including basic Geneva Convention rights governing wartime captures and requiring humane treatment. To forestall any challenge to this novel legal regime, administration lawyers sought to create a "legal black hole" or "the legal equivalent of outer space"—explicitly outside the jurisdiction of US courts.[7]

Avoiding court jurisdiction over the detentions was necessary to deny substantive rights and to prevent exposure of the administration's interrogation and torture program. For interrogations to be successful, the administration believed prisoners should be completely isolated, disoriented, and hopeless about their prospects for human contact or release, thus making them maximally dependent upon their captors and compliant with questioning.[8] Critical to this dehumanization project was denying access to lawyers and the corresponding possibility of believing help is on the way. Not only could lawyers counsel clients not to speak to interrogators; they could inject something even more threatening into the interrogation room: hope. Lawyers say "Tell me your story," "I am on your side," "You are not alone," and "I can help you."

The administration's legal architecture was dangerous not only because of the grotesque instrumental ends it was designed to protect—the torture and debasement of prisoners—but also because of its authoritarian logic. In developing these legal positions, the administration arrogated to itself all the power it saw in international law—that is to say, the authority to undertake the temporary detainment of battlefield captures—while disregarding corresponding constraints on that authority—the predetention determination of an individual's legal status and the universal obligation of humane treatment.

It represented, in an essential way, the definition of tyranny.

And whatever the merits of this legal position, denying individuals the entitlement to any rights required a public spin. This narrative is what Muneer Ahmad has called the "Iconography of Terror"[9] and Joe Margulies has called the "Myth of the Superhuman Terrorist."[10] Administration officials routinely described the detainees in Guantánamo as "the worst of the worst," "hard core, well-trained terrorist[s],"[11] and, in the colorful phrasing of the Joint Chiefs of Staff, the kind of monsters who could "gnaw the hydraulic lines in the back of a C-17 [military plane] to bring it down."[12] This metanarrative painted a frightening picture of depraved, transnational networks committed and able to destroy the United States, melding the otherwise individual identities of 780 men into this totalizing narrative of a Muslim menace. Such a narrative—which actually suppressed the emerging understanding among administration officials that the military actually had transferred very few bona fide terrorist suspects to Guantánamo[13]—nevertheless justified the total denial of rights and reconciled the apparent anomaly of lawless detention with the imagined moral superiority of the United States.[14] And this muscular claim to have captured and imprisoned hundreds of Muslim detainees helped a presidential administration that was otherwise self-conscious about being caught off-guard on 9/11.[15] As Ahmad observes, much like the racialized internment and debasement of Japanese Americans during World War II and the mass incarceration of African Americans today, Guantánamo fed an existential need for security.[16]

The Radical Lawyers' Response

Michael Ratner, CCR's longtime legal director, read the news about the Bush administration's Military Order No. 1 with considerable (but familiar) alarm. Ratner was one of the country's foremost radical, anti-imperialist lawyers, a man who cut his teeth representing social justice activists, prisoner-victims of the Attica attacks, and communities terrorized by atrocities in Central America during President Ronald Reagan's administration.[17] As a deeply politically engaged lawyer with a rich historical understanding of the ways in which executive power initiates needless war and commits war crimes, accelerates public fear, and criminalizes domestic communities (as was happening in the neighboring immigrant Muslim communities of Brooklyn), Ratner felt compelled to challenge what he regarded as the functional abandonment of the most elementary due process principles codified since the Magna Carta.[18] According to Ratner:

> The President's claim that he had unlimited and unchecked power to combat terrorism was by far the most serious threat to human rights in the post 9/11 world. It was of a different character than the granting of more powers to the CIA and FBI [of the kind Ratner had challenged in earlier years]. The president, under the military order, was claiming that he had the authority to arrest and detain people forever. This claim to unlimited detention power undercuts the key principle underlying democracy: the principle that authority (the president, the prime minister or king) is under law.[19]

Ratner and staff at the Center for Constitutional Rights debated and ultimately agreed to mount a legal challenge to this perceived executive lawlessness.[20] It was not a self-evident decision. As Ratner recalls, CCR was more accustomed to "defending the rights of those we generally agreed with, those involved in making progressive social change such as civil rights workers in the South or opponents of the US contra war in Nicaragua."[21] The principle that CCR was seeking to vindicate might lead it to represent those responsible for the horrific 9/11 attacks. Ratner sought to form a coalition to mount a challenge, but no other legal organization in the country would consider taking on the president at this politically fraught time. He ultimately connected with a small handful of lawyers, including the seasoned death penalty lawyers Joe Margulies and Clive Stafford Smith—both accustomed to absorbing public wrath while pressing for legal recognition of reviled clients—as well as the legendarily genius icon of the death penalty defense movement and New York University law school professor Anthony Amsterdam.

When the US military delivered the first three dozen prisoners to Guantánamo on January 11, 2002—intentionally shown in the US media as hooded, bound, and chained to the floor of a C-17 cargo transport plane—Ratner and his team of radicals knew what they would do. They sought to check a seemingly unprecedented executive action through a seemingly unprecedented legal challenge. They intended to file legal petitions for habeas corpus on behalf of men the administration had accused of orchestrating the cataclysm of 9/11. Habeas corpus is an ancient legal protection, derived from the Magna Carta, inherited in US common law from British law, and expressly protected by the United States Constitution (which prohibits the "suspension" of habeas corpus "unless when in cases of rebellion or invasion the public safety may require it").[22] At its essence the habeas petition is designed to prevent and remediate arbitrary executive detention by authorizing a court to question and nullify the asserted authorization for such detention.[23] As Guantánamo revealed, the idea of military detention without charge strikes at the heart of constitutional legitimacy.[24]

Ratner harbored no illusions about the possibility of immediate judicial relief. In fact, he viewed the initial filings as "hopeless" in light of seemingly overwhelming obstacles. To begin with, the lawyers had no clients. Since the point of incommunicado detention at Guantánamo was to isolate, disorient, and dehumanize detainees, they were denied any contact with the outside world, let alone lawyers. Still, the governments of the United Kingdom and Australia received notice of their citizens' detentions in Guantánamo, so family members who were correspondingly informed contacted human rights lawyers at home who in turn connected with CCR. But how would we to file a habeas petition when we were not permitted to communicate with clients and obtain their authorization? In one of a number of times in which we would resort to obscure and ancient common law principles throughout the litigation, the first habeas petitions were filed on behalf of detainees' parents as their "Next Friend." Under ancient common law, when the King locks you in the Tower and throws away the key, someone—a Next Friend—must be able to get into court. For these twenty-first-century lawyers, the Tower was Guantánamo.[25]

A second obstacle to the initial filings was the state of the legal doctrine involved. Following World War II, the US Supreme Court ruled that a convicted German war criminal, Lothar Eisentrager, detained on a US military base in Germany, could not access US courts to challenge his imprisonment.[26] This precedent was problematic, but unlike the *Eisentrager* case these UK and Australian Guantánamo petitioners were not from "enemy" nations, did not have the benefit of even a military trial, and, most fundamentally, unlike Germany, Guantánamo was, practically speaking, as much a part of the

United States as was Florida. Also, with age, bad precedent can become good. Some World War II legal architecture has been discredited by history, as any first-year law student studying the Supreme Court's shameful sanctioning of Japanese Americans' internment would know. Indeed, the initial legal team strategically extracted from these discredited decisions an important political warning: courts should not reflexively trust the executive's claim to unbridled power in wartime.

The final obstacle confronting Ratner must have appeared as daunting as Mount Everest. The habeas petitions were filed in February 2002, just five months after the 9/11 attacks. President Bush enjoyed massive popularity in large part *because* of his bellicose discourse; by assuming a wartime posture, Bush lustily advocated imposing maximal pain on and destruction of terrorist enemies (and those who would even harbor or defend them) and thereby sent the public's trust in military judgment soaring. Also, for the Bush administration, containment and humiliation of the Guantánamo detainees were central to the projection of an iconography of terror.[27] The earliest legal filings thus represented not a challenge to some individually incorrect detention decision but rather an attack on the president's constructed war-making architecture itself. CCR struggled to find local counsel in Washington who would even dare to put their name on such a filing. After it was lodged, Michael Ratner received enough hate mail and death threats to fill a suitcase.

Despite these uncertainties, Ratner and company filed "100% on principle."[28] At this historical moment, few lawyers possessed Ratner's gifts as a radical lawyer: his faith in the potentially redemptive power of law both as a means to critique power and articulate principle, his understanding of the real human consequences of war and unchecked executive power, and his belief in the enduring power of empathy and love as fuel for movements and justice. His example inspired an army of other lawyers—including me.

The challenge for the Guantánamo lawyers was to leverage a legal ruling ensuring the jurisdiction of the courts—and thus the possibility of lawyers—so as to dismantle the dominant political narrative justifying the legal anomaly of Guantánamo.

This first case challenging lawless executive detention was captioned *Rasul v. Bush*.

Phase 2—A Right to Law and a Lawyer

As Michael Ratner predicted, the initial stages of the *Rasul* litigation generated little more than hate mail and death threats. The federal district court and court of appeals made quick dispatch of the petitioners' arguments, largely agreeing with the government that US courts had no jurisdiction over habeas petitions filed by foreign nationals detained in a place those courts considered—despite all practical appearances—outside the formal territory of the United States. The lawyers for *Rasul* and the now-consolidated case *Al Odah v. United States* (brought by Tom Wilner, Neil Koslowe, and Kristine Huskey of the elite DC firm Shearman & Sterling at the behest of the Kuwaiti government seeking representation of Kuwaiti nationals) sought Supreme Court review almost two years to the date after the September 11 attacks.[29]

With support from various powerful voices filing amicus (or "friend of the court") briefs, including retired generals, former POWs, and Fred Korematsu—the civil rights icon who, having been subject to the mass internment of Japanese Americans, perhaps most embodied the danger of judicial acquiescence to (often false) claims of "military necessity"—the petitioners in *Rasul* avoided framing the case in terms of the rights of terrorist suspects versus the national security. Instead, they framed the case in terms of the "rule of law," the most transcendent and fundamental American value, versus the power-hungry Bush presidency, comprising a set of arrogant and bellicose officials. For a variety of regrettable reasons, the former narrative is rarely successful in American legal-political spheres. By contrast, the narrative that the Bush administration had been dangerously and arrogantly consolidating power was becoming increasingly plausible.

In a series of so-called enemy combatant cases before the Supreme Court, all challenging Bush administration military detention practices, advocates argued that the administration's legal architecture did not merely ignore the rights of detained individuals but, in so doing, betrayed foundational American principles. In defending itself, the administration took the most maximalist legal position, aggressively rejecting the relevance of the coordinate branches of government in a way that would make Alexander Hamilton and James Madison turn over in their graves. Beyond its overreach, the administration's position suffered a dramatic hit when shattering images of degraded, contorted, agonized Iraqi citizens tormented by US military officers in the Abu Ghraib prison came to light. The pictures took on extra salience given that the US deputy solicitor general, in response to Justice Ginsburg's observation during oral argument in the contemporaneous case *Rumsfeld v. Padilla*, that the government's absolutist legal position would arguably permit torture, confidently asserted: "Our Executive doesn't."[30] As Joe Margulies observed, the Abu Ghraib photos served as the most powerful amicus brief of all.[31]

On June 28, 2004, in *Rasul v. Bush*, the Supreme Court ruled against the Bush administration, holding that detainees possessed rights under the habeas corpus statute to challenge the legality of their detention without charge. Importantly, it would destroy the "legal black hole" narrative, finding that Guantánamo was "in every practical respect "within 'the territorial jurisdiction' of the United States."[32] Because of that, law and the US Constitution still applied. The opinion, written by Justice Stevens, who served in World War II and clerked for Justice Wiley Rutledge (who came to regret his vote in support of Japanese internment), turned on some highly technical jurisdictional maneuvers, but it also invoked the profound importance of the "Great Writ" of habeas as a check on arbitrary imprisonment. Indeed, it sent this powerful normative message: in a country committed to the rule of law, there could be no prisons beyond the law. The *New York Times* noted that the combined enemy combatant decisions issued by the Court represented "the court's most important statement in decades on the balance between personal liberties and national security."[33] Though its full parameters would be contested in the coming years, at a minimum the ruling introduced the antidote to Guantánamo's authoritarian logic: lawyers. The *Rasul* lawyers' successful strategy, once seemingly hopeless, now seemed inevitable. The detainees would no longer languish in silence, reliant on Next Friends and lawyers they had never met. Despite the initial, seemingly insurmountable obstacles, the strategy behind the *Rasul* decision represented one of the most canny and audacious crisis lawyering efforts in memory.

Although the *Rasul* decision contained a clear and resounding legal ruling, a central lesson from this episode—translatable to all emergency lawyering efforts—is that one cannot measure success by judicial vindication alone. As we shall see, the Bush administration accepted little of what seemed a stinging judicial rebuke. It did not shut down Guantánamo. A second phase of creative crisis lawyering had to emerge—one that expanded the team of legal actors from a handful to hundreds.

Building Networks, Shifting Narratives

Phase 2 Lawyering: Seeking Meaningful Access to the Writ

While *Rasul* was pending, lawyers from CCR had either reached out to or been contacted by other families with loved ones in Guantánamo. By the time *Rasul* was decided, there were sixty-five detainees whose families wanted representation, including the Kuwaitis represented by Shearman & Sterling. Lawyers from CCR and the Gibbons law firm in Newark, New Jersey, that had represented the detainees in the Supreme Court, alongside Margulies, Stafford-Smith, and other renowned habeas corpus experts such as Anthony Amsterdam and Eric Freedman, parceled out the habeas petitions, largely grouping nationals together, among thirteen sets of lawyers. Among these sixty-five detainees was Murat Kurnaz, a twenty-four-year-old Turkish resident of Germany. Even though I knew nothing about his case, he was assigned to me.

All these cases were assigned to Judge Joyce Hens Green of the federal district court for the District of Columbia. Speaking for the lawyers representing all of the detainees, Joe Margulies articulated our simple demands: access and answers. We wanted immediate access to our clients in Guantánamo, and we wanted answers to our habeas petitions—our clients had a right to know what they were accused of. The government reluctantly agreed to permit lawyers to visit their clients even as it vigorously fought all the cases, seeking again to dismiss them across the board.

Murat's Case

It was during this time, in October 2004, that I first met Murat. After our first meeting, I spent three long days with him developing trust. He spoke about his family, his childhood, his obsession with exercise, clean air, and healthy food. He had a rooted faith in Islam that helped him manage the brutality, solitude, and air of forever that hung over the prison. He was also hilariously funny—so much so that my friends eagerly awaited the government censors' review of my notes so I could share his jokes. Everything out of his mouth—any joke or message of love to his family—was deemed presumptively classified by the military and could be made public only after clearance by censors.

Soon after I returned home, the government filed with the court the unclassified reasons for his detention, which rested on an utterly preposterous accusation. In October 2001, while on a religious pilgrimage in Pakistan, Murat was apprehended on a civilian bus. Eventually, he was sold to the US military for the bounty it was offering for individuals allegedly connected to al-Qaeda or the Taliban. Because there was no actual evidence of violence or wrongdoing, the US government claimed that Murat's hometown friend, Selcuk Bilgin, committed a suicide bombing in Istanbul in the fall of 2003. Setting aside the legal absurdity of the government's claim—that it could indefinitely detain someone because of the act of a friend, allegedly carried out *while* Murat was incommunicado in Guantánamo—the government's claim was factually absurd as well. As a quick conversation with German authorities revealed, Selcuk Bilgin was alive and well. Several months later, I met him.

No Right to Substantive Rights

We assumed the *Rasul* decision would allow us to engage in hearings to challenge the evidence against our clients and that, if it was found to be insufficient, to obtain their release. Given the preposterously fabricated claim against Murat, I was particularly eager to engage the court in an age-old practice of producing evidence and vindicating *rights*. The government thought otherwise, moving to dismiss the sixty-five consolidated petitions. But these proceedings also revealed continuing overreach by the government, which claimed authority to denominate anyone an "enemy combatant" if he was merely "supporting Taliban or al Qaida forces, or [any] associated forces."[34] Indeed, at the oral argument on the government's motion to dismiss, the government conceded in response to a series of hypothetical questions that it could detain anyone at Guantánamo as an enemy combatant, including: "A little old lady in Switzerland" who sends a check to an orphanage "that turns out to be a front for al-Qaeda."[35] This was not a theoretical overreach on the part of the government but rather a legal necessity. As lawyer after lawyer would reveal, Guantánamo was filled with, figuratively speaking, many little old ladies from Switzerland.

Judge Green denied the government's motion to dismiss all of the then-filed habeas cases, concluding that detainees enjoyed basic due process rights to challenge the evidence against them and test the legality of their detention. She singled out the thinness of the evidence against my client and highlighted evidence from the classified portion of his file, which I was later able to publicize through parallel Freedom of Information Act litigation,[36] demonstrating that intelligence officials had long ago concluded that my client had "no connection to Al Qaida or the Taliban."[37]

Wholesale Lawyering Versus Retail Lawyering

The government immediately appealed Judge Green's decision, which set off a five-year battle in Congress, in the DC Circuit Court of Appeals, and in the Supreme Court, all in a quest to secure meaningful access to the rights-affirming protections of habeas corpus for our clients. I call this the "wholesale lawyering" process, and it was led by the original post-*Rasul* set of lawyers who had appeared before Judge Green.

Concurrently, there was what I call a robust "retail lawyering" process, engaged in by hundreds of lawyers whose efforts would over time lend them the moniker the "Guantánamo Bay Bar Association."[38] Handling case by case, client by client, they slowly picked away at the government's political and narrative defense of Guantánamo. The brilliance of the wholesale lawyering strategy, the dynamism of the retail lawyering process, and, more important, their continuing interactivity represented one of the most important collective legal efforts in memory.

Wholesale Lawyering

In the appellate proceedings, the wholesale lawyering team argued that even if the US Constitution's Due Process Clause did not protect detainees, those detainees possessed independent rights stemming from the habeas corpus statute itself, which specifically authorizes a judicial process to investigate the factual and legal basis for detention. The Justice Department lawyers had almost no response to the force of this simple argument. But for the pols and bureaucrats in the Bush administration, the fact that the habeas statute conferred rights was no obstacle—they just demanded a supplicant Congress to wipe away that statute. So, with little debate and no hearings, Congress repealed the habeas statute as it applied to detainees in the Detainee Treatment Act of 2005.[39] When the Supreme Court invalidated that retroactive repeal of rights,[40] Congress simply tried again to strip the courts of jurisdiction to hear any cases brought under the habeas corpus statute via the Military Commissions Act of 2006.[41] Congress thus sought two suspensions of habeas corpus within two years—more than had been attempted in the prior 200 years.

The wholesale legal team went back to court to argue that the Military Commissions Act of 2006 was an unlawful suspension of the constitutional requirement that habeas corpus remains available in cases of executive detention. We lost in the DC Circuit Court of Appeals. Our initial attempt to secure Supreme Court review failed. The litigation effort to secure fundamental habeas rights for our clients seemed doomed.

But that didn't mean there was no lawyering to be done.

Retail Lawyering: Building a Movement of Guantánamo Lawyers

As the machinations in the courts regarding the scope and meaning of the Great Writ moved apace, CCR took the lead in the massive effort to find representation for all the unrepresented Guantánamo detainees, numbering, at the time of *Rasul* in 2004, approximately 600 (from a peak of 779 in 2003). CCR lawyers, led by Gita Gutierrez, fanned across the country to convenings of prominent lawyers to recruit a geographically diverse set of firms and practitioners to represent detainees. At the same time, other CCR lawyers traveled to Afghanistan, Yemen, and the Gulf States to get Next Friend authorizations allowing family members to file for other detainees. To help grow and solidify the network, CCR held regular training sessions about all facets of lawyering at Guantánamo (which brought in the growing network of lawyers as trainers themselves), addressing topics from the restrictions the government had placed on our communications with our clients to the culture- and gender-based sensitivities they might encounter during meetings with clients.

No accurate count has ever been made, but I would estimate that no less than a thousand lawyers from across the country were engaged in representing detainees.[42] Crediting Michael Ratner's vision and leadership, David Cole has called this group "Michael Ratner's Army."[43] In my estimation, this represented the greatest mass legal defense effort in US history.

Because the merits of all the habeas petitions were stalled, these lawyers engaged in other litigation and advocacy activities that might help shift the administration's narrative about Guantánamo. A study by Mark Denbeaux and a talented team of students at Seton Hall Law School shattered the government's "worst of the worst" narrative by proving that only 8 percent of detainees were even alleged to be al-Qaeda fighters and that 55 percent were alleged to not even have engaged in a hostile act.[44] Lawyers representing ethnic Uighurs from China, whom the US government publicly admitted were not enemy combatants, argued in court and in the national media about the absurdity of detaining those even the jailer acknowledged to be innocent.[45] The evidence proving Murat Kurnaz's innocence became front-page national and network news.[46] Repeated, individual stories about clients in Guantánamo were cultivated by individual lawyers working all over the country, often with local media, to demonstrate time and again the attenuated basis for detention. These efforts steadily shifted understandings; the iconic image of Guantánamo detainees transformed from the "hardened terrorist" to the innocent "chicken farmer" in the "wrong place at the wrong time."[47]

Critically, Guantánamo lawyers and advocates increasingly recounted to the public details of the horrific treatment endured by their clients while in detention and facilitated the public airing of the detainee voices that the administration had done everything to silence.[48] For example, the Bahrain citizen detainee Jumah al Dosari wrote in the *Los Angeles Times*:

At Guantánamo, soldiers have assaulted me, placed me in solitary confinement, threatened to kill me, threatened to kill my daughter and told me I will stay in Cuba for the rest of my life. They have deprived me of sleep, forced me to listen to extremely loud music and shined intense lights in my face. They have placed me in cold rooms for hours without food, drink or the ability to go to the bathroom or wash for prayers. They have wrapped me in the Israeli flag and told me there is a holy war between the Cross and the Star of David on one hand and the Crescent on the other. They have beaten me unconscious.[49]

Alongside the legal advocacy on behalf of individual clients, and in many ways as a result of our newfound ability to speak with the detainees to learn and share their stories, international and DC-based advocacy groups joined the harsh criticism of Guantánamo. Amnesty International called Guantánamo the "gulag of our times,"[50] while Human Rights Watch and Human Rights First wrote deeply critical reports and engaged in advocacy with legislators on Capitol Hill.[51] Activist psychiatrists became highly critical of the American Psychological Association's collaboration in interrogations.[52] The libertarian Cato Institute repeatedly criticized indefinite detention without trial as contrary to the Madisonian plan.[53] A growing number of senior retired military generals spoke out about the dangers of abandoning principle and the Geneva Conventions—marking a rare occasion when the military and radical lawyers like Michael Ratner or the ACLU would be on the same side.[54] Military defense lawyers like Charles Swift heroically defied command pressure to aggressively fight for their clients accused in an otherwise closed military system.[55]

Pressure from foreign lawyers and international organizations was yielding concrete results on behalf of detainees as well. Clive Stafford Smith and lawyers at his new nonprofit organization, Reprieve, were ruthlessly successful in suing and shaming the British government for its failure to negotiate for the release of British detainees. Dan Mori, counsel for Aussie detainee David Hicks, waged a creative and resilient campaign to pressure the Australian government to insist on Hicks's repatriation.[56]

With the wholesale habeas litigation stayed and no immediate prospect of a judicial hearing on the merits of his case, I worked with my German cocounsel, Bernhard Docke, to pressure the German government to demand the release of our client, Murat Kurnaz. That meant repeated trips to Germany—to Murat's hometown and to Berlin alongside Bernhard—to hold press conferences, public convenings, and private meetings with diplomats and legislators to tell Murat's story. I sought to humanize him, despite the press's inclination to accept him as a terrorist (right-wing papers called him "Der Bremen Taliban," referring to his hometown). I showed the press and German government officials documents proving his innocence; I detailed his torture to anyone who would listen and at press conferences (including once while his mother silently wept beside me). Over a three-year period, Bernhard and I probably spoke to fifty German journalists and filmmakers. Our message was clear: Guantánamo was an evil institution, and Germans would be responsible—indeed complicit—if they did not press for his release. The liberal government of Chancellor Gerhard Schröder was cowardly in its response to these humanitarian demands, but within weeks of entering office, in 2006, Angela Merkel started negotiations for Murat's release. On August

24, 2006, Bernhard and I stood with Murat's family in Germany as he walked into their arms, finally free after five years in lawless military detention.

In 2002 Michael Ratner, the Center for Constitutional Rights, and just a few other courageous lawyers waved a writ of habeas corpus almost by themselves. By 2006 a national and global movement emerged, albeit one directed by legal and policy elites, demanding the end to Guantánamo and its related injustices. Instead of facing death threats like Michael Ratner in 2002, this movement had the support of civil society groups and even other nations' governments that came to understand the critical nature of maintaining constitutionalism and human rights.[57]

Phase 3—Victory and Loss

A Victorious Judicial and Political Consensus and Then Retrenchment

While hundreds of "retail lawyers" and advocates were surfacing stories about their clients, the "wholesale" quest for meaningful access to the writ of habeas corpus—a right to a hearing—proceeded. The wholesale legal team, myself included, sought to show that detainees did, in fact, enjoy constitutional rights in Guantánamo, including the protections of the Constitution's Suspension Clause.[58] If the Suspension Clause applied to the geographic space of Guantánamo, Congress's attempts to suspend the habeas statute, without providing an adequate substitute, would be unconstitutional. The team fought with the administration over historical understandings about the reach of the writ of habeas corpus, contesting the meaning of eighteenth- and nineteenth-century English cases involving far-flung imperial locations and disputing whether the extremely limited form of judicial review contemplated by the Military Commissions Act of 2006 was an adequate substitute for traditional habeas review. This part of the litigation was novel, important, and dizzyingly complex. But at a level of remove from these technicalities, for public consumption we had a seemingly unassailable position: if the government thinks a detainee did something wrong, it should give him a fair hearing. You cannot punish someone indefinitely based on mere executive say-so.

After initially denying our request for review, the Supreme Court took the very unusual step of reconsidering and granted our petition for certiorari in the summer of 2007.[59] At a packed and highly anticipated oral argument in January 2008, Seth Waxman, former solicitor general during the Bill Clinton administration, argued for the detainees; his argument featured prominently Murat Kurnaz's story—that the government claimed authority to detain him based on the manifestly false allegation that his friend was a suicide bomber—in challenging the illogic of the government's position.[60]

In what was assumed to be historic decision, *Boumediene v. Bush*,[61] the Supreme Court ruled in favor of the detainees again, concluding that the Constitution protects their access to habeas corpus and, in a rarity in legal history, rejected the concerted efforts of the executive and legislative branches during wartime, favoring instead robust judicial review.[62] The Court chastised the administration for its attempts to "govern without legal constraint"[63] and "switch the Constitution on and off at will"[64] and proclaimed that detainees should have "meaningful" access to the writ, which must include a right to present exculpatory evidence and the authority of the court to order release.[65]

It was a legal earthquake.

Around the same time, in the summer of 2008, then-Senator Barack Obama and Senator John McCain committed to closing Guantánamo as part of their presidential campaigns, albeit with different levels of emphasis.

It bears recalling that, in 2002, Michael Ratner could not even locate local counsel to put their name on CCR's "hopeless" legal filing because it was so toxically controversial. Yet a mere six years later, the concerted effort to build a dynamic movement of lawyers, activists, and rule-of-law advocates had produce a legal and political consensus that Guantánamo was illegitimate.

The Ultimate Retrenchment: A Limited Discourse of Rights

Almost immediately after the *Boumediene* decision, retail and wholesale lawyers alike moved in quick coordination to set up their cases for individual habeas hearings of the kind we had been fighting for since 2002. The federal district court in the District of Columbia, where these cases were set for hearings, set evidentiary standards and procedural requirements to constrain the government and also authorized detainee lawyers to obtain limited discovery to test the government's facts.[66] During this period, the district courts were articulating what I have elsewhere called a "New Common Law of Habeas."[67] It was a deep and rigorous set of common law–style adjudication that, among other things: (1) limited the scope of the government's detention authority (no more little old ladies from Switzerland); (2) critically scrutinized the quantity and quality of evidence, rejecting evidence obtained by torture and rank hearsay; and (3) issued an order in the case of concededly innocent ethnic Uighur detainees who faced a risk of persecution if returned home to China that their unlawful detention in Guantánamo be remediated by their supervised release into the United States.[68] Within approximately the first year after *Boumediene*, of the forty petitions adjudicated by the district courts, the court granted the writ thirty-one times—in other words, it ordered the liberty of *75 percent* of the detainees who had their cases heard post-*Boumediene*.[69]

At the same time, President Barack Obama's administration—which inherited the remaining 242 detainees who had not been released by the Bush administration—signaled a dramatic shift in detainee policy. On his second day in office, Obama issued an order that mandated the closure of the prison within one year.[70] He established the Guantánamo Review Task Force to evaluate the status of each detainee and appointed a State Department special envoy to negotiate detainee transfers. During the first two years of the Obama presidency, about fifty detainees were transferred from Guantánamo, about half to their home countries and the rest to third countries for resettlement, mostly in Europe.

Yet despite all of this early optimism, within two years of the *Boumediene* decision and Obama's election, we faced retrenchment in the courts and in politics. As many political science scholars will explain, legal claims of liberty and the recognition of disfavored persons are rarely sustainable over the long term. For the Guantánamo detainees, as in so many social justice struggles, the entitlement to rights is degraded by powerful actors in the legal and political systems, deploying a narrative and a legal architecture that would deny meaningful—let alone equal—access to justice. This retrenchment would draw legal—though ultimately artificial—distinctions around citizenship. It was sustained by a parallel narrative heightening fear and dehumanizing the detainees, making them monstrous and treating them as the "other." So, what seemed like both an inevitable and durable victory in 2008, a full and *final* reclamation of American values, would not come to be—calling into question our naïve assumption that Guantánamo was, in fact, contrary to American values.

On the legal front, the DC Circuit Court of Appeals (which was, during this time, even more conservative than the Supreme Court) eviscerated *Boumediene*'s promise of meaningful judicial scrutiny of the president's detention decisions. By 2013, the DC Circuit reversed every district court decision granting the writ and affirmed nearly every decision denying the writ.[71] It set up a de facto principle of total deference to the executive branch through decisions that, among other things, reversed careful fact-finding by lower courts,[72] accepted the authenticity of the government's evidence,[73] rejected the relevance of international law,[74] and largely limited the authority of courts to order a detainee released.[75] As the appellate judge David Tatel observed in a dissenting opinion in *Latif v. Obama*, the DC Circuit's post-*Boumediene* jurisprudence "comes perilously close to suggesting that whatever the government says must be treated as true."[76]

The conservative judges on the DC Circuit made no secret of their open defiance of the Supreme Court. One judge on the circuit described *Boumediene* as full of "airy suppositions" about the practicality of judicial review, while Judge Raymond Randolph, whose decisions had been overturned by the Supreme Court in detainee cases on three separate occasions and who led the charge to dismantle *Boumediene* in case after case, compared the Supreme Court justices in *Boumediene* to Tom and Daisy Buchanan in *The Great Gatsby*—"careless people, who smashed things up [and] let other people clean up the mess they made."[77] It was as if *Boumediene* had never been decided. For Guantánamo detentions, the writ no longer exists as a mechanism of accountability.[78]

This had tragic consequences, as the case of Adnan Latif reveals. Like so many Guantánamo detainees, Latif was in Afghanistan for utterly innocuous reasons and was captured fleeing the US bombing campaign in that country. Following *Boumediene*, the federal district court in his case found the government's evidence of his affiliation with al-Qaeda "not convincing" and ruled his detention unlawful. Even though the Guantánamo Task Force had cleared Adnan for release, the Obama administration itself appealed the district court's decision to the government-friendly DC Circuit. Predictably, another conservative panel of the DC Circuit reversed the decision, basically adopting a "Guantánamo-only" rule that accepted the government's evidence on its say-so. Adnan Latif filed a compelling petition for certiorari, pleading with the Supreme Court to correct the steady evisceration of its *Boumediene* decision by the DC Circuit. The Court declined, relegating *Boumediene* to nothing more than an empty promise.[79] Adnan, who had earlier written to his lawyer that "I am a prisoner of death," killed himself in his cell not long after.[80]

While detainees were experiencing judicial abdication, they saw political retrenchment as well. Despite his early promise—and action—toward closing Guantánamo, President Obama lost his will. Republicans in Congress demonized his plan to repatriate Uighurs in Virginia and realized that conservatives could be effective in painting Obama as weak on national security.[81] Congress also passed laws imposing challenging—albeit not insurmountable—conditions on transferring detainees to third countries. By 2013, judicial relief was impossible and diplomatic attempts to repatriate detainees had effectively stopped. No lawyers had grounds to litigate habeas cases, as *Boumediene* had seemed to promise.

Given the futility of law during this period, in February 2013 detainees took matters into their own hands. Seizing control over the only aspect of the life they retained, detainees engaged in a hunger strike that reached more than a hundred men—two-thirds of the prison population. More than forty-five were painfully force-fed through plastic tubes inserted through their noses and into their stomachs. This collective action by the detainees got the president's attention when he was asked about it at a press conference. Obama again articulated the "this is not who we are" trope—that is to say, we don't hold people indefinitely without trial or force-feed them.[82] One would have to question the belated and increasingly mythical invocation of American values. Inside the administration, however, the strike put some pressure to restart the transfer and resettlement process.

In the last two years of his administration, Obama transferred eighty-one men—still not enough to close the prison. The consequences of prolonged indefinite detention for those implicated by that continuing judicial and political abdication are severe.[83] The forty-one men who Obama could not release by the end of his term now face Donald Trump's Islamophobic administration, empowered by the DC Circuit's judicial rulings and the Supreme Court's abandonment of Guantánamo to do what the president wants without legal constraint.

Longer Lessons from Crisis Lawyering

As we can see, this story about the search for law in a lawless place is complex and far from triumphalist, as it failed in its ultimate aspiration to end indefinite detention and close the prison. Indeed, as Jack Goldsmith has argued—with a considerable sting to this human rights lawyer—the initial challenges to the illegality of Guantánamo have, per the DC Circuit's reckoning, actually instantiated a legal regime that *justifies* continuing detention *pursuant to legal process*.[84]

But let me stress: I have absolutely no regret for the role that CCR, I, and hundreds of other lawyers and activists played in representing Guantánamo detainees and challenging other aspects of the war on terrorism. This was a courageous and principled response to a genuine human rights crisis, motivated by the highest aspirations of conscientious lawyering. It was not only consequential—I dare say it was often heroic. This legal effort exposed incompetence, cruelty, torture, and deeply misguided executive policies; it narrated the experiences of humans who would otherwise have remained voiceless and demonized; it captured the attention of the highest decision makers in the land and across the world; and it led to the release of 750 men from the brutality and indignity of indefinite detention. Personally, it was the most meaningful, morally engaging, and challenging work I have ever done, made more so because it was in coordination with an awe-inspiring coalition of creative and committed lawyers, activists, and clients.

Still, as this story of lawyering and rights was playing out, I had considerable frustration that important basic rights—including those we thought we first obtained in *Rasul* and then substantiated in *Boumediene*—did not take hold in Guantánamo or as part of our broader struggle against excesses in the war on terrorism. Rights were held out before us repeatedly, like Lucy with Charlie Brown's football, only to be taken away at the last second. In the end, we learned a difficult lesson about what it means to fight for law in a lawless place. The reason for this may not be surprising to political scientists and anthropologists, but for those who are trained in the imagined neutrality of legal doctrine and have faith in a linear story of progressive American constitutionalism, this can be a lesson worth recalibrating.

After all, rights do not exist in a vacuum. They are not freestanding, three-dimensional objects, with a shape and mass that endure once they are recognized. Instead, rights are utterly contingent on politics—not the other way around. They depend on membership in a political community. Hannah Arendt famously defined citizenship as the "right to have rights,"[85] by which she meant one could not access rights such as freedom from deprivation of life and liberty if not recognized as a legitimate member of the political community.[86] Drawing from this framework, Muneer Ahmad has observed that the problem for Guantánamo detainees, for victims of drone strikes, and for Muslims unfairly treated in the United States is that, politically dispossessed as they continue to be, they have "no right to have rights."[87] Without corresponding political legitimacy, any jurisprudentially recognized rights can be taken away soon thereafter.

If this is true, it suggests we need a more modulated approach to long-term struggles for justice. It causes me to think about rights tactics and strategies slightly differently and to offer a more optimistic take on the struggles since 9/11. As Michael Ratner and the other Guantánamo pioneers recognized, the law started and remained a critical articulation of principle, carrying a narrative force about the value of democracy, human rights, and human dignity that can override claims of raw state power. But legal principle alone will rarely be enough. The success of the Guantánamo work, by any measure—releases, changed narratives, historical memory—came from the mass mobilization of lawyers, activists, and advocates who offered a sustained critique of all aspects of the institution, leveraging stories of clients and exposing the cruelty and contradiction of the Guantánamo experiment. Thus, it was the legal mobilization and advocacy that *Rasul* unleashed (far more that the "rights" purportedly promised by *Boumediene*) that had the most consequence in this now decades-old struggle for justice. And for this remarkable reckoning of law and movement-building to be sustained into the future in any context, it has to be fueled by the deeply human, by the enduring and reinforcing values that stand opposite to repression: hope, empathy, and solidarity.

And after almost two decades of lawyering in a lawless space, I recognize other, more critical modes of lawyering outside the rights-vindication paradigm. They include:

Lawyering as Principle. For a politically oriented and experienced lawyer like Michael Ratner, principles like democracy, rule of law, and human rights are not just worth fighting for; they also have a narrative force that can change minds and limit power. They can fuel long-term campaigns for justice.

Lawyering as Hope and Resistance. Authoritarian systems like Guantánamo seek to isolate victims from the rule of law and their lawyers simply because lawyers mean that "help is on the way." In other words, lawyers produce hope in systems that are otherwise dependent on desolation and despair. Indeed, the first set of the ultimately hundreds of lawyers that would enter Guantánamo fractured the prism of total power and ensured that the prison would never be the same. Lawyers can form a layer of resistance protecting clients from continuing applications of state violence.

Lawyering as Recognition. As Ahmad powerfully observes, the central tactic of the George W. Bush administration in creating Guantánamo was myth-making and erasure. To this end, detainees had no identity other than the one constructed upon them. In this myth, menacing Muslim terrorists are entitled to no rights and no recognition. As Ahmad also argues, even without conclusive courtroom victories, the simple filing of a case—*versus* the president of the United States of America or the secretary of defense—represents a demand for individualized recognition and rights in age-old legal traditions embodied in the Great Writ and in historical struggles for justice dating back to the Magna Carta. It is akin to the existential assertion of rights as a form of bearing witness, as the brilliant death penalty lawyer Bryan Stevenson urges us to do when confronting racial injustice in the criminal justice system.[88] It is saying "I am not invisible" and "I am here" and "My client is here, and we are watching you." A demand for rights can be seen as a demand to blunt the force of the state, even if that demand cannot fundamentally alter state power.

Lawyering as Critique. Law in its greatest practical force can produce judicial decrees ordering the government to do something, including releasing someone from detention. But even in cases involving an unjust state, lawyers can use law to critique and destabilize a practice and, if successful, surface enough contradictions to make the practice unsustainable. The first Guantánamo filing in 2002 is a perfect example of this. Despite being "hopeless" at the time, the long-term litigation strategy challenging the Bush administration's practices opened political space to talk about the legality of its practices, inside and outside the courtroom. And after the *Rasul* decision, the influx of lawyers—and the retail lawyering and advocacy it produced—unleashed a torrent of critique about the incompetence and cruelty of administration officials, the innocence of our clients, the torture, and the interrogation that rendered Guantánamo politically unsustainable for some time.

Lawyering as Storytelling. Once lawyers were paired with clients, human stories could be told. Stories of suffering, despair, dignity, and families left behind could all be channeled into the public sphere. This had a powerful neutralizing effect on the administration's efforts to paint detainees with an undifferentiated wash of dangerousness, and on its own it had the effect of affirming detainees' dignity. Lawyers facilitated one detainee's pleas to the outside world by circulating detainee poetry and art, and they channeled clients' humanity from a dark cell on the edge of the world directly into the American public consciousness.[89]

Lawyering as Movement Support. CCR did not seek to hold onto the Guantánamo cases to advance its own institutional prerogatives. Along with others, CCR sought to democratize the representation of detainees. This had obvious administrative and resourcing benefits, but it also had another intentional aim that was functionally realized: it produced a collective, organized, and dynamic—indeed, global—movement of lawyers and advocates in a concerted effort to close Guantánamo. This mutually reinforcing effort of lawyers, human rights advocates, and institutions built its own momentum to successfully mitigate the excessive power claimed by the Bush administration.[90] The formidable collective known as the Guantánamo Bay Bar Association became so legitimized that administration attempts to criticize or intimidate it were an instant failure. The international nonprofit community that mobilized for Guantánamo still exists and collaborates on a range of practices related to excessive state power. I personally know several dozen since-radicalized big law firm partners ready to channel their Guantánamo-inspired outrage to challenge Trump administration practices. Indeed, I believe one of the reasons for the success of rapid responses to the Trump administration's lawlessness is the movement of politically oriented lawyers and organizations that have practiced and organized collectively in response to the Bush administration's excesses.

Lawyering as Liberation, Reunification, and Love. Earlier, I told you the story of meeting my client Murat Kurnaz for the first time and what it was like to break the seal of isolation and hopelessness together. That moment was transcendent—if abstract—and it felt like a crack in the force field of militarism, violence, and degradation. I'd like to end with another story about my client that I hope reinforces how, despite its monumental frustrations, lawyering can be life-altering for those engaged in it—a process of liberation, solidarity, and affirmation of basic human dignity.

In August 2006, German officials told my German cocounsel, Bernhard Docke, and I that Murat would likely be released. On August 24, 2006, I met the Kurnaz family at a gas station outside of Murat's hometown of Bremen for the six-hour drive south toward Ramstein Air Force Base. We were told he would be arriving in the early evening on a C-17 transport plane. The day was full of intrigue—secret meetings with German officials; constant, intrusive calls from German and American reporters; and almost overwhelming anxiety. While we waited in a Red Cross facility for seniors, we saw a huge C-17 military plane descending from the sky. It was Murat.

Murat's mother, Rabiye (who had been fighting tirelessly and courageously for her son's release for years), Murat's father, and his two brothers assembled in a hallway on the fourth floor to greet Murat. Rabiye stood in front of the creaky elevator doors, where her anticipation built to an almost unbearable level as the elevator repeatedly started and stopped, huffed and creaked. When the doors finally opened, Rabiye latched on to her son as if he might be taken away from her again at any moment. With Murat in her arms, she wept.

In the incredible excitement of that very long day, including a 3 A.M. rush to get the Kurnaz family home past a swarm of waiting journalists, I remember one thing more clearly than any other: during the dozens of hours that Murat and I had spent together in Guantánamo, his ankle had always been chained to the floor.

That day, for the first time, I saw Murat walk.

NOTES

1 *See* Center for Constitutional Rights, https://ccrjustice.org.

2 *Id.*

3 *Id.*

4 Military Order of November 13, 2001, 66 Fed. Reg. 222 (Nov. 13, 2001).

5 The president claimed authority to do so—and to override both congressional and constitutional strictures on the use of military trials—upon his administration's robust understanding of the commander-in-chief powers of Article II of the Constitution—an authority that administration lawyers deemed could override virtually every codified legal constraint in the war on terror. He also based it on the ample and elastic authority conferred by Congress via the Authorization for Use of Military Force, which provided—and, incredibly, still authorizes the president to use—"all necessary and appropriate force against those nations, organizations, or persons he determines planned, authorized, committed, or aided the terrorist attacks that occurred on September 11, 2001." Authorization for Use of Military Force, Pub. L. No. 107-40, 115 Stat. 224 (2001).

6 JOSEPH MARGULIES, GUANTÁNAMO AND THE ABUSE OF PRESIDENTIAL POWER (2007) (arguing that prolonged, preventive detention, coercive

interrogations, and secrecy were hallmarks of the administration detention policy commencing after 9/11 and carrying through to Abu Ghraib).

7   Michael Isikoff, *The Gitmo Fallout*, NEWSWEEK (July 16, 2006), www.newsweek. com. *See also* Memorandum for William J. Haynes, II, General Counsel, Department of Defense, from Patrick F. Philbin & John C. Yoo, Deputy Assistant Attorneys General, Office of Legal Counsel (Dec. 28, 2001), *reprinted in* THE TORTURE PAPERS: THE ROAD TO ABU GHRAIB, 29—37 (Karen J. Greenberg & Joshua L. Dratel eds. 2005) (stating their belief that a federal district court cannot properly exercise *habeus corpus* jurisdiction over detainees on Guantánamo because the United States does not have sovereignty over the island under its lease with Cuba (Agreement Between United States of America and the Republic of Cuba for the Lease to the United States of Lands in Cuba for Coaling and Naval Stations, Feb. 16–23, 1903, U.S.-Cuba, T.S. No. 418, 6 Bevans 1113 [hereinafter "lease agreement"]); *Vermilya-Brown Co. v. Connell*, 335 U.S. 377, 380 (1948) (stating that the United States has no sovereignty over Guantánamo Bay).

8   *See* Neil A. Lewis, *Red Cross Finds Detainee Abuse in Guantánamo*, N.Y. TIMES (Nov. 30, 2004) (reporting conclusions of the ICRC, whose investigative team spent most of June 2004 at Guantánamo, that "investigators had found a system devised to break the will of the prisoners at Guantánamo . . . through 'humiliating acts, solitary confinement, temperature extremes, [and] use of forced positions.'").

9   Muneer Ahmad, *Resisting Guantánamo*, 103 NW. U. L. REV. 1683, 1696 (2009).

10 Joseph Margulies, *The Myth of the Superhuman Terrorist*, NATL. L.J. (Nov. 23, 2009).

11 *See* Ahmad, *Resisting Guantánamo*, 1695.

12 Katharine Q. Seelye, *A Nation Challenged: The Prisoners; First 'Unlawful Combatants' Seized in Afghanistan Arrive at U.S. Base in Cuba*, N.Y. TIMES (Jan. 12, 2002).

13 *See* Greg Miller, *Many Held in Guantánamo Likely Not Terrorist Suspects*, L.A. TIMES (Dec. 22, 2002) (reporting that Maj. Gen. Dunleavy traveled to Afghanistan to complain about the number of "Mickey Mouse" detainees being sent to Guantánamo).

14 Margulies, *The Myth*.

15 And, because as we shall later see, lawyers would eventually expose the reality that very few detainees were bona fide terrorist suspects, the administration needed to continue to deny rights—and corresponding visability—to feed the (false) narrative that these detentions were necessary to prevent another terrorist attack.

16 Ahmad, *Resisting Guantánamo*, 1695.

17 *See generally* MICHAEL SMITH, LAWYERS OF THE LEFT (2019); BRANDT GOLDSTEIN, STORMING THE COURT (2005). Tragically, in 2016, Michael, who never shied away from a fight, battled but ultimately succumbed to cancer. Vincent Warren, *CCR Mourns The Loss of a Hero—Michael Ratner* (May 11, 2016), https://ccrjustice.org; David Cole, *Michael Ratner, RIP*, JUST SECURITY (May 11,

2016), www.justsecurity.org; Harold Koh, *Michael Ratner: The Leading Progressive Lawyer of a Generation*, JUST SECURITY (May 12, 2016), www.justsecurity.org.

18 Critically, as an experienced human rights lawyer, he had seen this play out before. Just about ten years prior, following a coup and resulting humanitarian crisis in Haiti, hundreds of Haitians fled in overcrowded boats in search of American shorelines—and asylum. The first Bush administration (George H. W. Bush) deployed the Coast Guard to interdict the Haitians and house them in prison-like pens in Guantánamo Bay. Ratner, along with the brilliant, young Yale law professor (and future dean) Harold Koh supervising students in the Human Rights Law Clinic there (including many who would continue the radical lawyering tradition learned during that case and three of whom—Christy Lopez, Ray Brescia, and Michael Wishnie—are contributors to this volume), filed a legal challenge arguing that the indeterminate detention without access to the asylum process violated U.S. and international law. The first Bush administration took the position that, as foreign nationals located on foreign soil (i.e., Cuba), they were not entitled to assert rights in U.S. courts—a position Ratner knew he would encounter again this time. The broader litigation and advocacy campaign on behalf of the Haitians was largely successful; many were allowed to seek asylum in Florida. *See* GOLDSTEIN, STORMING THE COURT.

19 Michael Ratner, *Litigating Guantánamo, in* INTERNATIONAL PROSECUTION OF HUMAN RIGHTS CRIMES 202 (2007).

20 Other CCR lawyers who were central to the initial filing were then-legal director Bill Goodman, Barbara Olshansky, and Steven Watt. In subsequent years, dozens of CCR staff spent thousands of hours representing detainees and fighting in the courts of law and public opinion, including: Seema Ahmad, Jesse Baen, Liz Bradley, Kevi Brannelly, Annette Dickerson, Wells Dixon, Abigail Downs, Omar Farah, Tina Foster, Susan Hu, Aliya Hussain, Gita Gutierrez, Shayana Kadidal, Pardiss Kebriaei, Rachel Meeropol, Jen Nessel, Ibraham Qatabi, Omar Shakir, Vince Warren, Noor Zafar, and numerous others.

21 Ratner, *Litigating Guantánamo.*

22 U.S. CONST. art I, § 9, cl. 2; *Rasul v. Bush*, 542 U.S. 466, 474 (2004).

23 *See Rasul*, 542 U.S. at 474; *see generally* JONATHAN HAFETZ, HABEAS CORPUS AFTER 9/11: CONFRONTING AMERICA'S NEW GLOBAL DETENTION SYSTEM (2011)

24 *Rasul*, 542 U.S. at 476–77.

25 Another case was brought by a team of lawyers, including constitutional scholar and advocate Erwin Chemerinsky, asserting "Next Friend" status for a group of clergy seeking to bring habeas claims on all of the detainees' behalf. That case was dismissed for lack of standing. *Coalition of Clergy v. Bush*, 189 F.Supp.2d 1036 (C.D. Cal. 2002), *aff'd* 310 F.3d 1153 (9th Cir. 2002), *cert. denied*, 538 U.S. 1031.

26 *See Johnson v. Eisentrager*, 339 U.S. 763, 790–91 (1950).

27 *See* Ahmad, *Resisting Guantánamo*, 1695.

28 DAVID COLE, ENGINES OF LIBERTY: THE POWER OF CITIZEN ACTIVISTS TO MAKE CONSTITUTIONAL LAW (2016).

29 *Al Odah v. United States*, 321 F.3d 1134 (D.C. Cir. 2003), *rev'd sub nom. Rasul v. Bush*, 542 U.S. 466 (2004).

30 Supreme Court of the United States, *Rumsfeld v. Padilla*, No. 03–1027, Tr. Of Oral Argument, 23 (Apr. 28, 2004).

31 JOSEPH MARGULIES, GUÁNTANAMO AND THE ABUSE OF PRESIDENTIAL POWER (2007).

32 *Rasul*, 542 U.S. at 480.

33 David Stout, *Supreme Court Affirms Detainees Rights to Use Courts*, N.Y. TIMES (June 28, 2004).

34 Memorandum from Paul Wolfowitz, Deputy Sec'y of Def., Order Establishing Combatant Status Review Tribunal (July 7, 2004) ("The term "enemy combatant" shall mean an individual who was part of or supporting Taliban or al-Qaeda forces, or associated forces that are engaged in hostilities against the United States or its coalition partners. This includes any person who has committed a belligerent act or has directly supported hostilities in aid of enemy armed forces.")

35 *In re Guantánamo Detainee Cases*, 355 F. Supp. 2d 443, 475 (D.D.C. 2005).

36 *Azmy v. U.S. Department of Defense*, 562 F. Supp. 2d590 (S.D.N.Y. 2008).

37 *Id.*

38 Stacy Sullivan, *Minutes of the Guantánamo Bay Bar Association*, N.Y. MAG. (June 16, 2016), http://nymag.com.

39 Detainee Treatment Act of 2005, Pub. L. No. 109-148, §§ 1001–1006 (2005).

40 *See Hamdan v. Rumsfeld*, 548 U.S. 557, 635 (2006).

41 Military Commissions Act of 2006, Pub. L. 109-366, 120 Stat. 2600 (2006).

42 Later, the ACLU would start the John Adams Project to recruit lawyers to represent the so-called 9/11 conspirators who were moved to Guantánamo in 2006 from secret CIA detention and who faced death-eligible charges in military commissions proceedings.

43 David Cole, *Michael Ratner's Army*, NEW YORK REVIEW OF BOOKS (May 15, 2016), www.nybooks.com.

44 Mark Denbeaux et al., *Report on Guantánamo Detainees: A Profile of 517 Detainees Through Analysis of Department of Defense Data*, SETON HALL U. SCH. OF L. (2006).

45 *Kiyemba v. Obama*, 563 U.S. 954 (2011) (noting the Uighurs had "been held for several years in custody at Guantánamo Bay, Cuba—a detention that the Government agrees was without lawful cause") (Breyer, J., statement re denial of certiorari); Editorial, *The Rule of Law in Guantánamo*, N.Y. TIMES (Oct. 11, 2008) (criticizing the U.S. government for continuing to detain indivduals even the government thinks innocent).

46 *See* Carol D. Leonnig, *Panel Ignored Evidence on Detainee; U.S. Military Intelligence, German Authorities Found No Ties to Terrorists*, WASH. POST (Mar. 27, 2005) (quoting once-classified statements in Kurnaz's classified file

demonstrating that both the U.S. military and his home German government recognize he had no connections to terrorist groups); see also Richard Bernstein, *One Man's Odyssey to Guantánamo*, N.Y. TIMES (June 2, 2005) (describing conclusions of German officials that Kurnaz has no connections to terrorism or al-Qaeda). In an interview with *60 Minutes*, Kurnaz detailed his experience as a prisoner in Guantánamo, as well as his claims of torture and the government's own evidence proving his innocence. *Ex-Terror Detainee Says U.S. Tortured Him*, CBS NEWS (Mar. 28, 2008), www.cbsnews.com.

47 *They Came for the Chicken Farmer*, N.Y. TIMES (Mar. 8, 2006) 9 (describing the case of a chicken farmer in Pakistan, detained because his name resembled the Taliban deputy foreign minister's name); Tom Lasseter, *Day 1: America's Prison for Terrorists Often Held the Wrong Men*, MCCLATCHY NEWSPAPERS (June 15, 2008), www.mcclatchydc.com ("An eight-month McClatchy investigation in 11 countries on three continents has found that [there are] perhaps hundreds [of men] whom the U.S. has wrongfully imprisoned in Afghanistan, Cuba and elsewhere on the basis of flimsy or fabricated evidence, old personal scores or bounty payments.")

48 *See Tipton Three Complain of Beatings*, BBC NEWS (Mar. 14, 2004), http://news. bbc.co.uk (referring to Omar Kadhr, Kurnaz, and al Qatani).

49 Juma Al-Dassari, *A Voice From Gitmo's Darkness*, L.A. TIMES (Jan. 11, 2007), www.latimes.com.

50 Alan Cowell, *U.S. 'Thumbs Its Nose' at Rights, Amnesty Says*, N.Y. TIMES (May 26, 2005).

51 *See* HUMAN RIGHTS WATCH, GUANTÁNAMO TEN YEARS ON (2012), www. hrw.org. *See also* the materials on Guantánamo compiled by Human Rights First at www.humanrightsfirst.org.

52 *See* Stephen Soldz, *When American Psychologists Use Their Skills for Torture*, QUARTZ (July 26, 2015), https://qz.com. (recounting infighting around deployment of mental health professionals in military interrogations).

53 *See* Brief of the Cato Institute as Amicus Curiae in Support of Petitioners, *Boumediene v. Bush*, 2007 WL 2441584 (U.S.).

54 *See* Brief of Retired Generals and Admirals, Washington Legal Foundation, Allied Educational Foundation, and the National Defense Committee as Amici Curiae in Support of Respondents, *Boumediene v. Bush*, 2007 WL 2986451 (U.S.).

55 In one of the most important constitutional cases of the era, which was initiated by Swift's brave defiance of unethical military pressure, *Hamdan v. Rumsfeld* struck down the then-existing military commissions system. *See generally* JONATHAN MAHLER, THE CHALLENGE: HAMDAN V. RUMSFELD AND THE FIGHT OVER PRESIDENTIAL POWER (2008).

56 *See* David Marr, *David Hicks' Lawyer Michael "Dan" Mori on the PR Campaign That Saved His Client*, THE GUARDIAN (Dec. 4, 2014), www.theguardian.com.

57 One of the clearest examples of this involved a statement made by Cully Stimpson, the deputy director of defense for detainee affairs in 2007, in which he identified about a dozen major American law firms representing detainees and

with some measure of shock suggested that CEOs represented by such firms drop the firms or "make those law firms choose between representing terrorists or representing reputable firms[.]" David Luban, *Lawfare and Legal Ethics in Guantánamo*, 60 STAN. L. REV. 1981 (2008). As Luban put it, the bullying tactic was a signal failure:

> Within days, newspaper editorials and bar groups denounced Stimson's crude attempt to pressure the Guantánamo lawyers to abandon their clients; Charles Fried, the conservative former Solicitor General, wrote a blistering op-ed against Stimson; and the Defense Department embarrassedly disowned Stimson's comments. Stimson apologized; and three weeks after the interview he was out of a job.

> *Id.*, at 1982.

The ethical mission of the Guantánamo Bar Association had become invulnerable to questioning.

58 U.S. CONST. art I, § 9, cl. 2.

59 That change of direction is attributable to the interplay between wholesale and retail lawyering. David Cynammon, a commercial lawyer at a commercial D.C. firm, joined the Guantánamo Bar Association around 2006, representing Kuwaiti detainees. Through a series of personal and professional connections, Cynammon located Stephen Abraham, a former naval intelligence officer who had been involved in a number of the CSRT military administrative panels and who was willing to blow the whistle at that moment in time about that laughably one-sided and outcome-determinative process. Abraham's whistleblowing, which showed that the military could not be trusted to dispense justice without judicial review, was a product of retail lawyering. Yet, the wholesale lawyering team relied on Abraham's testimonial in urging the Supreme Court to reconsider its position, which likely caused the Court to change course and grant the original petitioners' additional request for review. *See Gitmo Panelist Slams Hearing Process*, CBS (Feb. 11, 2009), www.cbsnews.com.

60 *See* Marty Lederman, *Quick Reactions to* Boumediene *Oral Argument*, SCOTUSBLOG (Dec. 5, 2007), www.scotusblog.com (calling this portion of Waxman's argument "one of the more powerful and effective rebuttals I've ever seen").

61 *See Boumediene v. Bush*, 553 U.S. 723 (2008).

62 *See* Baher Azmy, *Boumediene, Executive Detention and the New Common Law of Habeas*, 95 IOWA L. REV. 445 (2010).

63 *Boumediene*, 553 U.S. at 765

64 *Id.* at 727.

65 *Id.* at 728.

66 *In re Guantánamo Bay Detainee Litig.*, No. 08-MC-442, 2008 WL 4858241 (D.D.C. Nov. 6, 2008).

67 Azmy, *Boumediene*.

68 *In re Guantánamo Bay Detainee Litig.*, 581 F. Supp. 2d 33 (D.D.C. 2008), *rev'd and remanded sub nom. Kiyemba v. Obama*, 555 F.3d 1022 (D.C. Cir. 2009), vacated, 559 U.S. 131 (2010).

69 *See* Azmy, *Boumediene.*

70 *See* Exec. Order No. 13492, 3 C.F.R. § 101 (2010).

71 For comprehensive treatment of the DC Circuit's dismantling of habeas, *see generally* Stephen I. Vladeck, *The D.C. Circuit After Boumediene*, 42 Seton Hall L. Rev. 1 (2011).

72 *See generally Al-Adahi v. Obama*, 613 F.3d 1102 (D.C. Cir. 2010) (overturning a district court's factual finding that detainee was not a member of al-Qaeda).

73 *See Latif v. Obama*, 666 F.3d 746, 748–49 (D.C. Cir. 2011).

74 *See Al-Bihani v. Obama*, 590 F.3d 866, 871 (D. C. Cir. 2010).

75 *See Kiyemba v. Obama*, 555 F.3d 1022, 1026 (D.C. Cir. 2009)

76 *See Latif*, 666 F.3d at 779 (Tatel, J., dissenting) (quoting *Parhat v. Gates*, 532 F.3d. 834, 849 (D.C. Cir. 2008).

77 Raymond Randolph, *Joseph Story Distinguished Lecture: The Guantánamo Mess*, Address Delivered to the Heritage Foundation (Oct. 20, 2010). Arch conservative stalwart Judge Silberman wrote in an opinion that, unlike with criminal defendants, the risk of erroneous decision to release terrorist suspects compels that they be afforded fewer legal protections. *Esmail v. Obama*, 639 F.3d 1075, 1078 (D.C. Cir. 2011) (Silberman, J., concurring) ("I doubt any of my colleagues will vote to grant a petition if he or she believes that it is somewhat likely that the petitioner is an al Qaeda adherent or an active supporter.")

78 Linda Greenhouse, *Goodbye to Gitmo*, N.Y. Times (May 16, 2012) (discussing D.C. Circuit's disdain for the Supreme Court's ruling and its refusal to intervene post-*Boumediene*).

79 Notably, the Supreme Court granted certiorari *seven* times to review "enemy combatant" cases during a four-year period of the George W. Bush administration. *See Rasul v. Bush*, 542 U.S 466 (2004), *Rumsfeld v. Padilla*, 542 U.S. 426 (2004), *Hamdi v. Rumsfeld*, 542 U.S. 507 (2004), *Hamdan v. Rumsfeld*, 548 U.S. 557 (2006), *Rumsfield v. Padilla*, 542 U.S. 426 (2004), *Al Marri v. Spagone*, 555 U.S. 2020 (2009), and *Boumediene v. Bush*, 553 U.S. 723 (2008). During the eight years of the Barack Obama administration, despite numerous requests from detainees, the Court took no cases involving military detention. This dynamic underscores a critical narrative point: as long as Guantánamo was perceived to be exceptional—a perception aided by the bellicosity and arrogance of the Bush administration's legal positions—the Court would see itself having a role to intervene and course-correct. But, with Obama, who seemed measured, obedient to the law, and pledged to do the work himself to close the prison, the Court must have perceived it had no necessary role to superintend military affairs. Thus, far from the exceptional institution the Court seemed to reject in 2004, throughout the Obama administration the Court accepted the increasing normalization of Guantánamo into American life and law.

80 Baher Azmy, *The Face of Indefinite Detention*, N.Y. Times (Sept. 14, 2012).

81 *See, e.g.*, Charlie Savage, Power Wars: Inside Obama's Post-9/11 Presidency (2017).

82 Paul Harris, *Guantánamo 'Not In the Best Interests of the American People,' Says Obama*, THE GUARDIAN (May 1, 2013), www.thegaurdian.com.

83 *See, e.g.*, Sudarsan Raghavan, *Long After His Release, an Ex-Detainee Struggles With Guantánamo's Torturous Clutches*, WASH. POST (Apr. 25, 2018).

84 JACK GOLDSMITH, POWER AND CONSTRAINT: THE ACCOUNTABLE PRESIDENCY AFTER 9/11 (2012). For a critique of Goldsmith's sunny perspective on the state of checks on executive power, *see* Baher Azmy, *An Insufficiently Accountable Presidency*, 45 CASE W. RES. J. INT'L L. 23 (2012)

85 *See* Masha Gessen, *"The Right to Have Rights" and the Plight of the Stateless*, THE NEW YORKER (May 3, 2018), www.newyorker.com.

86 For exploration of this principle in the context of Guantánamo, see Ahmad, *Resisting Guantánamo.*

87 *Id.*

88 *See generally* BRYAN STEVENSON, JUST MERCY (2014).

89 *See, e.g.*, POEMS FROM GUANTÁNAMO (Marc Falkoff ed., 2007); *Ode to the Sea: Art from Guantánamo Bay*, www.artfromGuantánamo.com.

90 As professor Jules Lobell has explained, the winner-take-all model of American law does not sufficiently capture the power of lawyering even in loss. Even losing cases, he observes, "have helped to create a community and a culture dedicated to litigating the constitutional aspirations of oppressed groups," and "communities often gain their identities not in celebrating their victories but in remembering their defeats." JULES LOBELL, SUCCESS WITHOUT VICTORY: LOST LEGAL BATTLES AND THE LONG ROAD TO JUSTICE IN AMERICA 6–7 (2003).

3

Responding to the (Dual) Policing Crisis in Ferguson

CHRISTY E. LOPEZ

The United States Department of Justice (DOJ) has the ability to investigate law enforcement agencies and demand civil relief to eliminate of patterns or practices of misconduct, pursuant to 34 United States Code § 12601 (formerly 42 United States Code § 14141). Enforcement of this statute has been delegated to DOJ's Civil Rights Division. At its most robust, this enforcement has led to findings reports that detail what DOJ learned during its investigations of law enforcement agencies, followed by the negotiation and implementation of federal court orders called "consent decrees." In this chapter, I analyze the events that occurred in Ferguson, Missouri, in 2014 related to the police killing of Michael Brown Jr. as a way to explore how DOJ's pattern-or-practice investigations and subsequent consent decrees relate to broader efforts to transform policing. I led the Civil Rights Division team that investigated the Ferguson Police Department.

Introduction

In August 2014, the St. Louis suburb of Ferguson, Missouri, began to flash across screens as a city in crisis. Michael Brown Jr., an unarmed eighteen-year-old African American Ferguson resident, had been shot and killed by a white Ferguson police officer named Darren Wilson. People rose up in response to the killing, and there were peaceful and nonpeaceful protests, with some significant property damage. The response of law enforcement to the protests was viewed by much of the nation to be disproportionate and unnecessarily forceful, inflaming tensions rather than promoting peace and protecting people. For some, the law enforcement response—which included the use of canines and tactical vehicles and placing snipers on rooftops—was disturbingly reminiscent of law enforcement brutality during the civil rights movement of the 1960s or the quelling of protests in dictatorial nations.[1] This crisis continued for weeks, with renewed large-scale protests—and more property damage—occurring later in response to announcements that a St. Louis grand jury had declined to indict Darren Wilson for violation of state law and, following that, the decision by the US Department of Justice not to prosecute Wilson for violations of federal civil rights laws.

But DOJ's criminal investigation of Darren Wilson was only part of the department's response to the crisis in Ferguson. DOJ's broader response included a pattern-or-practice investigation of the entire Ferguson Police Department (FPD), which DOJ's Civil Rights Division[2] opened in September 2014. It is this broader response by DOJ that is the topic of this chapter.

The pattern-or-practice investigation of the FPD focused on whether there was systemic law enforcement misconduct by the police department. In early spring 2015, DOJ issued a 102-page documentation of the Civil Rights Division's findings regarding unconstitutional conduct by the Ferguson Police Department (the "Ferguson Report" or the "Findings Report")[3]. The Ferguson Report made clear that underneath the widely visible crisis following Michael Brown's killing was a deeper crisis manifested, in part, in longstanding, systemic, and unlawful conduct by the FPD. The report showed how this deeper crisis had created a "powder keg," in the words of United States Attorney General Eric Holder, that ignited when Darren Wilson shot Mike Brown and his body was left on the street in the August sun for several hours. Or, as put by law professor and Ferguson activist Justin Hansford, the Report was affirmation that, indeed, "water is wet."

Although the news that the policing crisis in Ferguson during the summer of 2014 was rooted in something much deeper was utterly unsurprising to some, it came as a disturbing revelation to many. The Ferguson Report was thus able to serve not only as the basis of a broad federal consent decree (approved in April 2016) requiring extensive changes to Ferguson's police department and municipal court system but also as a catalyst for reckoning and change in police departments and court systems nationwide.

This chapter uses DOJ's work in Ferguson as a case study to explore the proper role for DOJ more broadly in addressing the policing crisis in the United States in the twenty-first century. I argue that it is helpful to this assessment to think of this policing crisis as a *dual* crisis in which one crisis is acute, the other chronic. The *acute policing crisis* involves a city—or cities—in turmoil after a tragic use of state violence, as was the case in Ferguson during the summer of 2014 and as has been the case many times since then, from Baltimore to Minneapolis and beyond. The chronic policing crisis is extraordinarily complex and entrenched. The *chronic policing crisis* is inextricably interwoven with our history as a country. It involves police conduct that is lawful as well as unlawful and implicates actors and practices far beyond the police department or even policing. The chronic crisis of policing exists whether or not it is simultaneously accompanied by an acute policing crisis.

As discussed below, DOJ's pattern-or-practice investigation was largely instigated by the acute crisis that existed in Ferguson. But that investigation also provided DOJ the opportunity to address—incompletely but with significant impact—the chronic crisis of policing not only in Ferguson but in the United States more broadly. This is often the case, as it should be. That is to say, while a DOJ law enforcement misconduct investigation is often prompted by an acute crisis, and the investigation may help ameliorate some of the effects of that crisis, addressing the acute crisis is not and should not be the intent or focus of a DOJ law enforcement misconduct investigation. Nor should DOJ seek, or be expected, to address the chronic policing crisis in its entirety. Rather, the work of a DOJ law enforcement misconduct investigation is to address a relatively narrow aspect of that chronic crisis: unlawful patterns or practices of policing. At the same time, if we conceptualize a policing crisis as a dual crisis and recognize the complexity of the chronic aspect of that crisis in particular, we can explore ways that DOJ's work can and should impact the policing crisis beyond its focus on patterns of illegality. Further, we can better recognize that the potential impact of DOJ's pattern-or-practice police reform work lies not only in the consent decrees it negotiates but also in how it conducts its investigations as well as in any findings reports it issues.

This chapter first describes how DOJ went about addressing the acute and chronic crisis of policing in Ferguson through its law enforcement misconduct investigation and then explores what we might learn from this effort about how DOJ should conduct such investigations in the future. The hope is that this exploration might allow all of us—not only lawyers within DOJ or in civil rights and social justice organizations but also community organizers, police reform and abolition activists, and other criminal justice stakeholders interested in meaningful changes to policing—to learn how to more effectively work together, or at least alongside each other, toward goals that we largely share.

DOJ and the Crisis in Ferguson: 2014–2015[4]

Midday on Saturday, August 9, 2014, after a brief altercation that began when Ferguson Police Department officer Darren Wilson profanely[5] confronted Michael Brown and a friend because they were walking in the street of a residential neighborhood, Wilson shot and killed Michael Brown. Crowds gathered as Michael's body laid on Canfield Drive for hours in the hot August sun. There was word that Brown had been surrendering, with his "hands up," when shot. There was no dispute that the eighteen-year-old African American was unarmed. As evening fell, a fleet of police SUVs descended on Canfield

Drive. Officers wearing black gloves and bulletproof vests and bringing long guns, police dogs, and pepper spray jumped out of the SUVs. This militaristic intrusion into the grieving neighborhood confirmed for some that police either did not understand or did not care how painful Mike Brown's death was.[6] By early Sunday morning large groups of protesters began gathering outside the Ferguson Police Department.

Peaceful and nonpeaceful protests and direct action that would ebb and flow for more than a year had begun. There were incidents of violence and property damage. Perhaps most notable among the first few days was when "armed vandals," in the words of the reporter Wesley Lowrey, "took advantage of raging protests to break into the QuikTrip petrol station" a block away from where Michael Brown was killed. "Before long," Lowrey wrote, "the store was ablaze."[7]

News cameras rolled as the St. Louis County Police Department came into Ferguson with armored vehicles and SWAT officers who trained their guns on peacefully protesting crowds. Police used tear gas and rubber bullets against marching protesters. Snipers were placed on rooftops, and police canines were deployed alongside their handlers. Scores of arrests were made—more than 150 in the first week or so.

On Tuesday, August 12, President Barack Obama made a statement acknowledging concerns about the killing while urging a peaceful response. Both the Department of Justice and the FBI announced they would investigate the shooting for possible federal civil rights violations. Attorney General Eric Holder expressed concern about the equipment and tactics used by local police to handle protests, and Missouri governor Jay Nixon announced that the Missouri State Highway Patrol would take over security operations in Ferguson. The governor then declared a state of emergency, requiring Ferguson residents to stay in their homes between midnight and 5 A.M. The ACLU immediately released a statement expressing civil liberties concerns with the curfew. The next day, the governor rescinded the curfew and, later, ordered in the National Guard.

In the first few days, protests in Ferguson and elsewhere in St. Louis County were, by most accounts, organic and unorganized, which contributed to their unpredictability. Soon, they became more structured, as local activists and organizers went into action. Direct action—from vigils, to picketing the Ferguson Police Department, to blocking traffic on Interstate 70—took place. Protests began to occur in other cities in the United States. Black Lives Matter organized its first in-person national protest, the "Black Lives Matter Freedom Ride," to Ferguson. The Freedom Ride brought more than 500 people from across the country to Ferguson to provide support to activists already on the ground there. Amnesty International deployed a human rights team to Ferguson. Organizers used social media to circulate real-time updates across the country and around the globe. Journalists documented being arrested for their attempts to report on the protests and police response. A student journalist was threatened at gunpoint by a police officer who did not want to be recorded on camera.

Civil rights lawyers were on the ground in Ferguson virtually from the outset of the protests. Some had been there for years. ArchCity Defenders released a white paper, based on its work representing clients in municipal courts across St. Louis County, documenting the long history of abusive fines and fees in municipalities including Ferguson and how this abuse was disproportionately borne by people living in poverty and by African Americans.

In response to the protests, the National Lawyers Guild deployed nearly a hundred legal observers to monitor police conduct during demonstrations. Some of these legal observers were arrested. The Lawyers Guild, along with others, hosted Know Your Rights training sessions and built coalitions of lawyers, students, movement organizers, and others. On August 14, the ACLU of Missouri filed a lawsuit challenging as unconstitutional the police policy of ordering members of the media and public not to record the police acting in their official duty on public streets and sidewalks. On August 18, the ACLU of Missouri filed another First Amendment lawsuit, moving for a temporary restraining order to stop police from requiring people to keep moving on sidewalks and thoroughfares in Ferguson unless gathered in a designated protest area. The temporary restraining order against the "five-second rule" was denied, but a later motion for preliminary injunction, issued after the court heard evidence on the motion, was granted. This injunction was signed later by a federal judge as a permanent order.[8] Similarly, after an initial agreement to resolve the August lawsuit filed by the ACLU for the right to record police proved ineffective, the ACLU moved for a preliminary injunction in November. A federal district judge granted three court orders against the Missouri State Highway Patrol, the county of St. Louis, and the city of Ferguson.

On August 18, Attorney General Eric Holder traveled to Ferguson, accompanied by attorneys from DOJ's Civil Rights Division. During this trip, Holder met with community members but not with Ferguson police officers. Before his trip, Holder had issued a statement condemning "unequivocally" violence by protesters and announcing that DOJ had deployed officials from the Community Relations Service (CRS) to Ferguson. CRS operates pursuant to a statutory mandate to help resolve tensions that arise because of allegations of discriminatory practices.[9] Prior to his trip, Holder also published an op-ed in the *St. Louis Post-Dispatch* in which he wrote: "We understand the need for an independent investigation, and we hope that the independence and thoroughness of our investigation will bring some measure of calm to the tensions in Ferguson." The Attorney General was speaking of the criminal investigation led by the FBI and the Civil Rights Division's Criminal Section into whether Darren Wilson violated Mike Brown's federal civil rights. Upon returning from his trip to Ferguson, Holder announced that DOJ's Community Oriented Policing Service (COPS) Office would send representatives to Ferguson to continue providing technical assistance on crowd-control techniques and facilitating communication between law enforcement and communities.

On August 20, the ACLU of Missouri faxed a letter to the superintendent of the Missouri State Highway Patrol, asking him to identify and remove the police officer who pointed an assault weapon at individuals and threatened to kill them and then, when asked to identify himself, responded with profanity. The Highway Patrol responded the same day that the officer, identified as a St. Ann police officer, had been removed from duty in Ferguson. Also, on August 20 a grand jury in St. Louis began investigating whether Darren Wilson had violated any state criminal laws.[10]

In the midst of this turmoil, DOJ announced, on September 4, that it would investigate the Ferguson Police Department to determine whether it was systematically violating the law. This investigation was brought pursuant to the "law enforcement misconduct" provision of the Violent Crime Control and Law Enforcement Act of 1994. This statute authorizes the United States Attorney General to bring a civil action for equitable and declaratory relief to "eliminate" any "pattern or practice of conduct by law enforcement officers" that violates the United States Constitution or other federal law.[11] DOJ delegated this statutory authority to the Civil Rights Division, which in turn delegated it to the division's Special Litigation Section. The day before the announcement, two federal officials from the Special Litigation Section traveled to Ferguson to meet with city leadership privately to inform them that an investigation was likely. By the time the officials (of whom I was one) had set foot back in Washington, news of the impending investigation was out. The *Washington Post* reported that the launch of the Ferguson pattern-or-practice investigation "will represent the Obama administration's most aggressive step to address the Ferguson shooting, which set off days of often-violent clashes between police and demonstrators in the streets of the St. Louis suburb." Citing federal officials speaking on the condition of anonymity, the *Post* reported that the probe would "look not only at Ferguson but also at other police departments in St. Louis County."[12] While the Civil Rights Division pattern-or-practice investigation included only Ferguson, this statement underscores

DOJ's sensitivity from the outset that the problem was not just in that one city. At the same time it initiated its Ferguson investigation, DOJ's COPS Office also launched the "Collaborative Reform Initiative" with the St. Louis County Police Department, and, as part of its separate "Critical Response Initiative," the COPS Office conducted an after-action assessment of the regional police response to the Ferguson protests.

The Civil Rights Division's pattern-or-practice investigation of Ferguson was exhaustive. As documented in the official Findings Report, over the course of six months, the Civil Rights Division investigation team, with the assistance of policing and statistical experts, spent more than a hundred person-days on the ground in Ferguson, plus countless hours off site reviewing and analyzing documents and information. The onsite team interviewed city, court, and police officials, more than half of Ferguson's sworn officers, and dozens of people charged with municipal offenses; met with community groups, advocates, and neighborhood associations; and conducted hundreds of in-person and telephone interviews of people who lived in Ferguson or who had interacted with the Ferguson police and court system. The team participated in police ride-alongs, observed court sessions, and spent days with police and court officials painstakingly poring through drawers of court and policing records to establish peoples' experience with the Ferguson police and court system. Offsite, the team reviewed more than 35,000 pages of police records, including incident reports, investigations, and policies, plus thousands of emails and other electronic materials provided by the police department. The team analyzed FPD's data on stops, searches, citations, and arrests, as well as data collected by the municipal court.

Unstated in the Findings Report is the unprecedented backdrop against which this investigation took place. The Civil Rights Division's investigative team, which consisted of four attorneys, an investigator, a paralegal, several retained policing and statistical experts, and an intern, was operating in a crisis climate unlike the setting for any previous pattern-or-practice investigation. Initial site visits and community meetings were beset by confusion among community groups about who this new "DOJ" group was, even as DOJ's Community Relations Service was reluctant to share information about the groups with whom they had been meeting prior to the Civil Rights Division's arrival. As a result, while community members and activists often assumed everyone from DOJ was working together, these groups often knew more about what each DOJ component was doing than the components knew about each other. This led to frustration among the various DOJ components on the ground, an inability to fully leverage the work of the entire department, and skepticism among local groups and activists about whether DOJ had a clue.

Tensions and media scrutiny remained high throughout the investigation, complicating the usual investigative work of gaining information and insights from community members, police, and other stakeholders. At one of the first large community meetings, a gathering of 300-plus people at St. Louis Community College's Florissant Valley campus, team members balanced the transparency concerns of the dozen or so TV cameras and other media outlets in attendance with the need to allow the one-on-one exchange of information among persons directly impacted by Ferguson policing and members of the DOJ investigative team. The team explicitly affirmed the importance of a free press in a democracy to the media representatives present while at the same time advising them they would not be allowed to intrude on conversations between community members and the DOJ investigative team.

The investigative team had to contend with local interpretations of media statements made by DOJ and other federal officials. In late October, for example, Attorney General Holder called for "wholesale change" in the FPD during a talk in Washington. This statement, alongside the stressors of policing protests for months (and a healthy dose of entitlement), doomed any possibility of collaboration and support that sometimes occurs in DOJ's pattern-or-practice investigations. It culminated with vitriolic outbursts from Ferguson police officers during a meeting between those officers and members of DOJ's investigative team in early November. Officers angrily told DOJ lawyers that DOJ had "prejudged" the FPD and that the investigation was a political sham fueled by media bias.

Civil Rights Division lawyers and other members of the team also sought to balance the demands of the investigation itself with interim events that required immediate attention. The day prior to the large community meeting at the community college, the Civil Rights Division sent a letter to Ferguson police chief Tom Jackson asking him to address immediately the failure of the city's officers to wear their identification nameplates while policing protests. It was our view that this practice was exacerbating tension at ongoing protests. At the community group meeting in Florissant we became aware of another concerning practice: officers wearing "I am Darren Wilson" bracelets while policing protests. Community members told the investigative team they had seen officers, some of whom had black tape over their nameplates, the previous day, and they showed the team pictures of the bracelets. These bracelets were apparently worn in response to the "I am Mike Brown" mantra that had become widespread among protesters and activists. The officers' expression echoed the false equivalency of "blue lives matters" to "black lives matter," and even worse it inflamed tensions by insinuating approval for, and possibly a desire to replicate, Wilson's shooting of Mike Brown. The team wrote another letter to Chief Jackson on September 26, confirming a conversation with him in which he committed to ensuring officers would no longer wear those bracelets. The letter noted: "These bracelets reinforce the very 'us versus them' mentality that many residents of Ferguson believe exists." The team coordinated with the CRS and COPS, and COPS secured a commitment from the county police that their officers also would not wear these bracelets. We noted at the end of the letter that we would publicly release both the bracelet and the nameplate letters "due to the strong interest in this issue."[13]

On other occasions during the investigation, as part of their investigative fact-finding, DOJ investigative team members would observe interactions between police and protesters. At times, the police appeared to be violating protesters' First Amendment rights. The National Lawyers Guild had legal observers on site, and the ACLU had several related lawsuits already pending in federal court. Nonetheless, it exasperated protesters that the DOJ team did nothing in immediate response to the apparently unlawful conduct of Ferguson police officers.

As night fell in St. Louis on November 24, the Monday before Thanksgiving, St. Louis County prosecutor Robert P. McCulloch announced that a grand jury had decided not to indict Darren Wilson on any criminal charges. Protests, property destruction, and violence began almost immediately. Many businesses in Ferguson were burned, and the windows of others were smashed. A few people threw bottles and rocks at police carrying riot shields, and several police cars were burned. Protesters blocked Interstate 44 in St. Louis. Heavily armed and militarized police in Ferguson deployed tear gas. Gunfire, including automatic gunfire, was reported, and flights to nearby St. Louis International airport were suspended. Approximately thirty people were arrested. St. Louis County chief of police Jon Belmar stated that he "didn't foresee an evening like this." The violence following the grand jury's decision not to indict Wilson for shooting Mike Brown dwarfed the weeks of unrest that had occurred after the shooting itself. Across the country, other protests took place. The grand jury's announcement in St. Louis occurred the day after the sickening killing of twelve-year-old Tamir Rice by a police officer in Cleveland. A little more than a week after the announcement in St. Louis, a grand jury in Staten Island declined to indict Daniel Pantaleo for killing Eric Garner less than a month before Michael Brown was killed. Thousands of people again took to the streets across the country.

Several months later, on March 4, 2015, DOJ released two reports. The first was its report documenting the Civil Rights Division's criminal investigation of Darren Wilson. The report by the division's Criminal Section concluded that the evidence did not establish that Wilson violated any applicable federal criminal civil rights statutes and that DOJ would not seek to prosecute him. The second report released was the 102-page Findings Report regarding unconstitutional conduct by the Ferguson Police Department. The report found that the FPD engaged in a pattern or practice of conduct that violated the First, Fourth, and Fourteenth Amendments of the Constitution. More specifically, DOJ found that the FPD had engaged in a pattern or practice of conducting stops without reasonable suspicion and of making arrests without probable cause in violation of the Fourth Amendment; interfering with the right to free expression in violation of the First Amendment; and using unreasonable force in violation of the Fourth Amendment. DOJ found also that the Ferguson Municipal Court had a pattern or practice of focusing on revenue over public safety, leading to court practices that violated the Fourteenth Amendment's due process and equal protection requirements. The Findings Report documented how Ferguson's court practices exacerbated the harm of the city's unconstitutional police practices and imposed particular hardship on its most vulnerable residents, especially those living in or near poverty. Using statistical evidence and illustrative examples, the report showed how minor offenses generated crippling debts, resulting in jail time because of an inability to pay as well as the loss of driver's licenses, employment, and housing.

The Ferguson Report also documented DOJ's finding of a pattern or practice of racial bias in both the FPD and the municipal court. Again using statistical evidence and illustrative examples, the investigation showed how the harms of Ferguson's police and court practices were borne disproportionately by African Americans and that this disproportionate impact was avoidable. The Ferguson Report further set out how these harmful disparities in Ferguson's court and police practices were due, at least in part, to intentional discrimination, as demonstrated by direct evidence of racial bias and stereotyping about African Americans by certain Ferguson police and municipal court officials. DOJ's Ferguson Report also affirmed and expanded upon what the ArchCity Defenders white paper had documented about St. Louis's municipal court system.

The immediate response to the release of these reports was mixed. In Ferguson, the announcement that DOJ would not prosecute Darren Wilson was met with renewed protests, and the turmoil continued. As for the Ferguson Report, concerns among the DOJ team conducting the pattern-or-practice investigation that the import of their findings would be buried underneath the news that Darren Wilson would not be federally prosecuted proved unfounded. News that DOJ had found that broadly abusive and sometimes brutal police conduct permeated the FPD, and that this conduct was fueled both by racial animus and a desire to raise revenue for the city through fines and fees disproportionately imposed on Ferguson's black residents, reverberated across the country and around the globe.

Perhaps the most direct impact of the Findings Report was to demonstrate the appropriateness of broad, court-ordered reform to eliminate the pattern of unlawful police conduct documented. A public accounting of what DOJ found proved invaluable when, after nearly a year of negotiations to reach an agreement and several public hearings on the consent decree, the Ferguson City Council voted not to approve the decree. United States Attorney General Loretta Lynch, who, as noted in the *New York Times*, had a "reputation for delivering impassive and guarded public remarks," was "as animated as she has been in nearly a year as attorney general" in announcing DOJ's decision to immediately file suit against the city to remedy the patterns of unlawful conduct set out in the Ferguson Report. "The City of Ferguson had a real opportunity here to step forward, and instead they've turned backwards," she said. "They've chosen to live in the past."[14] After several weeks of contested litigation, the city reconsidered and unanimously voted to accept the consent decree that it had originally negotiated with DOJ. "This is Mike Brown's legacy," Michael Brown Sr. said. The image of Michael Brown Jr.'s father gripping hands with Ferguson mayor Tony Knowles in the moments after the vote brought home this point even more than the words.[15] As detailed below, as this book goes to print, that consent decree is being implemented.

Learning from Ferguson: DOJ and Policing's Dual Crisis

Ferguson was of course neither the first nor the last city to find itself thrust, in an instant, into the center of a crisis caused by a police killing. Just a few weeks after the release of the Ferguson Report, Baltimore found itself in similar upheaval when Freddie Gray, a twenty-five-year-old African American Baltimore resident, sustained fatal injuries to his neck and spine while in transport inside a police van after being arrested by police officers. Gray's death became a flashpoint in the city as Brown's death had been in Ferguson.[16] The reasons for the public reaction are complex but, like Brown's death, are also illustrated by the way Gray died. Baltimore police chose to chase Freddie Gray on foot because he had run away. When police caught up with and searched Freddie, they arrested him for having an illegal knife clipped to the inside of his pants pocket. (The knife would turn out to be legal.) DOJ responded in Baltimore largely as it had in Ferguson: launching a pattern-or-practice investigation that culminated in a consent decree that currently is being implemented.

More recently, the police killing of George Floyd in Minneapolis, during his arrest for allegedly passing a counterfeit $20 bill, ignited protests not only in Minneapolis but across the country and around the world. The scope and impact of the protests in response to George Floyd's death is unprecedented. On one day alone—June 6, 2020—more than half a million people protested in nearly 550 different locations in the United States.[17] These protests have been widely accompanied by demands to "defund" or "abolish" the police, and, in their wake, polls have found that 95 percent of Americans now believe that we need police reform—a percentage of Americans calling for change that would have been unimaginable a week before Floyd's killing and that is astonishing in a nation as polarized as the United States in the spring and summer of 2020.[18] In contrast to both this broad public sentiment and DOJ's work during the Obama administration, DOJ has taken no action in Minneapolis and more generally has been hostile to pattern-or-practice investigations throughout the Trump administration.

There is little doubt that we have not yet seen the last of acute policing crises like those prompted by police killings in Ferguson, Baltimore, and Minneapolis. It is also likely that DOJ will one day return to enforcing the Law Enforcement Misconduct Statute (34 U.S.C. § 12601)[19] and that, when it does, some of these investigations will be in cities undergoing a policing crisis. The question is how effective DOJ's response will be, particularly after such a long hiatus.

Organizers, activists, and movement lawyers learned much from their work in Ferguson and elsewhere, and they began documenting much of that learning almost immediately. That intentional effort helped transform Ferguson from a moment to a movement, as the demands and protests following Floyd's death dramatically underscore.[20] DOJ's investigation, Findings Report, and consent decree were part of what happened in Ferguson, but there have been few holistic efforts to learn from DOJ's work there and even less documentation of that learning. This is unfortunate, because there were lessons learned that, if applied in the future, can not only improve the effectiveness and efficiency of DOJ's response but also bolster broader efforts to reshape policing and community safety. This chapter is an attempt to correct, at least partially, this omission. This section will first describe what I call a "dual crisis" in policing in the United States in the twenty-first century. It will then assess the tools the DOJ has to respond to this dual crisis—one acute and the other chronic—and conclude with an examination of the proper role for the DOJ in responding to the dual crisis.

The Dual Crisis

To learn from DOJ's response to the crisis in Ferguson, it is useful to conceptualize policing crises like the one in that city as a *dual crisis*: one acute and
one chronic. When we set DOJ's work against the backdrop of each of these
crises, we can better understand the unique value and significant limitations
of DOJ law enforcement misconduct investigations and better assess their
effectiveness.

An acute policing crisis occurs when: (1) the operations of a jurisdiction,
usually a city, are significantly and visibly disrupted by (2) large-scale protests, peaceable or otherwise, and/or the state response to those protests, and
(3) the protests are a response to an act of state violence, usually deadly and
whether legally justified or not. Several DOJ federal pattern-or-practice police
investigations have been preceded by acute policing crises.[21]

While not always the case (at least theoretically), an acute policing crisis
generally can be thought of as a conflagration of the chronic crisis of policing
that is discussed below. The incident sparking the acute crisis galvanizes a
community into immediate reaction and protest, but that incident—and the
responsive community outrage—have roots in the chronic crisis. Although
part of the chronic crisis, the acute crisis presents different challenges and
opportunities for addressing harmful policing than does the chronic crisis.
For this reason, it is useful to analyze the acute crisis separately.

The chronic crisis of policing is so longstanding and intertwined with
American history that it may seem odd to consider it a crisis.[22] But a "crisis"
is defined as "a time of intense difficulty, trouble or danger." Although the
difficulty, trouble, and danger that some communities and individuals experience at the hands of the police have become normalized, they nonetheless
have been, and remain, intense. Policing as it has been practiced in the United
States carries with it a severe—even existential—daily threat for many people
in many places.[23] And even where the impacts of policing are less extreme,
policing outcomes have long been grossly disparate among different cohorts
within the population, creating large groups of de facto second-class citizens
in the United States.[24] Many people and communities in the United States
have been experiencing a crisis in the policing they experience for decades,
even centuries. The chronic crisis of policing and the criminal justice system
has been explored by scholars, policy makers, and activists for decades, with
a resurgence that began after Ferguson and gathered more steam after George
Floyd's killing.[25] Yet, others deny that a chronic crisis in policing even exists.

One aspect of the chronic policing crisis is systemic unlawful conduct by
law enforcement within a particular law enforcement agency. When unlawful

conduct is closer to being the norm than an aberration, it can be thought of as systemic. Legally, it is sometimes called a "pattern or practice" of unlawful conduct" or an unlawful "custom or policy." This systemic misconduct is generally tolerated, or even facilitated and condoned, by the agency's culture. It can persist for decades, to the point where it is hard to remember that policing can be any different. It is this aspect of the policing crisis that DOJ has the most explicit authority to address through the law enforcement misconduct statute.

However, systemic police misconduct is only one aspect of the chronic crisis of policing. The chronic crisis stems also from conduct that is lawful and in accord with the rules. The chronic policing crisis is in fact caused largely by policing that furthers formal and arguably agreed-upon policing goals, even though that policing causes substantial and unnecessary harm.[26] This aspect of the chronic crisis of policing is perpetuated by United States Supreme Court holdings, legislation passed by duly elected leaders, and the informal norms that we tolerate and sometimes condone. One set of examples of how the chronic crisis is driven by legal rules and norms is the web of policing rules established by Supreme Court decisions. Many holdings contribute to a system of expansive police power in which police can significantly limit an individual's liberty in ways that have little connection to public safety or even seem to defy reason. For example, the Court has held that a police officer may unilaterally send someone to jail for an infraction that would not be punishable by jail even if the person were convicted of that offense. The Court has also held that a police officer may seek "consent" to search without advising individuals that they have the right to refuse consent and despite social science demonstrating that meaningful consent in the police/public interaction does not occur. The Court has also steadily degraded its consideration of officer use of force to the point where a police officer may constitutionally use force—including deadly force—even where it was clearly avoidable and otherwise unnecessary.

Relatedly, another dimension of the chronic crisis of policing is that, while it is reinforced by policing, its origins lay outside it. Legislators, prosecutors, and other actors in the criminal legal system incentivize and sometimes require harmful and unjust policing.[27] The role that nonpolice actors, like prosecutors and judges, play not only in perpetuating injustice throughout the criminal justice system but also specifically in incentivizing and tolerating *police* abuse has only recently broken through to the mainstream consciousness. And it has been accompanied by the election of a wave of "progressive prosecutors," like Kim Foxx in Chicago and Wesley Bell (a Ferguson City Council person and negotiator of the DOJ consent decree) in St. Louis, who often base their campaigns in large part on their predecessors' response to alleged police abuse.

Most fundamentally, the chronic crisis of policing stems from our nation's history of condoning economic and racial inequality, as well as the stories we tell ourselves about why this inequality is acceptable.[28] This topic is far too great to even begin to adequately address in this chapter. Suffice it to say that it is not a coincidence that the policing rules created by the Supreme Court cases described above—perpetuated by the criminal justice system more broadly and tolerated throughout our history—disproportionately harm people of color and people living in poverty.[29]

As this brief description of the chronic crisis underscores, the dual policing crisis is too broad and multifaceted to be fully addressed by any one actor or intervention.[30] No player—even a player with the power and resources of DOJ—can fully address the entire problem. To be most effective at resolving this dual crisis, we must determine the nature of the tools each actor brings to the project, and we must have some understanding of the challenges and opportunities presented by the various aspects of the crisis. If we can do that (however imperfectly), we can do a better job at matching each actor's strengths to the project of dismantling the policing crisis. In the context of DOJ's work in Ferguson, this requires us to understand the tools DOJ brings to this work as well as the challenges and opportunities presented by the policing crisis as it has played out in that city. Once we do this we can begin to evaluate DOJ's work in Ferguson and use that experience to inform how DOJ *should* address the dual crisis of policing in the future.

The next section describes the origin and nature of the primary tool DOJ has available to address the dual policing crisis.

DOJ's "Pattern-or-Practice" Authority

DOJ is a massive organization with significant power and resources. With more than ten thousand attorneys, it is sometimes referred to as the world's largest law office,[31] but it is really much more than that. For one thing, unlike any private law office, it has the coercive power of the state behind it. The Civil Rights Division was created in 1957, and it was expanded in 1964 so that the power of DOJ could be wielded to protect the rights of individuals, especially when local and state governments fail to do so.[32] Given the power of DOJ and its Civil Rights Division, it was not surprising that, from the out-set of the division's Special Litigation Section's work in Ferguson, there were unrealistic expectations about how the investigation would address the acute crisis even while conducting the pattern-or-practice investigation. Some hoped that the very fact that a Civil Rights Division team was on the ground would decrease tensions in the city. Some were hopeful that the release of a findings report would help Ferguson move beyond disruptive protests. Still others hoped that DOJ's intervention would more fundamentally "fix" policing in Ferguson and throughout the region.

Perhaps if there had been broader understanding of the tool the DOJ was using in Ferguson—the law enforcement misconduct statute—it would have been clear from the outset that the Civil Rights Division's pattern-or-practice work would have only ancillary impact on the acute crisis and that its real work would be to powerfully (albeit only partially) address the chronic crisis of policing.[33]

Gaining an understanding of this tool starts with a look at its history. DOJ's law enforcement misconduct statute is most directly the result of the beating of Rodney King by officers of the Los Angeles Police Department (LAPD) and the aftermath of that incident of unjustified state violence. In March 1991, Rodney King, a twenty-five-year-old African American man, was beaten for several minutes with batons, blows, and kicks by several LAPD officers following a high-speed chase. The beating was captured on video by bystander George Holliday who, after failing to find anyone at LAPD interested in the footage, provided it to a local television station, at which point, as we would say today, it went viral. Four officers prosecuted for the beating by the Los Angeles District Attorney's office were acquitted, sparking riots in Los Angeles that were deadly and caused a significant amount of property damage. The Criminal Section of the DOJ's Civil Rights Division then prosecuted the same four officers for violations of federal criminal civil rights statutes. A federal jury indicted two of the officers and acquitted two others.

As prosecutions of individual officers were under way, the Christopher Commission, established by Los Angeles mayor Tom Bradley to conduct a "full and fair examination of the operation of the LAPD including its recruitment and training practices, internal disciplinary system, and citizen complaint system," released a report documenting broad, entrenched patterns of officer misconduct within the LAPD—patterns that revealed a clear connection between the LAPD's institutional failings and the brutal behavior of officers like those indicted for beating Rodney King.[34]

The aftermath of Rodney King's beating highlighted both the difficulty of holding individual officers accountable for even egregious misconduct and created a better understanding of the complex dynamics surrounding police abuse. The prosecutions of the officers helped clarify the inadequacy of the criminal justice system either to *prevent* instances of abuse or to fully remedy them. The analysis provided by the Christopher Commission's report helped the nation better understand the link between *systemic* deficiencies and egregious *instances* of abuse. And the broad public outrage underscored that the conduct of officers in one law enforcement agency can impact interactions between police and the public in cities and towns large and small across the country.[35] The Christopher Commission's report also helped to explain the link between an acute policing crisis and some of its chronic crisis roots, including the failure of the criminal justice system to hold officers accountable as well as the tendency of policing systems to facilitate, rather than to prevent, police abuse.

The Rodney King incident exposed a lack of any enforcement mechanism giving the federal government the legal authority to address systemic police misconduct at the state and local levels either before or after the occurrence of a socially cataclysmic event. The federal government was limited instead to seeking to criminally prosecute individual officers after the fact—that is, to address one aspect of the crisis.

In response to the Rodney King incident, the United States Congress included the "law enforcement misconduct" provision in the Violent Crime Control and Law Enforcement Act of 1994. As described above, this statutory provision authorized DOJ to take action to "eliminate" any "pattern or practice of conduct by law enforcement officers" that violates the Constitution or other federal law. Thus, though born of an acute crisis, the law enforcement misconduct provision giving rise to DOJ's pattern-or-practice investigations in Ferguson and elsewhere is focused on addressing the chronic crisis of policing—or at least the portion of the chronic crisis that stems from systemic law enforcement misconduct.

Below, I discuss the extent to which this statute allows DOJ to effectively address the chronic crisis of policing. But Ferguson also provides an opportunity to look at the impact that DOJ's pattern-or-practice investigations can have on the acute crisis and vice versa. Understanding the relationship between DOJ's pattern-or-practice investigations and the acute crisis is important because it helps us more fairly evaluate DOJ's efforts overall and because understanding this relationship will help us make DOJ's pattern-or-practice work more effective. Thus, before turning to how DOJ's law enforcement misconduct investigations impact the chronic crisis, I explore the challenges and opportunities that acute crises create for DOJ's pattern-or-practice work.

DOJ and Ferguson's Acute Crisis

Conducting a DOJ pattern-or-practice investigation is generally less complicated in the absence of an ongoing acute crisis. But DOJ investigations will continue to occur in the midst of an acute crisis, for reasons that are described below. Further, as explained below, this is not a bad thing, as DOJ's police reform efforts conducted in the midst of an acute crisis can have greater impact.

A CATALYST FOR DOJ INTERVENTION

It would be inappropriate for the Department of Justice to initiate a pattern-or-practice investigation of a police department based solely on an acute crisis. As noted above, DOJ's authority to conduct law enforcement misconduct investigations stems from an act that authorizes the United States Attorney General to bring a civil action for equitable and declaratory relief to "eliminate" any "pattern or practice of conduct by law enforcement officers" that violates the Constitution or other federal law. Neither public protest—no matter how widespread—nor the incident that precipitated that protest—no matter how egregious—is a "pattern" or a "practice" requiring broad federal intervention. Thus, in Ferguson, as in every case, DOJ did not launch an investigation without first conducting a preliminary inquiry and determining that there were indications of systemic law enforcement misconduct.[36]

But it would be equally inappropriate for DOJ to ignore an acute policing crisis in determining when and where to initiate one of its relatively infrequent investigations. There are 18,000 law enforcement agencies in the United States, and DOJ has conducted fewer than seventy law enforcement misconduct investigations. There is no agreed-upon way to systematically select which law enforcement agencies should be subject to DOJ's enforcement attention. As Ferguson underscores, an acute crisis has often proven to be symptomatic of a pattern or practice of unlawful police conduct that is causing the precise harm the federal law enforcement misconduct statute was meant to eliminate. It would be (as during the Trump administration) troubling to see DOJ showing no interest in fulfilling its responsibility to investigating whether individuals' rights are being routinely violated in any of the communities in the throes of an acute policing crisis, particularly because acute crises often signal systemic misconduct in these communities' law enforcement agencies.

UNEARTHING INFORMATION

An acute crisis can enhance the depth and value of DOJ's investigative fact-finding and consent decree remedies. Just as an earthquake or landslide can expose the ground underlying the landscape, enhancing our understanding of how things came to be as they are, the upheaval caused by an acute crisis can reveal facts and dynamics that can allow us to better understand the nature or causes of a particular pattern or practice of policing harm. If we act quickly, before the ground is again changed or re-covered, we can gain insights that transform our understanding not only of the particular law enforcement agency being investigated but also of the nature of policing and its interactions with communities across the country and over time. A pattern or practice investigation puts the Civil Rights Division in the right place at the right time to make unique use of these insights. In Ferguson, hundreds of people spoke with DOJ about their experiences with the Ferguson police. This was extraordinary in light of how small Ferguson (21,000 people) and its police department (fifty officers) were yet completely unsurprising in light of the intense worldwide focus on this small city. In the first days and weeks of the Ferguson protests, advocates released reports documenting troubling practices, and journalists wrote innumerable articles documenting their own investigative findings about misconduct within the Ferguson Police Department and providing information about persons who had been recently harmed.[37] An acute crisis is certainly not necessary for advocates and journalists to compile this depth of information, and they often do surface such facts to no avail. But much of this information would not have been available to DOJ except for the attention brought to Ferguson by the acute crisis.

CREATING A CLIMATE FOR GREATER IMPACT

In addition to being a catalyst for a DOJ law enforcement misconduct investigation and helping to unearth information, an acute crisis also can create a climate in which a DOJ investigation can have a greater impact. An acute policing crisis can bring to the forefront the "fierce urgency of now."[38] Organizing and protests can awaken a broader portion of the public to the harm and injustice of police abuses, or at least make clear that these concerns can no longer be ignored. Too often, as Ferguson demonstrated, it seems that it is not the unnecessary police violence but the outraged public response that succeeds at gripping broad public attention. As Wes Lowrey wrote: "[I]t was the destruction of the QuikTrip, not the police shooting of Mike Brown, that brought the national media's focus to Ferguson. . . . [E]ven the breaking of a young black body left on public display . . . didn't catch the attention of the national media. It was the community's enraged response—broken windows and shattered storefronts—that drew the eyes of the nation." Once drawn to Ferguson, it was the police response to the protests (which, despite some significant property damage, were overwhelmingly nonviolent) that caused many to begin to wonder whether law enforcement in a town they had never heard of was as broken as it appeared to be and what that said about law enforcement elsewhere.

Whether because of interest convergence, moral enlightenment, or desperation, once this awakening happens, the climate has the potential to become more receptive to a deeper look at policing and the dynamics that drive it. There is political momentum for change that did not previously exist. In Ferguson, changing this political momentum was particularly difficult and remains far from complete to this day. The acute crisis did seem to contribute to the city council and mayor being more motivated to address longstanding law enforcement deficiencies. Similarly, new openness to change was evident in St. Louis County more broadly. This motivation, for many actors, doubtless stemmed from a desire to save one's own job; to prevent municipal insolvency; or to quell public unrest. Sometimes this political momentum for change has an arguably more noble font. Police executives or others in a law enforcement agency or government may have long known of the need for, and may have been seeking changes in, policing, but until the acute crisis the political momentum for significant change was not there. As one Chicago policing unit exasperated by that city's policing put it to a DOJ attorney, they "popped the champagne" when they heard DOJ had opened a pattern-or-practice investigation.

An acute crisis can force a conversation and bring key stakeholders to the table with a more serious mind-set than they had been able to muster previously. Officials may be willing to address more seriously the concerns of politically marginalized constituents and also be more willing to develop meaningful legislative or policy solutions to longstanding harms.

Although the catalyst for this motivation for change may have been the acute crisis, once activated there is an opportunity to explore the nexus between the acute crisis and the more fundamental chronic crisis. Communities may be more broadly primed to think expansively about the root causes of the acute crisis, including both institutionalized/structural policing harm, in addition to the unlawful conduct, as well as the interplay between police and other parts of the criminal justice system. Communities can begin to more broadly consider how policy decisions and social dynamics—from the war on drugs, to the dehumanization of Latinx and black people, to municipal revenue-collection decisions—impact policing.

In this way, the acute crisis creates an opportunity to address harm-causing policing at a more fundamental level. Because the opportunity provided by an acute crisis occurs infrequently, is unpredictable, and can have a brief shelf-life, it is important that stakeholders recognize the opportunity and be prepared to act when it presents itself.

DOJ should be no exception and should leverage the climate for change offered by an acute crisis to increase the impact of its enforcement work. One of the most potent ways to do so is through findings reports. As discussed below, DOJ's Ferguson Report had a significant impact on the policing and the criminal justice system not only in Ferguson but also across the country. While the investigative team worked hard to ensure the report was solid and persuasive, and while the facts in Ferguson indeed spoke for themselves, there is no question that without the attention already trained on Ferguson due to the acute crisis the Ferguson Report would not have been as broadly read or its import as fully understood.

CHALLENGES PRESENTED BY THE ACUTE CRISIS

DOJ's work in Ferguson underscores that while an acute crisis can appropriately serve as the catalyst for DOJ intervention that will have outsized impact, this work should not be expected to significantly decrease the immediate harm or impact of the acute crisis.

One of the most difficult challenges DOJ faces when it is asked to intervene in a policing crisis through a pattern-or-practice investigation is setting realistic expectations about which acute problems being faced by communities it can and cannot address in real time. While there are many examples of this phenomenon, what stands out about the Ferguson investigation is the tension and officer conduct during the protests that occurred throughout our investigation. In the midst of some of the most contentious protests, community members were dismayed and frustrated that DOJ investigative team members did nothing more than observe as Ferguson police officers appeared to blatantly violate court orders mandating protections for protesters. Some protesters and activists on the ground expected that, when DOJ civil rights attorneys saw civil rights violations committed right in front of them, they would immediately do something about it—after all, if the federal government wasn't going to do anything about it, who was? Although this was an understandable expectation, it was incompatible with the team's actual authority. It was also arguably inconsistent with the role that a pattern-or-practice investigation—and the attorneys and other team members who conduct it—should play during an acute crisis. As discussed below, the work of the Civil Rights Division should be focused primarily on addressing the chronic crisis. This means that the investigative team needs to remain focused on gathering information and analyzing that information so that it can make reliable findings about whether a pattern or practice of unlawful conduct exists. Attending to the immediate legal demands of the acute crisis distracts from that mission and risks undermining the legitimacy of the investigation by making DOJ's findings seem "prejudged." At the same time, not immediately responding to violations risks DOJ appearing uncaring or ineffective, also undermining legitimacy.

The team sought to educate all stakeholders that the DOJ investigation was neither designed to nor likely able to quell tensions in the near time or provide immediate relief to legal violations. The facts recounted above demonstrate that this was indeed the case in Ferguson: protests and property damage occurred upon release of DOJ's Ferguson Report. These renewed protests were largely in response to the announcement the same day that DOJ would not seek to prosecute Darren Wilson. And it is possible that the protests would have been worse had the Findings Report not been released at the same time. But the reaction demonstrates that a DOJ pattern-or-practice investigation does not inoculate against demonstrations, peaceable or otherwise.

The investigative team did seek to balance its longer-term, chronic-crisis focus with immediate focus on the acute crisis in various ways, including, for example, not only sending but also publishing the letters regarding officers covering their name plates and wearing the "I am Darren Wilson" bracelets. The team also sought to work with, and recommend strategies for, DOJ's Community Relations Service, which was on the ground in Ferguson before the Civil Rights Division and whose statutory mandate includes mediating to quell unrest. Nonetheless, this became a difficult aspect of the investigation as the team struggled to find the right balance between immediate action and long-term focus and sought to convince themselves, and others, that the balance they had struck was appropriate.

A second challenge the DOJ faces when it brings its pattern-or-practice investigatory authority to bear in a policing crisis is the fact that the protests and demonstrations that often arise in an acute crisis—especially the non-peaceable aspects and violence that can accompany them—are often polarizing. Ferguson demonstrates how acute crises facilitate turning protesters and police into caricatures. In Ferguson, officers calling protesters "animals" and aiming guns at peacefully assembling people, alongside the generally militarized response and disregard for First Amendment rights, undermined the legitimacy of all law enforcement and destroyed any proclivity toward a cooperative solution among many demonstrators in Ferguson. At the same time, many officers working the protests were subject to vitriolic personal attacks—especially African American officers, who were often the subject of racialized attacks. These officers—unaccustomed to being challenged, resistant to the need for self-care, and imbued in a racist policing culture—were ill-equipped to respond to this in any remotely constructive manner. And everybody was exhausted, literally and figuratively.

The team's interactions with Ferguson's officers, as recounted above, underscore the extreme level of defensiveness that can set in once the dynamics of an acute crisis are set in motion. The treatment of protesters can increase cynicism among activists and even unengaged members of the public about the possibility of meaningful change. Thus, even as the recognition of the need for change has been enhanced, as described above, confidence that this change can actually be achieved, especially by those at the center of the acute crisis, can dwindle.

DOJ and Chronic Policing Crises

As the previous discussion shows, acute crises present challenges to the effectiveness of DOJ's work, but they can also enhance it. Consistent with the origins of the DOJ's statutory authority to investigate systemic law enforcement misconduct, however, combating the chronic crisis is where the DOJ has greater potential to have real and lasting impact in the particular community facing the dual policing crisis and beyond.

Understanding the Chronic Aspects of the Ferguson Policing Crisis

The chronic crisis in policing is made up of several components. One is a *culture of unlawful police conduct* that may have been in place for decades. But *lawfully sanctioned police conduct* often causes significant harm, especially to people of color and people living in poverty. The chronic policing crisis is also *incentivized, and often created, by the work of legislators, prosecutors, judges,* and other criminal justice system actors. And the chronic crisis is intertwined with our nation's history of condoning *economic and racial inequality* and the stories we tell ourselves about why this inequality is acceptable.

Each of these elements of the chronic policing crisis was clearly evident in Ferguson. As set out above, there were clear patterns of unconstitutional conduct in violation of the First, Fourth, and Fourteenth Amendments as well as federal statutory law. But some of the most pervasively harmful aspects of Ferguson policing were lawful (for example, instructions to cite and arrest for violations of the municipal code so that revenue would remit to the city and the attendant use of arrest warrants as threats to push for payment of court fees). The extent to which non–police actors—from the mayor, to the city prosecutor, to the finance director, to the municipal court judges and clerk—incentivized and even demanded harmful policing was well-documented in the Ferguson Report and subsequent publications. And the use of racial tropes and stereotypes as old as the United States to explain and justify abusive economic practices was evident in Ferguson's reliance on a supposed dearth of "personal responsibility" among African Americans and people living in poverty as the explanation for the deeply harmful impact of its police and court practices.[39] As the Ferguson Report documented, Ferguson's history as a sundown town—in which black people were not welcome after dark—and as a newly majority-minority city, contributed to the dynamics in which abusive policing flourished.

Ferguson in many respects encapsulates the depth and complexity of the chronic crisis of policing. It is therefore a good vehicle for exploring the extent to which DOJ's pattern-or-practice work can serve its core function of addressing the chronic crisis and which elements of DOJ's work do this best.

How DOJ's Pattern-or-Practice Work Addresses the Chronic Crisis

The impact of DOJ's pattern-or-practice work is often assessed solely through the lens of the consent decrees that DOJ negotiates with state actors subsequent to most investigations.[40] But DOJ's pattern-or-practice investigation impact goes beyond whatever is achieved via the consent decree. In some instances, a DOJ investigation and findings report may have as great, and in some respects greater, impact than the subsequent consent decree. Further, as discussed below, consent decrees can have an impact beyond addressing unlawful police conduct. Thus, to fully appreciate the impact of DOJ's pattern-or-practice work on the chronic crisis, one must consider what can be achieved not only through a consent decree but also via a DOJ investigation and findings report. And one must consider how each of these elements of DOJ's work might address the chronic crisis more broadly than it does the systemic unlawful conduct by police.

The Central Importance of Addressing the Harm Caused by Systemic Police Misconduct

Notwithstanding the need to take this broader look at DOJ's pattern-or-practice work, it is worth pausing first to consider the urgent need to address the portion of the chronic crisis that is at the center of DOJ's work: changing police practices so that identified patterns of unconstitutional police conduct are eliminated. Given how much of the chronic policing crisis is fueled by lawful but harmful policing conduct, and nonpolicing actors, it might be easy to discount the import of DOJ's work developing and implementing consent decrees to eliminate unlawful police conduct. A consideration of the harm caused by systemic police misconduct, and the ability of consent decrees to reduce and perhaps even eliminate some of that harm, helps us to more fairly evaluate DOJ's work and also underscores the need to keep that work focused on using consent decrees to eliminate patterns of unlawful police conduct.

DOJ's policing consent decrees and similar settlement agreements generally require changes in how law enforcement agencies recruit, train, supervise, and hold officers accountable. These remedies do not require wholesale transformation of policing or the criminal justice system. Rather, as noted above, they are intended to eliminate the pattern or practice of unlawful conduct, not the chronic policing crisis in its entirety. To see the value of the remedies DOJ obtains notwithstanding this limited goal, it is important to recognize at the outset that *we do not need to disrupt every cause of the harm to prevent it.*

As a difficult but useful illustration, Timothy Loehmann, the Cleveland police officer who shot to death twelve-year-old Tamir Rice, may have done so because he consciously or unconsciously devalued black life, or was responding to our society's institutionalized association of blackness with criminality and danger, or for other reasons rooted in myriad aspects of the chronic crisis. But he was in a position to shoot and kill Tamir because the Cleveland Police Department hired him and gave him a gun. And it did so despite ample red flags that Loehmann should never have been allowed to be a police officer.[41] We must work to end the devaluing of the lives of people of color and unconscious and conscious bias, but we should also be clear about the difficulty of this task, as well as the need to take interim steps to prevent loss of life and liberty while that deeper struggle continues.[42] Even if court-imposed remedies resulting from a DOJ investigation cannot eliminate deadly race discrimination in policing, these remedies may still be able to bring about changes in hiring, accountability, and other systems that will save lives.

While it is impossible to know how many children like Tamir Rice are alive today because officers like Timothy Loehmann were either not hired or were fired because of changes brought about by DOJ consent decrees, we do know that many law enforcement agencies see far fewer police shootings after the implementation of consent decrees.[43] Law enforcement agencies also generally see a decrease in uses of force more broadly after implementation of a consent decree, although this decrease may sometimes be initially masked by better systems of accountability that result in higher numbers of force being *reported.*[44]

Similarly, DOJ consent decrees may reduce the harm of race bias even if they cannot eliminate it. It is difficult to imagine, for example, that a DOJ consent decree, in Ferguson or elsewhere, can ever "eliminate" racial, eth-nic, and socioeconomic disparities in policing except in tandem with success combating other elements of the chronic crisis (like legalized race discrimina-tion and embedded biases). As ArchCity Defenders executive director Blake Strode said in 2019: "[T]he status quo [is] one of structural racism, poverty, overinvestment in the carceral system, and policing and prosecution. That is as real today in 2019 as it was five years ago in 2014."[45] Nonetheless, DOJ consent decrees can reduce the harm of such disparities by requiring reforms that lower the rate of police stops, searches, citations, and arrests, especially unlawful ones. In Ferguson, for example, in 2013 and 2014 the Ferguson Police Department averaged about 21,000 citations a year, while from 2015 to 2018 it averaged approximately 3,500 citations per year.[46] The DOJ consent decree likely was central to this drastic reduction and likely increases the longevity of this change.[47] The fact that racial disparities persist should not eclipse the fact that far fewer black people in Ferguson—likely thousands fewer—have been ticketed in the years since the filing of the DOJ consent decree (April 2016) and that a federal court and federal monitors will continue to watch over these practices for several years. Particularly given the cascading impact of citations in St. Louis County, this is significant harm averted.[48]

By emphasizing the import of DOJ's consent decrees, in no way do I intend to discount the harm of the chronic crisis that consent decrees cannot reach. This harm is profound. It creates a de facto second-class citizenry and the Catch-22 "chokehold" articulated by professor Paul Butler in which the law is applied in a manner that makes it impossible to comply with or sometimes to even survive.[49] We should keep fighting this. But we should recognize that as much work as has been done, much work still remains, and we should at least consider the idea that a world of truly harmless policing may be unattainable in the foreseeable future. As professor Butler says: "[T]he Chokehold's genius is its mutability."[50] Its mutability stems from its roots in a society and culture that is still imbued by economic inequality and white supremacy with all it entails. Given the severity of current harm, and the uncertainty of truly rising above, we can and should seek to reduce harm however it manifests itself, even as we work to uproot the underlying causes. DOJ's consent decrees are one potent means of reducing current harm.

Consent Decrees' Potential to Address the Chronic Crisis More Broadly

Although DOJ's consent decrees are and should be focused on eliminating *unlawful* police conduct, to be effective at doing so they must address lawful police conduct and conduct by actors outside of policing. Thus, even though it would be unrealistic to expect DOJ's consent decrees to resolve the entire chronic crisis, in evaluating their full impact we should look not only at how they impact unlawful police conduct but also at how consent decrees impact policing and the criminal justice system more broadly.

It is important to be clear from the outset that this broader impact should not be the intent of the consent decree. Given that a considerable amount of policing harm is caused by lawful conduct by officers or by actors outside policing, it may be tempting to deliberately use DOJ's power as expansively as possible to address the chronic crisis more broadly than the pattern of unlawful law enforcement conduct. Indeed, some people in Ferguson and elsewhere think that is exactly what DOJ has done. One Ferguson resident opposed to the consent decree the city negotiated with DOJ questioned a provision about Ferguson's occupancy permits: "This has nothing to do with policing," he said. "They proposed changes to expand their powers. They were thinking, 'How do we use this to make radical change?'"[51] In fact, as discussed below, addressing occupancy permits was important to addressing systemic misconduct, but this and similar provisions have often resulted in DOJ being accused of misusing its statutory enforcement authority to implement an agenda that goes beyond ensuring that police abided by the law. In other words, this view posits that DOJ has sought, through its consent decrees, to get at too big a portion of the chronic crisis.

DOJ lawyers should indeed be mindful of not overstepping their statutory authority in carrying out their work. As David Luban writes: "Government has many constituencies, and if it orients itself to just one of them it ceases to be democratic and pluralist and instead veers in a dangerously ideological direction, one step removed from single-party repression."[52] One has only to remember that the George W. Bush administration drafted legal opinions that purported to justify torture, or read the newspaper any day of the week about the litigating positions and legal interpretations taken and made by the Trump administration, to be wary of the ease with which the state can dangerously overstep boundaries when it begins to serve an ideological agenda rather than the rule of law.[53]

But government attorneys can remain within the rule of law and still be energetic and creative in their efforts to enforce it. There is nothing improper per se about a consent decree provision that addresses the broader chronic crisis where this also furthers the Civil Rights Division's legitimate enforcement mission.[54]

Further, eliminating unlawful police conduct often *requires* addressing other elements of the chronic crisis, including confronting policing practices that may be lawful but cause unnecessary harm. Ensuring that police routinely adhere to the law sometimes requires that police be willing to restrain their own conduct more than is required by law. There is no law, for example, against using stop-and-frisk per se as a strategy for removing guns, or of adopting "zero tolerance" street enforcement. But when police agencies rely on these lawful strategies, they can become used to stopping people for no public safety purpose, with little or no suspicion of wrongdoing, and often on the basis of impermissible factors such as race. This can result in patterns of unconstitutional stops, searches, and arrests. Similarly, even if raising city revenue through ticketing is lawful, it can result in extensive harm. DOJ investigations demonstrated this in Ferguson, Baltimore, and elsewhere.[55]

Thus, to correct patterns of unlawful policing, consent decrees often *must* address practices and structures that may not themselves directly violate the law. Consent decrees generally do this by placing greater constraints on police conduct, or by requiring more of police, than does the law. Courts have affirmed this approach, holding that settlement agreements may hold wrongdoers to a higher or more restrictive standard than permitted by law in order to correct past violations.[56] In other words, where lawful conduct is causing or facilitating legal violations, courts may decree, or parties may negotiate, an order that prohibits police from undertaking even that lawful conduct. By the same token, law enforcement agencies may be required to do more than the law requires to correct patterns of unlawful conduct. A consent decree may, for example, prohibit or discourage a particular type of stop or search that would otherwise be legal because of the tendency of that form of police action to lead to unlawful racial profiling or unreasonable searches or seizures in violation of the Fourth Amendment. Examples of this in DOJ consent decrees include restrictions on pretext stops and consent searches in New Orleans, Ferguson, and elsewhere. Discouraging these sorts of stops can disrupt a culture of using stop-and-frisk or zero tolerance as an abusive policing strategy. It is apt that consent decrees are often referred to as "structural reform agreements."[57]

While included for the effect on systemic misconduct, these remedies, once in place, have the potential to get at some of the deeper causes of the chronic crisis. They may, for example, reveal misconceptions about the legal authority or tactical tools police require to keep us safe. The dramatic reduction in stops and frisks by the New York City Police Department during the litigation of *Floyd* is perhaps the most well-known example of a broad reduction in police intrusion being accompanied by public safety improvements rather than fruition of the dire predictions of "blood in the street"; many cities with police consent decrees have experienced similar dynamics. DOJ's consent decrees demonstrate this same dynamic in jurisdictions across the country. Indeed, the researcher credited with the term "Ferguson Effect"—whereby crime allegedly rises because of police inaction in the wake of controversy, has found that there is no apparent link between fewer arrests and increases in serious crime.[58]

Similarly, consent decree requirements for training in, for example, force de-escalation, implicit bias, and active bystandership may be necessary to eliminate patterns of Fourteenth and Fourth Amendment violations. These requirements aim to change officers' conduct by teaching them to exercise their discretion more judiciously, to rethink their relationship to the community they serve, and to be more empathetic. Take, for example, the Ferguson resident's critique, noted above, of the consent decree provision requiring Ferguson to reconsider its occupancy permit ordinance.[59] DOJ's investigation found that Ferguson police were enforcing Ferguson's occupancy permit rules in a manner that destroyed police legitimacy and, in so doing, undermined the ability to police lawfully and effectively:

> In one instance, for example, a woman called FPD to report a domestic disturbance. By the time the police arrived, the woman's boyfriend had left. The police looked through the house and saw indications that the boyfriend lived there. When the woman told police that only she and her brother were listed on the home's occupancy permit, the officer placed the woman under arrest for the permit violation and she was jailed. In another instance, after a woman called police to report a domestic disturbance and was given a summons for an occupancy permit violation, she said, according to the officer's report, that she "hated the Ferguson Police Department and will never call again, even if she is being killed."[60]

Each of these changes has the potential to make police culture—and the public more broadly—more amenable to policing transformation, even as it addresses the specifics of an unlawful policing culture.[61]

Even consent decree requirements that seem quintessentially reformist—such as the requirement in Ferguson's and many other decrees that police engage with communities in nonenforcement capacities—may actually be effective at disrupting one of the most intransigent, foundational elements of the chronic crisis: the automatic devaluation of people of color, or the association of people of color—especially black boys and men—with crime.[62] Positive nonenforcement interactions are one of the few interventions supported by research as having the potential to reduce the sorts of biases that cause police to assume danger or guilt when initiating contact with people of color.[63] Other consent decree requirements also encourage or require removing police from the public safety equation altogether in certain circumstances. The Ferguson Consent Decree, for example, requires that the city create a community mediation program that will "conduct neighborhood mediations that promote lasting resolutions of appropriately selected disputes among community members, while reducing the need for involvement in the criminal justice system."[64] This remedy, while meant to create a culture that would support lawful policing, also goes directly to one of the main features of the chronic crisis: general overcriminalization. Similarly, many DOJ policing consent decrees require the establishment of mechanisms to divert persons in mental health crisis, or young people, from police and criminal justice involvement.[65]

The DOJ's consent decrees sometimes address another component of the chronic crisis as well: the impact of nonpolice stakeholders on lawful policing. Ferguson is perhaps the most expansive example of this. To interrupt the harm being caused by years of unlawful policing practices, the DOJ insisted upon incorporating and expanding Ferguson's amnesty program as part of the consent decree.[66] Pursuant to this program, 44,000 municipal cases have been dismissed in Ferguson since 2014—75 percent of those from before 2014. More than $1 million in court debt has been dismissed by the city.[67] Beyond this amnesty program, the consent decree in Ferguson requires significant changes to the city's municipal court system and a rewriting of its municipal code—with community input.[68] The Ferguson Consent Decree specifically requires that the city rescind or revise several municipal rules, in addition to the occupancy permit provision noted above. These include "Failure to Comply with Order of Police Officer," which DOJ found unconstitutional on its face, as well as its "Crossing at Right Angles" and "Manner of Walking Along Roadway," requirements that DOJ found were enforced in an unlawful manner by the police, thereby causing unnecessary harm and undermining police legitimacy and community trust.[69]

Thus, even when hewing to its relatively narrow scope of implementing consent decrees meant to eliminate patterns of unlawful conduct, DOJ's work can have a broader impact. This is not only a legitimate use of DOJ authority; it is essential and even inevitable to DOJ's pursuit of its statutory mission.

The Impact of the Findings Report

While much of the attention to DOJ's pattern or practice police work is focused on the consent decrees it negotiates with the police departments it investigates, the broader impact of DOJ's work may be its so-called findings reports. DOJ has issued a findings report (sometimes styled as a letter) at the completion of every police misconduct investigation conducted since at least 2010. One cannot fully assess the import and impact of DOJ's work in Ferguson or elsewhere without considering these findings reports.

Findings reports are essential to effective enforcement of the law enforcement misconduct statute and can be a powerful tool in combating the chronic crisis of policing more broadly. The Civil Rights Division's investigations are fairly exhaustive, as they must be, to both determine whether there is a pattern or practice of misconduct and to assess the nature and breadth of the problem as necessary to develop remedies to eliminate patterns of unlawful conduct. The findings are accordingly substantial and often complex. A findings report is critical in helping the city, police department, and public assess whether a remedy is needed and what that remedy should look like. A findings report also helps the jurisdiction and the public to assess whether the agreed-upon remedies that make up any negotiated settlement agreement address the unlawful conduct that the Civil Rights Division found or whether such remedies go too far or fall short. By setting out the harm caused by the unlawful conduct, a findings report can make it more difficult for a party to back out of a consent decree it negotiated (as in Ferguson and in New Orleans). If a consent decree is entered, the findings report acts as a touchstone so that the parties to the agreement, as well as the public, can look back to see whether the consent decree has addressed the problem it was meant to address. This touchstone is particularly helpful if a party later seeks to modify terms of the consent decree itself. The findings report ensures that any information DOJ learned during its investigation is not lost.

The Ferguson Report has been the clearest example of the power of DOJ findings reports. Although many of us had not heard of Ferguson before August 9, 2014, thanks to the work of ArchCity Defenders and others it already was clear by then that cities in the St. Louis region were using municipal courts to fund towns at the expense of poor, overwhelmingly black, people.[70] While the attention to the region after Michael Brown was killed likely would have resulted in broader knowledge of this widespread abuse, it likely would not have been as broadly known if DOJ had not become involved; the connection to Ferguson's (and the surrounding towns') abusive use of fines, fees, and unconstitutional, racially discriminatory policing might have remained largely hidden. It was not the DOJ pattern-or-practice investigation that revealed the "powder keg" created in the region by these practices.[71] It was DOJ's findings report that seared knowledge of this conduct, its causes, and its consequences on the national and international psyches.

Notwithstanding the work that advocates had been undertaking in this area for many years, the publication of the Ferguson Report is widely viewed as the start of the broader movement to reform fines and fees in the United States.[72] Once Ferguson's police and court practices, and the harm they caused, became known, jurisdictions large and small in St. Louis County and across the United States began looking inward and assessing their own practices—and their own vulnerability to the kinds of police abuse and subsequent outrage—that the world saw in Ferguson. From statewide initiatives, to local initiatives around Ferguson and elsewhere, to national initiatives, some practices changed quickly, and this change has continued. It is unlikely that these changes—many of them transformative—would have taken place without the dramatic impact of the Ferguson Report on public awareness that policing was being done for revenue rather than public safety reasons; that this type of policing both reflected and reinforced racial disparities and stereotypes; and that we ignored these dynamics at our moral, economic, and physical peril.

While DOJ's other findings reports to date have not had the high-profile impact of the Ferguson Report, they have similarly served as critically important teaching and advocacy tools. The impact of findings reports has not been systematically documented (and perhaps it is not possible to do so), but there is considerable anecdotal evidence of their contribution to police learning and progress. Police officials and community advocates read them to see how their own law enforcement agencies measure up. Community groups use them to advocate for change in state and local legislatures. Previously, most large policing conferences included sessions on the Civil Rights Division's pattern-or-practice work, including highlighting recent findings reports.

DOJ's findings reports also inform—and perhaps in some cases transform—courts' and judges' understanding of policing generally and of police practices in particular departments. Courts will sometimes cite a findings report as consistent with a finding that the evidence supports suppression of evidence, for example. Justice Sotomayor cited several DOJ findings reports in her dissent in *Utah v. Strieff*, arguing that the majority's expansion of police power where an individual is subject to an outstanding warrant will have an outsized, cascading effect across the country due to the sheer number of people subject to warrants. In her dissent, Justice Sotomayor writes:

> Justice Department investigations across the country have illustrated how these astounding numbers of warrants can be used by police to stop people without cause. In a single year in New Orleans, officers "made nearly 60,000 arrests, of which about 20,000 were of people with outstanding traffic or misdemeanor warrants from neighboring parishes for such infractions as unpaid tickets." Dept. of Justice, Civil Rights Div., Investigation of the New Orleans Police De-

partment 29 (2011). In the St. Louis metropolitan area, officers "routinely" stop people—on the street, at bus stops, or even in court—for no reason other than "an officer's desire to check whether the subject had a municipal arrest warrant pending." Ferguson Report, at 49, 57. In Newark, New Jersey, officers stopped 52,235 pedestrians within a 4-year period and ran warrant checks on 39,308 of them. Dept. of Justice, Civil Rights Div., Investigation of the Newark Police Department 8, 19, n. 15 *2069 (2014). The Justice Department analyzed these warrant-checked stops and reported that "approximately 93% of the stops would have been considered unsupported by articulated reasonable suspicion."[73]

I do not doubt that most officers act in "good faith" and do not set out to break the law. That does not mean these stops are "isolated instance[s] of negligence," however. Many are the product of institutionalized training procedures. . . . The majority does not suggest what makes this case "isolated" from these and countless other examples. Nor does it offer guidance for how a defendant can prove that his arrest was the result of "widespread" misconduct. Surely it should not take a federal investigation of Salt Lake County before the Court would protect someone in Strieff's position.

This passage demonstrates not only Justice Sotomayor's tacit recognition that there is a chronic policing crisis that stems in part from Supreme Court decisions; it also underscores the collective power of DOJ findings reports to inform courts' understanding of the breadth and harm of some police practices. This understanding is essential (if not always sufficient on its own, as *Strieff* shows) to addressing the chronic crisis.

Lessons Learned

Recognize You're Not All That

Successfully addressing the dual policing crisis requires that the Civil Rights Division support police reform efforts that occur parallel to its investigative work—rather than trying to hem them in or shut them down—even though these efforts can sometimes complicate or be seen by some as diluting the import of a DOJ investigation. As in Ferguson, these efforts often are led by local activist, protest, and legal groups that have been working on—or lived through—police abuse for years. It is important that their deeper knowledge and import is acknowledged and appreciated. This does not mean that DOJ must always agree with the tactics or precise aims of these groups, but it should seek out common ground. This facilitates the investigation by minimizing the risk of local groups undermining or working counter to the DOJ investigation, and it also recognizes that DOJ's involvement can help create capacity and support for these groups. This capacity and growth will be important to transforming police in the long run: long after the current acute crisis is over, the investigation is done, and even after any resulting consent decree has run its course.

To genuinely support shared aims of local and nongovernmental groups, DOJ attorneys must be aware that the privilege and power conferred by virtue of their DOJ affiliation (not by any special abilities of the attorney) remove obstacles that have stood in the way of police transformation (like jurisdictions' willingness to share information, to give just one example). In other words: be humble about why you are able to achieve whatever it is you are able to achieve within any given police department.

DOJ does not face many of the legal hurdles that others seeking to combat police misconduct must contend with. The law enforcement misconduct statute has no private right of action. Private plaintiffs must contend with the formidable (and increasing) hurdles of qualified immunity, class-action lawsuit restrictions, and section 1983 limitations on injunctive relief. At the same time, DOJ status hardly removes all obstacles to police transformation and can throw up some additional ones—for example, shifting attention from more transformative local efforts to more reformist DOJ efforts. At heart, DOJ attorneys need to have the humility to recognize that—whatever their expertise, how hard they are working, and the potential scope of their legal authority—they are visitors that have been inserted into a community that has struggled with a policing crisis for decades before DOJ arrived and will continue that struggle after DOJ leaves. DOJ attorneys should strive to use their authority to lessen the harm of the crisis without disrupting the critically important efforts of others.

Support Community Partners

DOJ's pattern-or-practice investigations are meant to address the causes of the acute crisis in the long term by requiring, where appropriate, remedies to prevent unnecessary acts of state violence and abusive police conduct in the future. But, as Ferguson shows us, the team conducting those investigations and negotiating those remedies is not set up to resolve or lessen the immediate harm of the then-current acute crisis. Given the demonstrable need for immediate action, and the unsuitability of the investigative team to fulfill that need, DOJ and others should look to build up, and call upon, other entities for direct support during the acute crisis.

In Ferguson, this need was filled by legions of local activists. An organic movement built up almost overnight, not only to demand justice for Mike

Brown, but to do so in a manner that would have a lasting and just impact. The work done by local organizer-activists—Kayla Reed, Jonetta Elzie, Brittany Packnett, DeRay McKesson, Tef Poe, Montague Simmons, and Jon Chasnoff, to name just a few—and by scholar-activists such as Justin Hansford, among others, has been documented in articles, books, podcasts, and movies and is far too extensive to capture here. As discussed below, these individuals and the groups and communities they work with will be the ones to undertake the hard work of confronting the *entire* chronic crisis long after DOJ's relatively narrow (albeit critically important) scope of work has been completed. But it is important to acknowledge also that while individuals and groups like this *need* assistance during an acute crisis, they also can *provide* it *if* sufficiently supported.

Relatedly, Ferguson underscores the continuing import of groups such as the ACLU and National Lawyers' Guild, as well as other groups with hyper-localized focus, such as ArchCity Defenders, in addressing the acute crisis. DOJ's Ferguson Report and the COPS Critical Response Initiative report were useful in describing some of the rights violations that Ferguson and others committed before and during the acute crisis. And the consent decree requires changes meant to prevent similar rights violations in the future. But it was these advocacy groups that were able to take immediate action when individual rights were violated during the acute crisis.

Notwithstanding the import of other groups and individuals, Ferguson also underscored how DOJ could do more to address the acute crisis. DOJ's Community Relations Service should be resourced and directed in a manner that would allow it to better prepare for and respond to acute policing crises. The CRS is, according to its website, meant to be the Department of Justice's "Peacemaker" for "community conflicts and tensions arising from differences of race, color, national origin, gender, gender identity, sexual orientation, religion, and disability."

CRS fulfills its "peacemaker" role by:

> [W]ork[ing] with all parties, including State and local units of government, private and public organizations, civil rights groups, and local community leaders, to uncover the underlying interests of all of those involved in the conflict and facilitates the development of viable, mutual understandings and solutions to the community's challenges. In addition, CRS assists communities in developing local mechanisms and community capacity to prevent tension and violent hate crimes from occurring in the future. All CRS services are provided free of charge to the communities and are confidential. CRS works in all 50 states and the U.S. territories, and in communities large and small, rural, urban and suburban.

Since its creation in 1964, its website states, CRS has "worked to rectify civil rights disputes and respond to conflicts that poison communities and prohibit society from reaching its full potential."

CRS has the potential, and the mandate, to fill a role that is desperately needed in community conflicts across the country and was desperately needed in Ferguson in 2014. CRS staff was on the ground in Ferguson from nearly the first days of the protest. Several CRS specialists spent much of their time in Ferguson for months, and the CRS's Ferguson work had attention from the highest levels. But despite the diligence of staff efforts, CRS's impact was compromised by a lack of resources and an inability at the institutional level to adapt its work to the needs on the ground. There was a tremendous amount of misinformation among Ferguson police officers and protesters alike. There was a lack of communication between the various stakeholders with various levels of interaction during the nightly protests in downtown Ferguson. Inflammatory rhetoric and dehumanization were widespread. Yet CRS for the most part limited its role to facilitating formal meetings between city leadership and some community representatives, rather than meeting directly with Ferguson line officers to discuss their angers and concerns, or being present at nightly protests to engage in shuttle diplomacy as needed and to facilitate communication.

As tensions continued to rise in Ferguson, some began to urge the investigative team to use time on the ground in Ferguson to leverage community contacts they were developing to try to mediate protests and other interactions between community members and law enforcement. This was an understandable request. The sense that things could erupt at any time was palpable, and the ongoing tension made it more difficult for the team to develop the rapport useful to gather information from officers and members of the public about problems with policing and how to fix them. It was difficult to refocus people on moving forward and on solutions given the dynamics constantly dragging them back into a highly contentious here-and-now. When Ferguson police blatantly violated the rights of protesters by arresting individuals peacefully protesting, with DOJ observers standing there, it made the federal government appear powerless to stop abuse by local police. This is, unfortunately, to some extent true: The investigative team was not the National Guard; it was a group of civil rights attorneys and investigators whose mission was to diagnosis and develop remedies for broken systems, with the aim of preventing future civil rights violations. But had DOJ been better able to assist the relevant stakeholders in developing and implementing effective ground rules for protests, then DOJ might have been more helpful on the ground and gained some legitimacy in the process. But asking the investigative team to serve as a peacekeeping team presented opportunity costs (i.e., time spent as mediators or otherwise responding to the acute crisis was time not spent investigating), and playing the role of mediator seemed, in some respects, at tension with their role as investigators. And—no small thing—the investigative team was for the most part not trained as mediators or facilitators.

The obvious irony is that the need the investigative team was being asked to fill was precisely the need that Congress foresaw in 1964 and addressed via the establishment of the CRS. Unfortunately, it is difficult for a large bureaucracy to pivot in the middle of an acute crisis, and CRS lacks sufficient resources for such an approach anyway. As Ferguson and other cases have taught us, we need to provide resources and direction to CRS to allow it to fulfill its desperately important mission—and we should do so before the next acute crisis.

Set and Manage Expectations for DOJ's Role

Ferguson shows how there are often a variety of expectations for how DOJ's Civil Rights Division is and should be responding to a dual policing crisis. These expectations will drive interactions with the investigative team and DOJ more broadly and will impact evaluations of the efficacy of DOJ's pattern-or-practice investigations and consent decrees. It is thus important that the team manage those expectations from the outset. Perhaps most fundamentally, DOJ should convey that its work should be seen as an important—but certainly partial—response to the crisis that should serve as a catalyst for broader momentum and action, rather than as a comprehensive solution that supplants the need for broader action. Managing expectations about what a DOJ investigation can—and cannot—achieve, and then staying out of the way of those who *can* undertake broader transformative efforts, enhances DOJ's chances of success, even as it facilitates the efforts of others to address the chronic crisis more broadly.

DOJ can communicate its role during its outreach to community groups, individuals, and interest groups. In doing so, DOJ can help encourage the creation of space and momentum for communities to begin to think about their own role—separate from, as well as part of, any DOJ agreement—in defining and realizing policing transformation in their own communities.

Similarly, in their meetings with city and police officials, Civil Rights Division personnel should be clear that city and police officials can and should meet with concerned community members and activists to work on police-related issues that may be beyond the scope of the DOJ investigation. A DOJ investigation can enhance the "fierce urgency of now" created by the acute crisis. DOJ can impress upon the city and police the need to work directly with communities on issues that go beyond the DOJ investigation and consent decree. DOJ should encourage officials to use the energy and creativity that arises during a dual crisis, not only to end the pattern or practice of unlawful conduct but also to set about doing the deeper work that is necessary to ultimately reduce the harm of policing more broadly.

Educate Through Investigation; Educate Through Outreach

Outreach is essential to any DOJ pattern or practice investigation. Talking with individuals who have been harmed by policing is critical to developing the facts necessary to determining the existence and nature of police misconduct. During one-on-one or group meetings, attorneys and investigators can learn more about the particular police-related concerns of a given community, identifying patterns in stories of police treatment that guide document requests and other aspects of the investigation. In a pattern-or-practice investigation, meeting with individuals and groups—including local community groups, police affinity groups and unions, criminal justice stakeholders, and civil rights groups, among others—is an invaluable mechanism for learning which problematic practices appear to be widespread and for diagnosing the causes of these patterns, as well as potential solutions.

Although these meetings are thus meant to educate DOJ, it can use them to help educate about the chronic policing crisis, that is, how dynamics beyond a pattern of unlawful police conduct are impacting policing in that community. Much of this education must come after the release of any findings report, thereby allowing for an open discussion of what DOJ has found. DOJ can discuss the portion of the problem that might be addressed in a consent decree as well as what is beyond the scope of that decree. The more sophisticated the audience, the more in-depth these conversations can be. Indeed, public sophistication on policing topics has advanced so much since Ferguson that DOJ may learn more than it teaches in many of these conversations.

Educate Through the Findings Report

The Ferguson Report's impact on systems of fines and fees—far beyond how those fines and fees facilitate unlawful policing—is well-known and discussed above. We should not lose sight of the many other ways findings reports can confront some of the tenets of the chronic policing crisis. For example, one of the causes of the chronic policing crisis is economic inequality, as the Ferguson Report helps explain. But the Ferguson Report also directly confronts one of the reasons this system of economic inequality was allowed to persist for so long: because it was masked by a racial stereotypes. One stereotype documented in the report was that black people are dangerous and unruly and must be controlled and civilized by a network of rules regulating their lives down to how they crossed the streets (only at right angles in Ferguson).[74]

Another stereotype is that the reason that black people were the ones lined up outside Ferguson's municipal court at every session—and the ones being arrested and taken to jail for not paying their fines and fees—was not because of race bias or economic inequality but instead because of a lack of "personal responsibility."[75] In demonstrating the falsity of this excuse and how it was used to deflect attention from the city's actual use of fines and fees to raise revenue and control a racialized social order, the Ferguson Report provided concrete, current, and credible facts that supported the arguments of scholar-activists such as Keeanga-Yamahtta Taylor that it is not moral failures or a "culture" of poverty among black people that perpetuates disparately poor outcomes; it is how these stereotypes have been allowed to mask deliberately perpetuated economic inequality.[76]

Further, the act of making the findings of its investigation public can itself address the chronic crisis. A findings report is the state's affirmation of the voices and lived experiences of often-marginalized groups and represents a public call to disrupt the status quo. There is power in this tacit admission.

Conclusion

Although instigated by an acute crisis, DOJ's pattern-or-practice investigation of the Ferguson Police Department allowed DOJ to address—incompletely but with significant impact—the chronic crisis of policing not only in Ferguson but in the United States more broadly. This is often the case, as it should be. That is to say, while a DOJ law enforcement misconduct investigation may be prompted by an acute crisis, and the investigation may help ameliorate some of the effects of that crisis, addressing the acute crisis is not and should not be the intent or focus of a DOJ law enforcement misconduct investigation.

Neither should DOJ seek, or be expected, to address the chronic policing crisis in its entirety: no single entity can do that, especially when that entity is enmeshed in the power structures that give rise to the chronic crisis. Rather, the focus of a DOJ law enforcement misconduct investigation should be the more modest—but still critically important—goal of remedying unlawful patterns or practices of policing. As DOJ's work in Ferguson shows us, even this more modest goal leaves ample room for DOJ to push policing forward in the right direction. The lessons learned in Ferguson can help all actors interested in ending the chronic crisis of policing work together more effectively so that our efforts support shared goals.

NOTES

1 JENNIFER E. COBBINA, HANDS UP, DON'T SHOOT: WHY THE PROTESTS IN FERGUSON AND BALTIMORE MATTER, AND HOW THEY CHANGED AMERICA (2019).

2 As discussed below, numerous components of the United States Department of Justice were active in Ferguson in 2014. Where not otherwise noted, a general reference to "DOJ" involvement refers to the law enforcement misconduct investigation (also referred to as a "pattern-or-practice" investigation) conducted by the Special Litigation Section of the Civil Rights Division.

3 UNITED STATES DEPARTMENT OF JUSTICE, CIVIL RIGHTS DIVISION, INVESTIGATION OF THE FERGUSON POLICE DEPARTMENT (Mar. 4, 2015) (hereinafter "Ferguson Report").

4 My role investigating the Ferguson Police Department for DOJ provided me unique insights on what transpired there in 2014–2015. I acknowledge, however, that mine is just one perspective and that each person experienced these events differently, having access to insights that I did not, and drawing meaning from these events that may differ from mine in many respects. I do not presume to speak for any other person, including others on the DOJ investigative team.

5 Robynn Tysver, *Omahan: To Get Trust, Policy Should Keep a Civil Tongue*, OMAHA WORLD HERALD (Jan. 14, 2015).

6 Kayla Reed, *Under the Arch Podcast*, episode 2 at 5:00.

7 Wesley Lowery, *Black Lives Matter: Birth of a Movement*, THE GUARDIAN (Jan. 17, 2017).

8 Editorial Board, *Justice in St. Louis County*, N.Y. TIMES (Sep. 6, 2014).

9 *See* www.justice.org.

10 KEEANGA-YAMAHTTA TAYLOR, FROM #BLACKLIVESMATTER TO BLACK LIBERATION (2016); see also reports on National Public Radio at http://npr.org; on the website of the Missouri Chapter of the American Civil Liberties Union, www.aclu.mo.org; and on the website of the National Lawyers' Guild, www.nlg.org.

11 At the time of the Ferguson investigation, this statute was codified at 42 U.S.C. §14141. It is now codifed as 34 U.S.C. §12601.

12 Sari Hortwitz et al., *Justice Dept. to Probe Ferguson Police Force*, WASH. POST (Sep. 3, 2014).

13 Julie Bosman, *Police Behavior in Ferguson Draws Attention of Justice Department*, N.Y. TIMES (Sep. 26, 2014).

14 Matt Apuzzo, *Department of Justice Sues Ferguson, Which Reversed Course on Agreement*, N.Y. TIMES (Feb. 10, 2016).

15 Stephen Deere, *Ferguson Council Unanimously Approves Agreement With DOJ*, St.
    Louis Post-Dispatch (Mar. 15, 2016).
16 *See* Cobbina, Hands Up, Don't Shoot.
17 See www.nytimes.com/interactive/2020/07/03/us/george-floyd-protests-crowd-
    size.html.
18 See www.forbes.com/sites/
    carlieporterfield/2020/06/23/a-whopping-95-of-americans-polled-support-
    criminal-justice-reform/#6c6954e43ad2.
19 As of this writing, the DOJ under President Donald Trump has brought only one
    pattern-or-practice investigation—of a subunit of the Springfield, Massachusetts,
    police department. Although the DOJ investigation of the Springfield Police
    Department found a pattern or practice of constitutional violations, DOJ, without
    explanation, did not demand any remedy to eliminate that pattern or practice. See
    www.justice.gov/usao-ma/pr/
    justice-department-announces-findings-investigation-narcotics-bureau-
    springfield-police.
        The DOJ under Trump has sought to avoid, end, and prevent policing consent
    decrees.
20 *See, e.g.*, Taylor, From #BlackLivesMatter; Cobbina, Hands Up,
    Don't Shoot.
21 In addition to Ferguson and Baltimore, the DOJ investigation of the Chicago
    Police Department, among others, can be characterized as occurring in the midst
    of an acute crisis.
22 *See, e.g.*, Paul Butler, *The System Is Working the Way It Is Supposed To: The Limits
    of Criminal Justice Reform*, 104 Geo. L.J. 1419 (2016).
23 Paul Butler, Chokehold: Policing Black Men (2017); Devon
    Carbado, *From Stopping Black People to Killing Black People: The Fourth
    Amendment Pathways to Police Violence*, 105 Cal. L. Rev. 125 (2017).
24 Butler, *The System Is Working*; Charles R. Epp, Pulled Over: How
    Police Stops Define Race And Citizenship (2014); Andrea J.
    Ritchie, Invisible No More: Police Violence Against Black
    Women And Women Of Color (2017).
25 Critical legal scholars, including race-crit scholars, have long touched on what I
    am calling the "chronic crisis" of policing. The recent work of a few, including
    Amna Akbar, Monica Bell, Paul Butler, Devon Carbado, Tracey Meares, and
    Keeanga-Yamahtta Taylor, has explored it in depth. The Movement for Black
    Lives, Campaign Zero, ArchCity Defenders, and prominent policing activists such
    as DeRay McKesson, Patrice Cuellors, Alicia Garza, Derecka Purnell, Kayla Reed,
    and Brittany Packnett (among many others) also have emphasized the dynamics
    that I describe here as composing the chronic crisis. My understanding of the
    chronic crisis is indebted to their work, even as it is based primarily on my
    experiences investigating and attempting to change police conduct as an attorney
    in DOJ's Civil Rights Division.

26 Butler, *The System Is Working*; Carbado, *From Stopping Black People*; Monica Bell, *Police Reform and the Dismantling of Legal Estrangement*, 126 YALE L.J. 2054 (2017).

27 *See, e.g.*, MICHELLE ALEXANDER, THE NEW JIM CROW: MASS INCARCERATION IN THE AGE OF COLORBLINDNESS (2010); Naomi Murakawa, *The Racial Antecedents to Federal Sentencing Guidelines: How Congress Judged the Judges from Brown to Booker*, 11 ROG. WILL. U. L. REV. 473, 482 (2006); Elizabeth Hinton, *Creating Crime: The Rise and Impact of National Juvenile Delinquency Programs in Black Urban Neighborhoods*, 4 J. URBAN HIST. 808 (2015).

28 *See, e.g.*, Taylor, FROM #BLACKLIVESMATTER.

29 *See, e.g.*, Butler, *The System Is Working*; Carbado, *From Stopping Black People*; Bell, *Police Reform*.

30 Joanna C. Schwartz, *Who Can Police the Police?* 2016 U. OF CHI. LEG. FOR. 437 (2016).

31 U.S. Department of Justice, www.justice.gov.

32 *Id.*

33 My focus on the Civil Rights Division's pattern-or-practice work is not meant to discount the import of the Criminal Section's work investigating and prosecuting officers for criminal violations of federal civil rights. This work is critically important. As Ferguson itself underscores, however, the work of the Criminal Section has an even more narrow scope and its own hurdles to overcome. Its impact on the dual crisis is thus a topic for a different day.

34 HUMAN RIGHTS WATCH, SHIELDED FROM JUSTICE: POLICE BRUTALITY AND ACCOUNTABILITY IN THE UNITED STATES (1998); THE INDEPENDENT COMMISSION ON THE LOS ANGELES POLICE DEPARTMENT, REPORT OF THE INDEPENDENT COMMISSION ON THE LOS ANGELES POLICE DEPARTMENT (CHRISTOPHER COMMISSION REPORT) (1991).

35 Kenny Reich, *Police Throughout U.S. Feel the Effects of Events in L.A*, L.A. TIMES (July 15, 1991); *See also* Stephen Rushin, *Federal Enforcement of Police Reform*, 82 FORDHAM L. REV. 3189, 3207–15 (2014) (discussing history of federal police misconduct statute).

36 *See* U.S. DEPARTMENT OF JUSTICE OFFICE OF THE INSPECTOR GENERAL, AUDIT DIVISION, AUDIT OF THE DEPARTMENT OF JUSTICE'S EFFORTS TO ADDRESS PATTERNS OR PRACTICES OF POLICE MISCONDUCT AND PROVIDE TECHNICAL ASSISTANCE ON ACCOUNTABILITY REFORM TO POLICE DEPARTMENTS, 18–14 at 9 (Feb. 2019), https://oig.justice.gov.

37 There were many useful resources created during the first days and weeks of the crisis, but the one with the single greatest impact may have been the white paper by ArchCity Defenders documenting abusive fines and fees throughout St. Louis County, including in Ferguson. *See* www.archcitydefenders.org.

38 Martin Luther King Jr., March on Washington, August 28, 1963 ("We are now faced with the fact that tomorrow is today. We are confronted with the fierce urgency of now. In this unfolding conundrum of life and history, there "is" such a thing as being too late. This is no time for apathy or complacency. This is a time for vigorous and positive action.")

39 TAYLOR, FROM #BLACKLIVESMATTER; Ta-Nehisi Coates, *The Gangsters of Ferguson*, THE ATLANTIC (Mar. 5, 2015).

40 *See, e.g.*, Kimbriell Kelly, Sarah Childress & Steven Rich, *What Happens When Police Are Forced to Reform?* WASH. POST (Nov. 13, 2015).

41 Eric Heisig, *Tamir Rice Shooting: A Breakdown of the Events That Led to the 12-Year-Old's Death*, CLEVELAND.COM (Jan.13, 2017, updated Jan. 19, 2019), www.cleveland.com. ("In the wake of Tamir's shooting, the city said it was committed to improve its hiring practices. At the time he was hired, the police department had no policies for vetting recruits. Improving hiring practices is also something the city is required to do under a settlement it reached with the Justice Department.")

42 *See, e.g.*, Butler, *The System Is Working* (arguing that DOJ's pattern-or-practice investigations are "stopgap measures that provide limited help but fail to bring about the transformation demanded by the strongest articulations of the crisis [in American criminal justice].").

43 For example, in the five years before the DOJ investigation of Detroit's police department, Detroit police officers fatally shot at least 47 people. After extensively remaking use of force training, reporting, and investigation as part of the consent decree, this rate declined dramatically. Between 2009 and 2014, when the Detroit consent decree ended, there were a total of 17 fatal police shootings. Overall police shootings decreased from an average of 69 shootings per year in 2000, to an average of 28 shootings per year in 2014. Letter from Barbara L. McQuade, United States Attorney, and Molly J. Moran, Acting Assistant Attorney General, to Detroit Mayor Michael E. Duggan (Aug. 25, 2014).

44 *See, e.g.*, Kimbriell Kelly, Sarah Childress & Steven Rich, *Forced Reforms, Mixed Results*, WASH. POST (Nov. 13, 2015) (noting increase in use of force in Pittsburgh after consent decree but disregarding requirements that more minor levels of force be reported and more stringent requirements for force reporting).

45 John Eligon, *Stopped, Ticketed, Fined: The Pitfalls of Driving While Black in Ferguson*, N.Y. TIMES (Aug. 6, 2019).

46 *United States v. City of Ferguson*, No. 4:16-cv-0018-CDP, Transcript of Status Conference Before Judge Catherine D. Perry at 65 (Dec. 17, 2018).

47 Samuel Walker, *Institutionalizing Police Accountability Reforms: The Problem of Making Police Reforms Endure*, 32 ST. LOUIS U. PUB. L. REV. 57 (2012).

48 A lower rate of stops and other police intrusions occurs in many jurisdictions after a DOJ consent decree. This outcome appears to be uneven however. *See, e.g.*, Samuel Walker, *"Not Dead Yet": The National Police Crisis, A New Conversation About Policing, and the Prospects for Accountability-Related Police Reform*, 2018 U.

ILL. L. REV. 1777, 1837–38 (discussing decreases in LAPD stops after consent decree and increases in arrests).

49 Butler, *The System Is Working.*

50 *Id.,* at 7.

51 Rachel Lippmann, *Federal Judge Approves Ferguson Consent Decree*, ST. LOUIS PUBLIC RADIO (Apr. 19, 2016), https://news.stlpublicradio.org.

52 David Luban, *The Moral Complexity of Cause Lawyers Within the State*, 81 FORDHAM L. REV. 705, 712 (2012).

53 *Id.* ("One of the failings of the Bush Administration's Office of Legal Counsel (OLC) was the way that it aggressively pressed to build extreme legal positions into the fabric of the law by embedding them in OLC opinions.")

54 *See, e.g.*, Douglas NeJaime, *Cause Lawyers Inside the State*, 81 FORDHAM L. REV. 649, 654 (2013) (arguing that "cause lawyers" working for government can "harness state power to advance shared movement-state goals"). As David Luban points out, however, while lawyers who have chosen to pursue a law reform agenda may find government lawyering "a dream come true," lawyers pursuing a more radical agenda may have to "mask or transform their commitments." Luban, *The Moral Complexity*, 709–11.

55 *See, e.g.*, U.S. DEPARTMENT OF JUSTICE CIVIL RIGHTS DIVISION, INVESTIGATION OF THE BALTIMORE CITY POLICE DEPARTMENT REPORT 40–43 (Aug. 10, 2016).

56 *See, e.g.*, *Frew v. Hawkins*, 540 U.S. 431 (2004).

57 *See, e.g.*, Steven Rushin, *Structural Reform Litigation in American Police Departments*, 99 MINN. L. REV. 1343 (2015).

58 Richard Rosenfeld & Joel Wallman, *Did De-policing Cause the Increase in Homicide Rates?* 18 CRIMINOLOGY & PUB. POL'Y 51 (2019). ("We find no evidence of an effect of arrest rates on city homicide rates for any offense category for any year in this period [2010–2015], including 2015, the year of the spike in homicide levels.")

59 According to the consent decree: "To ensure constitutional enforcement of the Ferguson Municipal Code ("Code") and further promote community-oriented policing, the City agrees to revise the Code and ensure that it comports with the United States Constitution and other laws; establishes clearly defined municipal offenses and appropriate penalties for violations; and adequately protects the public health, safety, and welfare." The occupancy permit provision of the code was one of several specified provisions to be revised. Consent Decree, *United States v. City of Ferguson*, No. 4:16-cv-000180-CDP (E.D. Mo. 2016), ¶ 36 (hereinafter "Ferguson Consent Decree").

60 Ferguson Report, 81.

61 Bell, *Police Reform.*

62 *See, e.g.*, JENNIFER L. EBERHARDT, BIASED: UNCOVERING THE HIDDEN PREJUDICE THAT SHAPES WHAT WE SEE, THINK, AND DO (2019).

63 *See, e.g.*, JACK GLASER, SUSPECT RACE: CAUSES AND CONSEQUENCES OF RACIAL PROFILING (2015).

64 Ferguson Consent Decree, ¶32.

65 U.S. DEPARTMENT OF JUSTICE CIVIL RIGHTS DIVISION, THE CIVIL RIGHTS DIVISION'S PATTERN OR PRACTICE POLICE REFORM: 1994–PRESENT 33–34 (Jan. 2017) (describing how in recent years DOJ's settlement agreements "have attempted to more effectively and sustainably address police misconduct . . . by focusing on the links between such misconduct and institutional failures outside of police departments, in areas such as social services, medical and mental health care, jails, and court systems").

66 Ferguson Consent Decree, ¶¶ 326–27.

67 *United States v. City of Ferguson*, No. 4:16-cv-0018-CDP, Transcript of Status Conference Before Judge Catherine D. Perry at 64 (Dec.17, 2018).

68 *See* Ferguson Report, 9–11; 78–89.

69 Consent Decree, ¶¶36–40.

70 ARCHCITY DEFENDERS, MUNICIPAL COURTS WHITE PAPER (2014).

71 U.S. Department of Justice, *Attorney General Holder Delivers Update on Investigations in Ferguson, Missouri* (Mar. 4, 2015), https://justice.gov.

72 FINES AND FEES JUSTICE CENTER, INVESTIGATION OF THE FERGUSON POLICE DEPARTMENT (Mar. 1, 2015).

73 *Utah v. Strieff*, 136 S.Ct. 2056, 2068–69 (2016) (some internal citations omitted).

74 Ferguson Report, 70–75.

75 *Id.*

76 TAYLOR, FROM #BLACKLIVESMATTER, 29–32.

4

When Crisis Comes to the Newsroom

The Media Lawyer in a Time of Global Unrest

DAVID E. MCCRAW

[The Committee to Protect Journalists] annual report shows record # of journalists imprisoned worldwide in 2017, including 21 on "fake news" charges. @POTUS must understand his harmful rhetoric only empowers repressive regimes to jail reporters & silence the truth.
—Senator John McCain, December 17, 2017

The long-term economic downturn in the US newspaper industry has blown a hole in international news coverage by American media.[1] Most large-city American newspapers have shuttered their foreign bureaus and retreated to their home bases, leaving the increasingly perilous business of covering the world from an American perspective to a handful of big players like the Associated Press, the *Wall Street Journal*, the *Washington Post*, and the *New York Times*, helped along by a few gritty and brave freelancers.[2] For those news organizations that remain in the world's hardest places, journalists have become softer targets for hostile regimes. It's just math: silencing one voice isn't much of a lift for governments used to locking down their own people whenever they dared to resist, especially if no one is there to witness it. Added to that toxic equation is the vulnerability of journalists, often working alone, to kidnapping by terrorist groups–a shocking reality driven home to the world in 2014, when journalists Jim Foley and Steve Sotloff were among the hostages beheaded by ISIS in Syria.[3]

That is the reality that those of us tasked with international security for news organizations face in a world where both our industry and the threats that our journalists encounter have undergone dramatic change. When I first became a lawyer for the *New York Times* in 2002, it was not uncommon for the detention of a journalist by a hostile government or combatants to be resolved before we could act. More senior officials or commanders would intervene quickly on the scene. Journalists enjoyed an "honest broker" status in even the most perilous parts of the world because all sides in a conflict understood in some way they needed journalists to get their message out to the world. But the rise of social media fundamentally altered that reality. No side needed a reporter any longer to be its communication channel to the larger world. And as the brutality of terror and warfare ramped up, the journalists left to cover the front lines were made all the more vulnerable.

Lawyering for a national news organization often involves duties that extend beyond the metes and bounds of the law: dealing with irate readers unhappy with the day's news or their home delivery, helping editors sort through ethical quandaries, connecting reporters to sources in the legal profession who might be able to explain the law behind a news story. But when I became the *New York Times*'s de facto international crisis manager, I stepped into a role that went far beyond anything I had been trained for as a lawyer, but at the same time, and in significant ways, I drew on the core skills that a lawyer naturally brings to any task. As unprepared as I was to lead a response to a kidnapping, over time I came to understand that—though the stakes were life-and-death high—it had commonalities with so many other complex problems I had faced in my career. The situation required a mastery of the available information, an insistence on rationality despite the pull of emotional responses, a skeptical embrace of experts, and ultimately a willingness to make the hard decisions despite imperfect information and options that were never optimal.

That skill set was instrumental for me in leading the *Times*'s response in a range of international emergencies over the course of a decade, from the arrest of our local staff in Egypt to a helicopter accident that seriously injured one of our journalists in a remote part of Iraq. But the truest test of those skills came in three incidents—two kidnappings in Afghanistan and the seizure of four journalists by the Qaddafi government in the midst of the Libyan civil war. In more recent days, those skills continue to be tested as the *Times* and other news organizations enter a particularly fraught period for journalists covering a dangerous world.

A Kidnapping in Afghanistan

The fact that I found myself thrust into the role of response manager was more a matter of organizational fluke than corporate design. It began in October 2008, when I received a call from one of our editors, letting me know that our reporter David Rohde had been kidnapped in Afghanistan during a reporting trip he had taken with two Afghan colleagues to interview a Taliban leader.[4] After David missed a prearranged phone check-in, someone at our

Kabul bureau had called his cell phone and learned that the three of them had been seized after driving into a trap set by the militant they were meeting.

Three years earlier, I had been assigned as the legal department's representative to a company committee charged with drafting a crisis plan to deal with emergencies overseas. Because of the nature of our business, the committee's work largely focused on the perils of kidnappings and government detentions. It was natural that a lawyer would come to be the drafter of the document. Our department had oversight for many corporate policies, from record management to business ethics. Over several months, I collaborated with the committee and a consultant over a series of meetings and drafts. In the end, when we issued our plan, it was quickly tucked away in a drawer and pretty much forgotten. That, it turned out, was enough to put me in charge of managing our response to David's kidnapping three years later.

I had only the vaguest idea of what we were supposed to do. A group of editors and I sat in a conference room that first afternoon trying to find out what we could from Carlotta Gall, our bureau chief in Kabul. I knew we had crisis consultants we could call, but we had never done that before, and nobody at the *Times* had communicated with them in the six years I had been at the paper. Somebody mentioned that David was also working on a book about Afghanistan. Maybe we should find out what his publisher could do to help us, someone else suggested.

I stepped out of the room and tracked down the number for the publisher's general counsel. When I got through, I explained how David Rohde was writing a book for his company and how David had just been kidnapped by the Taliban. He agreed with me that it was a terrible situation. "I'm glad you're involved," he said. "We wouldn't know what to do."

For the next eight months, my life would be consumed by David's kidnapping. I would go to the FBI's New York operations center with our executive editor, Bill Keller, to watch hostage videos released by David's captors. I was on the phone or in meetings every day with David's wife, Kristen, and his brother, Lee, as we tried to figure out how to get David and his two Afghan colleagues home. Reporters at the *Times* with connections deep into the intelligence services gave us information that was always interesting but could never be verified. I worked with two outside security consulting firms. One was the *Times*'s regular consulting firm for crisis management. The other, introduced to us by a friend of David's relatives, was run by a former Green Beret who had as his top operations person a former CIA agent. The former agent had already been convicted of a felony; his boss would be convicted a few years later of defrauding the government on defense contracts. They came filled with promises of cowboy missions and deep-state intelligence. They conjured up one crazy scheme after another. They gave code names to people who they said were in Pakistan, where David was being held, and who were providing them with firsthand information on David's captors. They came up with mind-boggling plans to bribe Taliban guards, have them overpower the others, and spirit David and the two Afghans off in the night—going where and how . . . who knew? The details were not part of their game.

At one point, Kristen, Lee, and I were summoned on a Sunday afternoon to a New York hotel lobby to meet with a guy who claimed to work undercover for the CIA and was willing to go into Pakistan and bring David out. We sat in an isolated corner as he whispered about his plans and swept his eyes around the nearly empty room. We had no idea what was real and what was phony, what would work and what wouldn't.

It didn't help that the US government was mostly an enigma to us. The FBI is the lead agency when an American gets kidnapped—even in distant war zone–like Afghanistan, where the CIA, the US military, and the State Department know far more about what is going on and seem not very interested in sharing with others, particularly out-of-their-depth FBI agents. The agents would lecture us on the illegality of paying ransoms, and then an agent would call me later and tell me that I shouldn't be an idiot: these things got solved by money more often than not. Every so often, I would get invited down to the FBI operations center in the Chelsea neighborhood of Manhattan so agents could complain that I wasn't sharing information, and then I could complain that they weren't telling me and David's family anything, and then we would talk about sports. The FBI was unhappy that we had our own private security team working on the kidnapping, no matter how bungling that team might have been, no matter how little we actually knew about what the security consultants were doing, and no matter how sketchy they were. At times, individual FBI agents and US officials went out of their way to be helpful, reaching out directly to Kristen and David's family and meeting with them in Washington. Others put on their game faces, revealing nothing and—I suspected after a while—knowing nothing. There would be very occasional contact from the kidnappers, always seeking money or the release of detainees. At one point, David was able to make a call to his wife. Another time, the Red Cross showed up with a letter for Kristen from David. We spent seven months working blind, searching for some reason to hope, but never knowing what was really going on, not even with the people who were supposed to be helping us.

As a media organization, the *Times* faced problems unique to those in our industry. In the normal course of events, we would be covering an event like the kidnapping of a prominent journalist who worked at a prominent news organization. Our reporters would be determined to find out what was happening and writing about it for the world. But the *Times* managed to keep the Rohde kidnapping out of the press. It was a controversial decision, one of those things that cut hard against our DNA as a news organization.[5] Most kidnapping experts tell companies and families that they are better off not having the kidnapping in the papers. Little good can come from publicity. Worrying about what is going to be said and whether it could provoke the kidnappers to harm the victim or make more absurd demands is one more stressor in a situation that is minute-by-minute, day in, day out, a slow burn of tension. When so little is under your control, it makes no sense to bring on one more out-of-control factor. At the request of David's family, Keller and our corporate public relations people asked other news outlets to stand down and not report what they knew about the kidnapping. It was awkward—we were in the business of disclosing information, not hiding it—but lives were at stake, and we extended the same consideration to others who were kidnapped when we were asked. At one point during the kidnapping saga, Al Jazeera obtained a staged video clip of David marching through the mountains with his captors and put it on the air. Keller got on the phone to Al Jazeera editors and was able to get them to pull the piece. It was never broadcast again.

A Hybrid Role for a Lawyer

As days turned into weeks and David and his two Afghan colleagues remained hostages, little that I was doing had the look or feel of traditional lawyering. To be sure, there were, from time to time, straightforward legal issues to address. When the issue of paying a ransom came up after the kidnappers demanded millions of dollars, I did a deep dive into the law surrounding material aid to terrorists, looking not only at what the law said but also the practical considerations of whether the US government would really prosecute a family or American company for securing the release of a victim of terrorism.[6] There were other legal questions as well, most of them centered on employment law: where and how to pay David's salary, questions about his benefits, nagging issues about insurance policies.

But the hybrid role I had assumed—both legal adviser and operational manager—called on me to use lawyering skills in nontraditional ways. It is easy to frame a kidnapping as the antithesis of legal work. It is, by definition and by nature, lawless. Lawyers naturally gravitate to process, to documentation, to information-gathering, to the order imposed by templates and precedents. And, in fact, as any security consultant will advise, those very things matter in the chaos of an international crisis. In an event in which so much is beyond the control of the company and the family seeking to resolve the situation, it becomes critical to keep careful, day-by-day records of what happened and what was discussed: to establish a regular pattern of check-ins with the company and family stakeholders, to be persistent in the collection and organization of information, and to maintain a process for continual outreach to those in government and elsewhere who may be able to assist. Of course, while the chaos of the situation may demand such orderliness, that same chaos makes it difficult. Those involved invariably want real-time updates, not scheduled twice-a-day calls, and the need to document regularly gets shunted aside by the demands of the moment. But crisis management ultimately tests a different skill set: one's ability to operate as a creative problem-solver while working on a problem that has no ready or apparent solution. An international crisis is an overarching problem to be solved, but in the unfolding of the response there is a continual series of smaller, more discrete problems that need to be addressed—from the determination of how and where to obtain information and the implementation of communication strategies to the management of difficult relationships in times of unrelenting stress.

Lawyers may or may not feel suited to take on a leadership in all of that. Some do better, and play a more productive role, by advising the people in the operational roles, providing needed legal advice, calibrating liability, and staying mindful of any possible litigation that may lurk down the road when the event is over. I found the opposite to be true. The practice of law is, at base, an engagement in problem-solving and I have always seen it as such and been willing to embrace creativity, looking for solutions that sometime involve business as much as the law, diplomacy as much as advocacy.

So even though no one in the company thought of the kidnapping as a "legal matter" properly managed out of an in-house legal department, senior management did recognize that I came at my job in a way that could translate well into being the right person to oversee our response to the kidnapping. Overwhelmingly, crisis management centers on tasks that track the work of many lawyers: making strategic decisions about and implementing a response, supervising consultants, overseeing the collection of intelligence, being a liaison with the government, and—most critically—managing communications internally and externally and with his family.

It helped that I understood journalism and newsrooms. News organizations are not like other companies. In the years since David's kidnapping, I have sat through too many pitches from security firms that specialize in providing protection to American workers abroad, as they tried to impress me by how quickly they had moved their clients out of countries that had imploded with public unrest or terrorist attacks or the onset of war. I had little interest in any of that. I needed to know how good they were at keeping safe the people who planned to stay behind and run toward the fire. We were a news organization, not an oil company. We were in the world to be a witness to its troubles. Neither were our employees satisfied to passively go about their work, leaving the kidnap response to others. They were reporters, with incredible sources in the Pentagon, at the CIA, and elsewhere in the US government. They could get top foreign officials to come to the phone. They were professionally ordained to find out information and share it. Journalists inside a news organization may compete ruthlessly, fall prey to intra-office jealously, and whisper about the failings of others in their newsrooms, but when crisis comes, they are like Marines—personally invested in saving whoever has wandered into harm's way. There is no need-to-know ethos in a news organization; there is a working premise, for better or worse, that everyone needs to know everything and needs to know right away. That reality complicates crisis management for any news organization.

There was more to recommend having me take on operational duties. As the lead lawyer for the *Times* newsroom, I comfortably straddled the bifurcated world of a news organization, with its inevitable wall between the corporate and business offices on one side and its independent news operation on the other. I knew where to go on the corporate floors to get resources, and I had the hard-won trust of the journalists, who knew I was going to do what was right by David and not be a corporate-side functionary, cautiously cleaving to some company line. (In fact, our CEO, our publisher, and our entire business staff were endlessly supportive of me and of David's family, no matter what lingering and long-held suspicions may have colored newsroom sentiments.) Still, it took a long time, and several miscues, for me to realize the importance of keeping things confidential within a tight group of employees, of being strategic about the information that was going to be shared with employees, and of limiting the circle of decision makers who would play a role in managing the crisis. When information flows too freely in a crisis, false hope, false despair, and consuming distraction invariably follow. People act on those things, and the result is rarely good for them or for the crisis management team. It becomes its own problem, one more thing to manage in a situation that needs no further complications.

The single-most fraught issue in any kidnapping is the decision whether to pay a ransom, and there, undeniably, the law infuses the decision-making. Most obviously, a kidnapping for money becomes a form of extortion, and the family or company forced to pay is a crime victim. That is a fairly straightforward legal scenario when a kidnapping is done by criminals just seeking cash. But terrorism kidnappings are different. The US government at the time took the position that payments of ransom in terrorism cases were illegal, a form of material aid to terrorists.[7] The FBI agents advising us when calls came in from the kidnappers told us that they could not be part of any offer of a ransom—unless it was a scheme to lure the kidnappers out of hiding. Only later, thanks to the advocacy of Jim Foley's family and others after his death, did the government modify its position and publicly declare in 2015 that American families would not be prosecuted for paying ransoms.[8] The prohibition remains for corporations and non-family members.[9]

We were fortunate that we as a company never had to face the question of whether we would pay a ransom. (We made offers in the sporadic calls with the kidnappers to keep the lines of communication open but were never close to the amounts they were demanding.) Any discussion of ransom, legal concerns aside, is fraught. As close as a company may be to the family of a kidnap victim, as much as the parties are working in sync for a common goal, there is a simple hard truth at the center of the discussions: the family's interests and the company's interest are not necessarily aligned. The family has a single-minded goal: the safe return of a loved one. A company must look at a range of interests—some legal considerations, some business matters: whether a ransom payment will create an incentive for kidnappings of other employees going forward, what reputational harm could flow from paying terrorists, and what obligations the company has to its shareholders and its board.

Neither a company lawyer nor a crisis response manager was going to be in a position to make those hard calls for a corporation. It was a decision that had to be made by the most senior people in an organization. My ability to advise my corporate client on the legalities of ransom would always be useful but could never answer the actual question: Should we do it? We never got to that hard place in David's case.

The End of a Kidnapping, the Beginning of a Second

The Rohde kidnapping ended as abruptly as it had begun. For months we had spent hours upon hours turning over and over again what we could do to try to bring the kidnapping to an end, who might be able to intervene, what connections we could try to make to the kidnappers. Then, on a summer Friday evening in June 2009, eight months in, I was in a car heading to a dinner party when David's wife, Kristen, called my cell phone. David had just called home. "He's escaped and he needs help," she said. David and Tahir, his Afghan colleague, had gotten away by crawling down a rope and made their way through the town of Miranshah to a nearby Pakistani military garrison. They had convinced the Pakistani military officer in charge to let them in (after the sentries made sure they were not rigged with suicide vests)—but it didn't mean they were safe. In the lawless tribal areas of northern Pakistan, where the Taliban held sway and the Pakistani government maintained only a nominal presence, there was no guarantee that they wouldn't be handed back to their captors.

I called our security consultants. No one knew anything about the escape, and after months of bravado and wild plans, they had no ideas about what we should do in the much-too-real situation that was unfolding before me. Susan Chira, our foreign editor, was supposed to be hosting the dinner. She and I had stopped outside her building, the two of us on the sidewalk, making calls to *Times* people in Pakistan and Afghanistan and anyone else who might be able to help. We agreed that we needed to join Kristen at her apartment downtown. Susan and I dashed past her arriving guests and flagged down a cab. In the car, I called the US embassy in Kabul, talked my way past the switchboard, and finally got through to an official there. It was not yet daybreak on the other side of the world. I explained everything I knew so far, which wasn't much. I could hear the embassy official taking notes. He asked me for some basic information. And then he said: "Be assured, Mr. McCraw, we will do nothing to stand in the way of your operation." I was in a cab on the West Side of New York City. I was a media lawyer who had once written a corporate crisis management plan. I was trying to get two kidnap victims out of the tribal areas of northern Pakistan. This guy on the phone was, as far as I was concerned, the US government. "I don't have an operation," I said. "I need you to have an operation." He went off to find an operation, never to be heard from again.

We worked through the night calling everyone Kristen, Lee, and I knew in President Barack Obama's administration, asking for assistance. The calling was frantic, and it got to the point that someone at the Pentagon finally told Lee we needed to shut it down, because everybody was spending valuable minutes answering phone calls from the officials we had called rather than doing something useful to get David out. The plan, as it evolved over the early-morning hours, was to have a Pakistani military helicopter fly into Miranshah, pick up David and Tahir, and transport him to Islamabad, the Pakistani capital. The next morning, after spending most of the night on the phone, I received word that David and Tahir had made it to Islamabad, then been taken to Bagram Air Base in Afghanistan before David would return to America.[10]

Three months after David returned, I received a call on a Saturday morning outside a suburban grocery store. The *Times* reporter Stephen Farrell and Sultan Munadi, an Afghan journalist who also worked for the paper, had been taken by the Taliban in Afghanistan. It started all over again: making the difficult calls to family members, connecting with the right people in government, collecting whatever information we could about the reporting trip they had been on, seeking out advice from the consultants (although we were done with cowboys). Four days later, British paratroopers staged a night raid on the house where they were being held.[11] Steve was rescued. Sultan was killed in the battle, as was a British soldier, Corporal John Harrison.[12] In David's case, the American government had told David's family that it would advise them if a military raid was being considered. Steve's kidnapping was different. It was being handled by the UK government because he was a British citizen. The first time I knew of the military operation was when my contact at the British Foreign and Commonwealth Office called me as the helicopters were bringing Steve back to Kabul.

Neither kidnapping really ended with the return of the reporters to safety. In both instances, we were swept up in public controversies that served as pointed reminders of how crisis management has to outlive the crisis itself. In Steve Farrell's case, Afghan journalists quickly came to believe that the rescuers had purposely gone for the Caucasian Westerner but had no regard for the Afghans, whether they were the captors or Sultan.[13] In the United Kingdom, the British newspapers loudly proclaimed that a brave English soldier had died rescuing reckless journalists who had put themselves in harm's way.[14] The killing of Sultan was a tragedy, one deeply felt by those at the *Times* who knew him, but there was no evidence to suggest that his death was anything more than a grave tragedy in the heat of a firefight.[15] In the United Kingdom, the *Times* contributed to a fund established in honor of the fallen soldier and joined in recognizing the sacrifice he had made. Those decisions were easy. The harder decision was to avoid getting into a heated debate with British newspapers over the conduct of our reporting team. We had points we could make—and, despite the tragic death of the soldier, it was still unbecoming to blame the victims of a kidnapping—but little good would come from keeping the story alive.

The aftermath of the Rohde kidnapping was more complicated. People inside the US government started passing rumors, to reporters and others, that we had paid a ransom.[16] We hadn't. If someone else paid—the Saudis, the Pakistani intelligence service, the US government, persons unknown—we never knew about it, and the idea seemed particularly preposterous based on what was verifiable and known. David and Tahir showed up at a military garrison unannounced and had to plead to be let inside.[17] There was no plan in place to get them out of the Pakistan tribal areas and to safety, not until David's family and I prompted the US government to do something after Kristen's call to me in the car. None of that would make sense if someone had arranged for the release. It would be irrational and illogical for anyone to leave such critical loose ends. Ransom-payers don't want to have to pay twice. Over time, I heard the story of the escape—daring and without assistance—often enough from David and Tahir that I had no doubts it was true. Yet, nearly a decade after the kidnapping, I continued to field questions about "what really happened." Behind many of the inquiries was the not very veiled hope of some reporters and others to show that the *New York Times* had engaged in a cover-up and propagated a lie in covering the kidnapping in its pages.

It was a difficult position for me as a lawyer. The natural urge was to be an advocate and to lay out the facts and make our case. But there was no obvious forum. At one point, I invited two FBI agents to our offices to go over our financial books documenting the transfer of funds to and from Kabul over the relevant period. The FBI had heard that the alleged ransom was paid from our bank account in Afghanistan. The ledgers showed that there had been no unexplained disbursements, and the agents appeared convinced. But I knew through contacts (specifically contacts that David Rohde had) that the report of the ransom had circulated far beyond the FBI and into the intelligence community and State Department. David made his own personal missions to various officials to challenge the report, but the story of the ransom persisted. I did what I could at first. I phoned an ambassador who appeared to be one of the people spreading the story and had a difficult conversation. Occasionally stories would pop up on the internet, and we would respond, but the counternarrative persisted, no matter where the truth was.

As difficult as it was to navigate the post-kidnapping communication challenges, in the long view the experience was instructive for those of us who are typically on the receiving end of complaints about coverage. In the regular course of my work, I deal often with those incensed with *Times* articles. Even when the criticism is misguided and wrong, I think back to my experience of being on the other side, of the white heat of negative publicity, of how reporting can at times go off track, and of how important it is to make sure our reporters have their stories right.

Four Journalists Go Missing in Libya

After the incident with Steve and Sultan, we had no more kidnappings, but other crises kept coming. Anthony Shadid died while on a reporting trip inside Syria, Alissa Rubin was seriously injured in a helicopter crash on Mount Sinjar in Iraq, a freelancer was detained in Ethiopia, two other freelancers were jailed while reporting from the Sinai Peninsula, one of our stringers in the Democratic Republic of Congo had to be relocated to Kenya, and we were in a more-or-less constant showdown with the authorities in Turkey as the Erdogan government took a hard turn toward authoritarianism. The hard, dark turn of the Turkish government was particularly troubling. When four of our journalists disappeared in Libya during the war there in 2011, it was the Turkish embassy in Syria we turned to for help.[18] The US diplomatic corps had left the country, but the Turks had stayed and were instrumental in getting our people back home. They stood up for the journalists and for human rights in a way that now seems almost impossible to fathom.

The four—Tyler Hicks, Anthony Shadid, Lindsay Addario, and Steve Farrell—had vanished one afternoon, along with their driver Mohammed Shaglouf, as they covered the war from the rebels' side. About the only useful bit of information we had in the first hours was that they had been carrying a satellite phone. And we knew that for as long as the phone was on, it would be transmitting their geographical location—the longitude and latitude of where they were. It would be a critical clue to finding them. There was just one problem: the satellite phone company wouldn't give us the data from the phone. Our tech people kept calling; the phone company kept refusing. The most important lesson I had learned from dealing with foreign crises was to be persistent, to keep trying, anything and everything, no matter how hopeless. The company was headquartered in the Middle East, and I finally got a senior executive to come to the phone. It was early in the morning in New York and I sat in my office, alone on my floor, making the plea. I explained that we needed the geographic coordinates, that it was a matter of life and death. The executive was warm and courteous, courtly almost, but nothing I said could move him. He said it was illegal to give me the information. But it was our data, I protested. No, he said, that was wrong. The data did not belong to the *Times*, and it did not belong to his company. It belonged to the land that was Libya, to the planet earth. It was nonsensical, utterly stupid, and so around and around we went. There was no resort to legal principles or legal advocacy. That would have been futile. In the end, he gave up the location of the last transmission—an incredibly useful bit of evidence—but surrendered it only after my persistent appeal for a humanitarian response to my request.

We learned over the next day that the journalists had been rounded up during a fight between the rebels and Qadaffi's military at a checkpoint. In New York, my small team was working sixteen hours a day trying to get them freed, knowing that the United States and its allies were about to start bombing Qadaffi's strongholds and everything would be more complicated when that happened. Reporter Chris Chivers left his home in Rhode Island and showed up to assist. We were joined by one of our outside security consultants. The three of us sat hour after hour in my office brainstorming on how we could reach the Qadaffi government. Every morning and afternoon, I gave regularly scheduled updates to the four families. We sorted through Twitter trying to figure out which way the war was going. Four days into the crisis I learned of two people in New York who knew Qadaffi personally. I got them to the phone and persuaded them to call the Libyan leader even as the bombing of Tripoli started. I cajoled and pressed my contact in the State Department to do more to help us get to the right people in the Libyan government. We learned that our journalists had been mistreated, and we needed the US government to do more, faster. In the strange way these things unfold, I ended up one afternoon on the phone with a Libyan government official, who was in the same room with not only the four *Times* journalists being held but also David Kirkpatrick, who was covering the war for us from Tripoli and had been permitted to come see them.

Five days into the standoff, the Libyans finally committed to handing over the four to Turkish diplomats. A time was set, arrangements were made, and the Turks began traveling through the dark streets of Tripoli to the pickup point. And then the bombing resumed. The Libyans said the transfer could not go forward. It was late at night in New York. Chivers and I closed down my office and came dragging back in at four in the morning, when the Turks were to try again. Shortly after dawn, we got the news that the ordeal was over.[19] Our journalists had been handed over. The Turks had come through. They escorted the four to the Tunisian border and freedom.

There remained one task undone. Mohammed Shaglouf, the driver, had disappeared after the car was stopped at the checkpoint. He had worked for the *Times* for exactly one day, hired that morning to take the *Times* journalists to report on a hospital in a village near the front. Prodded by Chivers, a former Marine, I knew we had to help his family as they tried to find out what had happened to him. By then, Libya was attempting to pick up the pieces after the fall of Qaddafi and the rebels' victory. Mohammed's family had tried to sort through rumors and hazy reports of his whereabouts. Someone recalled hearing his name called out at a Qaddafi detention facility. That proved to be untrue. In fact, he had been shot and died at the checkpoint.

Not far from where Mohammed had died, a Libyan man had created a carefully tended cemetery of unmarked graves for those whose bodies had been left behind in battle. He had taken pictures of the interred in the hopes that, later, families might be able to identify their loved ones. Shane Bell, one of our in-country security advisers, volunteered to travel into the heart of Libya to get DNA samples from Mohammed's family and from a body that appeared to be his. I set about trying to find a lab anywhere in the Middle East that could do the DNA testing quickly. I got nowhere. Shane was due to take home leave, so he packed the samples in his suitcase and carried them half-way around the world to Australia, where he found a lab that did DNA work. The samples were not in good shape, and the lab told me it would be hard to do a proper analysis, but the technicians there finally managed to pull it off. They sent me the results. There was no chance that the body in the unmarked grave was Mohammed.

I carefully typed up an email to the Shaglouf family, hoping to cushion what I knew would be the harsh blow of learning that they had not found their son and brother. They had studied pictures of the corpse and were convinced that the DNA would confirm the identity. I expressed my regrets as best I could. I am sure I did not achieve the closure I was hoping for. Nothing in my legal training had prepared me for delivering that sort of heartbreaking message to a family in grief.

Our dealings with the Shaglouf family underscored once again that for those of us charged with managing a company's crisis response the work extends beyond the resolution of the immediate crisis. Others inside and outside the company will move on—and probably should. But for a company that cares about its standing in the world, as the New York Times does, these events may have long tails, and the need to do the right thing, as best we can, remains.

A World of Trouble

After the two kidnappings and the Libyan detention, I became converted to the most obvious of causes: preventing crises abroad. By 2014, when the world was horrified by ISIS's brutal executions of journalists Jim Foley and Steve Sotloff (along with two aid workers), we had resolved as a company to do better in protecting the safety of our journalists. The age of the swashbuckling foreign correspondent who drank hard, smoked to an excess, and moved about the world with reckless abandon to track down the story as the bombs fell and the bullets flew was over (if it ever existed at all). New security protocols were put in place, requiring journalists heading for dangerous places to provide us with copies of passports, basic information about their families, and a security memo to be signed off on by our in-house security adviser. Scheduled phone check-ins became commonplace. Reporters at times traveled with security advisers. We occasionally pulled people out of countries when the personal risk became unacceptable.

Inevitably in legal circles, the discussion of such protocols gets framed as meeting a duty of care.[20] We are confident we are meeting that standard, but we rarely frame our conversations in-house that way. It suggests an approach aimed at meeting some minimal standard, with an eye trained on the law rather than the safety and well-being of our people. We want those of us charged with looking out for reporters' safety—as well as the reporters themselves—to understand our first commitment is not avoiding a lawsuit but rather doing what we can to ensure the security of journalists reporting from the world's toughest places before an incident occurs.

This has made the dangerous rhetoric coming out of the White House since the presidential inauguration in 2017 all the more disturbing.

Throughout the course of the kidnappings and the detentions and the random mayhem our reporters encountered, I didn't always love the way we were treated by our government, but that was usually in the details—disagreements about what could be done reasonably and what could not. My experience had been that somebody in the US government would come to the phone when an American reporter was in trouble. Whatever unhappiness an administration may have had with our coverage, it got set aside. I also knew that as part of the core American diplomatic mission, under George W. Bush and under Barack Obama, the foreign service made a point to advocate for a freer press in countries struggling to find democracy. The Bush State Department, no fan of the *Times,* had sent me to speak in Jordan, Yemen, Kuwait, Bahrain, and various countries of the old Soviet bloc about how press freedom worked in the United States. It was part of spreading the secular American gospel of freedom.

The first time we had a problem in the Middle East while Donald Trump was in the White House, someone in the State Department called one of our editors. He wasn't authorized to speak but needed to tell us about a threat that was looming for one of our reporters who had offended the local government. The official had made the call on his own, because he wasn't convinced that in the new State Department we would be able to count on anyone at the local embassies to help us out. I was told by people at other news organizations with reporters in trouble that the Trump State Department had continued to be helpful, but I was not looking forward to finding out for myself the first time we really needed the backing of the US government in the midst of a crisis.

Then there was the president's obsessive denouncement of the US mainstream media as "fake news."[21] It was corrosive inside our borders. Beyond them, it was dangerous. The calculus for the world's worst autocrats was simple: if the American president could denounce independent news organizations in his country as enemies of the people and work to undermine a free press, there was no reason they should not deal with their own local journalists in exactly the same way. By the second year of the Trump administration, autocratic nations like Malaysia were enacting laws banning fake news, barely hiding what was really going on: there would now be another tool available for authoritarians to control the media and keep unpleasant truths from their people. The situation was also bleak for those American news organizations that happened to be working in repressive nations. When autocrats harassed or brought charges against American news organizations over stories that displeased a regime, they undoubtedly assumed they were ingratiating themselves with the government in Washington.

Steve Erlanger of the *Times* reported on how infectious the president's "fake news" diatribe had been among the world's worst leaders.[22] Syrian president Bashar al-Assad responding to reports of human rights abuses, said: "We are living in a fake-news era."[23] President Nicolás Maduro of Venezuela echoed his sentiments.[24] In Myanmar, where the government turned a blind eye to the military's savage killing of Rohingya Muslims, an official said it was all fake news.[25] Others joined the chorus in Poland, in Hungary, in Libya, in Russia, and in Somalia. Steve offered a chilling example from the *People's Daily*, the government propaganda organ of China, which wrote:

> *If the president of the United States claims that his nation's leading media out-lets are a stain on America, then negative news about China and other countries should be taken with a grain of salt, since it is likely that bias and political agendas are distorting the real picture.*[26]

America had often held itself as a model when it was out promoting democracy to the world. The authoritarians of the world didn't seem much interested in following our lead in those days. But now? They were suddenly eager to sign on to be like this new America.

In July 2018, *New York Times* publisher A. G. Sulzberger met with President Trump and discussed how denouncements of a free press were putting foreign correspondents at risk.[27] It appears the message did not get through. In his own tweet about the meeting, the president launched another broadside about fake news.[28] Soon after, he was back out on the rally circuit, issuing toxic sound bites about the dishonesty of the press, scolding reporters for daring to write critical articles, and portraying the American media as "enemies of the people."[29]

None of that fits neatly into the classic paradigm of a corporate crisis. But ironically, and sadly, it marries my dual roles at the *Times*: as a First Amendment lawyer, and as an executive responsible for the safety of our journalists. Wearing either hat, I see it as a crisis, or at least as a crisis in the making. Speaking out for press freedom may be the one crisis-management duty I am most qualified to perform after all these years as a First Amendment lawyer. And little seems more important at this juncture.

Lessons Learned

For those who end up two-hatted in times of crises—both lawyer and response manager—there can be an obvious tension at times. It is hardly surprising that the people directly involved in a crisis—the employees and their families—may wonder where our loyalties lie. Is a decision being made to protect the company's reputation and legal interests or the best interests of our employees in trouble? And how does a lawyer walk that line when what may be best for the employee may run counter to the interests of the company?

There are no easy answers to those kinds of questions, and fortunately they tend to be raised more in the abstract than in the actual unfolding of a crisis. It seems inevitable, however, that in a complex and drawn-out crisis in which possible legal conflicts emerged between an employee's family and the company, someone in my position would need to surrender the legal portfolio and take independent advice from another lawyer while continuing to be the day-to-day operator on crisis response. I have been fortunate to work for a company that has an unwavering commitment to putting the employee who is in crisis first. The *Times* has never been content to use the duty of care as the full measure of the response to be given. That has permitted me to focus not on meeting minimal legal standards but on the things that matter in resolving a crisis: clear and orderly communication inside and outside the company, strategic thinking, persistence in problem-solving, relentlessness in collecting and exploiting the available information, and forming alliances with those people and entities most likely to be of assistance. In crises, just as in litigation, much of what happens, good or bad, is beyond our control. And that immovable fact is what makes it all the more imperative to do what we can to be fully in control of the rest.

NOTES

This article is adapted from the book TRUTH IN OUR TIMES: INSIDE THE FIGHT FOR PRESS FREEDOM IN THE AGE OF ALTERNATIVE FACTS (2019).

1 For data on overall financial trends in the newspaper industry, *see* Michael Barthel, *Despite Subscription Surges for Largest U.S. Newspapers, Circulation and Revenue Fall for Industry Overall*, PEW RESEARCH CENTER (June 1, 2017), www.pewresearch.org. For data on the decline in foreign reporting, *see* Simon Kruse Rasmussen, *Is Anybody Out There? Crisis and Collaboration in Foreign Reporting*, REUTERS INSTITUTE FELLOWSHIP PAPER, UNIVERSITY OF OXFORD (2012), https://reutersinstitute.politics.ox.ac.uk.

2 Research shows that, in the period 1998 to 2011, twenty or more U.S. news outlets closed all their overseas bureaus. Anupe Kaphle, *The Foreign Desk in Transition*, COLUM. JOURNALISM REV. (Mar./Apr. 2015), www.cjr.org. At organizations

that were maintaining an international presence, the numbers of countries covered, and staff employed, were also in decline. *Id.*

3 *See generally* Lawrence Wright, *Five Hostages*, THE NEW YORKER (July 6 & 13, 2015), www.newyorker.com.

4 For a full account of the Rohde kidnapping, *see* DAVID S. ROHDE & KRISTEN MULVIHILL, A ROPE AND A PRAYER: THE STORY OF A KIDNAPPING (2010).

5 *See* Dan Murphy, *Rohde: Media Faces Tough Choices in Kidnap Cases*, CHRISTIAN SCIENCE MONITOR (June 20, 2009), www.csmonitor.com; Howard Kurtz, *Media Agreed to Stay Silent on Kidnapping of Reporter David Rohde*, WASH. POST (June 29, 2009), www.washingtonpost.com; Kelly McBride, *Journalists Can't Uphold Standard Set by News Blackout of Rohde Kidnapping*, POYNTER INSTITUTE (June 23, 2009), www.poynter.org.; Joel Simon, *Is It Time to End Media Blackouts?*, COLUM. JOURNALISM REV. (Sept. 3, 2014), https://archives.cjr.org.

6 While there are no known prosecution of Americans for payment of ransom to terrorists, asylum-seekers have faced legal obstacles when U.S. authorities have treated ransom payments made in their home countries as material aid. *See* Steven H. Schulman, *Asylum Seekers and the Material-Support Bar*, 59 CATH. UNIV. L. REV. 949 (2010).

7 Julie Hirschfeld Davis, *Obama Ordering Change in U.S. Hostage Policies*, N.Y. TIMES (June 23, 2015), www.nytimes.com; Julie Pace & Eric Tucker, *US Will No Longer Prosecute Hostages' Families for Paying Ransom to Terror Groups*, BUS. INSIDER (June 23, 2015), www.businessinsider.com. In fact, it was widely believed that, despite what the officials said publicly, the U.S. government had facilitated payment of ransoms in some circumstances. Shane Harris, *U.S. Pays Off Hostage Takers*, DAILY BEAST (Apr. 29, 2015), www.thedailybeast.com. For legal background on the issue of ransom and the prohibition on material aid to terrorists, *see* Schulman, *Asylum Seekers*.

8 Statement by the President on the U.S. Government's Hostage Policy Review (June 24, 2015); Office of the Press Secretary, The White House, *Executive Order: Hostage Recovery Activities* (June 24, 2015); Julie Hirschfeld Davis, *Families Press for Changes in Policy on Hostages*, N.Y. TIMES (May 29, 2015), www.nytimes.com.

9 In announcing the new policy, the White House made clear that the government's position ending prosecution of ransom-payers applied only to families of victims. *See* Office of the Press Secretary, The White House, *Fact Sheet: U.S. Government Hostage Policy* (June 24, 2015).

10 *See* Adam B. Ellick, *With a Plan and a Rope, Captives Escape Taliban*, N.Y. TIMES (June 21, 2009), www.nytimes.com.

11 *See* Eric Schmitt, *Seized Times Reporter Is Freed in Afghan Raid That Kills Aide*, N.Y. TIMES (Sept. 9, 2009), www.nytimes.com.

12 *See* Steven Morris, *Inquest Pays Tribute to British Soldier Who Died Rescuing Journalist*, THE GUARDIAN (Mar. 16, 2011), www.theguardian.com.

13 *See Death of Sultan Munadi, Journalist Killed During Raid, Angers Afghans,* HuffPost (Nov. 9, 2009), www.huffingtonpost.com; Bob Dietz, *Afghan Journalists Call for Justice in Mundi's Death,* COMMITTEE TO PROTECT JOURNALISTS (Sept. 14, 2009).

14 *See, e.g.,* Andrew Pierce, Thomas Harding & Ben Farmer, *Army Anger as Soldier Killed Saving Journalist Who Ignored Taliban Warning,* THE TELEGRAPH (Sept. 9, 2009), www.telegraph.co.uk; Tim Shipman, *Miliband Criticises Kidnapped Journalist for Ignoring 'Very Strong Advice' Against Travel in Afghanistan,* THE DAILY MAIL (Sept. 11, 2009), www.dailymail.co.uk.

15 *See Sultan Munandi,* REVOLVY, www.revolvy.com/page/Sultan-Munadi (citing inquest that finds Munadi was shot both by Taliban fighters and the British forces).

16 *See New York Times "Paid Millions" to Release David Rohde From Taliban: Reporter,* HuffPost (Mar. 18, 2010), www.huffingtonpost.com; John Cook, *Did the New York Times Lie about Paying a Ransom for David Rohde's Release?,* GAWKER (Nov. 2, 2009), https://gawker.com.

17 *See* ROHDE & MULVIHILL, A ROPE AND A PRAYER.

18 *See* Jeremy W. Peters, *Freed Times Journalists Give Account of Captivity,* N.Y. TIMES (Mar. 21, 2011), www.nytimes.com.

19 *See id.*

20 *See, e.g.,* International SOS Foundation, *U.S. Legal Brief: Duty of Care and Managing Liability for International Assignees* (June 25, 2015). *See also* Holly Young, *Steve Dennis and the Court Case That Sent Waves Through the Aid Industry,* THE GUARDIAN (Dec. 5, 2015), www.theguardian.com.

21 *See, e.g.,* Sabrina Siddiqui & David Smith, *Trump's Attacks on Media Raise Threat of Violence Against Reporters, UN Experts Warn,* THE GUARDIAN (Aug. 2, 2018), www.theguardian.com; Daniel Politi, *Trump Doubles Down on Attacking 'Dangerous and Sick' Journalists: 'They Can Also Cause War!',* SLATE (Aug. 5, 2018), slate.com.

22 Steve Erlanger, *'Fake News,' Trump's Obsession, Is Now a Cudgel for Strongmen,* N.Y. TIMES (Dec. 12, 2017), www.nytimes.com.

23 *Id.*

24 *Id.*

25 *Id.*

26 *Id.*

27 David Remnick, *Trump v. The Times: Inside an Off-the-Record Meeting,* THE NEW YORKER (July 30, 2018), www.newyorker.com; Mark Landler, *New York Times Publisher and Trump Clash Over President's Threats Against Journalism,* N.Y. TIMES (July 29, 2018), www.nytimes.com.

28 *Id.*

29 *Id.*

5

Crisis in the Courts

The Campaign to Get ICE Out of New York State Courts

LEE WANG

It had taken months, but finally Carlos[1] had gotten a measure of justice. That morning, a judge had dismissed all of the charges against him and Carlos clutched a piece of paper proving his innocence. Earlier that year, Carlos's husband, who had beaten Carlos for years, called the police to falsely accuse Carlos of assaulting him. The local district attorney had charged Carlos with misdemeanor assault and he had been fighting the case ever since.

In Carlos's case, it wasn't just the fabricated charges he was worried about. He also feared being arrested by US Immigration and Customs Enforcement (ICE) in the courthouse. He had read about ICE targeting domestic violence victims in the courts and worried that, because of his undocumented status, something similar could happen to him. For months, he swallowed his fear and made regular court appearances to fight the charges.

When Carlos walked out of the courthouse that morning, it seemed like this one chapter in his abusive relationship was over. Then, a woman in regular clothes whom he had never seen before approached him. "What's your name?" she asked. "What's your name? What's your name?" she repeated in rapid fire. Carlos asked why she was asking and she responded: "You're here illegally, right?" Moments later, two men, also dressed in regular clothes, surrounded Carlos, handcuffed him, and hustled him into a car. The three people who accosted him turned out to be a team of plainclothes ICE agents.

Carlos pleaded with the ICE agents to let him go. He explained that he was a domestic violence victim. The ICE agents only made fun of him and used slurs about his sexual orientation. Once he was fingerprinted, Carlos was sent to an immigration jail in another state where ICE locked him in solitary confinement for ten days. When he was finally released into the facility's general population, he was ostracized and harassed when the other detainees learned that he was gay.

Carlos is just one of hundreds of immigrants targeted by ICE in New York courthouses since the election of President Donald Trump. Although ICE has targeted immigrants in state courthouses during previous administrations, the number of ICE operations in New York courts has skyrocketed under President Trump. From 2016 to 2017, the Immigrant Defense Project documented a 1,200 percent increase in ICE operations in courts throughout the state. In 2018, ICE operations in the courts jumped another 17 percent compared to the previous year.[2]

In this chapter I recount the dramatic escalation in ICE courthouse arrests in New York and describe how a statewide campaign developed to stop ICE from targeting immigrants in the state's courts. The first two sections describe how the phenomena of ICE courthouse arrests unfolded over the first half of 2017 and finally exploded into public view after ICE targeted victims of human trafficking; the third section looks at the creative tactics that lawyers and other advocates embraced in response to the arrests; the fourth section analyzes ICE's response to the outcry over courthouse enforcement; and the final section looks at the conflict between the court administration and attorneys over neutrality and civil disobedience.

The Crisis Unfolds

In early 2017, as reports of courthouse arrests started to come in through the Immigrant Defense Project hotline, it was hard to tell that this was a new phenomena. On a daily basis, the Immigrant Defense Project's staff was receiving reports of ICE raids all over the state, and ICE's tactics seemed to evolve on a weekly basis. ICE was showing up at people's homes in the predawn hours, pretending to be police; sweeping through apartment complexes on Long Island with mobile fingerprint devices; targeting immigrants at Greyhound bus stations; and luring immigrant workers to fake construction sites. As the calls to the Immigrant Defense Project hotline tripled in the first few months of the Trump administration, it seemed like immigrant communities were under assault from every direction.[3] The phenomenon of courthouse arrests was also harder to detect because immigration authorities were deliberately operating under the radar. In baseball caps and jeans, ICE agents spied on immigrants during arraignments, lurked in hallways, and often waited until the moment that their target stepped out of the courthouse to make their move.

Despite ICE's attempts to cloak its operations, by early March of 2017, the numbers were getting hard to ignore. In the first three months of the year, the Immigrant Defense Project hotline received more reports than we had for all of 2016. ICE wasn't just increasing the number of courthouse arrests; it was also broadening its targets. ICE was going after documented and undocumented immigrants alike, sometimes targeting green-card holders who had been in the United States for forty years. It appeared to make no distinction about the type of criminal charge immigrants were facing, targeting people in court who showed up to resolve traffic tickets or charges for drinking in public. But the arrests didn't focus only on criminal courts. ICE was also encroaching on special youth courts, which provide alternatives to incarceration and rehabilitation services for young people charged with crimes. For the first time, ICE was also spotted going after parents in family court.[4]

The seemingly random pattern of arrests made it difficult for attorneys to advise their clients. Who was really at risk of being arrested in court? Who needed to be warned? How should they be advised? What could attorneys say and not say about whether it was safe for a client to appear in court? Was there anything attorneys could do to stop the arrests from happening?

As advocates in New York grappled with how to respond, state supreme court justices around the country began to sound warnings about the dangers of ICE's conduct in state courts. Chief Justice Tani Cantil-Sakauye of California spoke first. In a letter to United States Attorney General Jeff Sessions and secretary of the US Department of Homeland Security (DHS) John Kelly, she asked that courthouses "not be used as bait in the necessary enforcement of our country's immigration laws."[5] Noting that the state's courts are the "main point of contact for millions of the most vulnerable Californians in times of anxiety, stress, and crises in their lives," the chief justice observed that ICE was deterring immigrants in the state from getting the help they needed and the justice they deserved. After concluding that ICE operations "compromise our core value of fairness" and "undermine the judiciary's ability to provide equal access to justice,"[6] the chief justice requested that ICE refrain from continuing to make arrests in the courts. In quick succession, the chief justices of Connecticut[7], New Jersey[8], Oregon[9], and Washington[10] echoed Chief Justice Cantil-Sakauye's concerns.[11]

But after this flurry of impassioned letters from chief justices around the country, DHS appeared to harden its stance. Secretary Kelly fired back at California's top judge, accusing her of making "troubling" statements and blaming California's sanctuary policies that limit local cooperation with ICE agents for the courthouse operations.[12] As more heinous reports of ICE courthouse arrests poured in from around the country—including one targeting a transgender domestic violence survivor as she sought a protective order in Texas[13]—ICE seemed to double down, announcing that neither victims nor witnesses would be exempt from arrests in the courts. As Thomas Homan, who was chief of ICE at the time, told Congress, immigrants should be scared, and they should look over the shoulder, particularly when they went to court.[14]

When ICE Shows Up in Human Trafficking Court

Up until the summer of 2017, New York's chief judge, Janet DiFiore, remained silent. What finally prompted her to break this silence was an act that was low even for ICE. On June 16, 2017, three ICE agents were seen roaming the halls of the Queens Criminal Court. They were particularly interested in AP8, a courtroom designated for victims of human trafficking. The specialized diversion court provided alternatives to incarceration, rehabilitation, and immigration assistance for people accused of prostitution-related offenses. Most of those appearing in AP8 were young men and women who were trafficked to the United States and suffered from violence, coercion, and trauma.

As one of the ICE agents lurked in the back of the courtroom, a reporter named Beth Fertig from the local National Public Radio (NPR) station happened to be in the room. It was pure coincidence that placed the agent and the reporter in the same room. Fertig was shadowing a team of attorneys from the Legal Aid Society for a story when they discovered that a plainclothes ICE agent was in the room and planning on taking their client, a twenty-nine-year-old woman from China. With the client's family members watching in horror from the wooden benches in the back, the Legal Aid Attorneys scrambled to figure out how to protect their client's rights.[15]

Thinking quickly, the attorneys requested that the judge set bail for their client. If bail was set, their client could be taken to Rikers Island, the notorious New York City jail that is now being dismantled after decades of human rights abuses there. Perversely, she would be safer on Rikers than walking freely on the streets.[16] That was because New York's sanctuary laws prevented the state Department of Corrections from handing most immigrants over to ICE. The judge agreed to set bail, and their client was taken into custody. Losing patience, the ICE agent left. The Legal Aid client was later released from criminal custody and returned to her family. But she was the lucky one. ICE agents had snagged four other immigrants in and around the Queens court that day, including another woman who was a victim of human trafficking.[17]

By the next morning, the local NPR station was leading with a story headlined: "Outcry After Immigration Agents Seen at Queens Human Trafficking Court."[18] Within hours, it was national news, and calls from reporters and elected officials began flooding in.[19] The chief judge finally made a public statement, saying she was "greatly concerned" by the arrests.[20] And local city council members were so incensed that they called for public hearings.[21]

The Legal Aid Society approached the Immigrant Defense Project about organizing a press conference with them, and by the next week we were standing shoulder to shoulder with city council members on the steps of City Hall. I worried that people wouldn't show up for the event, but the outpouring from advocates surprised me. Attorneys and activists from all over New York came out in force. There were seasoned public defenders in well-worn suits; immigration attorneys lugging bags of case files; and community members waving signs reading "Ningún Más Deportado" ("No More Deportations"). There were also a number of other organizations there that we did not work with often: Safe Horizon, Her Justice, Legal Services NYC, and Sanctuary for Families. They were some of the biggest legal service providers in the city for victims of violence. To the ordinary passerby, we were a unified voice. But for advocates, this was an unusual coalition. People who typically were on opposite sides in court were now united by a common cause.

Rapid Response in the Age of Twitter

Unfortunately, the outcry from jurists, advocates, and elected officials did not get ICE to relent. Instead, ICE ratcheted up the arrests, and by November of 2017 the Immigrant Defense Project had documented a 900 percent increase in ICE courthouse operations compared to the previous year.[22] By the fall of 2017, arrests became a nearly daily occurrence, and ICE agents appeared to behave more and more brazenly. In one incident, a dozen plainclothes ICE agents swarmed four young undocumented men outside of the Brooklyn Criminal Court.[23] In another, four agents tackled a young man and his six-month-pregnant girlfriend while they were crossing the street. While the young man's girlfriend was bleeding and screaming for help, the ICE agents dragged him into an unmarked car.[24] Disturbingly, in some cases, court officers appeared to be assisting ICE, physically blocking attorneys while ICE interrogated their clients and giving ICE agents entry into private areas of the court, enabling ICE to secretly take immigrants out of the court.[25]

As news of the arrests spread, it was not just criminal defense practices that were affected. Attorneys working with immigrants in family court and housing court were reporting a broad chilling effect on their clients. One attorney who worked in the Hudson Valley told us of a woman who had been raped by her abuser in a parking lot but was now too fearful of ICE to seek an order of protection in court.[26] Other attorneys told us of clients in abusive relationships that were afraid to move forward with custody proceedings, or to seek child support, because of the possibility of ICE being in the courtroom.[27] Longtime housing attorneys were suddenly unable to move forward with cases against landlords because key witnesses, who were undocumented, were too afraid to testify.[28] Beyond attorneys, there was an entire constellation of legal service workers—social workers, parent advocates, and case managers—working with immigrants who were gripped with fear.

As ICE arrests became the new normal in New York's courts, legal services providers struggled to adapt. What could they tell clients who were afraid to go to court? Was there anything they could do to protect clients from ICE? What rights did their clients have when confronted by an ICE agent? What happened if an ICE agent came to one of their offices in a court building? And what would happen to their clients *after* ICE arrested them? Would their cases even continue?

To try and answer some of these questions, the Immigrant Defense Project started to hold training sessions across New York City with criminal defense and family attorneys. There were a few concrete suggestions we could offer for reducing the risks to clients, but every strategy came with a cost. Attorneys could ask to waive appearances or at least minimize the number of appearances a client had to make. This might work in some cases, but it also meant that clients could not participate in special rehabilitative courts—like mental health treatment and drug treatment courts—which required *more* appearances than regular criminal courts. Attorneys could recommend that clients enter pleas as quickly as possible, but that meant forgoing the chance of negotiating a better offer from a prosecutor and sacrificing the right to go to trial. And, of course, attorneys could seek bail for their clients, like the Legal Aid attorneys did in the case of the human trafficking victim, but that meant their client could spend months behind bars at Rikers.

As we grappled with *what* to tell clients, we were also looking for new ways of staying up to date on ICE operations in the courts. Email chains with subject headings like "ICE in AP5" or "Beware: ICE sighting in Queens" started to fill our inboxes. The Immigrant Defense Project became a de facto tip line for ICE courthouse sightings. To verify the reports we received, staff attorneys and intake specialists interviewed as many eyewitnesses as we could, speaking with attorneys, family members, friends, and, when possible, the immigrants who were targeted and detained by ICE. But for defense attorneys trying to make quick assessments about the risks that their clients faced on any given day, email chains and tip lines proved too clunky.

By the fall of 2017, attorneys began using Twitter to warn others of ICE sightings in the courts. Twitter turned out to be the ideal forum for attorneys to share real-time information and documentation on what was happening in the courts. That might sound like a hackneyed observation to the average millennial, but in a court system where many attorneys rely on paper calendars to schedule cases, turning to Twitter was a novelty. But desperate times call for creative tactics. In the age of Trump, Twitter became a newly essential tool for lawyers.

Real-time tweets helped attorneys track the movement of ICE agents in and around the courts. This helped attorneys to assess the risks that their clients could face in court, which was critical for accurately advising clients about their options. The tweets also provided the first visual documentation of the arrests because attorneys were occasionally able to snap photos and even videos of agents lurking around the courts. They also helped to capture the scale and complexity of ICE operations. For example, attorneys from Brooklyn Defender Services provided a stream of information about a large-scale sweep that involved nearly a dozen ICE agents in September 2017. The feed from one attorney started with a photo of a man being led into an unmarked black car by a man in a blue tee shirt.

The feed continued with photos of more ICE agents as they waited on the corner outside of the Brooklyn Criminal Court and then moved into the courthouse and sat on benches in the hallway. All told, ICE targeted and arrested four young men that day.

The Twitter updates on such courthouse updates quickly evolved into the first substantial source of information available to the mainstream media. Indeed, the tweets from the September 14 ICE operation in Brooklyn drew so much attention that several news outlets showed up at court to interview ICE. Local media outlets were able to document some of the ICE operation themselves, publishing photos and videos of the plainclothes agents at court.[29] The press also experienced firsthand what it was like to interact with ICE agents who acted, in the words of one reporter, like "secret police."[30]

Not long after, Twitter also became an organizing tool for attorneys who were fed up with ICE snatching away their clients. On November 28, 2017, after a particularly contentious incident where court officers allowed ICE agents to use a restricted area of the court to arrest a thirty-year-old man, dozens of public defenders staged an impromptu walkout.[31] As word spread of the walk out on social media, attorneys from the Legal Aid Society and Brooklyn Defender Services streamed out of the court. With makeshift signs scrawled on the backs of Manila envelopes, the attorneys picketed outside of the Brooklyn Criminal Court at 120 Schemerhorn Street, shouting "ICE Out of NYC!" and "Shame on You!"

The November 28 walkout turned out to be the first of many. In the next six months, there were walkouts in the Bronx, Queens, and Staten Island. In the Bronx, public defenders stormed out of the Hall of Justice after a team of ICE agents swarmed a twenty-seven-year-old man who had come from the Ivory Coast when he was three years old.[32] On Staten Island, public defenders protested after ICE agents targeted an undocumented immigrant with no prior criminal history whose criminal case was dismissed just minutes before ICE agents arrested him.[33] Videos of the walkouts quickly spread on social media, bringing new attention to ICE's shadowy operations in New York courts.

Although the walkouts brought attention to the issue, they also created tension with the New York State Office of Court Administration, which supervised operation of the courts. During one walkout in Queens, court administrators reassigned a handful of cases from the Legal Aid Society to private attorneys who act as assigned counsel in the courts. A spokesperson for the Office of Court Administration accused Legal Aid Attorneys of abandoning their clients and undermining the operation of the courts.[34] The Legal Aid Society, which said that the public defenders had made sure the court docket was covered during the walkout, described the reassignment as retaliation for attorneys speaking their mind. The conflict over the walkouts was emblematic of a deeper divide between advocates, who believed the court needed to do something to intervene, and the officials who ran the state court system, who insisted that they couldn't take sides.

ICE Refuses to Relent

By the spring of 2018, the crisis in the courts seemed to be at a breaking point. The steady stream of news accounts of ICE targeting domestic violence survivors, asylees, Dreamers, and human trafficking victims had led to widespread calls for ICE to add courthouses to its list of "sensitive locations." ICE had a longstanding "sensitive locations policy," which discouraged agents from arresting people at hospitals, schools, places of worship, funerals, and public demonstrations.[35] ICE could simply add courthouses to that list. Indeed, that had been the central request of half a dozen state chief justices,[36] the American Bar Association,[37] and numerous elected officials. Congressional Democrats had even introduced a bill to make courts off-limits for ICE.[38]

Despite all this pressure, ICE refused to relent. Rather than back away from courthouse enforcement, ICE made it in an official policy. At the beginning of 2018, ICE published a directive titled "Civil Immigration Enforcement Actions Inside Courthouses."[39] It was the agency's first formal acknowledgement that it had a policy for targeting immigrants in and around courthouses. The directive also spelled out the justification for the practice, in surprisingly blunt terms, blaming local sanctuary policies for the arrests. As the policy noted, "[C]ourthouse arrests are often necessitated by the unwillingness of jurisdictions to cooperate with ICE in the transfer of custody of aliens from prisons to jails." Because cities like New York had stopped holding and transferring immigrants from its local jails to ICE (a practice that numerous federal courts have ruled is unconstitutional), ICE reasoned that it had no choice but to raid the city's courts for "criminals and fugitives" who could be carrying "weapons and other contraband."[40]

The new ICE policy also purported to limit the scope of courthouse operations in a couple of key ways: First, it would focus on "specific targeted aliens" such as those with "criminal convictions, gang members, or those presenting a national security or public safety threat"; second, arrests at "non-criminal court" proceedings would be "generally avoid[ed]" unless they were deemed "operationally necessary." New York's Office of Court Administration appeared to accept these limitations as meaningful changes on the part of ICE.[41] Indeed, even the chief justice of California, who had spoken out first against ICE's practice, described the policy as a "good start."[42]

However, advocates were skeptical. The new directive was filled with loopholes so big that they seemed to create no meaningful limits on what ICE could and could not do. While the policy mentioned "specific, targeted aliens," it also left this list of targets open-ended, making it possible for ICE to go after a much wider range of immigrants. The purported limit on arrests in noncriminal courts was similarly slippery. When was an arrest "operationally necessary"? The document provided no definition or guidance on what this meant.

As problematic as ICE's new policy was, it sparked some tough conversations within advocacy circles. After a year of relentless ICE arrests, any limit to ICE's operations seemed like a positive. A statewide coalition formed that included many legal service providers that primarily worked in noncriminal courts. For this group, could this policy be progress? At the next ICE Out of Courts coalition meeting, we decided to raise this issue with the group. While more than forty people from organizations around the city and state squeezed into an office lunchroom that doubled as our conference space, we gingerly broached the subject.

What I assumed would be controversial turned out to be a surprising point of agreement. Advocates of all stripes agreed that ICE's pledge to act "discreetly" in the courts was a hollow promise and that the policy provided no meaningful protection to immigrants, whether in civil or criminal courts. Some attorneys raised principled objections, noting that the constitutional right to access courts applied to all immigrants, regardless of which type of court they needed to attend. Others raised more practical concerns. One attorney pointed out that the policy did not account for the fact that many family courts were housed in the same building or complex as criminal courts. ICE would still be present in the courts, even if just a hundred yards away. This was unlikely to boost immigrants' trust of the courts. Others who represented immigrant victims also emphasized that their clients were often defendants too, who were ensnared in the criminal justice system for many reasons. A case in point: the women that ICE targeted in the human trafficking court in Queens were victims of human trafficking but were also charged criminally for prostitution-related offenses.

By the end of the meeting, the coalition of advocates agreed that, as a basic principle, the group would reject ICE's new policy as an acceptable response to the crisis in the courts. The coalition would fight for the rights of all immigrants to access the courts, regardless of whether they were charged with a crime or seeking protection from the court. It was a pivotal moment for the campaign.

Neutrality and Civil Disobedience in the Age of Trump

With ICE digging in its heels, advocates in New York were increasingly convinced that the state needed to intervene. The state legislature was considering a bill that would make it unlawful for ICE to execute arrests in and around courthouses, but it was idling in Albany.[43] In the absence of legislative action, the Immigrant Defense Project and other organizations asked the chief judge of New York's courts to enact court rules that would limit ICE's operations. Specifically, the coalition proposed that the chief judge require ICE to present a judicial warrant from a federal judge before executing a civil arrest in court and proposed that she give explicit instructions to court staff and officers not to assist ICE agents.[44]

After months of meetings with advocates, it was clear that the courts were uncomfortable about being pulled into what they perceived as a political fight. When asked what the judiciary planned to do to stop ICE arrests in human trafficking courts, the chief administrative judge of New York's courts, Lawrence Marks, told a panel of New York legislators that his hands were tied. "We can't take a position about immigration policies in Washington whether they're good or bad. Individual people can take a position on that but, institutionally, we have to be neutral."[45]

While the Office of Court Administration adhered to its middle ground, the perception of the courts in immigrant communities was shifting. Advocates struggled to get immigrants to seek child support or orders of protection, and district attorneys reported that cases were falling apart because witnesses were terrified to come to court.[46] Surveys of law enforcement and legal service providers revealed that ICE's presence in the courts kept immigrants from seeking protection from the courts. In Los Angeles, San Francisco, and San Diego, law enforcement has reported drops in domestic violence reporting from Latinx communities; Houston also reported a 16 percent decrease in domestic violence reporting from its Latinx community. In a letter addressed to the acting director of ICE, close to seventy retired judges observed that ICE's presence interferes with the work of the courts. They wrote: "[W]e know that judges simply cannot do their jobs—and our justice system cannot function effectively—if victims, defendants, witnesses and family members do not feel secure in accessing the courthouse."[47]

The Office of Court Administration's insistence on neutrality was in growing tension with the position that many attorneys took as vocal critics of ICE's presence in the courts. This conflict was put into sharp relief during the attorney walkout from the Queens Criminal Court on April 10, 2018.[48] The walkout in Queens was part of a series of walkouts led by public defenders frustrated and angry about ICE's untrammeled ability to snatch their clients from the courts. When the Office of Court Administrations responded to the protest by reassigning cases at arraignments from defender offices such as the Legal Aid Society, to private attorneys, a spokesperson explained that this was in response to attorneys' "abandonment of cases."[49] Public defenders who walked out that day dispute the notion that they left their clients in the lurch during the walkout.[50] The walkout occurred during the court's lunch break.[51] However, at the root of the dispute was not a factual question about timing but instead more fundamental questions about ethics and professional responsibility.

Attorneys have started to question where their fundamental obligations lie, not only as members of the bar but also as public citizens with moral obligations. As key players in a court system that federal immigration officers have publicly identified as a hunting ground for immigrants, how were attorneys expected to responsibly serve their clients *and* their individual consciences?[52]

The professional codes of conduct that govern the bar are one source of guidance, but these rules provide no easy answers. A lawyer has overlapping responsibilities as a representative of their client's interest, as an officer of the court, and as a public citizen with a "special responsibility for the quality of justice."[53] But when ICE comes to arrest a client in court, these roles can directly conflict. For example, if an attorney spots ICE agents outside of a courtroom and discovers that they are there to apprehend her client, what should she do? As a zealous advocate for her client, the attorney has a duty to inform her client of the risks of attending court. But as an officer of the court, the attorney cannot ethically tell their clients *not* to come to a court-mandated appearance. She also has a "duty to uphold legal process."[54]

Compounding these dueling professional obligations is the potential threat of federal criminal prosecution for "harboring" a noncitizen. Under 8 U.S.C. §1324(a), it is a federal crime to knowingly conceal or shield a noncitizen who is unlawfully present in the United States from detection by immigration authorities. Before the appointment of Attorney General Sessions, harboring was seldom prosecuted, and there are many potential defenses to such a prosecution for attorneys.[55] But the professional rules forbid "even minor violations of law." Wherever attorneys land on this question, one thing is clear: the threat of this type of prosecution is not just bluster. In April 2019, a federal grand jury indicted a sitting Massachusetts state court judge and a state court officer for obstruction of justice for allegedly helping an undocumented immigrant avoid detection by ICE agents in the courthouse.[56]

What is a conscientious lawyer to do? The rules recognize that a lawyer's professional duties should be informed by "personal conscience," but they do not squarely answer whether civil disobedience is legally ethical in a situation where a client faces not only arrest but permanent exile from her family.

In the current moment, the codes of conduct may simply be insufficient. Showing obedience to the law is a difficult proposition at a time when the executive branch of the US government adopts policies that use courts as hunting grounds, tears away children from parents, denies refuge to survivors of persecution and violence, and bans entry based on religious belief. When the norms of human decency and fairness are routinely violated, attorneys may do better to look to the rich tradition of civil disobedience than to the professional rules.

In one of the most famous meditations on the duty to disobey unjust laws, *Letter from a Birmingham Jail*, Martin Luther King Jr. wrote that when a man breaks a law that "conscience tell him is unjust" and "willingly accepts the penalty" this is "in reality expressing the highest respect for law." For Mohandas Gandhi, an attorney trained in the English common law system, lawyers had a special obligation to engage in civil disobedience:

> Lawyers are the persons most able to appreciate the dangers of bad legislation. It must be with them a sacred duty by committing civil breach to prevent a criminal breach. Lawyers should be guardians of law and liberty and as such are interested in keeping the statute book of the country "pure and undefiled."[57]

Following this belief, during his noncooperation campaign of 1920, Gandhi called on India's lawyers to cease practicing and boycott the colonial court system.[58] The goal of the campaign was not only to challenge the legitimacy of the British colonial government but also to encourage the independence and moral growth of attorneys themselves.[59]

Gandhi's philosophy is an inspiring model for the current moment, not only because it speaks with moral clarity about the necessity of resistance to injustice but also because it considers the individual grappling with how to be a responsible lawyer and ethical human being.

One reason so many attorneys took part in the 2018 walkouts may be that they needed this transformation—an opportunity to express their outrage and to acknowledge the trauma that they are (or were) seeing and experiencing. I recently spoke with an attorney who told me she feels very apprehensive about going to court after seeing many of her clients taken away by ICE. She can't shake the image of two young children gripping their mother's hands as they watched ICE agents handcuffing their father in court. Another attorney described watching an arrest that looked like a "rendition" with a swarm of agents grabbing her client from the sidewalk outside of a court and hustling him into a car without saying a word about who they were or what they were doing. Watching ICE snatch people away day after day without being able to do anything to stop it is deeply affecting. Walking out of a court in protest may not change that reality today or tomorrow, but it does create an opportunity for attorneys to transform their experiences and give voice to what they have witnessed.

Conclusion

On April 17, 2019, the New York state judiciary made a surprise announcement. The chief administrative judge of the state's court system, Lawrence Marks, issued a one-page directive prohibiting arrests by ICE in any New York state courthouse without a federal judicial warrant of court order.[60] It was the first directive of its kind in the country and quickly become a model for other state judiciaries.[61] He credited a "comprehensive and well-documented report" put together by advocates in the ICE Out of Courts coalition for persuading the state judiciary to adopt the new policy.[62]

Two months later, federal district court judge Indira Talwani in Massachusetts issued a preliminary injunction prohibiting ICE from making civil immigration arrests in and around the state's courts.[63] The order, which applies to Massachusetts state courts, prohibits ICE from arresting individuals attending Massachusetts courthouses not only while they are inside of a courthouse but also while they are going to or leaving a courthouse as well. It was the first time that the federal courts weighed in on the legality of ICE's courthouse arrest policy, and it was a decisive statement for the need to limit ICE's unbridled approach to enforcement.

One shared trait of both of these victories is that they were born of creative coalition-building. Over two years, the New York State ICE Out of Courts coalition built itself into a statewide organization that included public defenders, advocates for victims of gender-based violence, civil rights advocates, immigration attorneys, and labor organizers. In Massachusetts, the plaintiffs that won the injunction from Judge Talwani included the Committee for Public Counsel Services, which serves as the statewide public defender; the Middlesex County District Attorney; the Suffolk County District Attorney; and the Chelsea Collaborative, a group representing noncitizens who are fearful of going to court as victims, witnesses, and supporters.

A key strength of these coalitions is their ability to provide a 360-degree view of how ICE's brazen enforcement tactics undermine the court system as a whole. In her decision, Judge Talwani describes the breadth of the damage that ICE's courthouse arrest policy imposes on the courts:

> Plaintiffs have made an unrebutted showing that each day that the threat of ICE civil arrests looms over Massachusetts courthouses impairs the [District Attorneys'] and [Committee for Public Counsel Services's] ability to successfully perform their functions within the judicial system, and Chelsea Collaborative's members' ability to enforce legal rights, and that absent an injunction, some state criminal and civil cases may well go unprosecuted for lack of victim or witness participation.[64]

However, while the New York State directive and the federal injunction in Massachusetts provide a foothold in the struggle against ICE's courthouse arrests, the fight is far from over. The directive, which has already become a model for other states,[65] has significantly limited ICE courthouse operations in New York, but it has not stopped them entirely. Despite the directive, ICE continues to remain a visible threat *outside* of courthouses in New York—even targeting a pregnant mother after an appearance in the Queens Criminal Court.[66] Due to limits in the state judiciary's control over town and village courts, the directive also does not protect immigrants in smaller courts outside of New York City, putting residents in more rural areas at risk.[67]

As the crisis in the courts continues, it has given rise to a newly creative style of lawyering. Unable to protect their clients from ICE inside the courtroom, attorneys are looking to innovative forms of advocacy—taking to the streets and to social media to plead their case. It has also challenged attorneys to consider their professional and ethical obligations to clients—and to fundamental fairness.

The crisis in the courts has also raised a host of questions about the role of the judiciary and the relationship between state and federal governments. The federal government's aggressive immigration policy continues to encroach on the courts, undermining the courts' operations and the fundamental rights that the judiciary is built to protect. In the face of this intrusion from ICE, state judiciaries may no longer have the option of staying on the sidelines. When ICE effectively shuts down access to justice, it may fall on the state judiciaries to find a way to keep the courthouse doors open.

NOTES

The author was formerly a Senior Staff Attorney at the Immigrant Defense Project where she helped to coordinate a statewide campaign to get ICE out of New York State Courts. She now directs a program at the Brooklyn Community Bail Fund that focuses on freeing immigrants from detention. The views expressed in this chapter are her own.

1 I have used a pseudonym to protect the individual's confidentiality.

2 See The Courthouse Trap: How ICE Enforcement Impacted New York's Courts in 2018, THE IMMIGRANT DEFENSE PROJECT (Jan. 2019), www.immigrantdefenseproject.org/wp-content/uploads/TheCourthouseTrap.pdf.

3 For a fuller description of ICE raids documented across New York State, see Ryan Devereaux, ICE Has Conducted Hundreds of Raids in New York Since Trump Came to Power. Here's What Those Operations Look Like., THE INTERCEPT (July 23, 2018), www.theintercept.com.

4 Courthouse arrest reports are on file with author.

5 Letter from Tani Cantil-Sakauye, C.J. of Cal. Sup. Ct., to Jeff Sessions, Att'y Gen., and John F. Kelly, Sec'y of Homeland Sec. (Mar. 16, 2017), www.newsroom.courts.ca.gov.

6 Letter from Tani G. Cantil-Sakauye, C.J. of California, to Jeff Sessions, Att'y Gen., and John F. Kelly, Sec'y of Homeland Security, March 16, 2017, https://newsroom.courts.ca.gov/news/chief-justice-cantil-sakauye-objects-to-immigration-enforcement-tactics-at-california-courthouses.

7 Letter from Chase T. Rogers, C.J. of Conn. Sup. Ct., to Jeff Sessions, Att'y Gen. and John F. Kelly, Sec'y of Homeland Sec. (May 15, 2017), www.ncsc.org.

8 Letter from Stuart Rabner, C.J. of N.J. Sup. Ct., to Jeff Sessions, Att'y Gen., and John F. Kelly, Sec'y of Homeland Sec. (Apr. 19, 2017), www.ncsc.org.

9 Letter from Thomas A. Balmer, C.J. of the Or. Sup. Ct., to Jeff Sessions, Att'y Gen., and John F. Kelly, Sec'y of Homeland Sec. (Apr. 6, 2017), www.ncsc.org.

10 Letter from Mary Fairhurst, C.J. of the Wash. Sup. Ct., to John F. Kelly, Sec'y of Homeland Sec. (Mar. 22, 2017), www.ncsc.org.

11 The C.J. of R.I. also publicly endorsed a call for ICE to designate courts as a "sensitive location" in statement to the R.I. Bar Ass'n. *See* www.courts.ri.gov.

12 Letter from Jeff Sessions, Att'y Gen., and John F, Kelly, Sec'y of Homeland Sec., to the Honorable Cantil-Sakauye, C.J. of the Cal. Sup. Ct. (Mar. 29, 2017), www.nytimes.com.

13 Marty Schladen, *ICE Detains Alleged Domestic Violence Victim*, EL PASO TIMES (Feb. 15, 2017), www.elpasotimes.com.

14 Elise Foley, *ICE Director to All Undocumented Immigrants: "You Need To Be Worried,"* HUFFPOST (June 13, 2017), www.huffingtonpost.com.

15 Liz Robbins, *A Game of Cat and Mouse With High Stakes: Deportation*, N.Y. TIMES (Aug. 3, 2017).

16 Sonja Sharp, *The Lawyers Trying to Get Their Clients Sent to Jail*, VICE (July 4, 2017), www.vice.com.

17 Beth Fertig, *Outcry After Immigration Agents Seen at Queens Human Trafficking Court*, WNYC (June 16, 2017), www.wnyc.org.

18 *Id.*

19 For an example of the reaction from elected officials, *see* Beth Fertig, *New York Democrats Tell ICE to Stay Away From Human Trafficking Courts*, WNYC (June 16, 2017), www.wnyc.org.

20 *Id.*

21 Corinne Ramey, *Immigrant Advocates Want*, WALL ST. J. (June 29, 2017), www.wsj.com.

22 *See* Stephen Rex Brown, *Courthouse Arrests of Immigrants by ICE Agents Have Risen 900% in New York This Year: Immigrant Defense Project*, N.Y. DAILY NEWS (Nov. 15, 2017), www.nydailynews.com.

23 Noah Hurowitz, *Immigration Agents Target Brooklyn Criminal Court, Lawyers Say*, DNA INFO (Sept. 14, 2017), www.dnainfo.com.

24 Courthouse arrest report on file with author.

25 Felipe De La Hoz & Emma Whitford, *Court Officers Are Aiding in Immigration Arrests Say Lawyers*, THE VILLAGE VOICE (Nov. 16, 2017), www.villagevoice.com.

26 Att'y affidavit on file with author.

27 Att'y affidavit on file with author.

28 Att'y affidavit on file with author.

29 A video posted by Andrew Paul Joyce, a reporter for *The Mic*, shows plainclothes ICE agents exiting the Brooklyn Crim. Ct. and leaving in an unmarked car. https://twitter.com/AndrewPaulJoyce/status/908350791022465024?ref_src=twsrc%5Etfw%7Ctwcamp%5Etweetembed%7Ctwterm%5E908350791022465024&ref_url=http%3A%2F%2Fgothamist.com%2F2017%2F09%2F14%2Fice_courthouse_arrests_brooklyn.php.

30 One reporter provided a firsthand account of his encounter with plainclothes ICE agents in a courtroom hallway who denied that they were immigration enforcement agents. *See* Leon Neyfakh, *Secret Police: ICE Agents Dressed in Plainclothes*

Staked Out a Courthouse in Brooklyn and Refused to Identify Themselves, SLATE (Sept. 14, 2017), www.slate.com.

31 Noah Hurowitz & Felipe De La Hoz, *Legal Aid Lawyers Stage Walkout After Yet Another ICE Court Arrest*, THE VILLAGE VOICE (Nov. 28, 2017), www.villagevoice.com.

32 Gwynne Hogan, *Public Defenders Walk Out of Bronx Courthouse After College Student Detained*, WNYC (Feb. 8, 2018), www.wnyc.org.

33 Chelsia Rose Marcius, Elizabeth Elizalde & Rich Schapiro, *Lawyers Protest as ICE Agents Detain Defendant at Staten Island Courthouse After Sweeping Raid*, N.Y. DAILY NEWS (Apr. 24, 2018), www.nydailynews.com.

34 Liz Robbins, *Lawyers Walk Out to Protest ICE, and Court Objects*, N.Y. TIMES (Apr. 11, 2018), www.nytimes.com

35 *See* Letter from Director John Morton on Enforcement Actions at or Focused on Sensitive Locations (Oct. 24, 2011), U.S. IMMIGRATION AND CUSTOMS ENFORCEMENT, www.ice.gov. For an excellent discussion of the origins of the "sensitive locations" policy, *see* Sarah Rogerson, *Sovereign Resistance to Federal Immigration Enforcement in State Courthouses*, GEO. IMMIGR. L.J. (Fall 2018).

36 *See* notes 3–7.

37 In August 2017, the A.B.A.'s House of Del. passed resolution 10C, calling on ICE to add courthouses to its list of "sensitive locations." *See ABA Urges Congress Add Courthouses to 'Sensitive Locations' to ICE Guidelines*, www.americanbar.org.

38 Rep. Espaillat (D-NY) introduced H.R. 1815, a bill that would amend the Immigration and National Act to forbid immigration arrests at courthouses and other sensitive locations. Sen. Blumenthal (D-CT) introduced a similar bill in the Senate, S. 845.

39 U.S. I.C.E., DIRECTIVE 11072.1: CIVIL IMMIGRATION ENFORCEMENT ACTIONS INSIDE COURTHOUSES (Jan. 10, 2018), www.ice.gov.

40 U.S. I.C.E., FAQ ON SENSITIVE LOCATIONS AND COURTHOUSE ARRESTS (last updated Sept. 25, 2018), www.ice.gov.

41 N.Y.S. ASSEMBLY & SENATE, JOINT BUDGET HEARING ON PUBLIC PROTECTION (Jan 30, 2018).

42 *New ICE Directive Formalizes Policy of Making Courthouse Arrests*, KQED (Jan.31, 2018), www.kqed.org.

43 *See* S.425A, Protect Our Courts Act, 2019–20 Leg. (NY 2019).

44 Additional information on judicial rules and policies regulating the conduct of immigration agents in and around courthouses is available in the Immigrant Defense Project's "ICE Out of Courts Model Toolkit," *available at* www.immigrantdefenseproject.org. The full text of the judicial rules proposed by the ICE Out of Courts Coalition to the N.Y. Off. of Ct. Admin. is below:

1) Expenditure of Resources to Assist with Immigration Law Enforcement Activities:

Employees of the Unified Court System shall not:

      i) Expend resources to assist with federal immigration enforcement activities in the course of their employment, in any courthouse of the New York State Unified Court System except to the extent they are described in Section (2).

     ii) Inquire into the immigration status of any individual within any courthouse of the Unified Court System unless such information about a person's immigration status is necessary for the determination of program, service or benefit eligibility or the provision of services.

    iii) Provide any information to immigration enforcement officers regarding persons appearing before the court, except information regarding citizenship or immigration status, as required by 8 U.S.C. § 1373, and then only if known.

  2) Civil arrests without judicial warrants: Civil arrests may only be executed within a courthouse of the Unified Court System when accompanied by a judicial warrant or judicial order authorizing them to take into custody the person who is the subject of such warrant. "Judicial warrant" is defined as a warrant issued by a magistrate sitting in the judicial branch of local, state, or federal government. "Judicial order" is defined as an order issued by a magistrate sitting in the judicial branch of local, state, or federal government.

45 N.Y.S. ASSEMBLY & SENATE, JOINT BUDGET HEARING ON PUBLIC PROTECTION (Jan. 30, 2018).

46 Eric Gonzalez & Judy Harris Kluger, *How ICE Harms the Justice System: The Feds' Aggressive Tactics in Our Courthouses Are Emboldening Violent Criminals*, N.Y. DAILY NEWS (Aug. 2, 2018), www.nydailynews.com.

47 *See Retired Judges Call on ICE To Halt Immigration Arrests*, BRENNAN CENTER FOR JUSTICE (Dec. 12, 2018), www.brennancenter.org.

48 Liz Robbins, *Lawyers Walk Out to Protest ICE, and Court Objects*, N.Y. TIMES (Apr. 11, 2018).

49 Beth Ferttig, *New York Courts Act Against Lawyers Protesting Immigration Agents*, WNYC (Apr. 10), 2018, www.wnyc.org.

50 *Id.*

51 *Id.*

52 *See* A.B.A., Model R. of Prof. Conduct: Preamble, Section 1(Aug. 15, 2018) ("A lawyer, as a member of the legal profession, is a representative of clients, an officer of the legal system and a public citizen having special responsibility for the quality of justice.").

53 *Id.*

54 *Id.* at Preamble para 5.

55 Before President Trump appointed Jeff Sessions to run the Justice Department, this was a seldom used provision, but during Sessions's tenure he identified harboring prosecutions as a priority for United States Attorneys. *See* U.S. DEP'T OF JUSTICE, ATTORNEY GENERAL JEFF SESSIONS ANNOUNCES THE DEPARTMENT OF JUSTICE'S RENEWED COMMITMENT TO CRIMINAL

IMMIGRATION ENFORCEMENT (Apr. 11, 2017). This has prompted concerns among the bar that attorneys could face prosecution for helping clients to avoid ICE. While this threat remains unfulfilled, the U.S. Attorney's office in Massachusetts is reportedly investigating a state jurist and other court staff for their alleged roles in helping an immigrant who was appearing in court to avoid ICE. *See* Andrea Estes & Maria Cramer, *Ice Agent Was in Courthouse. Did Judge and Others Help Man Flee?* BOS. GLOBE (Dec. 2, 2018).

56 Maria Cramer, Andrea Estes & Matt Stout, *Mass. Judge Faces Federal Charges Over Defendant's Evasion of ICE*, BOS. GLOBE (Apr. 26, 2019).

57 John Leubsdorf, *Gandhi's Legal Ethics*, 51 RUTGERS L. REV. 923. 928 (1999).

58 *Id.* at 929.

59 *Id.*

60 *See* Colby Hamilton, *New Rules Limit ICE's Arrest Ability in New York State Courts*, N.Y. L.J. (Apr. 17, 2019).

61 Nicholas Pugliese, *New Rules Seek to Limit ICE Arrests in N.J. Courthouses*, WHYY (May 24, 2019), https://whyy.org.

62 *Id.*

63 Danny McDonald, *Federal Judge Halts Immigration Arrests in Massachusetts Courts While Lawsuit Plays Out*, BOS. GLOBE (June 20, 2019).

64 *Marian Ryan v. U.S. Immigration and Customs Enforcement*, No. 19–11003-IT, Memorandum & Order Granting Plaintiffs' Motion for Preliminary Injunction (D. Mass filed June 20, 2019).

65 Nicholas Pugliese, *New Rules Seek to Limit ICE arrests in N.J. Courthouses*, WHYY (May 24, 2019), https://whyy.org.

66 Monsy Alvarado, *A Pregnant Mother of Two Is One Step Closer to Deportation*, USA TODAY (June 25, 2019), www.usatoday.com.

67 Christina Goldbaum, *When Paying a Traffic Ticket Can End in Deportation*, N.Y. TIMES (June 30, 2019).

6 ·

Preparation, Crisis, Struggle, Ideas

The Birth of the Detention Outreach Project

SARAH ROGERSON

There are more ideas on earth than intellectuals imagine. And these ideas are more active, stronger, more resistant, more passionate than "politicians" think. We have to be there at the birth of ideas, the bursting outward of their force: not in books expressing them, but in events manifesting this force, in struggles carried on around ideas, for or against them. Ideas do not rule the world. But it is because the world has ideas (and because it constantly produces them) that it is not passively ruled by those who are its leaders or those who would like to teach it, once and for all, what it must think.
—Michel Foucault

Rooted to a plastic chair in the lobby at the Albany County Correctional Facility (ACCF), a county jail in upstate New York, legs folded with the hope of channeling meditative calm, exhausted eyes desperately seeking clarity in the spreadsheets of immigrant detainees and volunteer lawyers crowding my laptop, my gaze wanders up and out of the window carrying the seal of the Albany County Sheriff's Office. The seal's six-pointed star circles the Dutch ship that carried the original immigrant settlers to the city of Albany.[1] I had passed by that seal hundreds of times over the previous five years and never took notice of it, but it now serves as the visual symbol of one of the most important teaching moments I have ever had as a student of crisis lawyering: that if we cultivate a strong foundation of relationships and collaborations around a known threat, crisis can serve as the birthplace of transformative ideas.

One of these moments presented itself to me in week four of a crisis lawyering response to a humanitarian disaster brought on by the Donald Trump administration's zero tolerance and family separation policies at the United States–Mexico border, which were exacerbated by broken immigration laws and systems favoring mass incarceration.[2] On the other side of the cinderblock wall providing me this brief moment of reflection, a team of attorneys from several major law firms across the state of New York are working diligently to triage and provide legal information to hundreds of immigrants fleeing violence, political unrest, and persecution. When this crisis subsides and there is time to assess our impact, a small group of dedicated immigration lawyers and advocates will have coordinated legal, religious, medical, and translation services to more than 300 individuals from more than thirty different countries, speaking nineteen different languages.[3] We will have organized hundreds of volunteer attorneys, clergy, and interpreters from across the country and leveraged their collective effort to restore a modicum of due process to an immigration system designed to separate immigrants from their individual constitutional rights, calling ourselves the "Detention Outreach Project" (DOP). And we will have done it with some of the most innovative partners in crisis lawyering, but also with some of the most unlikely partners imaginable: local law enforcement authorities.

Precisely one week prior to the individuals' arrival, the Albany County Sheriff had alerted me to the possibility of a phased-in influx of immigrant detainees to his jail over a period of six to eight weeks. Immigration authorities told the sheriff that the detainees would arrive in groups of thirty to sixty weekly until the jail was at capacity. This phasing cadence seemed manageable given that we had organized pro bono legal responses to similar-sized groups in the past. By combining the energy of enterprising law students at Albany Law School, the goodwill of local nonprofits such as The Legal Project, the efforts of area pro bono attorney volunteers, and tapping into additional networks of pro bono attorneys from large firms and nonprofit organizations in New York City, we had been able to manage. Because of the chaos at the border and the lack of transparency and accountability of US Customs and Border Patrol, the transfer was much more chaotic than planned.

Rather than an orderly, phased transfer, the US Department of Homeland Security (DHS) assembled more than 300 refugees from various countries who entered at the southern border of the United States, seemingly at random, and transported them, via airplane, in groups of a hundred, to the Albany County Jail over the course of eight days. Contrary to representations made to the sheriff by immigration authorities at the time, many were separated from family members, including parents forcibly separated from their children.[4] Nearly all of them were claiming a "credible fear of persecution," and many were seeking asylum at a port of entry, which is a lawful way to enter the United States.[5] However, due to President Trump's "Zero Tolerance" border policy, some of them were prosecuted for unlawful entry, some of them were unlawfully stripped of their documentation, and all of them were detained on arrival.[6] The conditions of their initial detention at the border were seemingly brutal, as they arrived in Albany in conditions that the sheriff described as "relatively disgustingly dirty . . . many of them had diseases, chicken pox, scabies, Chagas disease . . . it was a very, very sad situation."[7]

It was the largest influx of detainees in the state of New York—and one of the largest nationwide—presenting a massive challenge: to provide immigration legal services to an unprecedented number of individuals arriving en masse with skilled, but scarce, legal resources. Facing down this challenge would ultimately reveal points of weakness in the current immigrant legal services system in New York's capital. However, the innovation resulting from the crisis response would ultimately give birth to ideas, and leveraged grassroots organizing systems, designed to reclaim power from the federal immigration punishment system and place it back in the hands of immigrants and their advocates. Further, the relationships forged between law enforcement and immigration advocates would result in unprecedented county-level reallocation of punitive federal resources to restorative justice aims. In effect, the crisis that gave birth to the Detention Outreach Project would lead to some of the most rapid and progressive forms of reform in one of the most unlikely places: a county jail in upstate New York.

The Terrible Truth about Immigration Representation

Immigrants in the United States are not guaranteed legal representation at any stage of the deportation process. In fact, a process called "expedited removal" allows the government to deport certain individuals at the discretion of an individual immigration officer without being heard by an immigration judge at all.[8] Although immigrants in the United States have the right to hire a pro bono or paid attorney, there is no universal (or even limited) free representation at the federal level. The same is true even for children.[9] New York is an outlier among states, having launched the New York Immigrant Family Unity Project (NYIFUP), carving out several million dollars of state funding to provide free representation to unrepresented immigrants who are detained and in the process of removal proceedings.[10] Although NYIFUP is visionary and intrepid, its reach is limited to the most desperate stage of the removal process. Millions of undocumented immigrants in the United States would benefit from legal representation long before they are detained and the federal government actively seeks to deport them. There are few skilled immigration attorneys available generally, opening up a wide opportunity for *notarios*, or those engaging in the unlawful practice of law, to swindle desperate detainees and family members out of hard-earned dollars. Law school clinics are training future immigration attorneys, but the learning curve is steep—and the need is mounting.[11]

And yet, the presence of a lawyer is one of the most determinative factors for the success of cases in the American immigration system. Data from studies on the impact of an attorney in the immigration process show that an individual is much more likely to gain immigration status and/or defend against deportation if they are represented by counsel.[12] Furthermore, immigrants often face life-or-death consequences as a result of deportation, particularly asylum-seekers, who may be killed by their persecutors if returned to their country of origin.[13]

Civil immigration violations are increasingly met with consequences that mirror the criminal justice system in America, and the potential harm resulting from deportation in many cases is death. Given the quasi-criminal punishment doled out in the immigration context (detention and deportation) and the deadly consequences of being deported without representation by counsel, immigration cases merit the establishment of a right to government-appointed counsel.[14] Efforts to establish that right have thus far fallen short. In the meantime, volunteer lawyers across the country have come together to fill a void that need not, and should not, exist.

Unwitting Preparation: Forging Partnerships and Creating Best Practices

This particular crisis response would not have been as effective without a longstanding relationship between Albany Law School and the Albany County Sheriff's Office (with the consent of DHS). Five years prior, Chris Scoville, a law student, approached me with the little-known fact that immigrant detainees were being held in the local county jail. He wanted to explore ways that law students might effectively intervene in these cases. After doing some preliminary research, we discovered that a detainee had actually died in custody at the jail due to a combination of preexisting conditions and lack of access to medication as a result of a series of miscommunications between DHS and jail administration.[15] The case was the subject of a lawsuit brought by the American Civil Liberties Union (ACLU). After the suit was settled, the jail's improvements to its medical care and protocols were so significant that it was presented with an award by the ACLU shortly thereafter.

Nevertheless, I was not optimistic that the jail administration and the sheriff would be receptive to the idea of expanding legal information to immigrant detainees held in the facility. I challenged the students to create a pitch for a project under the new DHS "Parental Interest Directive," which was created under Barack Obama's administration in 2013 to operationalize certain procedures to allow parents to make arrangements for their children after being detained, including being present for any family court proceedings so that they did not lose their parental rights in absentia.[16] At the time, family separation by immigration authorities was not what we think of today. Rather, it was attributed to a lack of communication between the immigration enforcement machine and the family justice system in America, which resulted in a high number of immigrant children being wrongfully placed in foster care at the expense of the state.[17]

We were welcomed into the jail to present our ideas, the students and I nervous with anticipation of an unknown outcome. Much to our surprise, when the students finished their presentation, the sheriff's response was simple: "This is a no-brainer." We were all caught a little off-guard, but the sheriff embraced the idea and offered to help us obtain approval from DHS, which the jail would need in order to proceed as planned. As it turned out, convincing DHS would be a much more difficult undertaking due to the layers of bureaucracy required for the approval of this type of project. Once the final terms of our participation were negotiated, however, we were soon in the jail on a fairly regular basis, screening individuals picked up locally to see whether they needed to make arrangements for their children.

Over time, my communications with the sheriff expanded to other issues of immigrant safety and local policy. In tandem, I became an unofficial liaison between the private immigration bar, pro bono attorneys, and the local DHS leadership. We also partnered with free legal service providers at a local nonprofit (The Legal Project), whose attorneys and immigration legal professionals agreed to cover the intakes when the students were not in session or were otherwise unavailable. As we built trust between the jail and our project over time, one seemingly mundane but eventually critical development would serve as the logistical lynchpin for our operations in crisis: I was added to the list of individuals who received a list of immigrants being held by the jail for DHS every single morning. Early in the project, this allowed my students to track enforcement trends and to identify when we needed to make arrangements for trips into the jail. When crisis hit, these lists were our only window into the identities behind the souls DHS decided to transfer to the jail.

Beyond these menial lists, however, as advocates/attorneys on one side and law enforcement on the other, working through operational issues together (even and especially when it was uncomfortable), we created trusting relationships that would also turn out to be critical. Over the years, I would slowly accumulate the names, e-mails, and direct phone numbers of the individuals responsible for various things at DHS and at the jail. When private practitioners raised concerns about the strip-searching of immigrant women housed in the jail, we were able to carry their concerns to DHS and the jail administration, resolving the issue without exposing the complainant or engaging in expensive litigation tactics.

By and large, by working together, we were able to convert what could otherwise be a delicate land mine of mistrust and obstruction into a constructive relationship, realizing, of course, that each of us was operating within our own constraints and agendas. Upon reflection, these years of sporadic yet productive interactions not only were exceptional in nature but also proved critical in crisis.

As these relationships evolved, the students worked under my supervision to develop best practices for the project, which would become key instruments for success in crisis. First, students collected model intake protocols from immigrant detention outreach projects across the country, consolidated them, and then tailored them to the needs of the individuals that we most often encountered in the jail—largely Hispanic/Latinx individuals with myriad challenges to bonding out of detention to pursue lawful status. They also gathered a list of referral resources so that if individuals did not meet the criteria to benefit from the parental interest directive, we might direct them to other legal resources available to them, depending on their particular issue. Second, students developed a number of documents and releases, translated into Spanish, in order to be able to empower the individuals they met with additional information and connect them to resources.

In addition, the students began tracking the limited information we received from the individuals to identify systemic trends, which then fed into the priorities of the local advocacy coalition and pro bono networks to identify and implement systemic interventions. Some of these interventions were more successful than others, but essentially, the jail project became a hub of information that fed into the advocacy work of the immigrant rights community in ways that were not necessarily obvious or threatening to law enforcement.

After years of careful work and additional trust-building, we took one additional step that would allow for more fulsome use and development of the best practices developed by students and would lead to the creation of additional critical resources. After a regional program providing "Know Your Rights" presentations to individuals inside the jail ended, I approached DHS with the idea of formally expanding our project beyond the reach of the parental interest directive and into a model of intake and referral. Using the same intake protocol and the resources compiled and refined over the years, we were able to tailor the project to the shifting needs of the population as different groups ended up in the jail for different reasons with different legal needs. After some back-and-forth, DHS ultimately approved the project modification. This unshackled the project from its former, more limited scope and provided us the flexibility we would need for a crisis response.

Notably, and importantly, best practices being developed in other crisis lawyering scenarios across the state and nation would also enhance and deepen the impact of our response locally. This brings into focus the importance of another partnership that was not so much unlikely as it was underutilized. The regional collaborative had worked with a statewide immigrant advocacy network, the New York Immigration Coalition (NYIC), to provide joint trainings on a host of issues but had not yet had the opportunity to collaborate more substantively with the actual provision of legal services in the area. The NYIC is not a legal services organization; instead, it focuses on advocacy, generating funding, and supporting the legislative campaigns of its member organizations.

However, the immigration legal policy director at the NYIC, Camille Mackler, and I had become collaborators on a few smaller projects. Camille had recently organized a massive on-site legal response at JFK International Airport (JFK) on the same morning that the Trump administration's "Muslim Ban" went into effect in late January 2017, which garnered widespread national news attention.[18] As part of that massive pro bono attorney effort, Camille and her team at JFK had developed a number of crisis response protocols and technologies that will continue to inform these moments for as long as our immigration system remains this broken. Having had some time to reflect on the potential and pitfalls of those systems and technologies, Camille brought her perspective and experience to bear in Albany. Without her experience and generosity in sharing the resources that the JFK team built, we could not have been as successful as we were.

Outside of New York, attorney Stephen Manning was quietly building what is now one of the most powerful grassroots tools for immigration crisis lawyering and immigration advocacy created to date: a crowd-sourced case management system. His organization, Innovation Law Lab, has a bold mission statement that strives to counterbalance the gap in representation for refugees seeking asylum in the United States:

> We envision a world where every case that should win, does win, every time, everywhere. We work where the threat is greatest—where people and legal systems are most vulnerable to attack. We are deployed in immigrant detention centers and hostile judicial jurisdictions across the United States.

Like the NYIFUP program, Innovation Law Lab focuses on cases where individuals are detained and in active removal proceedings. During the JFK crisis, Camille had relied on Innovation Law Lab's powerful case management technology to allow multiple attorney volunteers to assist on dozens of cases in real time, in collaboration with one another, as details emerged. Paired with the power of Zen Desk, a hotline management technology with information sharing capabilities, this dual engine fueled a mass legal response for nearly two weeks at JFK with hundreds of volunteer lawyers working around the clock. These two developments, along with the power of the team communications app Slack, would provide the infrastructure for each major piece of the DOP's crisis response in Albany.

In so many ways, each immigration crisis that emerges anywhere in the country lends itself to new ideas for the next crisis. In effect, as each crisis plays out, the partnerships that Camille developed at JFK, and the technologies that Stephen developed in Oregon, are building a rapid response system that can be deployed anytime, anywhere, and within hours begin coordinating and applying thousands of hours of volunteer attorney power to bear on the immediate crisis moment. It was truly serendipity that we in Albany were able to benefit from this immensely powerful collaboration and, as will be discussed later, contribute meaningfully to the development of a larger crisis-response resistance machine. Without the foundation of these relationships and best practices, forged in the heat of crisis, the DOP would not have been as successful. With them, we were nearly unstoppable.

The Crisis and Struggle: Beyond Palliative Care

To understand the true impact of these relationships and the importance of incorporating the lessons learned from prior crisis collaborations, it is important to start at the very birth of the DOP. Riding in the quiet car of an Amtrak train, attempting to begin drafting this chapter, and on the way to teach a high school summer intensive course on immigration with Camille and journalist Liz Robbins from the *New York Times*, I received a phone call from the Albany County Sheriff. It being the quiet car, I darted to the nearest acceptable location to receive a telephone call—the bathroom. Huddled in the Amtrak quiet car's water closet, phone pressed up to one ear and a hand over the other, I heard the sheriff provide the details of the arriving influx of immigrants to the Albany County Correction Facility(ACCF). He then asked if I thought we could help. I told him I would need to check with our community partners but that I was pretty sure that we could. We set some ground rules to keep the details private and avoid press attention until we had a plan.[19] It was a call that would alter the trajectory of my summer, my career, and ultimately, this chapter. Because I was literally on my way to see Camille, she was among the first people I reached out to about the news from the sheriff. This would become critical as the crisis intensified and our existing protocols and initial resources would quickly collapse under the weight of the work ahead.

The irony is that the DOP and all that we would learn from it narrowly dodged extinction just days before. A local activist and I were mulling over the possibility of approaching the sheriff with a plan to phase out the boarding of immigrants and banning immigration authorities from the ACCF altogether. Our argument would be a moral one. We had hit a point in our project where the students were completely dejected. Although we were screening individuals for relief, none was available for most. As a result, the conversations would inevitably shift to a sort of palliative care: Were they receiving their medicine on a regular basis? Did they have access to clean underwear and feminine hygiene products? How were they being treated by the jail staff? Did they have contacts in the country that they were being deported to and did they have a way to support themselves? Would they mind telling us about their apprehension by ICE agents so that we could track trends and potentially help others?

It was brutally difficult work because it rarely felt like we were doing anything other than offering a bit of humanity in a desperately lacking process. Not that there isn't value in that kind of work, but as attorneys, we are used to being able to deliver a lot more to our clients. It was not hitting the marks for my law students' learning goals, and it wasn't really helping anyone achieve the goal of remaining in the United States. It felt like we were complicit, like we had become part of the system.

Less than forty-eight hours before that fateful quiet-car call, I was ready to try something more drastic: convince the sheriff that he is part of the problem and ask that he consider removing himself from the system altogether by refusing to board immigrants in his jail. I thought that we could make a compelling case, and I knew enough about his progressive agenda of lowering recidivism and diminishing the general jail population through critical interventions that I thought it was worth a shot—especially if we were thinking of pulling out of the project. I was considering coordinating this ask with the local "Abolish ICE" movement, called "ICE-Free Capital District." Together, I thought we could convince him that he was complicit and that the only morally justifiable thing to do would be to refuse to participate in the deportation machine.

Once faced with a national border emergency, disgusting conditions at the temporary facilities meant to house many fewer detainees near the border, and the subsequent transfer of more than 300 asylum-seekers away from those conditions and into the more humane environment of the ACCF, that calculation shifted. Without our legal interventions, many would have failed their Credible Fear Interview (CFI), which is the very first step in the asylum process, and many would be mistreated in a private federal detention facility without any medical care, without religious accommodations, and, most important, without legal counsel. Our impact was tangible, and we believed in our interventions because they produced favorable outcomes for the clients. Rather than acting in a more passive role in a broken system, the work was disruptive and impactful—ultimately leading to the release of many from immigration custody and control. We knew we were doing the "right thing."

Week One: Relationships and Technologies Pave the Way for Success

That first week was critical. Camille and I formed a small team of project managers, including Meredith Fortin, the director of immigration services support at the NYIC, as well as other JFK veteran volunteers, including Priya Gandhi, a lawyer who happens to excel at volunteer coordination and was willing to dedicate her free time pro bono. From New York City to Albany to London to Canada, our fledgling group began to plan. We knew we would need to dramatically scale up The Legal Project's existing pro bono recruitment efforts. We knew that a parallel effort to recruit skilled and experienced interpreters and translators, potentially in a number of different languages, would be part of the volunteer coordination effort. It soon occurred to me that the best way to harness the pro bono power in our area without a full-time legal coordinator (or any at all) had already been implemented by my son's elementary school Parent Teacher Organization. The volunteer organization platform, Sign-Up Genius, was the perfect tool for the job. A team of administrators could set up web pages that were very easy to disseminate via an automatically generated web link, offering volunteers the ability to sign up for shifts and roles as they were willing and able.

Volunteers literally poured out from every corner of the Capital District. That was the good news. The bad news was that we had no easy way to vet them for immigration law fluency, language fluency, or experience, and there was no easy way to pair them with interpreters and translators who were fluent in the languages spoken by the individuals seen during their appointed shifts. As a result, our core team familiarized ourselves with the various features of Sign-Up Genius to take better advantage of all the platform had to offer. Anticipating that many volunteers may not be immigration lawyers (and, in fact, most weren't), I had created a brief logistical and substantive training using Prezi, the online platform for presentations, which also could be shared easily via web link. Rather than hosting a PowerPoint on a website or mailing it to each volunteer individually, we could embed the link to the training into Sign-Up Genius and also in an auto-response to the volunteer coordination email, immediately providing our volunteers with self-guided basics upon sign-up. We were also able to use many of the resources students had already created, like the intake form and releases, so that we had a uniform method for all volunteers to use to gather the information we needed.

Shortly thereafter, Camille negotiated with Slack, the mobile and web-based team communication app, to provide us a free account in order to streamline our communications. These discoveries also happened to coincide with a critical connection (again, via Camille) to the Association of Pro Bono Counsel, a "mission-driven membership organization of over 200 attorneys and practice group managers who run pro bono practices in over 100 of the world's largest law firms."[20] Specifically, Harlene Katzman and Saralyn Cohen, pro bono counsel at the powerhouse law firms Simpson, Thacher, and Bartlett, LLP and Shearman & Sterling, LLP respectively. Harlene and Saralyn connected us, through APBCo, to a nearly unlimited supply of pretrained attorney volunteers, many of whom were trained in the protocols for refugees at the border and were eager to apply their skills closer to home. Those who were not trained would be trained by their firms, lessening the burden on us, the volunteer coordination team. Unfortunately, this meant that we ultimately turned away local attorney volunteers, but the benefits were massive: we were able to book multiple shifts at a time with the same attorneys who would take the train or fly in from their firms in order to help, providing continuity and stability to the project and avoiding the need to continuously respond to basic volunteer inquiries. As the DOP evolved and as new volunteer efforts needed to be rolled out, these early lessons proved invaluable.

Pinch-Points: Volunteer Coordination and Data Management

Of course, in crisis lawyering, once you solve one set of problems, another set develops. The next problem to solve: we had assumed written instructions to the volunteers would suffice, but it became very clear, very quickly that more complicated issues kept arising on the visitation floor. For example, volunteers did not have a way to communicate those issues to our team prior to the conclusion of their shift, leading to incomplete information and/or guidance to the detainee and leading to inefficiencies due to multiple detainees requiring additional volunteer visits. Another problem: our volunteers were collecting large amounts of information from multiple detainees each day, and we had no place to store it, organize it, and analyze it.

The first problem had a relatively easy solution: we began assigning experienced immigration attorney volunteers to serve as site supervisors for each

PREPARATION, CRISIS, STRUGGLE, IDEAS | 157

shift. The site supervisors were there to answer questions from volunteers, manage the flow of detainee visits with the jail staff, and handle any on-site problems, such as volunteer names being omitted from the gate clearance list at the jail and other technical difficulties. My colleagues at Albany Law School and law schools across the state, and an overwhelming number of experienced nonprofit immigration lawyers, took time away from their crushing workloads to dive into ours. There were times when the statewide and community support were completely awe-inspiring, but I had to wonder what might happen if these detainees had been placed in a less-resourced state. If, for example, these 300-plus individuals had landed in South Carolina or Mississippi, the situation might have been much different.

The data problem was much more complicated. Laptops and phones initially were not permitted in the visitation space. (We would later negotiate a change in that policy.) As a result, everything had to be completed on paper. This meant that each volunteer attorney had to print out her or his own intake form, write legibly, and deposit it at the nearby offices of The Legal Project, which had offered to organize the data gathered until we had a more permanent solution. Our early data management efforts were the epitome of the phrase "building the plane while flying it." Between volunteers lagging in dropping off the forms and a lack of real-time information regarding which detainees were being seen, the plane was veering off-course. We realized that we needed a secure place inside the jail to store intake documents, volunteer information, and completed forms. So again, we called upon our ever-evolving relationship with the sheriff, and he offered a solution: a set of lockers, drilled into the wall in the lobby, that only we would have the keys to, along with a coded lockbox to store an extra set of keys for shift volunteers. It was an elegant solution to a pressing need. The DOP team often joked about how ridiculously critical a set of lockers became for confidential data management when we were working with so many other high-tech experiments. The lockers were half of the solution; Innovation Law Lab provided the other.

Innovation Law Lab

With hundreds of clients and hundreds of lawyers in the constellation of the DOP, we needed a case management plan very early on. Within a week, Camille had secured a client management database from Innovation Law Lab to help us self-organize. Innovation Law Lab's database is an example of an idea forged in crisis. It is software that originally was developed in 2014 to manage the detention crisis at a family detention facility in Artesia, New Mexico, where thousands of women and children were detained until, using Innovation Law Lab's crowd-sourcing software, the asylum win rate exceeded 90 percent and the facility shut down.[21] The programmers, engineers, and attorneys that fuel the development of Innovation Law Lab, which is constantly evolving, are part of an iterative process of regular feedback that ultimately influences the design of the database to make it more responsive and user-friendly. Ultimately, Stephen Manning's goal with the Innovation Law Lab is to "crowdsource a refugee rights strategy."[22] In a sense, it is the prototypical example of an idea forged on the front lines of crisis that has the potential to revolutionize refugee rights advocacy and crisis lawyering.

Credible Fear, Zen Desk, and Remote Crisis Lawyering

In the first two weeks, we had interviewed more than half of the detainees. We knew that because they had not been fully processed at the border, they had not received their Credible Fear Interview, the first step in the longer process of seeking asylum in the United States. We would need to launch another phase of the project to make sure that all of the individuals we screened who were eligible for a CFI received one. We followed Stephen's lead, using the exact same Credible Fear Protocol that Innovation Law Lab used in the various family detention centers in which they operate, building on their best practices and implementing them for our purposes.

However, unlike the CFI process at the border, where asylum officers interview the detainees in person, and because Albany was located thousands of miles from the southern border typically staffed for those purposes, we learned that the CFIs would be conducted remotely, over the phone, through the Arlington Asylum Office in Virginia. This presented yet another challenge. Because the asylum officers would not be in the room with our clients, they were uncomfortable with attorneys being in the room. Alternatively, they were willing to allow attorneys to dial in to monitor the CFIs, explain their relationship with me (counsel of record) and the project, and take notes. This was a compromise we were willing to strike because the only other record of the CFI interview would be the notes that the asylum officers wrote down, which would not be provided to us or the clients until a decision had been made on whether they had passed the interview. The trick was to line up a bank of remote attorney volunteers and set up a central call center for all parties to dial in to.

Yet another JFK-tested platform came to our aid: Zen Desk. This software creates a single number that can be provided to multiple parties that automatically routes the call to standby volunteers sitting at dedicated phone lines. Our Albany Law School staff, NYIC partners, and pro bono lawyers at Shearman & Sterling stepped in once again to assist with staffing the hotline. This time, they didn't have to leave the comfort of their home offices. After a number of initial hurdles, including technology issues and human error (some of the asylum officers were slow adopters of the hotline model), we eventually were able to obtain real-time information as the CFIs occurred. This remote lawyering model, we hoped, might provide a way for more attorneys to be virtually present for CFIs all over the country. Ultimately, we achieved a positive CFI outcome for more than 90 percent of the cases we represented—well beyond the national average.

The Toll That Crisis Takes and the Ethic of Community Care

The early days of the DOP crisis response were not only operationally difficult but also pragmatically challenging and emotionally draining. Out of necessity, our core team forged an ethic of community care to sustain what we knew would be an intense lawyering response that would span many weeks, if not months. As it turned out, we would ultimately be functioning at a fairly high level of intensity for the first three months, tapering off in the last three until the last of the detainees were transferred out of the jail. Much of the intensity centered on the core team, particularly the project leads (myself included), the data team, and the volunteer coordination team. We decided early on that we would all allow for core team members to take their planned summer vacations, celebrate milestones, and, at times, be taken off of the project for an evening or two to take time away. We celebrated team victories, no matter how small, and we acknowledged when members of the team were facing pressures outside of the DOP.

It is remarkable that, within an all-volunteer effort, we were able to forge a relentless dedication to the project while also making sure that we cared for each other's well-being—in addition to the well-being of the people we were serving. We made a collective decision to augment our legal services with the coordination of religious services and the distribution of sacred texts, additional mental health support services, and the delivery of greeting cards distributed in several different languages during the holidays. We broached the topic of self-care and vicarious trauma with the sheriff and his jail administration, making some inroads and learning that there were some programs in place for jail employees. There are many more lessons yet to learn from this particular piece of the story, but at its core, our ethic of community care may have been a response to a shared suffering, which was felt not only by us and our clients but also by those tasked with incarcerating them.

New Ideas: Shared Suffering, from Abolish ICE to the Abolish
Prisons Movements

Outside the lobby of the jail's administrative offices, there is a series of plaques
hanging from the buff-colored cinderblock wall. On a particularly hectic day
in the thick of our operation, the jail superintendent's administrative assistant stops midsentence and points at the photos on the wall: "suicide, suicide,
suicide, overdose, motorcycle accident, drank himself to death, suicide, suicide, overdose. . . ." In ten seconds, she perfectly articulated the profoundly
upsetting reality that the entire system of incarceration is constructed within
a framework of shared suffering: those incarcerated, those who care about
them, and those who are hired to keep watch over them.

In the immigrant rights community, we often talk about the toll that prolonged detention takes on the individuals detained, their loved ones, and especially families—whether they are detained as a unit or separately.[23] Less
often discussed, but an area of recent inquiry, is the toll that removal defense
takes on the attorneys tasked to defend the detained.[24] And an even lesser-
known measure of shared suffering is that one in five corrections officers
suffers from post-traumatic stress disorder, a rate higher than Iraq and Afghanistan war veterans and much higher than rank-and-file police officers.[25]

One of the most unexpected outcomes of the partnership established with
the jail staff was the level of detail we would ultimately learn about their personal lives and struggles. The administration used a lot of overtime to provide
enough officers to facilitate attorney visits with multiple detainees from eight-
thirty in the morning until nine in the evening, sometimes on the weekends.
From union and national politics, to family matters, to whiskey and avocado
toast preferences, the small talk in the spaces between the work and the logistics provided rarely glimpsed insight into the lives of corrections officers.
The humanization of individuals who are so easily written off as cogs in the
prison industrial complex machinery created a cognitive dissonance for many
politically progressive volunteers that proved more inspiring than distracting.
It wasn't as though the volunteers became incarceration sympathizers, but
many learned that, on difficult days when things get overwhelming inside
the walls of a jail, it helps to find some common ground outside of the pain.

These discussions resulted in additional ideas and, eventually, programs
that would impact the entire jail population, not just the immigrants. For example, when discussing progressive criminal justice reform initiatives in other
states around the country, the sheriff disclosed that he was in the early stages
of envisioning a new approach to reentry that, unlike other programs around
New York, would begin at booking, rather than at release. He would also con-

vert some corrections officers positions into reentry caseworker positions. The caseworkers would be matched with an individual being booked into the jail and would help them create a reentry plan to be executed upon release.

It was serendipity that Elena Kilcullen, a student in my Poverty Law class who also was pursuing a joint degree in social work, had disclosed that creating just such a program was her career goal. During a previous internship, she had created a reentry manual for Albany County that she hoped would serve as the foundation for a program. Prior to the crisis, I had passed along her reentry manual to the sheriff, so he was familiar with her work. Postcrisis, the sheriff put Elena in touch with the jail personnel responsible for executing his vision for the "New Beginnings" reentry program, and she was able to create an independent study project that would allow her to revisit her manual, build on it, and convert it to an electronic format for ease of access by the men and women in the jail through wireless tablets that the sheriff provided through his contract with a communications firm.[26] She is now employed by the Sheriff's Office to implement the program.

This is one small example where a conversation about immigrant justice as racial justice during a moment of crisis downtime small talk gave birth to innovative ideas and collaborations. It's one step toward a broader shared agenda that has emerged in a series of conversations with the sheriff around reduction of the prison population through drastic reform of traditional corrections modalities within the ACCF. The goal: shrink the population and reduce recidivism in order to literally begin tearing down the older portions of the jail facility. The method: convert corrections into a more holistic, sustainable, and independence-centered reentry model, rather than one of punishment and containment. This is a critical component of the new Abolish Prisons movement, and I imagine that few in that movement have considered encountering willing partners in law enforcement.[27]

A related conversation emerging from this moment of crisis returns us to where we were forty-eight hours before that fateful call in the Amtrak quiet car: whether keeping bed space open for immigrant detainees empowers the immigration enforcement regime more than it disrupts it, even when part of filling the bed space includes better treatment than other facilities and the provision of legal services not available elsewhere. Postcrisis conversations among the advocacy team and with the sheriff were reminiscent of where we started just before the crisis hit: Does the value we provide by keeping the jail beds open to ICE outweigh the human suffering we enable by not taking a harder line on the issue? Recently, the sheriff took a stand, informing ICE that he would no longer house detainees without a valid judicial warrant, which has brought the population to zero.

The End Is the Beginning

The birth of ideas eventually results in the spawning of etiological reflections. How might we have come upon these ideas more quickly? What are the conditions under which we might come up with even better ideas building on those born of this moment? One consideration from the birth of the DOP is whether we could have been more intentional about building the relationships between the Albany Law School, the sheriff and jail administration, DHS, and community partners.

We certainly are doing so now.

The crisis in Albany ended just before Christmas, when the remaining detainees were transferred to the federal immigration detention facility in Batavia. But much of the work continues without the pressing crisis of new arrivals needing to be screened and prepped. We are exploring how to use the models we have developed to assist other areas of the country still receiving larger influxes of individuals from the border—mostly in the South, but also in southern New York and northern New Jersey. One of the most exciting developments was that our team convinced the sheriff to lobby the Albany County Legislature to rededicate a small portion of the more than $4 million of federal funding paid to the county to board the immigrants to a budget line in the sheriff's budget, with the idea that he would subcontract with a local legal services agency to have a full-time immigration attorney working for the Sheriff's Office.[28] If the unthinkable happens again, we can restart our own disruptive, injustice-righting machine with a full-time attorney lead and organizer on the ground from day one. That lawyer will not be left alone to serve in the wild but will benefit from a group of seasoned crisis leaders—ready to tackle the next challenge, birth ideas, and build useful new tools with every unexpected twist and turn.

This is a new kind of crisis lawyering. It is a kind of lawyering that can't anticipate every challenge, but it can produce and reproduce effective disruption leveraging tools by partnering with the very same people we've been told will fight us at every turn. By lawyering this way, we will find opportunity, trust, and a deeper dedication to the clients we serve because of the personal investments and ideological risks we choose to take. Crisis can be a revolutionary gift—if only we are brave enough to accept it.

NOTES

Epigraph. DIDIER ERIBON, MICHEL FOUCAULT 282 (1991) (quoting Michel Foucault, CORRIERE DELLA SERA, Nov. 1978).

1 See N.Y. JUD. LAW § 30-d (McKinney 2019); Albany County Sheriff, ALBANY CTY., www.albanycounty.com.

2 *See* Memorandum from Kevin K. McAleenan, Comm'n, U.S. Customs & Border Prot., L. Francis Cissna, Dir., U.S. Citizenship & Immigration Servs., Thomas D. Homan, U.S. Immigration & Customs Enf't, to Kirstjen Nielsen, Sec'y, U.S. Dep't of Homeland Sec., Increasing Prosecutions of Immigration Violations (Apr. 23, 2018), www.documentcloud.org/documents/4936568-FOIA-9-23-Family-Separation-Memo.html. This memo and others related to the crisis surfaced long after its height and only after significant prodding by Congress and the press. *See* Jeremy Stahl, *Newly Uncovered Memo Suggests Kirstjen Nielsen Lied to Congress About Family Separation*, SLATE (Sept. 25, 2018), https://slate.com.

3 *Southern Border in Our NY: Lawyers Screen 300+ Asylum Seekers in 1 Month at Albany Jail*, N.Y. IMMIGR. COALITION (Jul. 31, 2018), www.nyic.org.

4 *See* Brendan J. Lyons, *Many of the Immigrants at Albany County Jail Seeking Asylum*, TIMES UNION (Jul. 2, 2018), www.timesunion.com.

5 *See* Immigration & Nationality Act § 208(a)(1); 8 U.S.C. § 1158(a)(1) (2012).

6 *See, e.g.*, Miriam Jordan, *Family Separation May Have Hit Thousands More Migrant Children Than Reported*, N.Y. TIMES (Jan. 17, 2019), www.nytimes.com.

7 Tim Williams, *Albany County Sheriff Craig Apple and Sarah Rogerson on the Immigrant Detainees in Albany County*, CAPITOL NEWSROOM: WCNY 3:03–3:50 p.m. (July 12, 2018), www.wcny.org.

8 Immigration and Nationality Act 235(c), 8 U.S.C. 1225(c) (2012).

9 *See C.J.L.G. v. Sessions*, 880 F.3d 1122, 1129 (9th Cir. 2018); *J.E.F.M. v. Lynch*, 837 F.3d 1026 (9th Cir. 2016).

10 *New York Immigration Family Unity Project*, BRONX DEFS., www.bronxdefenders.org.

11 *Albany Law School Launches Immigration Law Clinic to Provide Free Legal Representation to Immigrants in the Capital Region*, ALB. L. SCH. (Apr. 9, 2015), www.albanylaw.edu.

12 Detained immigrants, and those formerly detained who were released, represented by counsel were respectively ten-and-a-half times and five-and-a-half times more likely to succeed in removal proceedings than their than unrepresented counterparts. INGRID EARLY & STEVEN SHAFER, ACCESS TO COUNSEL IN IMMIGRATION COURT 19 (2016).

13 *See Maria S. as Next Friend for E.H.F. v. Garza*, No. 17-40873, 2019 WL 101868 (5th Cir. Jan. 4, 2019); Sarah Stillman, *When Deportation Is a Death Sentence*, THE NEW YORKER (Jan. 15, 2018), www.newyorker.com.

14 Jennifer M. Chacón, *Overcriminalizing Immigration*, 102 J. CRIM. L. & CRIMINOLOGY 613 (2012); Kevin R. Johnson, *An Immigration Gideon for Lawful Permanent Residents*, 122 YALE L.J. 2394, 2405–14 (2013); Sarah Rogerson, *The Politics of Fear: Unaccompanied Immigrant Children and the Case of the Southern Border*, 61 VILL. L. REV. 843 (2016).

15 *See, e.g.*, Jordan Carleo-Evangelist, *Albany County Makes $1.1M Deal to End Jail Death Lawsuit*, TIMES UNION (Apr. 20, 2016), www.timesunion.com.

16 The Trump Administration revoked the Obama Administration's 2013 memo regarding the Parental Interests Directive and replaced it with another policy that provides fewer protections. *See* U.S. IMMIGRATION & CUSTOMS ENF'T, POLICY NUMBER 11064.2, DETENTION AND REMOVAL OF ALIEN PARENTS OR LEGAL GUARDIANS, www.ice.gov.

17 SETH FREED WESSLER, APPLIED RESEARCH CTR., SHATTERED FAMILIES: THE PERILOUS INTERSECTION OF IMMIGRATION ENFORCEMENT AND THE CHILD WELFARE SYSTEM 22–25, 42–43 (2011), www.raceforward.org.

18 *See* Wale Aliyu, *Coalition of Volunteers, Attorneys Camp Out at JFK in Wake of Trump Ban*, NBC N.Y. (Jan 30, 2017), www.nbcnewyork.com.

19 Joseph De Avila, *County Jail in New York Receives Hundreds of Asylum Seekers*, WALL ST. J. (Jul. 16, 2018), www.wsj.com.

20 ASS'N PRO BONO COUNS., https://apbco.org.

21 *The Artesia Report*, INNOVATION L. LAB, https://innovationlawlab.org/the-artesia-report.

22 Stephen Manning, *How to Crowdsource a Refugee Rights Strategy—Tedx Mt. Hood*, YOUTUBE (June 29, 2016), www.youtube.com/watch?time_continue=3&v=iX9fizsJfuU.

23 *See* J. M. von Werthern et al., *The Impact of Immigration Detention on Mental Health: A Systematic Review*, 18 BMC PSYCHIATRY 382, 396 (2018); Luis H. Zayas & Laurie Cook Heffron, *Disrupting Young Lives: How Detention and Deportation Affect US-born Children of Immigrants*, AM. PSYCHOL. ASS'N: CYF NEWSLETTER (Nov. 2016), www.apa.org.

24 *See* Lin Piwowarczyk et al., *Secondary Trauma in Asylum Lawyers*, 14 BENDER'S IMMIGR. BULL. 263 (2009).

25 RUTH DELANEY ET AL., VERA INST. JUST., REIMAGINING PRISON 28 (2018), https://storage.googleapis.com/vera-web-assets/downloads/Publications/reimagining-prison-print-report/legacy_downloads/Reimagining-Prison_FINAL2_digital.pdf.

26 *See* Jim Franco, *Sheriff: New Beginnings Will Change the Ending*, SPOTLIGHT NEWS (Jan. 24, 2019), www.spotlightnews.com.

27 *See* Ruarí Arrieta-Kenna, *'Abolish Prisons' Is the New 'Abolish ICE'*, POLITICO (Aug. 15, 2018), www.politico.com.

28 Mallory Moench, *Albany County Using Federal Funds to Pay for Legal Help to Immigrants in the County Jail*, TIMES UNION (Nov. 14, 2018), www.timesunion.com.

PART II

Crisis and Systemic Contexts

7

Key Considerations for Lawyers Shepherding Communities through Long-Term Recovery from Major Disasters

JOHN TRAVIS MARSHALL

Lawyers must play an active role in ensuring that state and local governments have the best possible legal infrastructure to support the long journey to recovery following a major disaster. Unfortunately, most communities have failed to evaluate whether essential laws and policies are in place to support long-term recovery from disaster events. This is a troubling oversight. At stake are a community's prospects for achieving equitable and efficient recovery. This chapter identifies several important steps to guide crisis lawyers in their ever-evolving responsibilities for guiding long-term recovery following crisis and disaster.

Introduction

Local and state governments responding to disasters require immediate assistance from a broad spectrum of organizations and professionals. But even with expert training and broad experience, few professionals find themselves fully prepared to help communities recover in a chaotic, postdisaster landscape. This is particularly true of lawyers. The previous several decades provide a long list of natural disasters that illustrate the extraordinary challenges that lawyers have faced in helping communities rebound. However, the large number of major disasters hasn't yielded any guiding principles. Lawyers who may find themselves working in long-term recovery are still largely flying blind when it comes to understanding the legal obstacles posed by major disasters and how those obstacles might be addressed or avoided.

The good news is that a growing literature about disaster recovery has begun to examine lawyers' concerns. Scholarly research and practitioner narratives have slowly emerged to help attorneys grasp the fundamental difficulties involved with lawyering in the *immediate* wake of disasters. However, these accounts of a disaster's emergency-response phase provide incomplete guidance to lawyers working in the protracted postdisaster phase known as the "long-term recovery." The emergency-response phase is a relatively short—albeit critical—phase of the disaster recovery journey. Attorneys working in the extended phase of long-term recovery have mainly shared practitioner war stories and other anecdotes describing the role a lawyer played in a years-long recovery from a disaster. Despite the recent frequency of major natural disasters, lawyers have struggled to create coherent and meaningful guidance regarding the challenges and opportunities faced in helping communities imagine and execute their long-term recovery from a major disaster.[1]

It is difficult to assess the cost of this deficit in understanding the work of long-term recovery lawyering. But it is probably accurate to say that inefficient or inept long-term recovery lawyering could delay a community's rebound from disaster. In this chapter I address the troubling knowledge gap surrounding lawyering in the long-term recovery context. I suggests several important considerations that lawyers who work with (and for) state and local governments need to consider in helping those governments navigate obstacles encountered during the community's journey to rebirth and renewal.

Long-Term Recovery—the Winding Road through the Community Rebuilding Process

Disaster scholars and professionals generally describe two parts to a community's recovery journey. In the first days and weeks following a disaster event, a city is focused on responding to the disaster's immediate impacts, including search and rescue, emergency housing, and debris removal. The second phase that follows is the long-term recovery.[2]

A community's long-term recovery from disaster begins as debris is removed from neighborhoods. Families begin to consider rebuilding or departing. Businesses weigh reopening, relocating, or closing shop. Local and state governments start evaluating the projects they can undertake to support individual, neighborhood, and community-wide recovery, including economic development and neighborhood redevelopment initiatives.

Unfortunately, the long-term recovery also tends to open an economic fissure between financially stable middle- and upper-income families (generally speaking, those earning more than 120 percent of area median income, or "AMI") and less financially secure moderate-, low-, and very-low-income families (those earning 120 percent all the way down to 30 percent of AMI). For many, but by no means all, middle- and upper-income families and businesses, the long-term recovery is self-propelling. Assistance from local and state governments hardly figures into these residents' rebuilding or relocation efforts. That's because "recovering" likely means tapping insurance, savings, or retirement accounts to pay for a family's move, temporary housing, or its rebuilding efforts.

But the experience of these families is only part of a community's long-term recovery story. A substantial number of a community's moderate-, low-, and very-low-income residents are not so fortunate. Lacking sufficient resources, many residents struggle to recover, cobbling together grants, donated labor and materials, and other assistance from state and local government, as well as philanthropic, nonprofit, and volunteer contributions. These individuals and families live paycheck to paycheck. Some rely on a modest fixed income due to age or disability. Many live in poverty.

Likewise, the small businesses owned by these moderate-, low-, and very-low-income families rarely have reserves to survive loss of their client or customer base. Minority families or small businesses are among the most likely to lack a postdisaster financial safety net.[3] Thus, a significant segment of the community faces dire postdisaster adversity, relying directly and indirectly on the work of local and state government attorneys responsible for formulating and implementing the city or state's long-term recovery plans.

The Responsibilities of Lawyers Working in Recovery Are Not Easily Defined

This chapter is written principally for lawyers working with (or for) local and state governments following major disasters. It also may prove a valuable resource for the diverse team of professionals with whom lawyers are embedded during long-term recovery. The reason it is pertinent to a wider professional audience is that long-term recovery requires an unusual level of interdisciplinary teamwork.

Lawyers play an integral role in a larger professional unit dedicated to addressing a natural disaster's impact. Consider the extreme level of destruction that accompanies major disasters. All, or a substantial part, of a city or region has been laid waste. A city's long-term recovery often involves re-creating or resurrecting almost every system on which a community relies, from roads to drinking water, stormwater, wastewater, streetlights, and the full range of public buildings and facilities. But it usually also includes a range of housing and community development responsibilities, including affordable housing, economic development, and neighborhood revitalization. Each of these initiatives is urgently important to community stakeholders. Each is also proceeding forward concurrently.

Long-term recovery lawyering forces attorneys to consider more broadly their roles as counselors. Following a disaster, it isn't unusual for local governments to find themselves creating and implementing housing and neighborhood redevelopment programs. Local government attorneys frequently help facilitate the acquisition and disposition of property. But in the wake of a disaster, lawyers must do much more than draft and negotiate agreements. Along with planners, real estate experts, and finance professionals, they must quickly design a program to deliver redevelopment projects to their city, county, or town. This means they must research state and local laws to make sure the city has the power to deploy real estate development tools, ranging from the power to use eminent domain in order to aid private redevelopment of affordable housing to the power to contribute publicly owned land for the redevelopment of city-owned property. Even if the proposed postdisaster program complies with state law, lawyers must vet the program for compliance with dozens of federal laws that control expenditure of federal disaster grant funds, including federal procurement, environmental review, and minimum wage and hour requirements. But that's not all. Lawyers also play an essential role in making sure that postdisaster redevelopment programs are implemented in a manner that is equitable, fair, and efficient—avoiding legal and political challenges that could slow delivery of projects to the vulnerable residents who are waiting patiently to return to the communities where they had lived and worked. In short, this kind of legal work is unusual for lawyers, who generally learn early in their training to set a precise scope for their client engagements. But this understandable inclination to define limits around lawyers' responsibilities cuts against long-term recovery's necessary fusion of complex law, planning, housing, community development, and management tasks.

Lawyers working in long-term recovery are, to be clear, carrying out their customary and ordinary tasks as city or county attorneys. They're prosecuting code enforcement cases and appearing before city councils, and they're writing statutes and testifying before legislative bodies. At the same time, however, lawyers are working elbow-to-elbow with colleagues from allied professions assessing community needs, crafting recovery plans, and helping to actively pursue and implement recovery goals. They are frequently cocreators of a community's recovery vision, not simply advocates for that vision.

Most local governments could not effectively or efficiently pursue recovery if their lawyers are narrowly engaged in law-related matters. Lawyers are thus instrumental members of a team entrusted with shepherding a community to recovery. They will be valued for their ability to see legal challenges present in a contract or in a federal regulation. Yet, long-term recovery lawyering is unusually dynamic in its nature. In service of the city's overarching goal of advancing community revitalization, local governments will also look to lawyers as part of their recovery team to guide projects through obstacles and opportunities that may affect the community's recovery.

Ideas for First Principles in Long-Term Recovery Lawyering: Lessons from Emergency Response Lawyering

There are few resources to which lawyers responsible for guiding a community's long-term recovery can look for guidance. The reason may be that the concept is relatively new to lawyers. Many war stories of lawyers working in long-term recovery flow from the challenges associated with the Hurricane Katrina and Superstorm Sandy recoveries.[4] It may also be that the chaos, urgency, and trauma accompanying major disasters make immediate disaster response a topic more compelling to practitioners and scholars examining lawyers' roles following disaster events. But scholarly and practice-focused studies of emergency response lawyering, although few in number, provide a valuable starting point for analyzing the challenges of long-term recovery lawyering.[5]

The growing literature on challenges faced by lawyers working in the immediate wake of disasters supplies at least three fundamental insights about our understanding of the important role that counsel play over the long-term recovery's extended time horizon. I explain these in the next few sections.

The Breadth of a Disaster Will Overwhelm Usual and Customary Legal Capacity

Lawyers engaged in immediate disaster response work are conscious of not only the enormous scope of destruction but also the human suffering that frequently accompanies disasters. A major hurricane or earthquake can paralyze a city or region, bringing down almost every major system, including the communications network, roads, the water supply, and wastewater and stormwater systems. At the same time, disaster upends communities in such a brutal way that it reveals abject human need on a scale not commonly encountered by most lawyers. That is why for lawyers, in coming to a community's aid immediately following a disaster, and later building that community back over a period of years, it is extraordinarily difficult to anticipate the issues they will be asked to address following major disasters.[6] So, the first insight that the existing body of disaster response lawyering literature shares is that responding to disasters and managing recovery raises a very broad spectrum of legal issues, ranging from animal law to zoning.[7] No single lawyer—and few law firms or city legal departments—can expect to have the substantive background and expertise necessary to serve a local or state government.

By Helping Communities Plan for Meaningful Long-Term Recovery
from Catastrophic Disasters, Lawyers Can Help Communities
Bounce Back More Quickly and Equitably

Emergency response planning has long been a required element of state government policies and procedures.[8] Although these emergency plans are required by the US Federal Emergency Management Agency (FEMA), legal practitioners and scholars are quick to note that they are not all prepared to the same level of rigor and forethought. Approximately 40 percent of the emergency response plans adopted by US states were judged to have lacked at least some important legal grounding.[9]

This comes as no surprise to some scholars and practitioners, who also note that lawyers have failed to engage earnestly with emergency response staff charged with carrying out planning processes.[10] Lawyers' absence or detachment, according to experts, has serious consequences for local government, not the least of which is potential exposure to tort claims associated with preparation or implementation of emergency plans.[11]

Hazard mitigation planning is a particularly important part of a community's comprehensive planning process because it helps communities avert development that puts residents at risk.[12] Such planning is informed by the understanding that most communities are continually growing or redeveloping. In fact, 50 percent of the built environment that surrounds us now will be replaced by 2050.[13] Prudent hazard mitigation planning helps minimize the need for postdisaster residential and commercial redevelopment initiatives that are so often major undertakings during a community's long-term recovery. It is imperative that lawyers play an active role in mitigation planning that will help local governments build more safely or less frequently in higher hazard areas. The stakes are high. As briefly discussed earlier in this chapter, moderate-, low-, and very-low-income families are often the most vulnerable to natural hazards, and they are also the population most likely to struggle during the long-term recovery. These families are also likely to live in vulnerable geographic areas, such as coastal or riverine plains. Effective hazard mitigation planning will provide an essential legal basis for communities to argue that their decisions concerning new and future settlement patterns protect lives and property and promote a more effective recovery from disaster.[14]

Planning with the long-term recovery in mind also means that communities think about the challenge of finding temporary and permanent housing for those displaced by a major disaster. Local governments can play a major role in laying the groundwork for a more successful long-term recovery by identifying and pursuing better postdisaster housing options for their communities. As part of their legal oversight of a required comprehensive planning process, counsel should ensure that comprehensive plan housing elements should include a section concerning temporary and permanent postdisaster housing. Consider, for example, the challenges faced in communities like the town of Lyons, Colorado, which had a very small inventory of vacant land for temporary housing and permanent housing.[15] After a substantial number of the town's 2,000 residents were displaced by a September 2013 flood event, those who lost their homes had nowhere to live in Lyons and were forced to make a long drive to nearby towns and cities. As the 2013 flood event made clear, homes could not be rebuilt in the high-hazard areas adjacent to the St. Vrain River. To make matters worse, these displaced families had little prospect for returning permanently to Lyons. The city had no provision to convert publicly owned land to private homeownership short of a voter referendum.[16] Without any plan in place for replacement housing, city residents rejected a proposal to swap existing city parkland for residents' former riverside homesites.

Local Political Pressures and Media Coverage Heighten Scrutiny of Postdisaster Lawyering

The role politics and the media play in disaster response and recovery is well documented, particularly in the days immediately following a disaster.[17] However, the literature focuses mainly on national politics and its influence on the level of federal funding that will be delivered to storm-affected communities. As for the media coverage of disasters and their immediate after-effects, the press has been blamed for disaster fatigue, which recognizes that Americans' interest in disaster-related stories usually wanes shortly after the disaster. At the same time, the press has been hailed for highlighting the injustice and inequity often associated with the chaos immediately following a disaster. These treatments of postdisaster media and politics are incomplete.

There is another dimension to postdisaster politics and media coverage of which lawyers working long-term recovery should be aware. Legal and policy decisions that lawyers assist in making on the local level are frequently influenced over the long term by pressure exerted by local political actors and media coverage. Lawyers working in long-term recovery must be mindful that their work is continually subject to the push and pull of political considerations and media scrutiny.

Current emergency-response literature notes that politics influences lawyers' recovery work in many ways. Postdisaster neighborhood redevelopment decisions have historically invited widespread redevelopment of high-hazard areas due to short-term political concerns associated with angering residents. This politics of pleasing the electorate has prevailed, even when the decision to allow rebuilding across a disaster area could potentially subject a local government to liability for future disaster-related losses.[18]

Local politics and the media also influenced the evolution of post-Katrina decision-making on a range of law-related recovery matters. In a city where 80 percent of the city's land area saw significant flooding and where 134,000 housing units were damaged or destroyed, neighborhood rebuilding and recovery loomed as enormous undertakings. Residents, their elected representatives, and state and local officials were all eager to see progress toward a return to normal.

In an effort to facilitate a more robust recovery, the City of New Orleans made an early and initial decision in late 2006 to place responsibility for carrying out certain housing-related redevelopment projects to the New Orleans Redevelopment Authority (NORA). NORA is a putatively independent redevelopment authority created under Louisiana state law in the 1960s to serve the city's redevelopment needs, and community stakeholders hoped that recovery projects administered by NORA could be insulated from local political pressures.[19] In many respects, this hope was not realized. The city's slowly unfolding long-term recovery helped create, for example, an environment where local politics nudged NORA to consider a redevelopment strategy that it and its community-based stakeholders initially disfavored: neighborhood redevelopment using public auctions' storm-damaged and formerly occupied Road Home properties.[20] Although NORA was created to operate independently of the direct control of the mayor and city council, it received much of its post-Katrina redevelopment moneys in its role as a subgrantee of the city's $440+ million allocation of disaster relief under the federal Community Development Block Grant (CDBG) program. As the City's subgrantee, NORA was required to negotiate a new cooperative endeavor agreement with the City each year, and it was frequently asked to appear before the New Orleans City Council in public hearings to answer questions about its progress on assigned post-Katrina redevelopment responsibilities. The chance that the city could decide year to year to reduce or eliminate NORA's main source of funding, and the spectacle of public hearings, necessarily made NORA responsive to competing efforts for control by the mayor and council.

NORA's overarching plan for redevelopment of the city's storm-damaged properties was set forth in the Parish Redevelopment and Disposition Plan.[21] As a part of each parish's long-term recovery plan, Orleans Parish was required by law to create a parish-wide plan articulating strategies for reuse or redevelopment of residential properties returned to New Orleans through

Louisiana's post-Katrina Road Home Program. Road Home was considered a lynchpin of neighborhood recovery, offering residents the choice to rebuild their storm-damaged property, sell their property to the state and rebuild elsewhere in Louisiana, or sell their property to the state and move out of state. Most New Orleans residents accepted the state's offer to stay and help rebuild, but a substantial number of homeowners decided to cash out (eventually totaling about 4,500 homeowners). Those newly orphaned residential properties were scattered across the city, but they were mainly situated in relatively low-lying neighborhoods, and virtually all of them were left with storm-damaged structures.

NORA was designated as the recipient of the Road Home Program's roughly 4,500 so-called buyout properties. As a recipient, it was responsible for drafting the state-mandated Orleans Parish Disposition Plan. This plan highlighted NORA staff's preference for legal strategies that would dispose of properties according to the strength of individual neighborhood real estate markets and the condition of surrounding homes. Importantly, the plan also memorialized the wish of New Orleans' neighborhoods to create affordable housing while retaining the longstanding homeownership character of the storm-damaged residential properties. The plan was approved by the New Orleans City Council and the state's Louisiana Recovery Authority in December 2007. To achieve the plan's goals, NORA pledged to use neighborhood-tailored disposition strategies, including using requests for proposals to attract private and nonprofit developers to particular neighborhood redevelopment opportunities. NORA also agreed to help implement an innovative law adopted by the New Orleans City Council. The city's Lot Next Door ordinance gave returning homeowners the chance to expand the existing footprint of the homes by purchasing the adjacent lot of a neighbor who decided not to rebuild. These and other aspects of NORA's redevelopment strategy were intended to support residential redevelopment at a pace that reflected market demand for residential redevelopment. Significantly, the state-mandated NORA plan did not specifically call for disposition of properties by public auction. Agency staff believed that auctions increased the chance that speculative investors—property purchasers with no connection to the neighborhood or perhaps even the New Orleans region or Louisiana—would purchase a majority of the property and have the chance to do so relatively early in a neighborhood's post-Katrina redevelopment. In addition, NORA was concerned that neighborhoods with high levels of absentee landowners would likely lead to those new owners converting what had historically been homeownership units to rental units. By potentially promoting this nature of neighborhood change, the agency would be cutting against its pledge and the city's goal to preserve what had historically been homeownership units. NORA also noted real estate research suggesting that a public auction's effects on neighborhood redevelopment would be mixed.[22] Despite the agency's deeply held concerns, however, it was noteworthy that NORA's disposition plan did not categorically restrict auctions as a potential disposition method.

The long-term recovery environment is a landscape of dilapidation and despair. Need overwhelms capacity, and the list of essential projects far outstrips available funds. Ideal and preferred long-term redevelopment strategies can be overshadowed by the clouds of adversity that accompany major and complex redevelopment challenges. Although several variables may have influenced changes in NORA's redevelopment strategy, slow arrival of federal funding and three years of mounting pressure significantly altered NORA's redevelopment strategy. The first federal disaster CDBG funds earmarked for revitalization of neighborhood-based assets did not hit New Orleans streets until March 2009, nearly three and a half years after Katrina flooded the city. To make matters worse, it was estimated that nearly 25 percent of New Orleans's residential addresses were blighted, most of them being dilapidated and uninhabitable from years of pre-Katrina neglect and also the seemingly corrosive effects of Katrina's floodwaters.[23] Under these circumstances, the pressure on NORA to consider alternative legal and real estate tools mounted. At least one member of the New Orleans City Council strongly disagreed with the agency's initial strategy to forgo auctions and rely on clustered offerings of property for redevelopment. An influential NORA board member and radio talk-show host, who also ran against New Orleans's incumbent mayor, C. Ray Nagin, argued strongly that the agency was holding up the city's recovery by refusing to sell the storm-damaged properties to the highest bidder. The Louisiana Land Trust, which was and remains the state agency entrusted with holding title to the storm-damaged properties until ready for sale to private landowners, noted that it was bearing significant monthly costs maintaining and insuring properties—costs that could otherwise be borne by auction purchasers. And each of these stakeholders, together with other local stakeholders, cited lost local property tax revenues and favorable press that accompanied the decision of sister Louisiana parishes to auction their storm-damaged properties—auctions that regularly generated millions in sales receipts for the State of Louisiana. This evolution of NORA's legal and real estate strategy for neighborhood redevelopment demonstrates how political and media voices can influence local governments to adjust the course of a community's long-term recovery.

NORA held its first auction in the spring of 2011 and has continued to auction properties as part of its overall suite of legal and real estate tools for returning vacant, blighted, and abandoned properties back into the New Orleans real estate market. No analysis has yet been done to assess the neighborhood impact—pro or con—of the auction as a postdisaster property disposition tool.

Lessons for Lawyers from Recent Long-Term Recoveries

Hurricane Katrina's unprecedented widespread destruction led many researchers and professionals to turn their attention to long-term recovery. In the second half of this chapter I suggest three important considerations for lawyers working in long-term recovery. These are discussed in the next few sections.

Lawyers Are in the Best Position to Help Communities If They Are Familiar with Federal, State, and Local Laws Applicable to Long-Term Recovery

Lawyers working in the disaster context should be aware of certain core federal laws, including the federal Stafford Disaster Relief and Emergency Assistance Act and the Housing and Community Development Act, and key policies, such as the National Disaster Recovery Framework.[24] These federal laws define the general universe of recovery activities for which the federal government will reimburse local governments.

Familiarity with key federal laws, while necessary, is insufficient. Because disasters begin and end locally, it is also essential that lawyers have a working knowledge of local and state law.[25] State and local legal landscapes contain nuances that can have a significant effect on design and implementation of disaster recovery programs. A state's constitution may give local governments broad latitude to donate public property for redevelopment of affordable housing. But local ordinances may ultimately frustrate the ability of cities and towns to convert a public park to housing units for residents displaced by a flood.

Ensuring compliance with applicable laws is not an easy task. Catastrophic disasters demand whatever immediate attention local and state governments can muster. The fog of destruction and disorder that hangs over a community makes it difficult even for comparatively high-functioning governments to respond appropriately. This responsibility for following all applicable laws becomes a head-spinning responsibility for local and state governments scrambling to help communities jumpstart recovery following a catastrophic disaster. Almost overnight, counsel serving local and state governments must ensure that they honor dozens of federal statutes and regulations relating to disaster recovery.

The consequences can be severe for failure to follow all applicable laws. Even a legal misstep that some would deem technical and not directly related to the overarching goals of helping a community recover can jeopardize a community's ability to carry out recovery. If a local government fails to comply with federal, state, or local laws when carrying out any range of recovery activities, the local government faces both the prospect of not receiving reimbursement from the federal government for work the local government completed and, at a minimum, not being able to timely pay contractors (often local firms) for work they have completed.

These costly local government failures are rooted in noncompliance with straightforward legal requirements and often involve oversights in contract drafting. Federal audits of local and state government recovery programs are replete with examples:

- HUD's inspector general recommended that St. Tammany Parish, Louisiana, repay more than $450,000 in federal disaster recovery block grants because the parish did not always understand or follow HUD's disaster recovery program requirements, including the parish's *own* policies and procedures for implementing the recovery program;[26]
- FEMA's inspector general questioned whether a New Jersey township should be reimbursed for $748,000 because it engaged in "improper contracting," including failing to follow federal procurement regulations requiring, among other things, the local government to secure multiple bids for nonexigent recovery work and to take prescribed steps to attract bids from historically disadvantaged firms;[27]
- HUD's inspector general questioned reimbursing New York City for disaster recovery expenses because it could not confirm that it always paid certain workers hourly rates required under the federal Davis-Bacon Act, which "require[s] that all laborers and mechanics be paid prevailing wage rates on Federal construction projects;[28] and
- FEMA's inspector general recommended that Jackson County, Florida, not be reimbursed for more than $3 million for, among other errors, "misinterpret[ing] Federal regulations and guidelines" relating to "Federal procurement requirements when awarding a contract for professional consulting services." The local government explained that its error was due to its confusion of federal regulations with state guidelines.[29]

Failure to comply with applicable laws and procedures can threaten to delay a community's recovery and, in some instances, retard the recovery by leaving already cash-strapped local governments and local businesses in even more vulnerable positions. Counsel for local and state government have a special opportunity and responsibility to ensure that their clients satisfy highly detailed legal requirements associated with all aspects of a community's recovery. Local and state governments can avoid the kinds of missteps that derail community recovery by ensuring that basic legal requirements applicable to recovery programs are woven into the fabric of the policies and procedures that govern the local or state government's pre- and postdisaster work.

Lawyers Must Participate in Planning for Future Disaster Events, Including Creating a Blueprint to Adopt Laws and Creating Institutions Necessary to Support a Robust Recovery

It may not be sufficient for local governments merely to comply with the laws that are on the books. Major disasters also spotlight gaps in the legal landscape.

Before disaster strikes, there are at least three questions lawyers should encourage local governments to consider about their legal landscape. First, local and state governments must anticipate laws and institutions that may need to be in place to authorize and carry out recovery programs. If local laws are missing, the heat of a postdisaster crisis isn't the best time to draft, consider, and adopt a new ordinance.[30] Second and in the same vein, if a local government determines that an existing local law could pose an obstacle to efficient and equitable recovery, then at a minimum that ordinance or statute should be flagged for amendment or repeal. Third, if a city or county determines that its existing governing infrastructure is inadequate to manage a vital part of the postdisaster redevelopment, the preferred time to design and, if necessary, staff and task the new agency is before disaster strikes.[31]

In conjunction with their local or state government colleagues, private practitioners should take the lead in auditing laws and institutions. This audit would highlight the essential legal and institutional ingredients for successful recovery from disaster. The audit could begin with a review of the ordinances, statutes, and comprehensive plans that govern the community. And then it could proceed to a review of the best practices of peer local and state governments, particularly those that have previously navigated a long-term recovery. The audit's focus would be to determine if those sister jurisdictions possess capacities that have helped them bounce forward after catastrophe.

Local government lawyers, joined by their colleagues from allied professions, will likely have little trouble reading their jurisdiction's ordinances and policies and finding laws that might impede recovery. In other words, their review of local laws will remind them of what they know doesn't currently function well but would be crucial to a demanding long-term recovery. Consider the example of Lyons, Colorado, where a local ordinance prevented the city from swapping or otherwise conveying city parkland to allow for development of postdisaster affordable housing absent a public referendum. In a community such as Lyons, where public parkland and undeveloped land is at a premium, counsel and staff would no doubt appreciate that their local government might be well advised to draft an emergency ordinance that would allow the jurisdiction to convey city property for housing development based on approval of the city council.

A more challenging task for government counsel and city staff might be using this audit to assess the laws and policies that *should* be on the books but are missing. This is a more challenging inquiry, but it starts with counsel and staff looking at the current condition of the city's neighborhoods and discussing the extant factors associated with persistent vulnerability in residents' health, financial status, or social well-being. For instance, is the city comfortable with the current range of rental and homeownership options for its residents? It may be that the housing occupied by the city's low- and moderate-income community skews dramatically toward renters with comparatively few homeowners.[32] This imbalance puts the city and its residents in a precarious position in the event of a disaster. Renters are highly vulnerable to displacement.

Ideally, the audit process would trigger the city to consider potential legal interventions to address the identified vulnerability related to the city's unusually large community of renters. The solutions to create more homeownership opportunities for low- and moderate-income families might include, for example, creating an affordable housing trust financed by a small impact fee that will be charged to apartment and home developers on issuance of their building permits.

Taking stock of a city's laws—those missing that ideally should be in place and those in place that should be repealed or amended—gives local and state governments a blueprint for local governments' more resilient legal landscape.

Counsel Should Promote Collection and Safe Keeping of Housing and Community Development Data Vital to Postdisaster Recovery Efforts

Developing working familiarity with a shelf full of statutes, regulations, and policies is only part of the challenge faced by lawyers working in long-term recovery. More vexing are the circumstances under which counsel must provide advice to their public-sector clients.

Disasters cut power and destroy records. Disasters also sometimes expose a local government's failure to collect basic data about property conditions, property ownership, payment of taxes, or land use and zoning designation. In such cases, lawyers must render advice with the understanding that the information that their clients have been giving them may be incomplete or incorrect.[33]

An understanding of a community's pre- and postdisaster neighborhood characteristics is vital to making informed decisions about long-term recovery, and it is essential to a local government's argument for securing supplemental assistance from state and federal partners.[34] Information detailing the age, type, and condition of housing stock, the comparative proportion of homeownership and rental units that make up a community's housing, and the number of moderate-, low-, and very-low-income families living in a community can help local governments anticipate and address a community's housing vulnerabilities.[35] Counsel can then work with the local government to craft policies and build local institutions that can help meet existing and future housing needs.

Data isn't just helpful before disaster strikes. It is also essential for counseling local governments on efficient and equitable investment of scarce resources during the long-term recovery. Data is crucial for lawyers who must advocate for redevelopment, because it both enables them to deploy the appropriate legal and real estate strategies for housing development and to make the critical—but sometimes unpopular—argument for new affordable housing.

Lawyers working in long-term recovery cooperate closely with planners and housing professionals to lay the groundwork for redevelopment of homeowner and rental units. Neighborhood housing data, for example, aids local governments in efficiently and equitably allocating resources for rebuilding affordable housing. One of the New Orleans Redevelopment Authority's chief responsibilities was to replace storm-damaged homes with new or rehabilitated affordable homeownership units. NORA accomplished this objective by: (1) tapping the supply of state-owned Road Home buyout properties; (2) using its statutory power to expropriate blighted properties; and (3) deploying other legal tools for acquisition, including land swaps and clearing title on tax adjudicated properties. At the same time, NORA also transferred properties for affordable housing development to: (1) individuals; (2) private developers and nonprofit developers based on competitive proposals; (3) individual neighborhood residents under the Lot Next Door ordinance; and (4) land swaps.

With limited financial resources at its disposal, it was critical for NORA to inform its decisions about the most appropriate legal and real estate tools (e.g., expropriation, land banking, market purchase, tax lien foreclosure, land swap, etc.) to use the best available data. For example, agency resources would likely be conserved by land-banking properties in neighborhoods with relatively low property values and relatively high levels of vacancy or abandonment. The best legal and real estate strategy for the community would be for a community to hold properties and maintain them until the neighborhood begins to show stronger signs of recovery or the community controls enough properties to allow for the community to consider a catalytic redevelopment project. But a community can't make informed decisions about legal and real estate development tools unless it has accurate data regarding a neighborhood's status. This vital information is drawn from data on building permit issuances, code enforcement citations, home conditions, and home sales prices—just to name several. If, for instance, data gathered by a community indicated that residents of a neighborhood with high levels of vacancy and low property values were largely continuing to pay taxes and maintain yards, then this data may inform a local government to proceed quickly with infrastructure projects that would strongly signal to displaced residents the local government's intent to invest in reviving a heavily damaged neighborhood.

Unfortunately, data concerning New Orleans's neighborhoods was not always fully, widely, or immediately available (much less effectively shared or collected) until the nonprofit Greater New Orleans Community Data Center issued a report on New Orleans's vacant and abandoned properties in the spring of 2010.[36] Until that time, more than four years into the Katrina recovery, NORA's decisions regarding its housing initiatives were based on the best anecdotes and information that staff could gather from agency property inspection data, local residents and neighborhood associations, area real estate professionals, and city colleagues.

There is another dimension to the imperative that communities develop predisaster strategies for collecting important data concerning housing and community development. Debates concerning the need for affordable housing often center around questions about demand. If there is one truth that has emerged from recent long-term recovery journeys, it is that disasters hit the poor the hardest, particularly a city's extremely low-, very low-, low-, and moderate-income families.[37] These are families, for example, in which one or both parents work in the city's hospitality industry. They generally live in rental housing, sometimes subsidized, but just as often they live in small dwellings characterized as older, inexpensive duplex, triplex, and quadraplex units.[38] After a disaster, these low- and moderate-income families are frequently displaced from these small rental units because their apartment has been destroyed or the landlord cannot afford to make immediate repairs. Residents are left with tough choices, including paying inflated postdisaster rents, moving to another city, or moving in with family or friends whose homes did not suffer significant damage.

Building affordable housing is an imperative in the vast majority of American states. In 2011, nearly 23 percent of families in the United States were overburdened by housing costs because they had to pay more than 50 percent of their income to cover housing costs.[39] Disasters can make this situation even worse, damaging or destroying a significant portion of a city's affordable housing stock and leaving the community with a significant deficit of affordable units. This was the case in the year after Hurricane Katrina, when the percentage of New Orleans families overburdened by housing costs rose to 26 percent, spiking from 21 percent between 2008 and 2009.[40]

Helping disaster-impacted cities plan and develop affordable housing is an important role for local governments and their lawyers to fulfill. It is particularly noteworthy that the availability—or not—of adequate housing data played a critical role delaying development of thousands of units of affordable housing following Katrina. As the post-Katrina long-term recovery proved, however, building an adequate supply of affordable housing precipitated a battle with interests that oppose building apartments that would allow for low- and moderate-income families to concentrate in an urban area.

In October 2009, at the request of a well-known advocate for New Orleans–area landlords, the Louisiana Bond Commission imposed a multiyear moratorium on approval of bonds to support development of new affordable multifamily communities. In support of his argument for a moratorium, this landlord asserted that the Bond Commission lacked data showing that market demand in New Orleans and in other parts of Louisiana justified new affordable housing unit construction. The commission agreed with the landlord advocate and decided that it should procure a detailed housing market-demand report before it considered approval for more bonds to fund affordable housing. Although this moratorium was lifted for several affordable housing development projects for which the State later authorized an independent demand analysis, the moratorium continued for almost five years until 2014. The US Department of Justice later alleged that the state Bond Commission had engaged in impermissible housing discrimination, but it is noteworthy that uncertainty regarding affordable housing demand created the initial opening for affordable housing opponents to block much-needed replacement housing.

Conclusion

A wide range of professionals must cooperate to do the heavy lifting involved in long-term disaster recovery. The lawyers working in city halls, state agencies, nonprofits, and civic groups are always on the teams that help mend a city or state following disaster. Moreover, lawyers frequently play a leading role in creating and implementing a city's or a state's recovery plan and the redevelopment programs that implement those plans. Up until now, however, lawyers responsible for guiding communities through long-term recovery have had few resources to help highlight the important challenges and opportunities they will face. This isn't just unfortunate. It is also a deficiency that carries real human and economic costs for the communities lawyers are serving, not to mention the governments that are funding the recovery.

The imperative to educate and otherwise prepare lawyers to help lead communities through long-term recovery is gaining traction among members of the bar.[41] But it is important that these efforts are sustained and broadened. Law schools, for example, represent tremendous community resources. State governments, local governments, and community-based nonprofits represent potentially compelling partners for law school clinics, research seminars, and pro bono projects. Law students, law faculty, and staff attorneys are well-trained and ideally situated to conduct extended and in-depth audits of local and state laws to determine whether they are responsive to the urgent and extraordinary needs posed by major disaster events. Unfortunately, under the ongoing and looming threats associated with climate change and sea-level rise, the demand for lawyers to lead and staff long-term recovery efforts will only grow. Lawyers must continue to develop and improve their thinking as professionals who will be asked to serve communities emerging from disaster events. Together with local and state bar associations, nonprofits, and law schools, the profession must be prepared to assume this role.

NOTES

This author gives special thanks to Victor J. Franckiewicz Jr., Esq., partner in the New Orleans office of Butler Snow LLP. As chief outside counsel to the Louisiana Land Trust, a legislatively chartered nonprofit, Mr. Franckiewicz has played an essential role in helping the storm-impacted parishes of South Louisiana recover from the unprecedented destruction wrought by Hurricanes Katrina and Rita. This chapter is greatly informed by long-running conversations with Mr. Franckiewicz concerning the role of lawyers in regional and local long-term recovery.

1　Disaster recovery practitioners have noted that long-term disaster recovery has generally received less attention. *See* Claire B. Rubin, *Long-Term Recovery From Disasters—The Neglected Component of Emergency Management*, 6 J. OF HOMELAND SECURITY & EMERG. MGMNT. 1, 1–2 (2009) (reflecting that the base of knowledge concerning long-term recovery is "not adequate . . . there are very serious deficiencies in basic and applied research on the topic, and that means a weak foundation exists for current and future recovery planning and implementation").

2 *See* Gavin P. Smith & Dennis Wenger, *Sustainable Disaster Recovery: Operationalizing an Existing Agenda*, in Handbook of Disaster Research 234, 237 (H. Rodriguez et al. eds. 2006) (describing long-term recovery as "the process of restoring, rebuilding, and reshaping the physical, social, economic, and natural environment through pre-event planning and post-event actions").

3 John Travis Marshall, Ryan Rowberry & Ann-Margaret Esnard, *Core Capabilities and Capacities of Developer Nonprofits in Post-Disaster Community Rebuilding* 18 no. 2 Nat. Hazards Rev. 05016004-2 & 3 (2017).

4 *See, e.g.*, Melissa H. Luckman et al., *Three Years Later Sandy Survivors Remain Homeless*, 32 Touro L. Rev. 313, 346–49 (2016); William P. Quigley, *A Letter to Social Justice Advocates: Thirteen Lessons Learned by Katrina Social Justice Advocates Looking Back Ten Years Later*, 61 Loyola L. Rev. 623, 626–88 (2015).

5 William C. Nicholson, *Obtaining Competent Legal Advice: Challenges for Emergency Managers and Attorneys*, 46 Calif. W. L. Rev. 343, 362 (2010) (observing, for example, that there are no analyses of the working relationship between local government attorneys and local emergency managers).

6 *See* Joseph Jarret & Michele Lieberman, *"When the Wind Blows": The Role of the Local Government Attorney Before, During and in the Aftermath of a Disaster*, 36 Stetson L. Rev. 293, 324 (2007) (noting that "[d]isasters generate a wide array of crises, making it almost impossible to foresee even a substantial fraction of the situations that will mandate legal acumen and intervention").

7 *See* Clifford J. Villa, *The Practice of Disaster Law*, L. Practice Today (Mar. 2012).

8 Disaster mitigation planning is required of *both* state and local governments. *See* J. R. Nolon, *Disaster Mitigation Through Land Use Strategies*, 23 Pace Envtl. L. Rev. 959, 963–64 (2006).

9 William C. Nicholson, *Obtaining Competent Legal Advice: Challenges for Emergency Managers and Attorneys*, 46 Calif. W. L. Rev. 343, 353–54 (2010).

10 *Id.* at 355–56.

11 Denis Binder, *Emergency Action Plans: A Legal and Practical Blueprint "Failing to Plan is Planning to Fail,"* 63 U. Pitt. L. Rev. 791, 794–803 (2002).

12 *See, e.g.*, Nolon, *Disaster Mitigation*, 968–69.

13 Arthur C. Nelson, Ph.D., FAICP, Keynote Address, Rocky Mountain Land Use Institute (Mar. 13, 2015).

14 *See generally* Andrea McArdle, *Storm Surges, Disaster Planning, and Vulnerable Populations*, 50 Idaho L. Rev. 19 (2014).

15 *See* Andrew Rumbach & Carrie Makarewicz, *Affordable Housing and Disaster Recovery: A Case Study of the 2013 Colorado Floods*, in Coming Home After Disaster: Multiple Dimensions of Housing Recovery, 104 (Alka Sapat and Ann-Margaret Esnard eds. 2017); Panel Discussion, *Post-Disaster Long-Term Recovery: Critical Considerations for Resilient Communities*, Rocky Mountain Land Use Institute, University of Denver Strum College of Law, Denver

(with D. Bowman, D. Chandrasekhar, R. Ehrenfeucht, D. Finn & A. Rumbach) (Mar. 9, 2018) (transcript on file with the author).

16 *See id.*, Rumbach & Makarewicz, *Affordable Housing*, 104–05.

17 *See generally* DOUGLAS BRINKLEY, THE GREAT DELUGE: HURRICANE KATRINA, NEW ORLEANS, AND THE MISSISSIPPI GULF COAST (2007).

18 *See* Gerry Frug, *Why Rebuilding After Disasters Is Largely a Legal Challenge,* CITYLAB (Oct. 13, 2013), www.citylaw.com.

19 *See* NEW ORLEANS REDEVELOPMENT AUTHORITY: ABOUT, www. noraworks.org. The city itself retained some post-Katrina housing initiatives as well as a long list of highly visible citywide redevelopment projects. The city and NORA lacked access to any federal community development block grant funds for neighborhood revitalization projects until two years after Katrina and did not begin spending down that money until March 2009. *See* John Travis Marshall, *Rating the Cities: Constructing a City Resilience Index for Assessing the Effect of State and Local Laws on Long-Term Recovery From Crisis and Disaster,* 90 TULANE L. REV. 35, 37 (2015).

20 The State of Louisiana created the Road Home Homeowner Assistance Program ("Road Home") to compensate Louisiana homeowners whose houses were lost or damaged by Hurricanes Katrina and Rita. *See generally Greater New Orleans Fair Hous. Action Ctr., et al. v. U.S. Dep't of Hous. & Urb. Develop.,* 631 F.3d 1078, 1080 (D.C. Cir. 2011).

21 PARISH REDEVELOPMENT AND DISPOSITION PLAN FOR LOUISIANA LAND TRUST PROPERTIES (2007) (on file with author). This plan memorialized that the New Orleans City Council approved in December 2007 a disposition plan for the state, enumerating the New Orleans Redevelopment Authority's key disposition principles for returning the parish's 4,700-plus Road Home properties to commerce.

22 Raymond H. Brescia, Elizabeth A. Kelly & John Travis Marshall, *Crisis Management: Principles That Should Guide the Disposition of Federally Owned, Foreclosed Properties,* 45 IND. L. REV. 305, 331 & nn. 214–17 (2012).

23 Charles Chieppo, *New Orleans Winning Strategy in the War on Blight,* GOVERNING (Mar. 18, 2014), www.governing.com.

24 *See* Clifford J. Villa, *The Practice of Disaster Law,* L. PRACTICE TODAY (Mar. 2012).

25 *See generally* John Travis Marshall, *Rating the Cities: Constructing a City Resilience Index for Assessing the Effect of State and Local Laws on Long-Term Recovery From Crisis and Disaster,* 90 TULANE L. REV. 35 (2015).

26 *See* St. Tammany Parish, Mandeville, LA, Did Not Always Administer Its CDBG Disaster Recovery Grant in Accordance with HUD Requirements or as Certified (Apr. 6, 2017), Audit Report No. 2017-FW-1004.

27 *See* Office of Inspector General, Audit of FEMA Public Assistance Grant Funds Awarded to Downe Township, New Jersey (Sept. 17, 2017), OIG No.

OIG-17–106-D (the IG also cited the township's failure to follow regulations requiring the contractor to furnish invoices for work completed that are supported by documentation that describes hourly rate, equipment usage, and work activity logs).

28 *See* The City of New York, NY Did Not Always Use Disaster Recovery Funds Under Its Program for Eligible and Supported Expenses (Sept. 27, 2018) Audit Report No: 2018-NY-2007, 6.

29 *See* FEMA Should Recover $3,061,819 in Grant Funds Awarded to Jackson County, Florida (Dec. 4, 2018), OIG-19–12, 4.

30 *See* Ryan M. Seidemann, Megan M. Terrell & Christopher D. Matchett, *How Do We Deal With This Mess? A Primer for State and Local Governments on Navigating the Legal Complexities of Debris Issues Following Mass Disasters*, 61 U. MIAMI L. REV. 1135, 1147 (2007).

31 *See* Gerry Frug, *Why Rebuilding*. Frug explains that "[a]fter a major natural disaster, the redevelopment process opens up what might seem like intractable legal issues, including property buy-outs, beach access, insurance policy, and cross-jurisdictional governance."

32 This imbalance between low- and moderate-income renters and homeowners has been identified as a concern for Panama City, Florida, following Hurricane Michael. Panama City had an unusually high number of low- and moderate-income renters—a number that approached 75 percent of all residents. *See* Presentation by Mark McQueen, City Manager, City of Panama City, Florida; Bankers and Community Partners Forum Focusing on Hurricane Michael Disaster Recovery hosted by the Federal Deposit Insurance Corporation, the Federal Reserve Bank of Atlanta, and the Office of the Comptroller of the Currency (Jan. 29, 2019) (notes on file with author).

33 *See* Jarret & Lieberman, *"When the Wind Blows,"*293, 312 (2007).

34 *See* Interview with Christopher Cohilas, Esq., Chairman, County Commission, Dougherty County, GA (June 13, 2019) (notes on file with author).

35 *See, e.g.*, The Institute for Economic Development and Real Estate Research et. al., An Advisory Report: Housing Market Dynamics in the New Orleans Area (Feb. 15, 2010), 8–9.

36 Greater New Orleans Community Data Center, OPTIMIZING BLIGHT STRATEGIES: DEPLOYING LIMITED RESOURCES IN DIFFERENT NEIGHBORHOOD HOUSING MARKETS (2010).

37 Extremely low-income families earn less than 30 percent of area median income (AMI). Very low-income families earn 30–50 percent of AMI. Low-income families take home 50–80 percent AMI, and moderate-income families earn 80–100 percent of AMI.

38 In the United States in 2000, approximately 14.5% of Americans lived in single-family attached rentals, including duplexes, triplexes, or quadraplexes. In New Orleans, that number was dramatically higher. Almost 37 percent of families live

in small attached single-family units. *See, e.g.*, The Institute for Economic Development and Real Estate Research et. al., An Advisory Report: Housing Market Dynamics in the New Orleans Area (Feb. 15, 2010), 4.

39 Keith Wardrip, Center for Housing Policy Housing Landscape 2011: An Annual Look at the Housing Affordability Challenges of America's Working Households (Feb. 2011), 1.

40 *Id.* at 7.

41 *See* American Bar Association (ABA) House of Delegates' Resolution No. 108 (2017), encouraging lawyers to work with "communities to adopt standards, guidance, best practices, regulatory systems, and programs that will make communities more resilient to loss and damage from foreseeable hazards and enhance the disaster resilience of communities."

8

Judging and Mediating for the "Long Emergency"

Superstorm Sandy, New York State's Regulatory Response to the Climate Change Crisis, and Reforming the Energy Vision

ELEANOR STEIN

Not every crisis arrives full-blown, and some emergencies are processes, not events. When Superstorm Sandy hit New York City on October 29, 2012, it created an immediate and devastating crisis across the East Coast: 159 lives lost, $66 billion in storm damage, and 8.5 million without power. Lower Manhattan was blacked out for days, and homes were destroyed in borough neighborhoods. Automobiles and vans floated down East 13th Street in Manhattan, and waterfronts were destroyed in Brooklyn, Queens, and Long Island. Superstorm Sandy hit New York City at the Battery, sending floodwater into the streets, sewers, and subway tunnels of Lower Manhattan. At the time, Sandy was the second costliest and most destructive storm in US history.[1] The city's storm barrier at the Battery was built to withstand an 11-foot storm surge, the previous highest recorded in 1821; Sandy came in like a freight train at 14 feet.[2]

The federal government, New York State, New York City, and New York City's power company, Consolidated Edison, may have been well-prepared to meet the floods and storms of the past thirty years, but, as the climate change scientists had accurately warned, the past was no longer a guide to future cataclysmic weather events.

This chapter is a case study of post-Sandy decision-making by state regulators and government, closing with the transition to the subsequent project, New York State's Reforming the Energy Vision (REV).[3] It is written from the point of view of the administrative law judge (ALJ) charged with bringing diverse parties together, ensuring equitable participation for affected communities, and mobilizing climate scientists and thought leaders to advise and generate meaningful recommendations to decision makers—all with an eye to the high stakes of these projects.

When Sandy struck, I was an administrative law judge at the agency responsible for the regulation of the state's energy industry, the New York State

Public Service Commission (PSC). I had experience presiding over commission cases addressing renewable energy, energy efficiency, and extreme weather-related blackouts, and I had been teaching the law of climate change since 2005 at Albany Law School and the State University of New York at Albany. A catastrophe of the scale of Sandy created tragedies and losses, but it also created an opportunity for the state and the energy industry to acknowledge that climate change was a major contributor to the storm and to reexamine the rising ambient heat, extreme heat waves, floods, and storms the region had suffered in increasing intensity in the previous decade. Only with this realization could come the development of innovative measures aimed not only at planning for the last storm but also at mitigating the power and impact of future storms and other climate-change-related catastrophes by reducing our emissions from the combustion of fossil fuels and by prudent adaptation to safeguard the state from rapidly changing conditions.

Within my capacity as an ALJ and mediator at the PSC, I brought experience and expertise in climate change matters. I, along with many colleagues, hoped to move climate change to the forefront of the commission's agenda and the state's approach to Sandy's aftermath. The first vehicle presented to do so was a petition filed by leading legal climate change advocates. Calling on the PSC to recognize the new reality confronting the energy industry and the regulators, just weeks after Sandy, the Columbia Center for Climate Change Law[4] and others filed a letter petition to the commission.[5] It stated:

> Utilities are not currently required to engage in long-term hazard mitigation planning, which would consider future projections for the natural hazards that may affect New York State given changing climate conditions and then determine how best to mitigate risks to the reliable provision of utility services. The Public Service Commission, fulfilling its duty to encourage the formulation of long-range programs, care for the public safety and ensure reliability of service, should require all utility companies within its jurisdiction to take these steps. This petition asks that the Public Service Commission take action as soon as possible to require New York's utilities to consider how their infrastructure and service delivery may be impacted by the extreme weather scenarios that are predicted to occur in the future and to develop plans for how those risks can best be mitigated.[6]

The commission did not act on the Columbia petition; however, a second vehicle presented itself only weeks later in the form of a filing submitted by Consolidated Edison Company of New York, Inc. (Con Edison), specifically, a petition seeking an increase in its rates.[7] The Con Edison rate filing requested an increase in existing electric rates of approximately 3.3 percent, but it also included a request for roughly another $1 billion for what the company termed "storm hardening": "potential storm hardening structural improvements over the next four years that are intended to reduce the size and scope of service outages from major storms, as well as to improve responsiveness and expedite the recovery process to better serve our customers."[8] In the filing letter, Con Edison anticipated working with city and state governments, as well as other stakeholders, in finalizing storm-hardening plans.

Although New York and other state regulatory commissions establish policy through generic cases, it is in rate cases that policy determinations come to life in the specifics of how the utility will be spending the money it collects from its customers. Rate cases are expected to take at least eleven months to complete and have extensive requirements for public information, evidentiary filings, and procedure. After the utility files its initial case, PSC staff and other parties may file their own testimony, and evidentiary hearings provide for cross-examination. Because all the company's forecast future expenditures are reviewed—the subject of 1,000 exhibits in this case—a specific issue area such as resiliency is likely to get lost.[9]

Recognizing this difficulty, on July 1, 2013, the PSC established a separate collaborative track to ensure a full treatment of the resilience issues, to proceed in parallel with the litigated evidentiary proceedings.[10] In a collaborative track, there was evident potential to create a mediated process to bring together government, the energy industry, academia, customer advocates, and thought leaders on climate change. The participants included not only Con Edison and PSC staff within the Department of Public Service but also the city of New York, the state attorney general's office, the Columbia Law School Center for Climate Change Law, Pace Law School Climate Change and Energy Center (PACE), the Natural Resources Defense Council (NRDC), the Environmental Defense Fund (EDF), plus many other environmental and customer advocacy groups. The regulatory response to Sandy developed in the Con Edison rate case filed in January 2013, which included a resiliency collaborative and a reexamination of the role of renewable energy and energy efficiency, especially of the changes needed in the organization and regulation of the energy industry. I was also the initial ALJ assigned to that case, then became a policy adviser to Public Service Commission chair Audrey Zibelman and project manager. In that capacity, I was particularly engaged in the public participation process, reaching out to energy democracy and environmental justice advocates, as well as industry, government, and consumer representatives.

In the immediate post-Sandy crisis and its aftermath, my work stretched the limitations of the usual role of ALJs in administrative cases. That role is usually characterized by judges managing the calendar and discovery procedures in quasijudicial proceedings; conducting formal evidentiary hearings and presiding over public statement hearings; and analyzing the evidence and penning recommended decisions for the PSC, the final decision maker, to act. At its narrowest, one view of the role of the ALJ is similar to that posed by John Roberts, who observed during his nomination for the US Supreme Court chief justice position: "[J]udges are like umpires. Umpires don't make the rules, they apply them. The role of an umpire and a judge is critical. . . . [I]t's my job to call balls and strikes."[11]

But the ALJ role is not limited to procedural decisions or mechanically applying rules. That role encompasses two critical responsibilities: building a robust and complete record to support PSC decision-making, and ensuring the participation of all interested stakeholders. In the post-Sandy world, I interpreted these mandates expansively to entail including record evidence on climate change and welcoming full participation by the thought leaders in this field—including climate scientists and the climate advocacy community.

The expectation that a judge or mediator be "neutral" as to substantive policies, especially faced with crisis conditions, is misguided. We all have opinions, especially as to issues like climate change, the protection of low-income customers, and equity for communities of color. Being fair to all parties and points of view is a more relevant quality than an unattainable neutrality. My views on the urgency of addressing climate change were on full public view in my teaching and writings. There were situations, however, where it was important to reveal potential conflicts of interest. In a few cases my husband, Jeff Jones, an environmental advocate and communications strategist, consulted for organizations that were parties in my case. Working with the agency ethics officer, I disclosed this potential conflict in a letter to all parties, including my commitment that this would not jeopardize my fair judgment in the case. No party ever moved for my recusal.

Once I was charged with facilitating the resiliency collaborative, I was no longer serving as a judge in the administrative litigation. The PSC practice is to distinguish the role of a settlement judge, who may mediate disputes or establish schedules for negotiation but who does not make recommendations for outcomes to the commission. An ALJ serving as the litigation judge continues to oversee the ongoing litigation and may write a recommended decision or internal recommendations to the commission for the outcome of the litigation. This functional separation protects parties, as settlement judges will be privy to offers to settle and other off-the-record material that should play no role in the final commission determination. As facilitator, I had greater freedom to explore alternative solutions with the parties and to assist in their problem-solving.[12] And as the collaborative progressed, its work came to resemble mutual problem-solving more than litigation.

But over and above these considerations, I considered it my responsibility to do everything I could to advance the discussion of climate change in government and to push for more aggressive mitigation of the greenhouse gas emissions from the energy industry's combustion of fossil fuels. In my view, that is a moral imperative given the current and future suffering of those exposed to apocalyptic climate-induced floods, storms, rising sea levels, wildfires, and heat waves.

Background: Climate Change

In the case of climate change, this emergency has long been expected. Scientists predicted in the nineteenth century the consequences of adding carbon to the planet's atmosphere. When Superstorm Sandy (downgraded from a hurricane) hit New York City, the impact was disastrous, and the federal, state, and city authorities and Con Edison were ill-equipped to respond. Although government, utilities, and media generally described Sandy as not just unforeseen but unforeseeable, climate scientists had, in fact, anticipated just such a storm, and its impacts, for a long time. Corporate fossil fuel giants have been informed by their in-house scientists at least since the 1970s of the planet-altering result of burning fossil fuels and of the potentially disastrous consequences of releasing increasing tonnage of carbon dioxide and other greenhouse gases into the earth's atmosphere.[13] In 1978, senior Exxon scientist James Black warned the company that doubling atmospheric CO_2 would warm the planet by 2–3 degrees Celsius and that "present thinking holds that man has a time window of five to 10 years before the need for hard decisions regarding changes in energy strategies might become critical."[14]

Similarly, governments have long been on notice of the climate threat. Renowned climate scientist James Hansen, former director of NASA's Goddard Institute for Space Studies, testified before Congress in 1988. He explained how climate change had loaded the atmospheric dice in favor of extreme heat events.[15] But almost twenty years earlier, then–White House aide Daniel Patrick Moynihan sent a warning letter about greenhouse gas emissions to President Richard Nixon adviser John Ehrlichman: "[T]his very clearly is a problem, and, perhaps most particularly, is one that can seize the imagination of persons normally indifferent to projects of apocalyptic change."[16] By the late 1980s, visionary writers were already warning the rest of us of what was coming, including science writer Bill McKibben in *The End of Nature* and novelist Marge Piercy in *He, She and It*.

Superstorm Sandy awakened the state of New York to the urgency of climate change: it was not merely a problem of extreme, isolated weather events and vague, distant future predictions of harm but rather a long emergency with dire consequences in the here and now. "Climate change" became part of the state government's lexicon at last.

In addition, the storm heightened the mobilization of environmental justice, customer, and community advocates pressing for action, with many government agencies, corporations, and academics stepping up to assess the causes and consequences of the storm, the protracted power outages, and the extensive damage. Notably, while the utility grid was down in much of metropolitan New York, facilities relying on microgrids, on solar power, and on combined heat and power were conspicuously successful in keeping the lights and heat on during the crisis.[17] To prepare for future disasters based on the lessons from Sandy, the most important lesson becomes: in the Anthropocene Epoch, the past is no longer the best guide to the future.[18]

The Mediation Process at the Public Service Commission

The sources I rely on, documented here, can all be found in the public record. My role in the post-Sandy proceedings was as facilitator of a collaborative process established by the PSC. The outcome of this effort was a joint proposal entered into by most of the participating parties following settlement discussions on all rate case issues, including the resiliency issues stemming from the collaborative. The settlement discussions are subject to the PSC confidentiality rules, which provide:

> No discussion, admission, concession or offer to stipulate or settle, whether oral or written, made during any negotiation session concerning a stipulation or settlement shall be subject to discovery, or admissible in any evidentiary hearing against any participant who objects to its admission. Participating parties, their representatives and other persons attending settlement negotiations shall hold confidential such discussions, admissions, concessions, and offers to settle and shall not disclose them outside the negotiations.

Because the PSC encourages mediation and other forms of collaboration, its confidentiality regulations apply not only to participants but also to any "neutral" parties and to the disclosure by mediators of oral or written communications prepared for the purpose of a mediation.[19] Fortunately, the commission's public record makes publicly available testimony, comments and reply comments, as well as statements on the Con Edison resiliency report that followed the collaborative and on the joint proposal itself. Of course, the notices and orders issued by the commission itself are also instructive and, in this case, voluminous.[20]

Con Edison had been preparing to file its rate cases in November 2012, seeking rate increases for electric and gas service. After Superstorm Sandy struck, it postponed that filing in order to incorporate proposals for a new set of extraordinary measures designed to modify its construction practices and standards to prevent similar damage from future storms. The crisis, including billions in damages to energy infrastructure in the region, interrupted Con Edison's business as usual and opened its eyes to the new imperative posed by climate change: a hundred years of consistent weather patterns were no longer a guide to future storm events.

In Con Edison's rate filing, for example, it proposed to rebuild the storm-damaged infrastructure by raising ground-floor or otherwise vulnerable facilities.[21] But to many collaborative participants, the failures of the utility during the storm were traceable to outmoded standards and even to the fundamental configuration of utility design. The collaborative soon became a place to interrogate what a post-Sandy utility should look like, what kinds of changes were driven by the shortcomings of a system designed decades ago, and the potential of new technologies and a mobilized community—what was called the "utility of the future." Shaken by the crisis, Con Edison was willing to consider and adopt system changes it had not seriously entertained in the past—and it was willing to accept the intervention of collaborative members in areas that implicated historically guarded domains (in how the utility assessed risk, for example).

The collaborative process provided a blank canvas for the stakeholders to envision changes in risk assessment, alternatives to traditional utility capital investments, and the long-term impacts of climate change on the electric system. In the end, Con Edison and almost all other parties agreed to propose jointly to the PSC some innovative outcomes, including in areas the commission would have had no authority to order the utility to comply. The use of alternative dispute resolution collaboration—in the shadow of the crisis—created added value and opportunity beyond the reach of a typical regulatory rate case.

Mediators/ALJs at the PSC have had many opportunities to realize the value of collaborative conversation in times of crisis. For example, in the summer of 2006, in the course of a protracted and unanticipated heat wave, 175,000 Con Edison customers in Western Queens experienced a nine-day outage. The PSC mandated its staff to investigate whether the utility's decisions during the heat wave were reasonable; if not, shareholders rather than customers might have to pay the cost of recovery. A settlement process was begun in the course of the regulatory litigation on this investigation, and I was appointed settlement judge (or mediator). Normally adversarial, government, industry, utility, and community parties began a collaborative process that resulted in an extraordinary joint proposal to the commission. Critical to the collaboration was the participation of a newly formed neighborhood group, Western Queens Power to the People. That joint proposal provided for termination of the review of utility actions during the outage, in exchange for a $46 million rate benefit for all Con Edison customers—a remedy often applied in similar cases. But in addition to that remedy, Con Edison created a $17 million "community benefit fund" for the Western Queens community. This fund was dedicated as follows: half of it was returned to Western Queens customers as credits on their bills, and the other half was dedicated to a community fund for uses approved by community groups. This portion went toward planting trees in the affected neighborhoods, energy reduction enhancements, and other environmental benefits. Also included were funding for a study of the economic and health consequences of the outage and—of primary importance to the community negotiators—a personal letter of apology to affected customers from the utility's CEO. For me, this experience was an object lesson in the power of leading collective discussion and of nonpositional negotiation. But it was also an object lesson in how far we had to go to seriously address the impacts of climate change on our energy systems. In that case, there was little discussion about the causes of the extraordinary heat wave or about the lack of consideration by either the utility or the state of the patterns of increases in ambient temperatures and of extreme heat events in the Northeast—patterns well understood by climate scientists at the time. During a break in the hearings on utility prudence, I asked one young Con Edison engineer, off the record, whether the outage could have been prevented by anticipating the problem and ensuring significant reductions in electric usage: "In hindsight, wouldn't it have been cheaper to install free energy star air conditioners for everyone in the neighborhood?" in comparison to the costs of the outage and its aftermath. "Of course," he responded.

I had been an ALJ at the PSC since 1994, after three years as an appellate litigator and two as session counsel to the PSC chair at the time, Peter A. Bradford.[22] As a judge I presided over many cases with environmental dimensions, from the siting of electric transmission and natural gas pipelines to New York's first Renewable Portfolio Standard (RPS). It was this case that opened my eyes to the rolling crisis that is climate change.

In his 2003 State of the State address, Governor George Pataki announced the goal of obtaining 25 percent of the state's electricity from renewable resources—solar, wind, biofuel, and hydropower—by the year 2013. After a series of hearings and public meetings, the PSC issued, for comment, my recommended decision; although the commission neither used nor adopted my approach to climate change, it did adopt the RPS program. The 2004 recommended decision opened with this context:

> The earth's warming during the twentieth century is the greatest in the past millennium, and the 1990s were possibly the warmest decade in a thousand years. This extreme climate change is producing catastrophic storms, glacial melt, ocean warming, and species extinctions. Caused by human industrial activity—the release and concentration of greenhouse gases, predominantly carbon dioxide (CO_2) in the earth's atmosphere—this trend will not easily be reversed. The generation of electricity from fossil fuel is a major contributor."[23]

Shortly after, I designed and taught courses on climate change law at both Albany Law School and the State University of New York at Albany. I continue to teach these courses, increasingly with an international law, human rights, and climate justice bent. Teaching the subject both required and enabled me to stay abreast of the rapidly changing and evolving field of climate change law. There was no casebook for the first years I taught climate change, although there are many to choose from today. I coteach with climate scientists and find that engagement with climate science, with changing international, federal, and state laws, keeps me engaged and current. I was also able to bring these resources into my work and to make climate scientists available to commissioners and staff at the PSC.[24]

The Con Edison Resiliency Collaborative

As one of three ALJs assigned to the Con Edison rate case, I was responsible for managing a collaborative effort among all stakeholders to assess the utility's recovery and reconstruction plans.[25] These plans were characterized by Con Edison as "storm hardening" and were the underpinning of its request for $1 billion from its customers to recover the costs of rebuilding its network and better equipping it to withstand Sandy-type events. As in any rate case, a request by a utility to recover funds from its customers to cover construction projects was subject to scrutiny by the DPS staff. In this case, the storm-hardening request was also intensively assessed by the office of the New York State Attorney General, counsel for New York City and the city's Sustainability Task Force, Columbia Law School's climate change center, the

EDF, and the NRDC, as well as numerous other environmental advocacy NGOs, consumer groups, and federal and state agencies.[26]

Con Edison filed its rate case in January 2013. The utility informed the commission:

> [Based] on our experience with Sandy, these new rate filings focus on the need for investments and preventive measures to further strengthen critical infrastructure designed to reduce the impact of future major storms on our customers. Specifically, the filings include approximately $1 billion in potential storm hardening structural improvements over the next four years that are intended to reduce the size and scope of service outages from major storms.[27]

The NGO parties warned that the company's single-issue focus on its existing infrastructure and its response to the last storm precluded consideration of alternative approaches. These, advocates argued, would take into account a wide range of anticipated climate change impacts and birth a forward-looking energy system.

Columbia's expert witness, the climate change scientist Radley Horton, testified in the rate hearings as follows:

Q: In your opinion, would a past 30-year average of New York weather accurately reflect the predicted future climate of New York State?

A: No. As greenhouse gas concentrations continue to rise, the climate of New York State and New York City is projected to change as well. By the 2020s, we would expect the climate of New York State and New York City to be statistically different from the climate we have experienced over the past 30 years. This difference will only increase as we move further into the 2050s, 2080s, and to 2100. Using the past 30-year average of weather as a benchmark for risk management would be unwise and contrary to our current scientific understanding.

Q: How would you recommend that Con Edison prepare for future weather conditions?

A: I would encourage Con Edison to engage with scientists to understand the climate scenario predictions and what those predictions might mean for Con Edison's vulnerability. Based on these predictions, I would also encourage Con Edison to conduct a comprehensive evaluation of its current and projected future vulnerability both to temperature increase and extreme weather events. Long-term infrastructure investments should be guided by an understanding of the climate factors that the infrastructure will have to operate in.[28]

Electric utilities are legally responsible for the reliability of their service and traditionally file regular reliability plans and emergency response plans to ensure their preparedness for extraordinary, force majeure events that may require mobilization of forces and equipment or even calling in mutual aid from neighboring jurisdictions in case of extensive outages. But these protocols, as we are currently witnessing in post–Hurricane Maria Puerto Rico, are designed for short-term responses to weather aberrations and turn out to be inadequate for the patterns of severe impacts resulting from changes in the climate.[29] Yet regulators and utilities have been reluctant to develop new approaches for the new reality—until disasters strike.

A utility rate case entails almost a year of litigation, extensive filed testimony, and cross-examination of witnesses on a broad range of issues treating the justification for the company's request for an increase in rates. In this case, the entry of environmental parties, New York City, and the state attorney general, among others, guaranteed that momentous issues of policy would also be on the rate case agenda—that, in fact, the issues raised by Columbia's petition would be adjudicated in the rate case, a foreign forum for many who ultimately participated.

In the course of weeks of hard-fought evidentiary hearings on a range of rate issues, it became clear that the policy issues were not essentially evidentiary in nature and should be considered on a separate track from the traditional rate-case issues. Accordingly, the PSC instituted a collaborative process in July 2013 to consider "storm hardening and resiliency issues." The first charge to the collaborative was to establish ground rules, a working schedule, and the scope of collaboration in the context of the progress of the rate cases as a whole. By this notice, the commission appointed me facilitator of the collaborative.[30] Collaborative sessions continued until fall 2013, when parties began negotiation of an overall rate settlement that would encompass agreements on the resiliency issues.[31]

As noted, the Sandy experience exposed the vulnerability of a historically reliable power grid to threats that were not only new but also continually changing (then and now). The extended electrical outage also demonstrated the flexibility and value of solar facilities and other electric generation resources that were distributed—that is, decentralized—in comparison to the decades-old utility model of large, fossil-fueled, central generating stations.[32]

The collaborative and its working groups conducted activities from July 8, 2013, to November 19 of that year. Among the key issues addressed was that the utility's reliance on long outdated Federal Emergency Management Agency (FEMA) floodplain maps was urgent in order to ensure that updated maps were used in the upcoming utility rebuilds. The participants had agreed to 2014 projects and budgets for the utility. Con Edison, like New York City and many other jurisdictions and utilities, relied on FEMA floodplain maps developed in 1983.[33] Although updated, nonfinal, working maps were available, these were the basis for utility planning. The FEMA maps are the industry and government standard for all infrastructure construction and repair: they indicate floodplains where construction is inadvisable or dicey. Since a great deal of utility building is on waterfronts, these sources are critical. The floodplain maps are based on records of the worst flood in a hundred years or the worst in five hundred years as a proxy for the odds of such floods recurring. So, a hundred-year flood is estimated to have a 1 percent chance of occurring in a given year. The outdated FEMA maps indicated that 33 square miles might flood; in fact, Sandy flooding exceeded the hundred-year floodplain boundaries by 53 percent. The updated working maps doubled the number of buildings included in the floodplain in New York City—from 400,000 to 800,000. Through the collaborative, the parties most concerned about this issue negotiated a stipulation committing the utility to use the most current FEMA floodplain maps in its upcoming planning and construction. That said, FEMA apparently still does not reflect anticipated climate change impacts, including sea-level rise, in its updated flood maps, notwithstanding that 17 percent of the city's total land mass was flooded by Sandy.[34] In an innovative addition, the stipulation provided standards for construction in flood-vulnerable areas requiring FEMA protections, plus an additional 3 feet to take sea level–rise predictions into account.

Other major issues resolved collaboratively included a reassessment of utility risk calculations, to include consideration of probability of climate-related risks over time, and an agreement that Con Edison would contract with Columbia's Earth Institute to conduct a long-term study of adverse risks of climate change to its infrastructure and organization. The PSC also ordered all other New York utilities to likewise work with climate experts to craft evidence-based future climate resilience plans.[35]

Finally, after considerable controversy, Con Edison agreed to modify its original filing request for over $1 billion for the construction of a new substation to meet the growing electricity needs of customers in Brownsville, Brooklyn. In the collaborative, other parties counterproposed that Brownsville's needs could be met more economically and with greater resilience by a combination of strategies. These strategies included making the customers' energy usage more efficient and flexible, installation of solar power and other renewable energy, and relying on distributed resources from alternative sources, saving hundreds of millions of dollars and enabling communities to "island" from the central grid and maintain their own power system in times of crisis. These resolutions were also approved by the commission in its 2014 Con Edison rate order.[36]

Of these, the Brownville project, renamed Brooklyn/Queens Demand Management, became the symbol and front line of a new commission and state regulatory approach to reduction of greenhouse gas emissions, resiliency, energy affordability, and the distribution of energy resources: Reforming the Energy Vision.[37] After being appointed ALJ for this proceeding, in September 2014, I moved from the judge's role to be appointed by PSC Chair Audrey Zibelman as project manager for REV. In that capacity I joined the chair's policy team. But I saw my best contribution as establishing ties with, and accountability to, environmental justice and climate justice groups, as well as grassroots environmental organizations and representatives of low income New Yorkers—those hardest hit by climate change and its consequences.[38] For example, the New York City Environmental Justice Alliance convened the Sandy Regional Assembly to create its own "Recovery Agenda," with a critical analysis of New York City's post-Sandy efforts for low-income people and communities of color.[39]

Conclusion

In a recent talk, the *New Yorker* writer and author of two major books about climate change, Elizabeth Kolbert,[40] warned that all the major climate markers are arriving earlier than anticipated: the destruction of the Australian Great Barrier Reef was anticipated, but not for thirty to forty years; pollinator populations are crashing; and fish populations are being destroyed by warming waters.[41] Climate change is increasingly understood to be at the root of destabilizing population migrations[42] and as a force multiplier for social dislocation, international conflict, and war.[43]

My climate scientist colleagues have always told me that the United States will never make real progress in recognizing the immediacy of climate change and responding with appropriate urgency, priority, and resources until this country is consumed by cataclysmic climate change events—the implication being that it is pointless to agitate for the needed level of response before that time. However, Hurricane Katrina, Superstorm Sandy, Hurricane Harvey, and Hurricane Maria have come and gone, and our federal government today has withdrawn from the Paris Agreement and is intent upon rescuing the coal industry, the most dangerous energy resource on the planet.

In times like this, meaningful action by states and cities, as well as civil society protests and activism—in the United States and around the world—become even more critically important. The day after Donald Trump announced the US withdrawal from the Paris Agreement, New York, California, and a dozen other states proclaimed themselves the United States Climate

Alliance, pledging to continue to meet the Paris goals and adopt even stricter emission reduction policies.

Superstorm Sandy marked a crisis point: New York's lights went out, streets became flooded, and we witnessed how crisis can do terrible damage. Now, after Hurricane Maria, we are watching climate shock used in Puerto Rico by disaster capitalists[44] to consolidate and advance their privatization and austerity agenda that would be unattainable under a normal democratic process. Yet post-Sandy, we see that, with collective action to respond, crisis can also be a platform for profound positive change.

NOTES

The chapter title is drawn from James Howard Kunstler, THE LONG EMERGENCY: SURVIVING THE END OF OIL, CLIMATE CHANGE, AND OTHER CONVERGING CATASTROPHES OF THE TWENTY-FIRST CENTURY (2005).

1 Hurricane Katrina (2005) was the costliest, but Hurricane Harvey, causing immense damage to the Houston area, and then Hurricane Maria (both in 2017), set new records. The latest study by the Milliken Institute School of Public Health at the George Washington University puts the death toll six months after the event itself at 2,975. Milliken Institute School of Public Health, George Washington University, *Ascertainment of the Estimated Excess Mortality From Hurricane Maria in Puerto Rico*, iii, https://publichealth.gwu.edu.

2 James M. Van Nostrand, *Keeping the Lights on During Superstorm Sandy: Climate Change Adaptation and the Resiliency Benefits of Distributed Generation*, 23 N.Y.U. ENVTL. L.J., 92 (2015).

3 New York State Public Service Commission, *Reforming the Energy Vision*, No. 14-M-0101, Order Instituting Proceeding (Feb. 2014).

4 This center is now the Sabin Center for Climate Change Law at Columbia Law School; its PSC filings on the Con Edison case are filed as Columbia Law School Center for Climate Change Law, and for consistency's sake I identify the Center under that name or as Columbia.

5 In addition to Columbia, petitioners included the Natural Resources Defense Council, Earthjustice, New York League of Conservation Voters, Municipal Art Society of New York, and Hudson Riverkeeper.

6 Anne R. Siders, *Letter to Commission Secretary*, COLUM. CTR. FOR CLIMATE CHANGE L. 1 (Dec. 12, 2012), https://web.law.columbia.edu.

7 N.Y. P.S.C. Nos. 13-E-0030 Letter from Con Edison President Craig S. Ivey to Public Service Commission Acting Secretary Jeffrey C. Cohen, Jan. 25, 2013, 1 (hereinafter "Con Edison Rate Filing Letter") (on file with author).

8 *Id.*

9 New York's Public Service Law § 65 provides that utility rates and charges must be just and reasonable—that is, approved by the state regulator. The extensive regulations governing requirements for filing for new rates and adjudicating the

utility requests are found in 16 N.Y.C.R.R. The breadth and complexity of a Con Edison rate case makes participation by intervenors and the public difficult. This case concerned the company's three services—electric, natural gas, and steam, as well as issues ranging from increasing reliability to providing utility incentives to keeping rate increases (reflected in customer bills) manageable. *See* N.Y. P.S.C. Case 13-E-0030 et al., Order Approving Electric, Gas and Steam Rate Plans in Accord with Joint Proposal, 71 (Feb. 21, 2014), http://documents.dps.ny.gov.

10 Notice of Collaborative Meeting Concerning Storm Hardening and Resiliency Issues, Con Edison Rates, N.Y. P.S.C. Case 13-E-0030 et al., http://documents.dps.ny.gov.

11 *Chief Justice Roberts Statement—Nomination Process*, U.S. CTS. (2005), www.uscourts.gov.

12 This latitude may resemble that of problem-solving courts working in specialized areas of law, documented in Raymond H. Brescia, *Capital in Chaos: The Subprime Mortgage Crisis and the Social Capital Response*, 56 CLEV. ST. L. REV. 271, 308 (2008).

13 Shannon Hall, *Exxon Knew About Climate Change Almost 40 Years Ago*, SCI. AM. (Oct. 26, 2015); *see also* NAOMI ORESKES & ERIK M. CONWAY, MERCHANTS OF DOUBT (1st ed. 2010).

14 Hall, *Exxon Knew*.

15 Dr. James Hansen, *Statement*, NASA GODDARD INST. FOR SPACE STUD., https://climatechange.procon.org/sourcefiles/1988_Hansen_Senate_Testimony.pdf.

16 Letter from Daniel Patrick Moynihan to John Ehrlichman regarding carbon dioxide and climate change (Sept. 17, 1969), www.energyhistory.yale.edu.

17 Combined heat and power (CHP) technology provides customers with a fuel source, usually natural gas, capable of heating the premises and also generating electricity with that fuel. Along with solar installations, fourteen facilities in the Sandy-affected region functioned through the Sandy devastation. *See* Van Nostrand, *Keeping the Light*, 116.

18 Many scientists now refer to the current era as the "Anthropocene," based on observations that "human-kind has caused mass extinctions of plant and animal species, polluted the oceans and altered the atmosphere, among other lasting impacts." Joseph Stromberg, *The Age of Humans Living in the Anthropocene: What Is the Anthropocene and Are We in It?*, SMITHSONIAN (Jan. 2013),www.smithsonianmag.com. The Anthropocene follows the 11,700-year-old Holocene. Will Steffen, head of Australia National University's Climate Change Institute, writes about how to date this new geological era, discussing the work of the atmospheric chemist and Nobel laureate Paul Crutzen, who popularized the nomenclature in 2000. Steffen starts the epoch in the early 1800s with the Industrial Revolution or in the 1950s for the Atomic Age. Either way, he urges that the new naming is "another strong reminder to the general public that we are now having undeniable impacts on the environment at the scale of the planet as a whole, so much so that a new geological epoch has begun." *Id.*

19 Confidentiality of Settlement Discussions, 16 N.Y.C.R.R. 3.9(d) and (e).
20 The Commission Con Edison rate case record can be accessed at http://docu-ments.dps.ny.gov. All documents referred to in that case, 13-E-0030, are contained in this record, http://documents.dps.ny.gov/public/MatterManagement/CaseMaster.aspx?MatterCaseNo=13-E-0030&submit=Search.
21 Con Edison Filing Letter from Con Edison President Craig S. Ivey to PSC Secretary Jeffrey C. Cohen (Jan. 25, 2013).
22 Peter Bradford had served as chairman of the Maine Public Service Commission and then as a member of the Nuclear Regulatory Commission, appointed by President Jimmy Carter. As N.Y. P.S.C. chairman he instituted extensive energy efficiency and demand-side management initiatives to reduce the state's electricity usage.
23 Renewable Portfolio Standard, N.Y.P.S.C. Case 04-E-0188, Recommended Decision (June 4, 2004).
24 For my thoughts about teaching these courses, *see* Eleanor Stein, *Ignorance/Denial/Fear/Paralysis/Engagement/Commitment: Reflections on a Decade Teaching Climate Change Law*, 102 RADICAL TCHR (2015).
25 The Commission adopted a definition of resiliency from the report to the governor by his N.Y.S. 2100 Commission: "Resilience is the ability of a system to withstand shocks and stresses while still maintaining its essential functions." *Recommendations to Improve the Strength and Resilience of the Empire State's Infrastructure*, CON EDISON RATE ORDER, 63 www.governor.ny.gov/assets/documents/NYS2100.pdf. There are as many definitions of resiliency as there are definers, apparently. In my view, "resilience" is generally used as a euphemism for "climate adaptation": safeguarding against those impacts that are already baked into the climate system as a result of past greenhouse gas emissions.
26 Participants in the Collaborative were: DPS Staff, Con Edison, New York City (NYC), Office of the Attorney General (OAG), Department of State Utility Intervention Unit (UIU), Department of Environmental Conservation (DEC), Westchester County, NYU School of Law Guarini Center on Environmental and Land Use Law, Institute for Policy Integrity (NYU), Public Utility Law Project (PULP), NYECC, CPA, Utility Workers Union of America (UWUA) Local 1–2, Energy Initiative Group LLC, and the Non-Governmental Organizations (NGOs), comprising EDF, Pace, Columbia, and NRDC. *See* CON EDISON RATE ORDER, 63.
27 Filing Letter, Rates and Services of Consolidated Edison Company of New York, Inc., Nos. 13-M-0030 et al., (Jan. 25, 2013) (hereinafter "Con Edison Rate Case").
28 Dr. Horton was an associate research scientist at the Center for Climate System, part of Columbia University's Earth Institute. His testimony was also on behalf of the other environmental NGOs. Michael B. Gerrard, *Direct Testimony of Dr. Radley Horton*, CTR. FOR CLIMATE CHANGE L. & ENVTL. NGO GROUP (May 31, 2013), http://columbiaclimatelaw.com.

29 Frances Robles, *FEMA Was Not Ready for Puerto Rico Storm, Report Says*, N.Y. TIMES (July 13, 2018).

30 Con Edison Rates, Notice of Collaborative Meeting Concerning Storm Hardening and Resiliency Issues, Nos. 13-E-0030 et al. (issued July 1, 2013).

31 Van Nostrand, *Keeping the Lights*.

32 *Id.*

33 Joel Scata, *FEMA's Outdated and Backward-Looking Flood Maps*, NRDC EXPERT BLOG (Oct. 2017), www.nrdc.org.

34 *Sandy and Its Impacts*, A STRONGER, MORE RESILIENT N.Y., www.nyc.org.

35 New York City is dogged by storms, floods, extreme heat events, and sea-level rise. The other state utilities also face climate dangers, but they vary with the location and terrain and the configuration of their own infrastructure. Therefore, they must be assessed individually.

36 CON EDISON RATE ORDER.

37 *See Reforming the Energy Vision*, N.Y. P.S.C. No. 14-M-0101, Order Instituting Proceeding (Apr. 25, 2014); *see also* Order Adopting Regulatory Framework and Implementation Plan (Feb. 25, 2015).

38 This is a story about the power and possibility of collaborative and collective thought and action, and all the work described in this essay was based in the collaborative work of Chair Zibelman and the DPS staff. The Con Edison collaborative benefited from the hard work under crisis conditions of the Con Edison group, from the climate change advocacy of the office of the NYS Attorney General, and from the Special Initiative for Reconstruction and Resiliency team of the NYC Mayor. In the post-Sandy proceedings and REV, contributors included Rocky Mountain Institute, Regulatory Assistance Project, Energy Innovation, Michael Gerrard, Director of the Sabin Center for Climate Change Law at Columbia Law School, the Earth institute, Pace Energy and Climate Center, NRDC and EDF, We Act for Environmental Justice (WEACT), NYC-EJA, PUSH Buffalo, the Energy Democracy Alliance, and many more who are still fighting for NYS government to play a stronger and more effective role in mitigation of greenhouse gas emissions and adaptation to climate change's inevitable impacts. New York's 2019 Climate Leadership and Community Protection Act (CLCPA), requires total statewide greenhouse gas (GHG) emissions to be 40 percent below 1990 levels in 2030 and 85 percent below 1990 levels in 2050. There is an aspirational goal of a 100 percent reduction by 2050. CLCPA also mandates that 70 percent of electric power demand in 2030 be met by renewables, and 100 percent be from zero emissions in 2040.

39 *See Movers & Thinkers: Speakers Bureau, Eddie Bautista*, N.Y. FOUND., www.nyf.org.

40 Elizabeth Kolbert, FIELD NOTES FROM A CATASTROPHE (2006), and her Pulitzer Prize–winning THE SIXTH EXTINCTION (2014) are primers for the science of climate change for the nonscientist.

41 *See* Jacqueline Williams, *Damage to the Great Barrier Reef . . . Irreversible*, N.Y. TIMES (Apr. 19, 2018, www.nytimes.com/2018/04/19/world/australia/australia-barrier-reef.html.; and remarks of Elizabeth Kolbert, April 20, 2018, on the WAMC roundtable.

42 Lauren Markham, *A Warming World Creates Desperate People*, N.Y. TIMES (June 29, 2018).

43 *See, e.g.*, S. Hsiang, K. Meng, & M.A. Cane, *Civil Conflicts Are Associated With the Global Climate*, NATURE (2011), 476, 438–41.

44 *See* NAOMI KLEIN, THE BATTLE FOR PARADISE: PUERTO RICO TAKES ON THE DISASTER CAPITALISTS (2018).

9

Litigation for the Homeless in the 1980s

A Look Back

RICHARD PINNER

In this chapter I describe how a small nonprofit organization called the Coalition for the Homeless beginning in the late 1970s, but most notably in the 1980s, approached a social problem: the crisis of mass homelessness.[1]

"Crisis," by its very nature, connotes an emergency. For many crises, the primary characteristic is the unprecedented magnitude (how big is the problem). Also, in many crises, there is a precipitating event (earthquake, flood, invasion) with a specific date (the storm hit Wednesday) and that it exists (the government declared a disaster area). The mass homelessness that we currently have in the United States is atypical of many of the crises that are addressed in this volume. It is not new; in fact, when I worked at the Coalition for the Homeless in the late 1980s and early 1990s, we often started sentences with "Not since the Great Depression. . . ." Neither did modern homelessness result from a foreign aggressor, the storm of the century, or a radical change in technology. There is no date or threshold number that we can look at and say, "That's it, that's when it began." There is no December 7, 1941, for the homeless.

When a tornado hits, news reports quickly recount the damage (say, $2 billion). Knowing that number implies that if we spent that much money we'd put the community back to where it was before the storm. Contrast that with homelessness: even if we could definitively count the homeless population,[2] would the crisis begin when there are a million Americans? Or 2 million Americans? At any one time or as the socially vulnerable cycle in and out of homelessness in the course of a year?[3] Or is it when one homeless person sleeps on *your* doorstep?

Further complicating matters, its causes and characteristics can be viewed differently depending on whether you are looking at it on a local, regional, or national basis or in an urban, suburban, or rural setting.[4] Rather, modern mass homelessness is the product of a multitude of factors (none of which alone, or perhaps even in pairs, would have engendered this magnitude). For instance, mental illness has existed in humans since there have been humans, while modern psychiatric systems date to the early nineteenth century.[5] The general public did not talk about the homeless mentally ill in the late 1700s.

So what led a social phenomenon of long standing to rise to the level of crisis? Four factors, I think, were most important:

First, the homelessness crisis was evolutionary rather than revolutionary, creeping up on us; it did not have an obvious tipping point. In New York City in the 1960s, for example, the homeless consisted for the most part of "bag ladies and Bowery bums" (stereotyped as homeless mentally ill women and white male alcoholics, respectively). When young single men and women and then whole families began appearing on the streets in the late 1970s, the perception of the problem ratcheted up.

Second, with a few notable exceptions, extreme poverty has long been hidden in the shadows,[6] with a population lacking the income, wealth, and political clout that draws public attention. But homelessness is a very public event. People living on the streets and in abandoned cars are much more visible than people living in squalid apartments.

Third, the New Deal helped change the sense that government had a responsibility to care for its citizens. Social movements that began to gain prominence in the 1950s and 1960s led many to believe that citizen activists had a role in getting government to accept that responsibility. Homelessness became a crisis because activists called it a crisis to draw attention to the problem and get government to address it.

Fourth, and perhaps most important, homelessness stood out to the public more when compared to the affluence of the modern American society. It definitely undermined the sense that everyone could partake in the American Dream. Even with economic downturns in the late 1960s through the mid-1970s, the United States still had great affluence and a strong middle class. Maybe the Great Depression was not a good comparison. Because back then, nearly everyone was in the same (sinking) boat. But when you are doing relatively well and someone lives on your doorstep and the doorsteps of your friends, you take notice.

Once homelessness in the late 1970s/early 1980s was tagged as a crisis, the inquiry turned to how to remedy it. As Robert Hayes, the cofounder of the Coalition for the Homeless, put it: "Look, you see a problem. If you're a journalist, you write about it; if you're a poet, you probably write a poem about it." And if you're a lawyer, you take someone to court.[7] Which is exactly what happened.

The causes and characteristics of the homelessness crisis did not change the tools by which the legal community approached the problem; existing litigatory and nonlitigatory approaches were used and adapted, but none were really invented. They did, however, affect how those tools were deployed and in what sequence. For the practitioner, how this unspooled is important to understanding what worked and what didn't work during the fifteen to twenty years when homeless rights litigation was in its most visible state.

As a preliminary note, it is worth pointing out that because of how the crisis came about, when it came about, the lack of legal precedents, and general public sentiment, the legal advocacy strategies (both litigatory and nonlitigatory) had several notable characteristics:

- There was no established game plan;
- there was no established team;
- there was very little relevant case law;
- it was iterative and not comprehensive; and
- at least in the beginning, it was more reactive than logically sequential.

Despite this seeming ambiguity, every story needs to start somewhere, and the legal remedy to dealing with modern homelessness can be said to have begun with *Callahan v. Carey* (1981).[8] *Callahan* involved the right to shelter for homeless men in New York City. The first named plaintiff was a middle-aged man sleeping on the sidewalks on the city's up-and-coming Chelsea neighborhood. When Robert Hayes, then a young Wall Street associate at Sullivan & Cromwell, struck up conversation with Robert Callahan, Hayes learned that Callahan and others on the street avoided the municipal shelter at 8 East 3rd Street (just off the infamous Bowery[9]) due to its extreme danger and poor hygiene. Befriending Mr. Callahan and taking a lawyer's approach by asking questions, Hayes soon learned that the poor condition of the shelter was no accident: city officials had told him it was that way on purpose to minimize service-seekers. Still, he did not rush the courthouse steps. Rather he tried to investigate the situation and negotiate. Sensing that discussions were going to produce little, Hayes filed suit in New York supreme court (New York's trial court) on October 2, 1979.[10] Hayes asked the court to declare that Callahan and the other five named plaintiffs[11] had a right to shelter that was guaranteed under a host of state and federal constitutional provisions, statutes, and rules and regulations.

Not surprisingly, the federal claims did not to prevail. Seven years earlier, an increasingly conservative United States Supreme Court, in *San Antonio School District v. Rodriguez*,[12] declared that poverty was not a suspect classification. If cases such as *Goldberg v. Kelly*,[13] which greatly enhanced the notion of property rights and that due process was needed prior to the deprivation of those rights, gave advocates for the poor some hope that substantive rights were on the horizon, *Rodriguez* was a cold reminder that *substantive* due process under federal law was not an easy litigatory approach.

State law, by contrast, would prove to be a much more fruitful avenue. Article XVII, section 1 of the New York State Constitution provides:

> The aid, care and support of the needy are public concerns and shall be provided by the state and by such of its subdivisions, and in such manner and by such means, as the legislature may from time to time determine.[14]

As we all well know, brevity of a constitutional provision does not mean that it will not lead to substantial litigation; and generality does not mean that it will not be stretched to cover items and topics that cause strict constructionists to groan.

In an opinion and order dated December 5, 1979, state justice Andrew R. Tyler granted the *Callahan* plaintiffs' motion for a preliminary injunction. In a decision that was as short as it was un-heartwarming, Justice Tyler wrote that "the Bowery derelicts are entitled to board and lodging." Moreover, the entire legal analysis was confined to a single paragraph at the end, which stated:

> The legal authorities for the decision may be found in Article XVII, Sec. 1. of the New York State Constitution. Sections 61 (1) and (3) (1) and (3) of the Social Services Law. Section 604.1.0 (b) of the New York City Administrative Code. Matter of Jones vs. Berman, 37 N. Y. 2nd 42.

Generally, it is widely accepted that the foundational basis for the decision was Article XVII, section 1 of the state constitution. Justice Tyler's decision was only a preliminary injunction, so the parties still had to fully adjudicate the matter. The case then went to trial. By all accounts the city was not considered likely to prevail. Mayor Edward Koch agreed to enter into a consent decree with the plaintiffs. Those who read the consent decree often are struck by how little is actually in there. It is only twelve pages long. The performance standards are limited to thirteen items,[15] and standards are in an appendix.[16] When you're dealing with something for the first time—which is often true in a crisis—there are few places to turn to for advice and guidance. *Callahan* was truly a case of first impression, and the consent decree was definitely created on an ad hoc basis.

Callahan's state trial court[17] preliminary injunction (which was effectively the law of the case), however, was not going to be interpreted as creating a right to housing for anyone. Once the Coalition and other advocates realized that homelessness was not going to be quickly or easily resolved and that, even under the best circumstances, shelters were only a short-term emergency fix, the focus turned to how to address more systemic change. Essentially, if you look at much of the litigation that followed *Callahan* (and *Eldredge v. Koch*, filed by the Coalition, and *McCain v. Koch*, filed by the Legal Aid Society with the Coalition as cocounsel[18]), the theme was services for subpopulations. In other words, *Callahan* established a floor (i.e., shelter), but it was not the ceiling. Would the courts find that populations with special needs required a higher floor? Would a cot on an armory drill floor or on a basketball court be sufficient for the government to discharge its duties?

Focusing on subpopulations gave advocates the leverage that they would not otherwise have had pursuing generalized rights. A deeper look at two of these subpopulations—the homeless mentally ill, and those who were infected with the human immunodeficiency virus (HIV)—is illustrative of the methods that plaintiffs' counsel used.[19]

It would come as no surprise that a substantial portion of the homeless singles population suffered from serious mental illnesses.[20] Estimates vary, but a safe figure is one-third.[21] Litigating on behalf of this subgroup had several advantages. For one, you could deal with a substantial part of the population. With nearly 10,000 homeless single adults then in city shelters and thousands more on the streets, relief for this particular portion of the homeless population would result in a significant improvement for the overall homeless population. Moreover, the narrative of how the many mentally ill individuals had become homeless was fairly straightforward. While the public tended to think that the homeless mentally ill were all recent dischargees from hospitals,[22] in reality the sequence was a bit more drawn out, and the bulk of it occurred enough before street homelessness that it is not considered a direct factor by many.[23] Additionally, the consensus among advocates and researchers has been that as long as there were low-cost private accommodations in the community, then the mentally ill could hold on to their housing. But those accommodations dried up not long after deinstitutionalization was under way. New York City alone lost more than 100,000 single-room occupancy units (SROs) in the 1970s alone, with an overall loss, according to the Supportive Housing Network of New York City, of 160,000 SRO units (from 200,000 to less than 40,000) between 1955 and 1995. Many of the mentally ill population—without supportive family and the care that community mental health centers were to offer—ended up on the streets. And once on the streets, most mentally ill individuals would, not surprisingly, end up decompensating—their mental states becoming significantly worse and making it quite difficult to reverse their fortunes. (The converse scenario was also valid: homelessness could trigger otherwise dormant mental illness.)

And while mental illnesses were, and still are, not treated as sympathetically as physical ailments, it's not hard to make the simple case that schizophrenia and other mental illnesses are not the sufferers' fault and that the onus is then on society to deal with them. Similarly, because mental illness crosses many demographic categories, the families and friends of mentally ill individuals have been an effective lobbying group to change the perception of policy makers. Groups advocating for the rights of individuals with psychiatric disabilities effectively helped change the perception that just because mental illness does not show up on an X-ray, it is not an illness. Law schools generally don't teach you to find a sympathetic client, but any practitioner will know that it makes a difference. Finally, and perhaps most important, there were other laws aside from the state constitution.

Enter John Klostermann, a long-term, revolving-door user of the New York State mental health system. In 1981, in a case originally filed against Governor Hugh Carey of New York and that would ultimately take the name *Klostermann v. Cuomo*, the plaintiffs, including John Klostermann, brought their action in state supreme court (again, this is the state's trial court) claiming that their repeated discharge from state-run psychiatric facilities was in violation of section 29.15 of the New York State Mental Hygiene Law, which required a written "service plan" for each patient, including "a specific recommendation of the type of residence in which the patient is to live."[24] The state argued that the case was not justiciable, that is to say, these were functions that only the legislature could address. The New York State Court of Appeals, without addressing the underlying merits, disagreed, holding that while the method of delivering the service was within the ambit of the executive branch, whether or not it was delivered could be enforced by the plaintiffs.[25] Moreover—and this has been important in impact litigation in New York ever since—the legislature's failure to supply adequate resources is not an excuse.[26] On remand, Justice Richard Wallach granted some of the defendants' motions, striking certain causes of action and, more importantly, denying plaintiff's cross-motion for summary judgment. He wrote: "Plaintiffs' request under CPLR 3211 (subd [c]) for partial summary judgment that plaintiffs must be 'ensured a suitable residence' under the provisions of the Mental Hygiene Law is denied on the ground that such disposition would be entirely premature on the present record."[27]

Then the litigation stalled. The sense at the Coalition was that, following the *Klostermann* decision in the Court of Appeals and then Justice Wallach's opinion on remand, the state largely cleaned up its act. Whether that was true—or just hopeful—is difficult to parse out. But by 1987, the sentiment was that things were worse. Complicating matters, advocates realized that the city of New York, which is one of the few municipalities to operate its own hospital system (which generally provides acute care), was discharging its patients to the street or to the city's congregate shelter system (that *Callahan* engendered).[28]

The Coalition therefore retooled *Klostermann* to revisit the state's compliance and bring in New York City with a common law cause of action (i.e., that there is a baseline duty of care). With section 29.15 arguably applying only to state facilities, the argument against the city was considered to be more difficult. In November 1987, the Coalition filed *Heard v. Cuomo* (state) and *Koskinas v. Boufford* (city). After nearly three years of motion practice, none of which got to the substance of the case, these two actions were assigned trial dates.

Helpful to practitioners is that the *Heard* and *Koskinas* trials and subsequent appeals were not the only efforts. In fact, before the trial, plaintiffs' counsel met with the state (which did not like the negative attention) and offered to settle for a fixed number of housing units and an agreement to work on the claim against the city. While nothing came of the meeting, it was at least cordial. A similar meeting with New York City's corporation counsel included the threat that the city would "close Bellevue [Hospital]" if it had to undertake the discharge obligation. Those of us on the plaintiffs' side who were in the meeting hoped that the threat was an idle one (as it turned out to be).

Even then, the city and state attempted a flanking move, though they would deny it was in response to the litigation. Effective as of July 1, 1989, but formally signed on August 22, 1990, the New York/New York initiative was a city and state collaboration to create more than 3,600 units of supportive housing for homeless mentally ill individuals and another 1,600 (existing) units set aside for the population.[29] These numbers were well below the stated need but were still a significant step in the right direction.

The *Heard* and *Koskinas* trials began in early 1990. Following nearly two weeks of testimony, Justice Edward Lehner concluded that the state defendants were not in (substantial) violation of their statutory obligations. But the city defendants *were* obligated to create and implement written discharge plans (which included residential accommodations) under sections 29.15 (f), (g), (m), and (n) of the Mental Hygiene Law. And unlike its state counterparts, the city was not in compliance with those obligations. Justice Lehner did not address the common law claims. But, he concluded, given that "in view of the fact that there is not now in existence sufficient available housing

to enable [the New York City Health and Hospitals Corporation] to immediately fully comply, the judgment shall provide for implementation over a
period of time. Suggestions as to the appropriate time period for compliance
shall be submitted with the proposed judgment."[30]

Upheld on the first appeal at the appellate division,[31] following the Court
of Appeals' acceptance of the case, Judge Joseph Bellacosa cautioned that "at
this stage of this monumental social crisis and of this litigation, we deem it
advisable to observe that the injection of the building-of-housing argument
as a [New York City Health and Hospitals Corporation] governmental duty
constitutes an overreading of the judgment at issue as affirmed by the Appellate Division and, now, our Court."[32] In essence, the Court of Appeals, while
linguistically dinging the plaintiffs' hope for housing development, was actually adopting the narrow argument that threads the justiciability needle that
the plaintiffs opened: the obligation is proper for a court to enforce, and how
government gets there is up to the government. *Klostermann* and its successor
cases definitely go in the "win" column.

If homeless mentally ill persons were a relatively sympathetic cast, homeless adults who were HIV positive in the mid-1980s and through at least the
mid-1990s were probably on the opposite end of many spectrums. Without
getting into the same chicken-and-egg issue as mental illness—which was the
cause and which was the effect—it was clear that many homeless individuals
were HIV positive. It was also clear that the same congregate shelters that
were the fixture of the New York City shelter system were not optimal locations for people with compromised immune systems. For instance, beds were
required to be no closer than 30 inches apart under *Callahan's* consent decree
(see Exhibit A to *Callahan*).[33] A photo of the Fort Washington Armory in
Manhattan,[34] reveals where upwards of 1,000 homeless men were sheltered at
a time, providing quarters that were not exactly sterile.

Congregate shelters were natural laboratories for the opportunistic infections such as pneumocystis carini pneumonia (PCP), caused by a relatively
common airborne fungus, which was one of the leading causes of death. Prior
to the advent of antiretroviral drugs to treat HIV, it was estimated that approximately 75 percent of those who were HIV positive would get PCP. On
top of the stressors that come from homelessness in general, the chaos of
living with hundreds of others on a drill floor, coupled with the body's compromised immune system (a primary characteristic of HIV), would lead to an
HIV positive person having a very difficult time fighting off such an infection.
Death from an infection was not an uncommon result.

Unlike the mentally ill, however, there were no real specific statutory protections for the HIV population at the time. What legal remedies there were,

though, were usually around things like privacy issues and discrimination, but there was no comprehensive scheme designed to offer substantive services. In fact, while New York City did provide may social services, and even had its own governmental unit serving persons with HIV,[35] the adequacy of those services was often criticized. The ACT UP! movement grew out of this very critique, and Larry Kramer won a Pulitzer Prize for his play *The Normal Heart* that focused on Mayor Koch's early record on AIDS.

Those of us at the Coalition for the Homeless at the time learned that another advocacy group was using Fair Hearings (see note 36 for a definition) to establish that individuals with sickle cell anemia were entitled to "medically appropriate housing" (i.e., noncongregate) options.[36] One of the symptoms of sickle cell anemia is a compromised immune system. We surmised but did not know for sure that this was a prelude to seeking Fair Hearings for clients who were HIV positive. Not to be beaten to the punch, the decision was made to find our own clients who were HIV-positive and to seek private accommodations as the remedy. Sadly, the search for potential plaintiffs was not difficult. To cloak the nature of what we were doing, we did not use the office address on the request. Several clients who were HIV positive sought Fair Hearings, which they attended with a Coalition staff member, and later received favorable outcomes from the hearing officers.

If this seems like a time-intensive and inefficient way to go about helping a population that likely numbered in the thousands, there was in actuality a more ambitious plan. One of the quirks of New York law is that the determination by the agency's agents is given credence in determining rights. In other words, the plan was to have the Fair Hearing determinations serve as evidence in a class-action lawsuit that the city itself (by virtue of the Fair Hearing officers) determined that private accommodations were appropriate for individuals with compromised immune systems.

The resulting lawsuit, *Mixon v. Grinker*, began with a request for a preliminary injunction, which was granted by the trial judge, and the named plaintiffs were given the requested remedy.[37] The city made the distinction between those with AIDS and those who were HIV positive. As Justice Edward Lehner noted in his opinion:

> Prior to the institution of this action the City had adopted a policy of providing individuals diagnosed as having [the federal Centers for Disease Control, or CDC] defined AIDS with individual housing units or granting rent subsidies. Although recently, under State Department of Social Services regulations, all public assistance recipients who have an HIV related disease have been declared eligible for rent subsidies, they are not entitled to other benefits, which include

individual housing and a cash allowance for nutrition and transportation expenses, unless their condition constitutes AIDS under the CDC definition.[38]

To deal with the HIV-positive (but non-AIDS) population and other frail homeless individuals, the city, "apparently as a result of the institution of [the] suit," as Justice Lehner noted, created dormitory-style facilities with no more than twelve individuals to a room. In a decision that one might say harkens back to Justice Lehner's days as a politician (he had been a long-serving member of the New York State Assembly), he wrote:

> I conclude that under the circumstances it would be irrational to place more than four persons of the plaintiff class in one room, whether it be in the [the state approved the Comprehensive Care Program, i.e., one with the twelve-bed limit] or other facility. Further, beds in the room should never be less than eight feet apart. Crucial to the appropriateness of such living arrangements is that the ventilation be adequate for the medical needs of the residents. Since I am unable to state any rules for determining such adequacy, the judgment to be settled hereon should order that the housing to be provided to plaintiffs contain adequate ventilation, with the adequacy to be certified by the City Commissioner of Health, employing recognized standards appropriate to the illness of the residents. Finally, arrangements should be made for persons in the program to have the option to eat and have bathroom facilities separate from the general population of the facility.

That decision was affirmed on appeal, but the Court of Appeals distinguished it from its holding in *McCain*:

> In explaining its holding, the [*McCain*] Court was careful to differentiate between [the trial court's] equitable authority to craft standards of minimal habitability, which is an extraordinary judicial task reserved for a situation when no departmental guidelines exist, and [the trial court's] authority to ensure compliance with the governing standards, which would always be proper.
>
> . . .
>
> In this case, by contrast to McCain, the City has implemented a comprehensive program, formulated with input from public health experts including the director of the AIDS Institute, for housing HIV-ill and other medically frail individuals. Under these circumstances, McCain does not confer upon plaintiffs the right to plenary judicial review of the merits of this special medical needs housing program embodied in departmental guidelines (cf., Matter of New York State Socy. of Surgeons v Axelrod, 77 N.Y.2d 677).[39]

As in *Klostermann*, *Heard*, and *Koskinas*, the ultimate written opinion in *Mixon* is not a clear-cut victory. But the pressure from the lawsuit, even to a casual observer, forced the government to provide more extensive services than it would have if left to its own devices. The breakthrough antiretroviral drug azidothymidine (commonly known as AZT), approved by the US Food and Drug Administration on March 20, 1987, and in wide use by the early 1990s,[40] helped dramatically to stem the tide of AIDS and AIDS-related conditions.

With the *Callahan* through *Mixon* cases creating substantive rights seemingly out of thin statutory and regulatory bases and some very successful use of the media, one would think that it was just the beginning of a long run of litigatory successes. Rather, it's fair to say that this was the pinnacle, that *Mixon* may have been the last, and that since then major, broad impacts in homeless rights litigation in New York have been rare. There are several reasons, I think, for this. First, the cases filed after *Callahan* and into the early 1990s dealt with many of the large issues that were capable of being litigated. After that, short of trying to secure housing as a right (which is a dead end in litigation), many of the open "impact" issues were on the periphery. Second, even at the time, advocates at the Coalition got the sense that public fatigue was beginning to set in. The city and state were spending billions, and the problem seemed to get worse. Third and similarly, there was a sense that the state judiciary was less willing to issue broad, sweeping victories. With victories in hand came responsibility for ensuring implementation, which is in and of itself a very large task and one that put a damper on taking on additional cases. The city finally settled the *McCain* litigation after twenty-five years.[41] Yet the *Callahan* litigation continues, with eligibility screening and ejection issues continuing more than forty years after the case was filed. Despite the oxymoron of a crisis entering (at least) its fortieth year, there are several takeaways from the height of the litigation period that are of general application to crisis lawyering:

How Do You Characterize Your Agenda?

Most homelessness litigation didn't really have another side. Rather, it was a battle for securing resources. Few would argue that litigating on behalf of homeless children is more difficult than defending the right of Nazis wanting to march in Skokie, Illinois. (Of course, just because someone is less sympathetic does not mean you don't take on the case.)

Litigating on behalf of certain populations can change the amount of input the clients have. If your clients are a bunch of university professors suing for tenure, they are likely to be fairly sophisticated even if they are not experts on labor law. By contrast, you can't ask a homeless child about how to write the statute and regulations on where they attend school. In cases such as the latter, lawyers have to be much more careful that they are not substituting their biases for what is in the best interest of their clients. If you represent both an organization and an individual, how do you handle a settlement offer that might be good for the individual but might not be good for the organization or future clients?

Still, you can decide on how broad (or narrow) you want your representation to be. Do you only take the large substantive cases? Do you only take individual cases? Do you take cases involving ancillary but important symbolic issues? There are no right answers to these questions, but mission confusion can undermine organizational clarity.

Getting Started: What Factors Should You Consider?

The optimal time to bring a lawsuit borne of crisis will oftentimes be unclear. (If your client is at the airport about to be deported the only answer as to when to start is "now.") But if true emergency is not the case, you may be able to strike while the iron is hot.

While you may have groundwork to do (remember, *Brown v. Board of Education* was not the first case on the docket), you have to guesstimate when to make your big move. Similarly, while we often used the preliminary injunction as a fast way of getting a favorable ruling, you can't wait too long and then claim irreparable harm. The perfect plaintiff, the perfect brief, and the perfect media campaign may have to give way to "good enough to get in the courthouse door" at the right time. Some things are more achievable in a crisis situation, when the public's attention is galvanized and there is sympathy toward the afflicted party, but you still have to frame the issue: "Better shelter for homeless children" is a good short-term rallying cry. "Build more housing" is not.

Also, how do you (or your organization) position yourself (or itself)? Are you an outsider or an insider? Litigation by its nature is adversarial. But even then, some litigators are more part of the system than others. There isn't necessarily a correct answer, but it does help establish your identity. It would come as a surprise to many that the Coalition for the Homeless, even during times when it was its most aggressive in the courts, was also the recipient of New York City funds for programs, such as a food program (for people on the streets) and the summer camp (for homeless children). So while the litigation was adversarial, and the implication was that government officials could do more, we tried to avoid the politics of ad hominem attacks.

Finally, there are the brass tacks of initiating any litigation. You may have a choice on venue. The late 1980s, for example, was a time with an increasingly conservative federal judiciary. In contrast, New York State laws, and its judges, were not. It is not that we didn't know where the federal courts were located—it's just that we thought we would get a more sympathetic hearing in state court. Important in the *Callahan* trial, for instance, was the fact that, in New York State, reputation is an exception to the hearsay doctrine. That testimony—included compelling testimonial evidence that the city's existing shelters were inhumane—is considered one of the reasons the city chose to enter into the consent decree.

It is not a coincidence that some of the same judges heard many of the cases. In New York, most cases are assigned by a lottery system. But if you have a *related* case, you can request the same judge. That does not mean that every decision by that judge is a foregone conclusion. Recall that Justice Lehner's decision in *Mixon* also was reversed on organizational standing. Similarly, a decision on discovery in *Heard* agreed with the city and state's position that psychiatric records did not have to be turned over, but that too was largely reversed.[42] At the later trial, those records were key in establishing the factual basis for the city's noncompliance. Rather, having the same judge can mean that you have someone who understands the issues, which Justice Lehner, for example, certainly did.

What Strategic Partnerships Can You Form?

Odds are your legal issues will overlap with those of other lawyers pursuing the same or similar ones. Very rarely will you be the only one in the space. Do you collaborate? Do you avoid others?[43] Again, no right answer here, but it's best to pick a method.

Perhaps you have the resources to go it alone. Yet nearly all the major lawsuits mentioned in this chapter had cocounsel from large corporate firms. While balancing competing needs (e.g., firms want their associates to gain experience), it is inarguable that the firms had legal research and document production and management capabilities that far exceeded ours.

Then there are the insiders. It is not a surprise that those of us on the plaintiffs' side had allies within the administrations we were suing. We did receive memos that were not intended for us to see that were helpful.[44] Those sympathetic insiders were also helpful in framing the issues (fairly, but to our advantage) to their superiors.

Complementary programs—your own or with other partners—can help. The Coalition also ran or supported a set of direct service programs, such as three single-room occupancy buildings it was awarded as part of the sentence in a criminal proceeding against the landlords,[45] many of which survive to this date. Not only did the programs provide benefits to their recipients, but they helped demonstrate that the remedies sought in litigation were possible. And they were often possible *and* better run and less expensive than the city's claims.[46]

Lastly, there are unofficial partnerships, most notably the media and elected officials. All lawyering can benefit from favorable public opinion. How that public opinion is formed, and what it favors, are generally more helpful if you're the one doing the framing. Likewise, politicians might be able to deliver the victory you want. Just because you don't get a clear judicial victory doesn't mean you haven't been successful as a lawyer if your work led to an uncredited legislative fix.

Are You Litigating Effectively?

A crisis is not an excuse to think only one step at a time. As with a good chess player, you have to think several steps ahead.

It is not always necessary—or advisable—to bring the "ultimate" case first. As one can tell from the description of homeless litigation, the cases built off of each other. Sometimes the groundwork was fairly large in scope, such as the justiciability victory in *Klostermann*. Other times it was as simple as knowing how to use Fair Hearings to establish a factual basis for relief. This is nothing new. Perhaps the most famous example is *Brown v. Board of Education*. *Brown* was not only a consolidation of five cases from around the country; it was also the culmination of years of precursor cases that set the stage. Neither was *Brown* the final word, as decades of cases have been brought since to implement and enforce its ruling.

Nor is it true that every claim has to be dealt with at once in an omnibus lawsuit. It would be easy to have concluded that discharges from hospitals are the main point of attack. In the wake of *Heard*, however, we got the sense that one way the city and state were dealing with pressure on discharge was to make admissions even more difficult. We met individuals who, for instance, ate broken glass without being admitted to an acute psychiatric ward, and we also met persons who could spend days on a gurney in a hospital hallway before getting a bed. Clearly there was pressure on admissions. Accordingly, the Coalition brought the related case of *Love v. Koch*, which sought appropriate care and treatment, including in-patient treatment when warranted. Not only would they be better cared for; once admitted, they would be ensured of a residential placement.

Have more than one plaintiff with more than one set of circumstances; you never know what set of facts will appeal to a particular court. And be prepared for rounds of interlocutory appeals as the case bounces back and forth.

Timing is another issue to factor. Crises can make it more difficult to plot out a desired timeline. But that does not mean that there are no time factors that can be considered. A relatively simple one we used, for example, was never to file a case on a Friday, since Saturday's newspaper is less widely read.

Unintended consequences can vex any litigation. If one could use the "way back machine" to revisit *Callahan*, it would be a long line. Mayor Koch regretted settling, and the plaintiffs' counsel certainly would have included a host of other items in the settlement—such as capping the size of the shelter—had he known how things would unfold. *Callahan* is frequently criticized for the shelter system that followed it. Particularly for cases of first impression, predicting the future is not an easy task.[47]

What Are Your Remedies?

Balancing short-term and long-term goals can be difficult. Are you trying to change the outcome for a single client, or perhaps for a small cohort, or are you trying to change the world?

If you are in an advocacy organization and are about to undertake a multiyear litigation strategy, decide if you can also help your clients with their short-term needs. As the appellate division noted in *Mixon*, the Coalition provided funding to named plaintiff Wayne Phillips.[48] While such support was important in establishing organizational standing (and did not result in a mootness claim, as the claim certainly was capable of repetition yet evading review), it was also the right thing to do. It is very difficult for a lawyer to tell a person in crisis to wait five years as the case winds its way through the court system. It is even more difficult for the person in crisis to hear that.

You can also choose to stay on a certain path, or you can allow yourself to address issues as they unfold. I worked with a lot of clever individuals, and we would often brainstorm ideas. If we collectively thought an idea was worth pursuing, we invariably did the legal research. For instance, New York City at various times auctions *in rem* properties on the open market. These sales come with an obligation to repair the property. We learned an important fact from a colleague who simply wondered about—and then researched—the backstory of a seemingly abandoned property that he saw in his neighborhood. It had been sold at auction, but the required repairs had not been made, leading to continued disrepair instead of adding to the city's housing stock. Our legal research concluded that the only litigatory method was a taxpayer lawsuit, but unfortunately that was not an easy path in New York State. Instead, we issued a report, which garnered a fair amount of local attention. It may not have helped, but it certainly didn't hurt.

When Is the Crisis Over?

There's an old joke about a lawyer representing a man convicted of a crime. After the verdict is handed down, the defendant asks his attorney: "Where do we go from here?" The defense lawyer responds, "You go to jail, I go back to my office." All of us who worked with homeless people at the time I did were acutely aware that, at the end of the day, we went home. Our clients were generally not that fortunate. That dissonance not only helped drive our work; it also helped us to understand a bit better the predicament our clients were in. If they were late for a meeting, we waited. If they had no shoes, we dipped into petty cash to buy them some.

As noted above, litigation is rarely a straight line. Cases bounce up and down from trial courts to appellate courts and back. Issues get narrowed as cases progress. Other issues get identified in the course of litigation. Some of them will be the result of things that you notice in your work. For example, homeless people were not allowed to vote, because you needed an address to vote. In *Pitts v. Black*, the argument that a post office box was sufficient to establish residency for voting purposes was accepted by the court. No one knows if that victory has even changed the outcome of any election, but for symbolic and basic human decency purposes, it was an important right to establish. Some side issues are more than symbolic. As provided in the *Callahan* consent decree, the plaintiffs' attorneys retained an ongoing monitoring function. Over many years, significant resources were expended to ensure that the city was living up to its (arguably scant) set of standards. Several times, the city attempted to have the court reopen the settlement. In short, it is safe to assume that nothing is ever "settled." But how you balance your work between chronic versus crisis and large versus small applicability is important.

Most on point: When do you call it a day? Is it when no one is living on the street or in shelters? Or is it when the problem is "manageable"? It's fairly easy to say, "Our mission is obsolescence." Realistically, many crises are not over in the short term. Physical infrastructure may be built, but the legacy issues (such as psychological impacts) can linger. Dr. Ellen Bassuk, who worked at Harvard Medical School for more than three decades, is a leading voice on the sustained trauma that homelessness has on children, even after they become formerly homeless.

Finally, remember that litigation is only one of the tools. For many years, the notion that homelessness was only, or mostly, a housing problem was in disfavor. Government officials seemed to use the argument as a cudgel—that since the needy needed so much, they shouldn't get anything. Or that providing them with housing won't solve all their problems, so there's no need to do that. Skip ahead a few decades, and one finds the Housing First! model, which is characterized as follows:

> Housing First is an approach to quickly and successfully connect individuals and families experiencing homelessness to permanent housing without preconditions and barriers to entry, such as sobriety, treatment or service participation requirements. Supportive services are offered to maximize housing stability and prevent returns to homelessness as opposed to addressing predetermined treatment goals prior to permanent housing entry.[49]

Forty years after *Callahan*, after countless therapeutic models, we are back to recognizing that homelessness should be a short-term condition that can be addressed by providing sufficient low-cost housing. And if that was not exactly the original intent of *Callahan v. Carey*, it definitely was the intent of its progeny.

NOTES

1 I have chosen to focus on those cases and events with which I'm more personally familiar. That does not mean, for example, that the cases discussed here are the only important ones, although they are all significant. But it is certainly easier to provide insight into strategy on things I more closely worked on or witnessed.

2 The most widely accepted definition of a homeless person is one "who lacks a fixed, regular, and adequate nighttime residence." U.S. DEPARTMENT OF HOUSING AND URBAN DEVELOPMENT, OFFICE OF COMMUNITY PLANNING AND DEVELOPMENT, THE 2017 ANNUAL HOMELESS ASSESSMENT REPORT (AHAR) TO CONGRESS 2 (Dec. 2017) (hereinafter "HUD Report").

3 A popular count used is the United States Department of Housing and Urban Development's snapshot homelessness census, cited in the HUD Report. The 2017 report states, for example: "On a single night in 2017, 553,742 people were experiencing homelessness in the United States." *Id.*, at 2. But most experts note that multiples of that figure *experience homelessness* during a year; *see* www.nationalhomeless.org.

4 For example, in many cities there is a lack of affordable housing. In others, there is sufficient inventory but wages are not high enough to afford even that.

5 During the nineteenth century and Victorian era, conceptions of who was responsible for the mentally ill shifted from the individual to society, precipitating the asylum movement.

6 *See* JACOB RIIS, HOW THE OTHER HALF LIVES: STUDIES AMONG THE TENEMENTS OF NEW YORK (1890), an important example of bringing public attention to the underclass.

7 *See* Noel King, *Behind New York's Right to Shelter Policy*, MARKETPLACE (Sep. 30, 2015), www.marketplace.org.

8 *Callahan v. Carey*, Index no. 42582/79 (Sup. Ct. N.Y. Co. 1981). A notable precursor to *Callahan* was the seminal Supreme Court decision in *Papachristou v. City of Jacksonville*, 456 U.S. 156 (1972), which dealt with a vagrancy ordinance. While *Papachristou* did not seek to accord any substantive benefits, it did successfully shield "[r]ogues and vagabonds, or dissolute persons who go about begging . . . persons who use juggling or unlawful games or plays . . . common night walkers . . . common railers and brawlers, persons wandering or strolling around from place to place without any lawful purpose or object, [and] habitual loafers" from criminal prosecution as vagrants.

9 This street being the one to give rise to the phrase "Bowery Bum."

10 An amended complaint was filed on March 31, 1980.

11 Due to a quirk of New York law commonly known as the "government exception doctrine," suits plead for class-action status, but it is seldom granted, on the theory that government is benign and of course will treat similarly situated people the same way.

12 411 U.S. 1 (1973).

13 397 U.S. 254 (1970).

14 It should not be surprising that this provision was the result of a Depression-era state constitutional convention (New York State Constitutional Convention of 1938) and approved by popular vote on November 8, 1938.

15 The requirements are: (a) Each resident shall receive a bed of a minimum of 30 inches in width, substantially constructed, in good repair and equipped with clean springs. (b) Each bed shall be equipped with both a clean, comfortable, well-constructed mattress standard in size for the bed and a clean, comfortable pillow of average size. (c) Each resident shall receive two clean sheets, a clean blanket, a clean pillow case, a clean towel, soap and toilet tissue. A complete change of bed linens and towels will be made for each new resident and at least once a week and more often as needed on an individual basis. (d) Each resident shall receive a lockable storage unit. (e) Laundry services shall be available to each resident not less than twice a week. (f) A staff attendant to resident ratio of at least 2 percent shall be maintained in each shelter facility at all times. (g) A staff attendant trained in first aid shall be on duty in each shelter facility at all times. (h) A minimum of ten hours per week of group recreation shall be available for each resident at each shelter facility. (i) Residents shall be permitted to leave and to return to shelter facilities at reasonable hours and without hindrance. (j)

Residents of shelter facilities shall be provided transportation (public or private) to enable them to return to the site where they applied for shelter. (k) Residents of shelter facilities shall be permitted to leave the facility by 7 A.M. if they so desire. (l) Residents shall be permitted to receive and send mail and other correspondence without interception or interference. (m) The City defendants shall make a good faith effort to provide pay telephones for use by the residents at each shelter facility. The City defendants shall bear any reasonable cost for the installation and maintenance of such telephones.

In the appendix are standards such as the spacing of the beds and the ratio of toilets and sinks (6 to 1) and showers of bathtubs (10 to 1) to shelter residents.

16 Out of those dozen pages grew an enormous municipal agency (the New York City Department of Homeless Services) that today has an annual operating budget that exceeds $1.29 billion.

17 One word on nomenclature: generally speaking, in New York State, the Supreme Court is a general trial court, with the Appellate Division (split into one four regions) as the first appellate court; the single Court of Appeals sitting in Albany is the state's highest court.

18 *Eldredge* was brought to extend *Callahan* to women. *McCain* was brought to extend *Callahan* and *Eldredge* to families. Without spending too much time editorializing, the fact that separate cases had to be brought on equal protection grounds is a fairly good indication of how aggressively the government litigated these cases.

19 Two other subpopulations included youth in foster care (*Palmer v. Cuomo*) and children in danger of being placed into foster care (*Grant v. Cuomo*). *Palmer* was brought by a group of homeless young people under the age of 21 discharged from foster care onto the streets. The plaintiffs sought care until age 21 and the education and training while in foster care that they would need to live independently. In granting a preliminary injunction to plaintiffs in July 1985, the court held that foster children are entitled to care until age 21 and to "career counseling and training in a marketable skill or trade." The Appellate Division affirmed that ruling. New York State subsequently issued regulations defining this responsibility. *Grant* sought to require New York City to provide basic protective (reports of suspected incidents of child abuse or neglect to be investigated within 24 hours) and preventive (actual delivery of City-identified support services) services to needy children. Ultimately, the Court of Appeals decided that protective services were required to be timely but that the defendants were not statutorily required to provide preventive services (73 N.Y.2d 820 (1988)).

20 Initially, the focus primarily was on the mental illness aspect of the population. Later, as more became known about the population, the focus was expanded to include those who were mentally ill and had a chemical dependency (either drugs or alcohol—Mentally Ill Chemical Abusers (MICAs), in the vernacular of the time, later known as Dually Diagnosed).

21 Oftentimes, critics would add up the percentages (e.g., 33 percent mentally ill and 40 percent alcoholics gets to 73 percent with serious drinking or mental problems) without realizing that there is great overlap among the subgroups.

22 One cliché was "Greyhound Therapy"—providing a discharged psychiatric with a bus ticket to someplace else.

23 Institutionalization in state hospitals in New York topped out at about 93,000 in 1955 when the first psychotropic drugs were introduced; today the adult inpatient population in New York State hovers around 10,000. The deinstitutionalization movement was a product of many factors, including: (i) litigation that required the least restrictive alternative (*see, e.g., Covington v. Harris*, 419 F.2d 617, at 623 (1969)); (ii) governmental desire to save money; and (iii) a movement toward care in the community (the Community Mental Health Act of 1963, also known as the Community Mental Health Centers Construction Act, Mental Retardation Facilities and Construction Act, Public Law 88-164, was to provide federal funding for community mental health centers and research facilities in the United States), and the utility of psychotropic medications, the inpatient population dropped steadily. As with many good ideas, the initial part happened (deinstitutionalization), but not the replacement (community mental health centers). Looking at the numbers, the major drops in inpatient populations began in 1955 with the introduction of psychotropic medications and picked up stream in 1965 when Medicare and Medicaid were enacted.

24 New York Mental Hygiene Law, § 29.15, subd (g), par 2.

25 The *Klostermann* named plaintiffs and putative class were all homeless individuals who had been discharged without a residential placement. As part of its decision in *Klostermann*, the New York Court of Appeals also found justiciable claims in *Joanne S. v. Carey*, in which New York State's Mental Hygiene Legal Service—a unit within the Appellate Division of the New York State Supreme Court—had represented current residents of state psychiatric facilities who were seeking clinically appropriate community placements.

26 Recognizing how many former state hospital patients ended up on the streets, section 29.15(j) ordered the commissioner of the New York State Office of Mental Health to try and locate those who had been inpatients for at least two years and had been discharged after 1972 without a written service plan and to seek to have services provided for that population.

27 126 Misc.2d 247 (1984).

28 Complicating matters, at least in the public's eyes, on October 18, 1987, Mayor Ed Koch instituted a program to forcibly remove mentally ill people from the streets if they were unable to care for themselves. While the initiative spoke in terms of danger to one's self or others (the legal basis for involuntarily hospitalization), the endeavor soon took on a carnival-like feeling. The first person picked up by Project HELP was a middle-aged woman named Joyce Brown, who also went by the name Billie Boggs, a nod to her favorite daytime talk-show host, Bill Boggs. Whether she was a real danger to herself or not (she claimed she was a "political

prisoner"), the courts soon released her; the underlying problem was that the city was allocating a few resources to this initiative but not really addressing the problem for the thousands of others who would have gladly taken assistance had it been available.

29 The program has been renewed twice more under different city and state administrations. It is without a doubt a success, having helped thousands of mentally ill individuals get off of and/or stay off the streets and out of congregate shelters.

30 150 Misc.2d 257, 264–65 (1991).

31 179 A.D.2d 429 (1992)

32 80 N.Y.2d 684, 610 N.E.2d 348, 594 N.Y.S.2d 675 (1993).

33 On file with the author.

34 See www.nytsyn.com/archives/photos/751308.html.

35 Within the Human Resources Administration, the City's general welfare agency, there was the Medical Assistance System–Division of AIDS Services, commonly known as MAP DAS.

36 "Fair Hearing" is the name given to the administrative procedure that is used to determine entitlement to many public benefits. The term is derived from *Goldberg v. Kelly*, which found that welfare benefits are "property" within the meaning of the Fourteenth Amendment to the United States Constitution and that they could not be terminated without some form of evidentiary hearing.

37 There are two New York specific elements that are worth noting. First, the court also granted the city's request to dismiss the Coalition as a named plaintiff on the grounds that it lacked standing. But that dismissal was unanimously reversed on appeal. 157 A.D.2d 423 (1990). Organizational standing is a powerful tool in impact litigation. Not only can it make bringing the lawsuit easier; it can also serve as a central organizing tool for the organization.

Second, a well-settled (and vexing) aspect of New York law is the governmental exception doctrine to class actions. Plaintiffs can plead a class action, but the court will not certify the class because, the theory goes, that government is benign and, once the named plaintiff is granted the remedy, the government will, of course, treat similarly situated individuals the same away. *McCain v Koch*, 117 A.D.2d 198, 221 (1st Dept 1986) (reversed on other grounds), 70 N.Y.2d 109, 114, n.2 (1987). Only after one has proven that similarly situated individuals (which is a matter to be adjudicated) have not in fact been treated the same way would a class be certified. While this pas de deux would seem to be a relatively minor inconvenience, it can add substantial time and effort to legal redress. And because this book is dealing with situations that are crises, that is not the type of time that counsel desires to spend.

38 157 Misc.2d 68 (1993).

39 88 N.Y.2d 907 (1996).

40 AZT was developed more than two decades earlier as a cancer drug.

41 New York City, Office of the Mayor, *Mayor Bloomberg Announces Statement With Legal Aid Socity Ending 25-Year Litigation and Court Oversight of Homeless Family Services System* (Sept. 17, 2008), www1.nyc.gov.

42 142 A.D.2d 537 (1988).

43 About Robert Hayes, it was said: "Among his fellow advocates, Mr. Hayes has developed a reputation for having sharp elbows. He has intervened in their lawsuits when he thought they were going poorly and sought to have some lawyers removed from cases if they disagreed with him." Suzanne M. Daley, *Robert Hayes: Anatomy of a Crusader*, N.Y. TIMES (Oct. 2, 1987).

44 In one rather humorous exchange, city lawyers were practically apoplectic during a deposition, as they could tell we were reading from the deponent's résumé, which they had not sent us. (Why they thought this was a secret document was lost on me.) During the break, my colleague asked where I got it from. I replied: "They attached it to his affidavit in the other case."

45 130 Misc.2d 987 (1985).

46 Terrence McNally (the screenwriter, not the playwright of the same name) calls this "change the story, change the world."

47 One unintended consequence, it can reasonably be argued, was a major positive. To comply with the right-to-shelter cases, the city relied on "welfare hotels," which were often tourist-class hotels that had fallen into disrepair. Paying upward of $3,000 per month for a family (in 1980s dollars) allowed advocates to show the sharp contrast in the economics of shelters versus permanent housing. This would lead New York City to spend billions of its own tax dollars to create affordable housing, including rehabilitating thousands dilapidated city *in rem* buildings; many of these had tin panels in the windows with painted flower pots so that passing motorists would having something better to look at. While Mayor Ed Koch would not admit that litigation was an impetus, the rehabilitation of thousands of city-owned buildings that were once slated for demolition as albatrosses was a major contributor to the revitalization of many neighborhoods. As Mayor Ed Koch often bragged: "In fiscal year 1989 alone . . . New York City spent $740 million in capital funds—more than three and one half times the amount of the local funds expended on housing by the nation's next 50 largest cities combined!"

48 157 A.D.2d 423 (1990).

49 U.S. Department of Housing and Urban Development, *Housing First in Permanent Supportive Housing*, www.hudexchange.info.

10

Scaling Worker Cooperatives as an Economic Justice Tool for Communities in Crises

Carmen Huertas-Noble, Missy Risser-Lovings, and
Christopher Adams

Worker cooperatives can be used as tools to address many of the socioeconomic harms we face today, and the crises of capitalism that undergird them,
providing an effective crises-response approach that lawyers working with
the most directly impacted communities can deploy in their efforts to shift
economic and political power to their clients and the communities in which
their clients live and work. In this chapter, written before the COVID-19 crisis
hit, we describe roles that attorneys are playing in recent efforts to establish worker-owned and -directed enterprises that can be brought to scale to
benefit those in crisis, especially those most marginalized by the prevailing
political and economic order.

Introduction

This case study analyzes the roles community coalitions and medical centers in Brooklyn, New York, have played in serving as anchor institutions for
worker cooperatives, addressing many of the negative social determinants of
health—particularly those that affect Black, Indigenous, and People of Color
(BIPOC) communities, immigrant communities, Muslim American communities, and the LGBTQI community. Negative social determinants of health
include a growing dearth in quality employment, poor workplace conditions,
racism, worsening poverty, inadequate access to quality health care, and a
lack of access to healthy food. Our experiences working in communities that
are disproportionately affected by these interconnected crises reveal what we
believe are the deeper crises—late capitalism, rising income inequality, and
their impacts on democratic institutions and democracy itself—that bring
about many of the severe inequities affecting marginalized communities.

   In addition, we explain how worker cooperatives can be used as tools to address many of these harms, and the crises that cause them, providing an effective crisis-response approach that lawyers working with such communities can

deploy in their efforts to shift economic and political power to their clients and the communities in which their clients live and work. We end with a description of the challenges lawyers who develop and represent worker cooperatives as a response to the crises affecting marginalized communities might face. We also include some best practices through which lawyers can maximize and operationalize principles of economic democracy in the form of cooperatively owned and governed union co-ops that center labor as sovereign and serve as bulwarks against the crises caused by capitalism, particularly in those communities we see as marginalized by capitalism's worst excesses.

The Crisis in Marginalized Communities:
Political and Economic Inequality

The crises of the current states of political and economic democracy—or, more precisely, the crises that arise from the lack thereof—are two sides of the same coin. On one side is the crisis of rising authoritarianism throughout the world.[1] On the other is a capitalist system that was formed to operate on the dependence and normalization of the use of brutality to expropriate land and exploit labor.[2] For example, in response to the global financial crisis of 2008, the United States sponsored the bailout of corporate actors who created the crisis (an economic injustice), without requiring accountability measures or promises for democratic control over the use of those funds for a larger public good (a political injustice), thereby reinforcing the political and economic structures that created the conditions for the crisis.[3] As Gautum Mukunda explained in the pages of the *Harvard Business Review*: "If you were a player in the American financial system, the government did everything possible to make sure that you did not suffer consequences from the crash your industry had caused. . . . Perhaps even worse was the extent to which the government focused its efforts on stabilizing the financial sector instead of directly aiding most Americans."[4]

Not surprisingly, the 2008 crisis was preceded by the greatest income inequality gap the United States had seen since immediately before the Great Depression, a gap that continues to widen.[5] Additionally, because of systemic attacks on many of our public institutions, most Americans are dealing with multiple crises at once without some of the traditional safety nets provided by programs originally designed to alleviate poverty. As a result, working people cannot afford to pay for basic necessities. For example, the US Department of Agriculture is creating increasingly stringent eligibility requirements for Supplemental Nutrition Assistance Program (SNAP) benefits, which could lead to 3 million people no longer qualifying and not being able to feed themselves and/or their families, increasing the already prevalent crisis of food insecurity.[6] Additionally, the unemployment rate is staggering in many communities. Others work multiple jobs and still are unable to afford the basics. This confluence of forces creates extreme economic insecurity and makes those in marginalized communities even more vulnerable to workplace abuses, such as wage theft, arduous work schedules, and low pay. An example of this is the exploitation of people who are incarcerated (who are disproportionately people of color) being forced to work dangerous jobs for almost no pay while in prison and being denied the same job once they are released.[7] In addition, economic inequality also makes access to quality, affordable, and effective medical care a challenge for those subjugated by capitalism, contributing to negative health outcomes.[8] Meanwhile, corporations receive increasing corporate welfare and unnecessary tax breaks.[9]

Health Disparities and Food Insecurity

Research has shown that only 20 percent of an individual's health can be attributed to medical care, while social and economic factors account for 40 percent. These factors, commonly called "SDOH," are the conditions in the places where people live, learn, work, and play, which affect health. Negative SDOH include things such as precarious and/or unsafe housing, substandard education, underresourced and overpoliced neighborhoods, poverty, and lack of access to healthy foods. In addition to the obvious outcomes these factors have on a person's life, all of these factors cause stress, which harms health and increase the likelihood of substance use. As one example of a community made up predominantly of people of color, where health disparities are dramatic, residents of Central Brooklyn "suffer disproportionately from every single category of health problem that the [New York City's] department of health keeps statistics on: from chronic diseases like diabetes, to violence, to mental health problems and drug related conditions. People in the area are hospitalized at a 30 percent higher rate than the city as a whole, and still 30,000 Central Brooklyn residents go without necessary medical care."[10] Many of these chronic diseases are impacted by access to healthy food.

Medical centers in communities with high concentrations of poverty, such as those in Central Brooklyn, are often considered safety-net providers and serve primarily underpaid and underresourced residents, providing critical access to health care that would otherwise be unaffordable and/or inaccessible. The closures of such medical centers—a crisis within itself in terms of access to care—exacerbate the various crises underresourced communities face, including poor health and high unemployment to name just two (albeit two that often cause a domino effect of problems in peoples' lives).

When safety-net providers close, communities already suffering from high concentrations of poverty and inadequate access to health care experience even higher unemployment, which is a negative social determinant of health itself along with all the social ills associated with not having adequate income to sustain oneself and/or one's family. And people who are impoverished, which includes the working poor (a term that should not exist if corporations were held more accountable), have a high risk of poor health and often face food insecurity.

The Department of Agriculture defines "food insecurity" as a household-level economic and social condition of limited or uncertain access to adequate food with either disrupted eating patterns or reduced food intake. Food insecurity can have permanent effects on the health of individuals and often causes increased health care costs. Food insecurity can lead to obesity, diabetes, hypertension, cardiovascular disease, asthma, tooth decay, anemia, birth defects, stress, anxiety, depression, and some cancers. Those who are food insecure are not necessarily all suffering from hunger—food insecurity also includes lack of nutritious foods and instead consuming foods with higher counts of calories and carbohydrates, which contributes to the adverse risk of acquiring chronic health conditions. This is a particular challenge for those living in "food deserts" (where the availability of fresh and healthy food is lacking or limited), "food swamps" (where there is a high density of stores selling high-calorie fast food), or "food mirages" (where there is abundant, high-quality food but it is priced out of the reach of lower-income residents)—which is disproportionately likely for people who are underpaid, who are also disproportionately people of color.

Food insecurity has additional consequences for children, impacting growth, ability to learn and focus, energy, delaying development, and leading to increased stress levels and behavioral health issues. Fast-food chains in predominantly Black neighborhoods have been shown to be more than 60 percent more likely to advertise to children than in predominantly white neighborhoods. Food insecurity in children has resulted in $1.8 billion in additional child hospitalizations and $5.9 billion in additional special education services for students in public, primary, and secondary schools. Food-insecure households spend 45 percent more on medical care than people in food-secure households.

Hospitals and health care can play a role in addressing food insecurity. While many insurance providers have covered nutritional counseling, a few recent initiatives attempted to also address food insecurity. Some hospitals bring healthy foods to patients who face barriers to accessing nutritious foods by hosting farmers markets on site, by providing vouchers for families to purchase healthy foods at these markets, and/or by ensuring that the vendors accept public benefits. Some hospitals offer on-site food pantries. Some have gone so far as to host on-site farms and food "pharmacies." Other insurance companies and hospitals are exploring the "food as medicine" movement. NYC Health + Hospitals/Bellevue recently announced that it will offer New York City residents personalized support in making the potential transition to a whole-food plant-based diet to improve/reverse chronic conditions such as heart disease, obesity, high cholesterol, and high blood pressure, providing $400,000 in pilot program funding. The Plant-Based Lifestyle Medicine Program partners with Health Bucks to provide coupons distributed by the New York City Department of Health and Mental Hygiene for patients to purchase fresh fruits and vegetables at farmers markets in the city. It also partners with the Healthy Savings Program, which offers discounts on produce at local supermarkets. An enterprise that employs some of these strategies to provide healthy food for Brooklyn health-care system patients and local residents could help improve health outcomes by addressing food insecurity, unemployment, and poverty and promoting food sovereignty.

Cooperatives: An Economic Equalizer

In many respects, these power imbalances that lead to the range of crises affecting marginalized communities flow from these communities' lack of political power, which, more and more in an age of skyrocketing economic inequality, is a product of a lack of economic power. The centerpiece of the American economic order is the corporation, which the United States Supreme Court has recognized as having political rights, a decision that has led to a greater concentration of political power that flows from greater concentrations of economic power, thereby subordinating human rights and creating marginalized communities.[11] And it is this concentration of political and economic power that has led to many of the broader societal inequalities described above.

In order to acquire a just share in the benefits of our economic systems and to address the various crises too many communities face, such as food insecurity, poor health, and poverty, working people must gain control over the aggregate political power of the corporations that form the core of our political economy. Because the power to control a corporation is based on the ownership of governing shares of its stock, working people must own those governing shares. An organization owned and controlled in such a way is often referred to as a "cooperative." Thus, cooperatives are one strategy that those who engage in a legal practice that focuses on *community economic development* (i.e., so-called CED practitioners) employ to help redistribute economic and political power.

Worker Cooperatives as Tools for Political and Economic Justice

Worker Cooperatives Defined

Worker cooperatives are distinct from traditional corporations because workers have governance rights based on the democratic principle of one worker, one vote. Workers also share equitably in the profits of the business, usually based on patronage. The cooperative structure stands in stark contrast to the traditional corporate model, where the primary concern of the business is usually maximizing the wealth of shareholders and where it is the shareholders who have governance rights. In traditional businesses, workers' wages are typically seen as expenses to be minimized as much as possible, and workers typically have no governance rights.

A vehicle to generate wealth for workers who are lower-income and have less wealth, worker cooperatives subordinate capital to labor—profits are distributed based on the workers' labor, not their capital investment. The extent to which nonworkers can participate in the governance and profit distributions of a cooperative business varies, but usually workers have at least a controlling voice in governance and receive a majority of profit distributions.

As businesses that prioritize the humanity of workers, worker cooperatives create meaningful, long-term, safe, sustainable, and dignified jobs with increased job security and reduced workplace abuse. Profit-sharing limits income disparities within the business and provides asset-building opportunities for all workers. Equitable pay structures are also more common in worker cooperatives. Furthermore, profits tend to remain local, so wealth-building occurs for both individuals and communities.[12] As worker-owners have more control over their work by democratically managing the business, they are more engaged than in traditional workplaces. Worker cooperatives also value community and thus tend to be more environmentally conscious of their practices compared to traditional businesses.[13]

While worker cooperatives are not a panacea to the multitude of crises we are facing, as workplaces where real democracy is practiced on a daily basis, worker cooperatives can serve as a model for building a meaningful movement for economic democracy and transformative economic and social justice. In the short term, they provide opportunities to address economic inequality and insecurity, especially for people with barriers to safe, stable jobs, like BIPOC, immigrants, the LGBTQ+ community, and people who were formerly incarcerated.

CED and Cooperative Lawyering—Strategies to Scale

A major discussion in cooperative lawyering is how best to develop cooperatives at scale to maximize their impact as social justice tools for communities in crises and to achieve systemic change. There are various strategies being undertaken to scale up the cooperative movement in the United States, including sectoral/industry approaches, such as replicable franchise-like models; maximizing the purchasing power of "anchor institutions" like hospitals and universities; structuring networks or federations of cooperatives to promote intercooperation; leveraging the assets of unions to develop union cooperatives; encouraging municipal investment and cooperative-friendly legislation, especially tax incentives; improving access to capital; leveraging technology and platforms; targeting retiring business owners who are open to their workers converting the business to a worker cooperative; and expanding educational initiatives to make cooperatives more mainstream and to build skills specific to cooperative businesses. We will focus on the sectoral or industry transformation approach and the anchor institution strategy, because they are the core strategies used in our case study and can serve as a model for industry transformation at scale.

The sectoral or industry transformation strategy involves benefiting from economies of scale; when done in combination with policy advocacy, it can have broad implications industrywide in terms of improved work practices. Some advocates of this approach suggest that, if you replicate businesses in a single industry, you can minimize the need for industry-specific training and can avoid reinventing the wheel. Others approach industry transformation while including co-operatizing the supply chains for that industry, developing multiple co-ops in a variety of industries, all in support of the broader sector.

The anchor institution strategy leverages the support and economic power of universities, hospitals, and other major institutions to support the development of the local community via procurement of goods and services from cooperatives. Nonprofit hospitals own assets in excess of $600 billion and have annual revenues greater than $500 billion.[14] By purchasing locally from cooperative businesses, anchor institutions can ensure that their expenditures circulate within the local economy and help create wealth in the communities they serve. As local businesses, with local worker-owners, this money tends to further circulate in the local economy—for every dollar a person spends at a local business, there is a two-to-four multiplier effect on the local economy through hiring and purchasing.[15] Additionally, purchasing locally creates reduced carbon emissions, as goods have less distance to travel. Purchasing local also allows for a lower likelihood of service disruption due to weather and disasters.

Case Study: Brooklyn Sprout

Our case study for this chapter focuses on Brooklyn Sprout, a union co-op founded by community members to grow hydroponic produce in food deserts or food swamps to provide healthier food options to hospitals, homebound patients, and other residents. The union co-op is intentionally designed to empower workers and to help ensure that profits remain in the community to benefit the local economy and its residents.

Identifying the Need: Health Disparities and Food Insecurity in Brooklyn

Despite the government's recently stated policy goal to "revitalize" Brooklyn through development and improve residents' quality of life, the fact is that such policies were designed to maximize capital investment, resulting in new high-income residents moving in, with existing Brooklyn residents being displaced or having their quality of life diminished (e.g., when local businesses such as grocery stores cater to new residents' palates and raise price points). In reality, nearly one in four Brooklyn residents still lives in poverty. Nearly half of Brooklyn's residents are Medicaid beneficiaries, the majority of whom are located in predominantly Black and Brown communities. Brooklyn has the highest concentration of low-paying jobs in New York City. Only one in five households has an annual median income above $100,000, while the same percentage receives food stamp (SNAP) benefits. Brooklyn's incarceration rates in predominantly Black and Brown neighborhoods are significantly higher than the average across the city. Bedford-Stuyvesant residents' average life expectancy is 4.4 years shorter than the citywide average. Canarsie's rate of severe maternal morbidity is almost double the rate of New York City overall. East New York's rate of hospitalization for preventable diabetes issues is more than twice the city average. Brownsville's rates of hospitalization for asthma among children is nearly twice that of the city overall.[16]

Despite these statistics—or perhaps because of them—health care is the largest industry in the borough of Brooklyn. Not only does it employ more than 293,000 people in Brooklyn; the New York health-care sector supply chain (of which Brooklyn is a part) spends a substantial portion of its $10 billion investments in goods and services in support of Brooklyn's hospitals, medical centers, and ambulatory care services. Furthermore, the central and northeast Brooklyn public hospital system recently underwent a major restructuring to create a new regional health system, which decentralizes hospital care in exchange for heightened local, ambulatory, and preventative care services. Part of this restructuring includes the goal of focusing on preventative healthy living by addressing the social determinants of health (known as "SDOH"—the conditions in the places where people live, learn, work, and play that affect health).

One social determinant of health in Brooklyn is the state of food security in the borough, or rather food *insecurity* (especially in marginalized communities). One in four Central Brooklynites lacks access to quality and varied food, which is almost twice the state average.[17] Food insecurity is widespread and is a product of the various crises that communities that are marginalized in the United States face today. Food justice activists use the phrase "food apartheid" to reflect the systemic racism permeating America's food system and its related political and economic systems.[18] Not only are there racial disparities in food insecurity;[19] they are exacerbated by gentrification,[20] which changes the food retailers that compose the local food environment—and Central Brooklyn has been gentrifying rapidly.

Given the economic might of the health-care industry in Brooklyn, creating enterprises that can contract with Brooklyn's health-care system would build local wealth for Central Brooklyn residents with wide economic disparities from unemployment and poverty levels, inadequate access to quality health care and mental health services,[21] measurably higher rates of obesity, diabetes, and high blood pressure, and limited access to healthy foods or opportunities for physical activity. It could also address some of the negative SDOH, including unemployment, poverty, and food insecurity.

Identifying the Community of Purpose: The Coalition to Save Interfaith

The Coalition to Save Interfaith (the Coalition) began to prevent the closings of safety-net hospitals and medical centers in Central Brooklyn and thus sparked an effort to keep one such medical center open—Interfaith Medical Center (IMC). IMC was slated to close due to "long-running underfunding, cuts to Medicaid and Medicare and changing market conditions." The Coalition, composed of local residents, health-care workers, community-based organizations, unions, business leaders, elected officials, and faith-based institutions, fought hard to keep IMC open in order to sustain access to health care, prevent job loss, and avoid the consequent spiraling crises associated with job losses in already hard-hit communities. The Coalition developed a community-driven, asset-based approach with a highly participatory design, which called for a greater emphasis to be placed on SDOH. One strategy to achieve this included sustaining local assets like the hospital itself, as well as increasing the supply of family-supporting, wealth-creating jobs and local ownership opportunities, with a goal of building a robust, community-owned entrepreneurial ecosystem.

While the Coalition was formed to save IMC, its work would also benefit its neighboring medical centers in Central Brooklyn, as the Central Brooklyn medical centers would become integrated as One Brooklyn Health Systems. After funding stabilized to keep the medical centers open, the Coalition to Save Interfaith changed its name to the Coalition to Transform Interfaith. The "transformation" would occur by making Interfaith an anchor institution for community wealth generation, starting with examining the supply chain to determine whether worker-owned cooperative entities could produce goods as part of a grassroots, community-led supply chain. And it was out of that desire to create such institutions that Brooklyn Sprout, worker-owned cooperative, was formed.

The Emergence of Brooklyn Sprout

Brooklyn Sprout was conceived of as a union co-op that would grow produce through hydroponic farming to source IMC's cafeteria and to deliver produce to homebound patients. The owners would be current residents and returning citizens, and the profits would largely remain within the community, thereby benefiting the local economy. As a worker-owned cooperative, Brooklyn Sprout aims to secure the right to affordable healthy food for those who do not have access. The enterprise's broader goals are to improve local residents' wellness by targeting the social determinants of health. The enterprise addresses poverty, unemployment, mass incarceration's impact on employment, and lack of access to healthy foods by creating an urban farm-worker cooperative that partners with IMC to grow food, so that local residents can be prescribed healthy foods instead of medicine and pay for such foods with either health insurance or other public benefit funds. Potential worker-owners include local residents from the neighborhood (which has a disproportionately high unemployment rate), and particularly returning citizens, or people who were formerly incarcerated (Central Brooklyn also has a disproportionately high incarceration rate). Brooklyn Sprout will also partner with nonprofit organizations that provide job training programs and other reentry services to help ensure success.

The Brooklyn Sprout farm will be located on the grounds of IMC and will be constructed of modified shipping containers that are primarily powered by renewable energy (specifically, solar). The food prescriptions will be available at farmers markets at IMC, as well as at farmers markets at nearby ambulatory care facilities. Produce will also be available for purchase by local residents without a prescription. The enterprise also has an educational element—urban hydroponic farms in public schools—where students will learn about farming and how to leverage technological innovations that are altering the sector with the potential for greater production. In addition to providing STEAM training for students, the farms can serve as a potential bulwark against the probable collapse of the current agricultural system and consequent food scarcity due to the climate crisis.

As a cooperative, the enterprise should, at a minimum, have the means and rights of distribution of the product, and any surplus value is to be owned and controlled by the workers—people who, without such rights, would otherwise be deprived of some of the most important benefits generated by the production process. Furthermore, because the farm will be located on public land, the rights to access and use the land on which the production is located should not be able to be transferred, revoked, or otherwise rendered useless without the consent of a very high percentage of those who benefit from its productive capacity. Because one of the goals of the enterprise is to generate wealth for the community in common, the rights of ownership and control to the means of production (seeds, energy, water etc.) should also be protected from transfer or appropriation by means of capital exchange or contribution without a clear and equitable public benefit.

The idea of Brooklyn Sprout is in many ways a product of the food sovereignty movement. "Food sovereignty" is the right of peoples to healthy and culturally appropriate food produced through ecologically sound and sustainable methods, as well as the right to define their own food and agriculture systems. It allows communities control over the way food is produced, traded, and consumed. It puts the aspirations and needs of those who produce, distribute, and consume food at the heart of food systems and policies rather than the profits of multinational corporations.

Food sovereignty movements explicitly support Black farmers, who receive a disproportionately low percentage of farm subsidies.[22] The Movement for Black Lives describes "food justice" as "a process whereby communities most impacted and exploited by our current corporate-controlled, extractive agricultural system shift power to re-shape, re-define, and provide indigenous, community based solutions to accessing and controlling food that are humanizing, fair, healthy, accessible, racially equitable, environmentally sound and just."[23] Framed this way, food sovereignty goes "beyond access to ensure that our communities have not only the right, but the ability to have community control of our food including the means of production and distribution."[24]

Cooperatives are a natural fit for the food sovereignty movement, as they place the means of production and distribution in the owners. Indeed, there has been a call recently for cooperatives to help address inequitable access to healthy and nutritious foods. Cooperatives can serve as community-based alternatives to the global industrial food complex. As local community institutions, they can become local food hubs and support regional food networks.[25] Some have questioned the ability of worker cooperatives to make much of an impact, given that issues of food access center on poverty, and not just proximity, and worker cooperatives are designed, at least in part, to provide fair wages for the workers.[26] However, while worker cooperatives are for-profit businesses, one of the cooperative principles is concern for community, and it is probable that worker cooperatives may consequently offer more reasonably priced food. There is also the potential for multi-stakeholder cooperatives to meet the needs of both consumers and workers.

In its work forming Brooklyn Sprout, one of the first actions of the legal team was to identify a potential opportunity in the nascent AgTech sector—a company developing hydroponic farming systems within shipping containers, which could help facilitate the inception of the enterprise. Because of the potential to scale (compared to traditional, vertical, and/or rooftop farms) with a small physical footprint and relatively small start-up costs, a modified shipping container farming flowers or vegetables could quickly generate a product to supply the hospital. This, in turn, would allow the enterprise to begin navigating the city and state procurement systems early in their operations, improving their chances of success.

The team helped locate public land for the farm to facilitate access to capital and operating expenses for a proof of concept. The team also developed a business plan in collaboration with one of the initial worker-owners. As the plan was being evaluated by funders, the team counseled initial members of the organization through entity-type selection, helped form the legal entity, and developed a framework for implementing a cooperative governance structure as the enterprise developed. Additionally, the team considered how the enterprise could position itself to coordinate with the hospital, local farmers markets, and community-supported agricultural programs and also comply with New York City's soon-to-be implemented food prescription program. The team also helped the client apply for status as a Minority and Women-Owned Enterprise (M/WBE)—another way to help secure resources and bring the organization to scale.

Challenges and Best Practices in Crisis Lawyering on Behalf of Worker Cooperatives

In our work with the Coalition and Brooklyn Sprout, there were several challenges that helped us establish some best practices for representing worker cooperatives moving forward. In reflecting on our work with the Coalition, a few notable issues arose: the idea of working with conceivers of worker cooperative projects, versus the members of that cooperative; the need for clarity of roles and adequate staffing to execute projects; the variety of lawyering approaches that may be appropriate for cooperative projects; and the need for inclusive legal problem-solving skills regardless of which lawyering approach is used. We will discuss each of these issues and challenges, in turn, and our proactive efforts to deal with them.

Working with Conceivers versus Members

Lawyers must clearly identify who their client is. When representing start-up worker cooperatives that are being supported by an organization or group of people who will not ultimately be the members of the cooperative, lawyers have the choice of representing those cooperative "conceivers," or the actual cooperative (working with its members) once the entity is being formed.[27] Several factors may influence the choice to work with conceivers: the accessibility of lawyers to conceivers working at nonprofits as opposed to for-profit cooperatives (as it may be easier to get pro bono representation for nonprofits than for-profit entities); the legal versus general informational needs of the conceiver (i.e., do they need legal representation or some other role, based on general sharing of information or idea or model generation); the legal complexity of the project (as it may be necessary for legal work to be performed before the co-op launches for certain complex projects); the need for cooperative expertise in legal representation (versus contract, license, real estate, or other legal work); the long-term relationship between the conceivers and the cooperative (e.g., some incubation models last a year or more before the co-op officially launches); the desire of the attorneys to represent and prioritize the voice of worker-owners (which may not be as centered when representing founders but may be addressed once worker-owners are on board); the desire of attorneys to support large-scale projects for maximum reach and impact (which are more likely to be developed by conceivers and not just members); and the list goes on.

For larger-scale worker cooperative projects, it is likely that there will be conceivers providing support. Conceivers often seek out the input of cooperative attorneys regarding entity type, governance, organizational structure, contracts, intellectual property, and other regulatory and compliance issues. Especially for complex projects, a lot of pre-formation work must be done to ensure the viability of the project. Many prospective worker-owners may not have the capacity to be very active during the entire pre-formation stage, especially if they are not yet being paid by the cooperative and thus likely have other work obligations.

Thus, for larger-scale projects particularly, it makes sense for cooperative attorneys to work with conceivers, at least at first. They can help troubleshoot potential issues for cooperative projects (e.g., around licensure in highly regulated industries) and embed structural protections to ensure the co-op remains a co-op and is democratically owned and operated. Cooperative attorneys associated with academic institutions can also provide research support on models and issues that arise and can leverage their networks for various needs.

The main drawback for cooperative attorneys working with conceivers is running the risk that the cooperative is dominated by the conceivers, thereby diminishing the value of a democratic workplace and lessening the empowerment of workers. Or worse yet, working closely with conceivers can raise the possibility that cooperative attorneys support a project that ultimately more closely resembles a traditional corporation, despite everyone's original and best intentions. Lawyers can implement a few strategies that can address this concern: serving as a project partner or consultant on cooperative projects, as opposed to assuming the role of counsel for the project; including language in a letter of engagement that ensures that the entity must be democratically governed or the lawyer has the right to end representation; and ensuring the lawyer has a major role, potentially even a governing role, in the cooperative start-up, so that she may help facilitate the actualization of cooperative values in the project until the worker-owners have legally become members of the cooperative. This would also allow for the lawyer to go over governance and employment issues with the worker-owners and help shape any amendments to the governance documents as appropriate.

The Need for Clarity of Roles and Adequate Staffing

A related issue is the need for adequate staffing to see a cooperative project through to launch. A successful large-scale cooperative has many needs: people who bring the ideas/theory/philosophy of cooperative economics; business people who help develop viable business plans and assist with branding and marketing; project managers who ensure those ideas become a reality and who handle day-to-day logistics; people who perform outreach to potential worker-owners and, if applicable, unions; people who train worker-owners in their trade and in cooperative management; people who leverage political networks; lawyers; fund-raisers; and others. A large-scale successful cooperative often takes multiple years to conceive of and launch, and these various roles must be staffed and funded.

These roles must be identified so that sufficient expertise is contributed to each area. And each role must be funded in the pre-formation stage of cooperative development. When they are not, projects are very slow to launch. Lawyers can sometimes take on some of these roles during the pre-formation stage, as discussed in the following two sections, but lawyers' resources are also limited, and clarity of roles is key to a smooth collaboration.

Different Lawyering Approaches May Be Useful, Depending on the Context

We also acknowledge that different lawyering approaches are called for in different circumstances, and there is not a one-size-fits-all strategy for the legal team to utilize. In the case of Brooklyn Sprout, an integrative lawyering approach worked well. In our practice, we often embrace a client-centered and/or CED-empowerment approach to lawyering, which is characterized by emphasizing the "role of marginalized stakeholders as decision makers and beneficiaries in a community's development process."[28] Indeed, the CED-empowerment approach fosters the collective action and active democratic participation of community residents to reshape their social, economic, and political systems.[29]

While this project recognized community voices as the inspiration for and source of the representation,[30] given the scale, the knowledge base of the co-alition, and the tight time frames we faced, we took an integrative lawyering approach. This approach did not and does not focus exclusively on the law-yer's counseling role, through which she strives to ensure that that the client has enough information to make its own decision, to which the lawyer then ultimately defers. The integrative lawyering approach allows for the lawyer to be an equal contributor to the representation and the discussions that flow from that representation, but she does not assume the role of final decision maker. When the lawyer assumes an integrative role with a client, she should make sure she feels comfortable giving advice based on the lawyer's expertise, but she should also commit to empowering the client to push back on and reject the lawyer's advice. Thus, the lawyer may play a larger role in various parts of the project[31]—helping conceive of models, develop strategy, advo-cate, provide public education and outreach, fund-raise, and give legal advice. Throughout this process, the lawyer gives her opinion and/or advice more directly to the client and assumes a robust deliberative and dialogic role with the client. Conceivers with a clear vision for the work tend to defer less to the lawyers' opinion, thus lawyers can more freely debate strategy with such individuals, ultimately playing a larger role in the decision-making process that informs and guides the representation, with the recognition, always, that the client makes the ultimate decisions regarding the representation, with the client and lawyer discussing the means of how to accomplish the client's goals in a collaborative and meaningful way.

Embracing an integrative lawyering approach requires applying a flexible mixture of skills, which is referred to as "role integration."[32] For this project, we had to integrate a broad range of intersectional practice areas, skills, and roles. At times we helped fund-raise, advocate, and develop budgets and business plans, in addition to acting as transactional attorneys advising on matters such as entity type, governance, contracts, and intellectual property. Under the integrative lawyering approach, the attorney is "expected to do more than translate the organization/community's grievance into discreet legal frameworks and discourse."[33] The attorney may participate in activities on behalf of or in partnership with the client from which the client may benefit from the presence of an attorney for any number of reasons. This approach requires a "shifting, flexible mix of skills and a more dynamic interaction with the organization and its varied functions—policy, community education, lobbying, and organizing"[34] as well as fund-raising and strategic planning. Indeed, because the Coalition had a complex and clearly communicated vision but was operating with limited resources, the lawyering team was deployed in all of these settings, particularly the last two. Faculty and students strategized with the Coalition on: how to build out a Central Brooklyn health-care ecosystem that would have the medical centers serve as anchor institutions that generate community health and wealth; how to create a plan that made sense of all the moving parts; and how and in what order to tackle them. As part of our work, we also helped the client take advantage of an opportunity to secure needed start-up capital, which is often one of the major obstacles to co-op formation. We did this by helping the client write a business plan and successfully secure funding. The client could not obtain these services in the market in the time frame needed, so we provided those services with the full disclosure that this was not our area of expertise—but we were willing to do what we could so the deal did not fall through. And we are fortunate enough that we had an attorney on our team with experience writing business plans and fund-raising. We consider this nonlawyering as part of our work when a client needs to build capacity and is operating under time pressures. We do the work, however, as a capacity-building tool to help the client get off the ground. It is not work that we would continue to do for the same client in future projects.

The Need for Inclusive Legal Problem-Solving Skills

Regardless of the lawyering approach selected, we see a need for inclusive, holistic legal problem-solving skills, including skills that may not traditionally be seen as legal. The authors recognize that inclusive legal problem-solving skills, including "metacognitive self-awareness, robust information gathering, active listening, language reframing, facilitation, problem-solving, and consensus-building skills,"[35] are essential skills for effective lawyering and produce the best outcomes for their clients. Part of problem-solving includes performing capacity-building work, such as drafting a business plan and securing financing that may not be traditionally viewed as legal work. Capacity-building work is often needed in a systems-change context. It is critical in helping the community turn their dreams into reality, and while some clients may not have these particular skills at first, they do have the business skills and need only temporary assistance in getting their business off the ground before they either develop these skills themselves or can afford to pay for them.

One might argue that a lawyer's expertise lies in legal representation and that lawyers should not spend their time fund-raising, relationship-building, or acting as business consultants. However, in our work generally, we have found that refusing to take on these roles can result in stalled or even failed projects. Furthermore, an expanded role for lawyers, including public education and other nonlegal responsibilities, is widely observed and advocated for in community-lawyering settings.[36] The authors also note that this critique seems to be applied mainly to the social justice–lawyering context, but not to an equal extent in a private, for-profit corporate context. Corporate lawyers have long played more expansive roles on behalf of their private-sector clients: "[I]t is an established, successful corporate law convention for lawyers to have a more expansive professional role. CED lawyers, like business lawyers, act as strategist[s], counselors, and facilitators before a variety of involved third parties."[37] In addition:

> [L]awyers can advance client empowerment by providing additional expert guidance on these [non-legal] matters in order to supplement the client's abilities. Providing this assistance fosters the actual development of client autonomy. The lawyer's involvement educates the client on how to approach such matters on their own in the future, especially if the client organization and its members have not acquired these skills in the past.[38]

We do believe that lawyers should perform only work that they are competent to perform, whether that is legal or nonlegal. However, we stand behind our choice to take on various roles in this project. When performing such tasks, however, it is important to clarify with the client what role the client wants to assume when taking on those tasks, especially whether it is legal or nonlegal. We also encourage clients to consider building into their project budgets line items for services such as project management staff and for activities that foster collaboration among subject-matter experts who may provide additional needed technical services. We are very intentional in our efforts to ensure that we are not assuming too large a role in carrying out the tasks necessary to see a project through to completion, because we do not want to crowd out or displace the role that community members should play in ensuring that the outcome of the representation adequately reflects and embodies their interests.

Conclusion

Many in the worker cooperative movement are grappling with how to increase the size and scope of worker cooperatives. We hope that our approach can serve as guidance for those who wish to build out a model that combines an anchor-institution approach with a sectoral approach to maximize the reach and impact of the benefits of the model, including contributing to larger economic democracy and social justice movements, as well as laying a foundation for a robust cooperative ecosystem. In the health-care sector, this is an approach that can sustain access to health care and address the social determinants of health, including by preventing job loss and its consequent associated crises, while also creating sustainable, safe, and dignified jobs and building collective wealth. Given the multitude of crises simultaneously occurring today, particularly in communities that are marginalized, focusing on anchor institutions and specific sectors can address the intersection of various crises through worker ownership, including the lack of economic security, food sovereignty, and improved health outcomes, which are all exacerbated by racial disparities and the political-economic crises of our time.

NOTES

1 On growing authoritarianism in the twenty-first century, *see* YASCHA MOUNK, THE PEOPLE VS. DEMOCRACY: WHY OUR FREEDOM IS IN DANGER AND HOW TO SAVE IT (2018).

2 Matthew Desmond, *In Order to Understand the Brutality of American Capitalism, You Have to Start on the Plantation*, N.Y. TIMES (Aug. 14, 2019) (tracing the brutality of the American system of capitalism to its origins in slavery).

3 On the interplay between economic inequality and political inequality generally, *see* JACOB S. HACKER & PAUL PIERSON, WINNER-TAKE-ALL POLITICS: HOW WASHINGTON MADE THE RICH RICHER—AND TURNED ITS BACK ON THE MIDDLE CLASS (2011).

4 *See, e.g.,* Gautam Mukunda, *The Social and Political Costs of the Financial Crisis, 10 Years Later*, HARV. BUS. REV. (Sep. 25, 2018).

5 JOSEPH E. STIGLITZ: PROGRESSIVE CAPITALISM FOR AN AGE OF
   DISCONTENT 35–38 (2019) (discussing ever-rising inequality in the United
   States).

6 Pam Fessler, *3 Million Could Lose Food Stamp Benefits Under Trump
   Administration Proposal*, NPR (Jul 23, 2019, 12:07pm ET).

7 KALI AKUNO & AJAMU NANGWAYA, JACKSON RISING: THE STRUGGLE
   FOR ECONOMIC DEMOCRACY AND BLACK SELF-DETERMINATION IN
   JACKSON, MISSISSIPPI 8–9 (2017). Akuno and Nangwaya describe how the
   capitalist system can no longer absorb the Black working class into productive
   endeavors, leading to "correction and contraction," which excludes and if
   necessary disposes of all the surpluses that cannot be absorbed or consumed at a
   profit (essentially illustrating that capitalism after slavery views Black labor as a
   surplus, which they seek to remove from the market via imprisonment). *Id.*

8 On the relationship between economic inequality and adverse health outcomes,
   see STIGLITZ, PEOPLE, POWER, AND PROFITS, 40–43.

9 *See, e.g.*, Louise Matsakis, *The Truth About Amazon, Food Stamps, and Tax Breaks*,
   WIRED (Sep. 6, 2018, 07:27P.M. ET) (explaining that, despite being valued at $1
   trillion, Amazon makes the Top 20 list of companies with full-time workers who
   receive SNAP benefits). Despite Amazon claiming $11.2 billion in profits in 2018,
   it also paid no corporate taxes.

10 Joshua Brustein, *Hospitals in Crisis*, GOTHAM GAZETTE (Sept. 26, 2005, www.
   gothamgazette.com/health/3004-hospitals-in-crisis.

11 On the role of corporate support for conservative politicians and policies that are
   hostile to working people, let alone the environment and public health, see Jane
   Mayer, Dark Money: The Hidden History of the Billionaires Behind the Rise of
   The Radical Right (2016).

12 *See, e.g.*, Carmen Huertas-Noble, Jessica Rose & Brian Glick, *The Greening of
   Community and Economic Development: Dispatches From New York City*, 31 W.
   NEW ENG. L. REV. 645, 654 (2009).

13 *Id.*

14 *See, e.g.*, COMMUNITY-WEALTH.ORG, www.community-wealth.org.

15 *See, e.g.*, Priya Baskaran, *Introduction to Worker Cooperatives and Their Role in the
   Changing Economy*, 24 J. AFFORDABLE HOUSING & COMMUNITY DEV. L.
   355, 366 (2015).

16 NEW YORK CITY, DEPARTMENT OF HEALTH AND MENTAL HYGIENE,
   COMMUNITY HEALTH PROFILES 2018 (2018).

17 *See Governor Cuomo Announces Next Step in $1.4 Billion Vital Brooklyn Initiative*,
   GOVERNOR ANDREW M. CUOMO (Aug. 16, 2018), www.governor.ny.gov.

18 *See, e.g.*, Anna Brones, *Food Apartheid: the Roots of the Problem With America's
   Groceries*, THE GUARDIAN (May 15, 2018).

19 *See, e.g.*, Rashid Njai et al., *Prevalence of Perceived Food and Housing Security—15
   States, 2013*, 66 MMWR MORB. MORTAL. WKLY. REP. 12, 12 (2017).

20 *See generally* Daniel Sullivan, *From Food Desert to Food Mirage: Race, Social Class, and Food Shopping in a Gentrifying Neighborhood*, 4 ADVANCES IN APPLIED SOC. 30 (2014).

21 *See, e.g.,* BROOKLYN COMMUNITY FOUNDATION, BROOKLYN FACTS, www. brooklyncommunityfoundation.org.

22 *See* Brones, *Food Apartheid.*

23 *Just Food, Justice From the Ground Up's Tipsheet: Defining Food Security, Justice and Sovereignty*, 2 (quoting the Movement for Black Lives) (on file with the author).

24 *Id.* at 4.

25 Dan DePasquale et al., *Forging Food Justice Through Cooperatives in New York City*, 45 FORDHAM URB. L.J. 909, 910 (2018).

26 *See* Jonathan Brown, *Beyond Corporate Form: A Response to Dan Depasquale, Surbhi Sarang, and Natalie Bump Vena's Forging Food Justice Through Cooperatives in New York City*, 45 FORDHAM URB. L.J. 1121, 1123 (2018).

27 Note that this is not a discussion on the legal ethics of this choice but a reflection on strategy and logistics. The authors note that legal ethics are always a part of our considerations when weighing strategic and logistical decisions with clients.

28 Carmen Huertas-Noble, *Promoting Worker-Owned Cooperatives as a CED Empowerment Strategy: A Case Study of Colors and Lawyering in Support of Participatory Decision-Making and Meaningful Social Change*, 17 CLINICAL L. REV. 255, 258 (2010).

29 *Id.* at 284.

30 NYS DOH convened a series of community engagement sessions in which Northwell Health participated to inform its study, which included three major activities: (1) conducting surveys of community perceptions; (2) facilitating small group discussions on specific health issues (e.g., cancer, diabetes, asthma, etc.); and (3) eight community engagement meetings where individuals provided testimonials on a wide range of topics, including their vision of what type of health care system would best serve them. The NYS Commissioner of Health led community engagement meetings with representatives of the governor's office, NYS DOH, and elected officials.

31 Sheila R. Foster & Brian Glick, *Integrative Lawyering: Navigating the Political Economy of Urban Redevelopment*, 95 CALIF. L. REV. 1999, 2057–59 (2007).

32 *Id.*

33 *Id.* at 2004.

34 *Id.* at 2004–05.

35 Beryl Blaustone & Carmen Huertas-Noble, *Lawyering at the Intersection of Mediation and Community Economic Development: Interweaving Inclusive Legal Problem-Solving Skills in the Training of Effective Lawyers*, 34 WASH. U. J.L. & POL'Y 157, 160 (2010).

36 *See* Foster & Brian Glick, *Integrative Lawyering*, 2057.

37 *Id.*, 159.

38 *Id.* , 159.

11

The Crisis Comes Once a Year

Lawyering on Election Day

DAVID S. TURETSKY

Elections are fundamental to the maintenance of democracy. Election monitoring poses significant challenges to lawyers, challenges parallel in many respects to crisis lawyering. I have been a lawyer for more than thirty-five years. Over my entire career, my principal pro bono area has been voting rights and protection. Voting is a fundamental right, secured through struggle. It is foundational to our other rights and the legitimacy of our government. For many, it is central to their personal dignity. For decades, I have worked to protect voters' rights on, and sometimes before and after, the vast majority of Election Days. In this chapter, I present a personal account of my experience of election (day) lawyering and conclude with a more generalized list of lessons-learned picked up over the years.

My election work has been organized around a simple principle: everyone who is eligible to cast a ballot should be able to do so and have it counted. A subsidiary principle is to keep the lines moving on Election Day because delays inevitably lead to reduced voter participation. In my experience, my political party uses its limited voter protection resources on Election Day to monitor the precincts that are likely to perform the best for our candidates. We often do not know a voter's intentions and we do not ask, but we do know that every vote prevented from being cast and counted in those precincts is more likely than not to be one of ours.

Unlike some crises discussed in other chapters of this volume, we know the arrival and duration of Election Day far in advance. We often know which problems may arise and the applicable laws, rules, and policies.

I was hooked on voter protection early. Indeed, the very first case I worked on to protect voting rights came when I was still a law student—a summer associate at a big New York City law firm. That case included an emergency hearing at the United States Supreme Court after a decision by a three-judge court required under the terms of the Voting Rights Act that resulted in postponement of the New York City primary elections in 1981. New York City argued early in the case that my colleagues were asking too soon for relief for

New York City's failure to obtain preclearance under the Voting Rights Act for changes it had made to polling locations. Then the City argued a few days before the election that we were too late. The three-judge court sided with us, dramatically enjoining the New York City primary election from proceeding only a few days before it was supposed to take place. One judge asked exactly when the City thought the time to decide the case was just right.

That same day, with the New York City media and political world ablaze, I joined the second-year associate who led the case, Kim Sperduto, and the third-year associate who was next in charge, Gwenellen Janov, on the shuttle to Washington, DC, and the Supreme Court to respond to what we knew would be New York City's imminent request for an emergency stay. As we arrived with books and a typewriter, the guards at the Court loaned us use of their locker room. That enabled us to quickly pull together a set of responsive papers to file on a moment's notice when New York City sought an emergency stay from the Court not long after our arrival. Unfortunately for New York City, the Supreme Court justice responsible for hearing its emergency request was Associate Justice Thurgood Marshall, one of the prime architects of the landmark Voting Rights Act. I was happy not to be a lawyer for New York City trying to explain its version of the Voting Rights Act to him. He polled the Court after the lawyers left, and the three-judge court's injunction remained in place.[1]

My commitment and involvement grew. Some years, I monitored a precinct. Other years, I helped lead or coordinate parts of voter protection efforts, as I did for Senator Bill Bradley in his final campaign for US Senate in New Jersey in 1990.

I also helped to respond to some unusual election emergencies. For a part of the 2000 presidential election circus in Florida, I had a good but unsatisfying seat. I was involved in the postelection review of the troubling "butterfly ballot." The design of that ballot confused a substantial number of would-be Al Gore voters in Palm Beach County into casting votes for third-party candidate Pat Buchanan. Notwithstanding the affidavits we obtained and the interviews we conducted—which documented the confusion, anger, and sadness of voters who mistakenly voted for someone whom some of them considered to be a racist—there was no remedy found after the election sufficient to address that particular problem.

In 2004, I was based in Harrisburg to help the coordinator of voter protection efforts in central Pennsylvania. Mobilized in significant part by the 2000 election mess in Florida, we deployed an unprecedented number of volunteer monitors who we trained on the law, process, and practicalities and instructed them how to enter information into a sophisticated computer data system that enhanced our situational awareness and response.

In this chapter I will highlight the lessons learned from these experiences. As a primary case study, I use events that occurred in Chesterfield County, Virginia, in 2008, from the primary contest to the general election. Although I helped solve some problems on Primary Day that year, the ones that got away are the heart of the story. We then acted aggressively and successfully to make sure that these problems would not recur in the 2008 general election.

As lawyers, we try to plan and anticipate. As election rights lawyers, we work to get the rules right, to solve as many problems as possible before Election Day, and to ensure that strategies and pathways for communications are in place to address the problems that may occur anyway. Unfortunately, we often have to grapple with problems on or even after Election Day that have the potential to affect the integrity or outcome of an election.

As citizens and likely voters, we are equity holders ourselves in the process of voting. We bring our own experiences and plans as voters. Our personal experience as voters can help us understand—as lawyers—what is happening and what is at stake, but it may also make some of us feel we have all the tools we need to act and the authority to do so. It may leave us fuzzy about who, exactly, is our client. As lawyers—beyond our role as citizens—we usually bring an additional tool kit, which includes some ability to read and understand the US and state constitutions, statutes, cases, rules, interpretations, and other components of the law. We may bring experience in advocacy and an understanding of legal processes. Some of us may be comfortable appearing before agencies and in courtrooms.

The equities that lawyers bring to the situation as professionals are usually very helpful. Sometimes they are not. They may not be helpful when lawyers of varying skill and experience unilaterally decide to take on local election officials aggressively in a hostile or threatening manner or communicate to the media with limited information and without much of a plan—or maybe even a bad one. Lawyers may accomplish great things, but they may also not be practical and may instead complicate the ability to solve problems and may even create new ones. The following case study describes my work in one series of elections; I try also to draw on these experiences to highlight larger lessons for crisis lawyering on Election Day and beyond.

Chesterfield County, VA, and the 2008 Democratic Primary and General Elections

As the 2008 primary and general elections approached, I had worked in voter protection for decades. I was a partner then in the Washington, DC, office of a large law firm. There, I organized (together with another lawyer) a pro bono Election Day monitoring program, which supplied Election Day volunteer legal monitors to the Democrats, Republicans, and other organizations, depending on the individual preferences of our attorneys.[2] Participants focused strictly on voter protection and not get-out-the-vote or other partisan activities.

Background: Observing on Election Day at the Virginia State Board of Elections

From about 2008 through 2015, I played the same role in Virginia every Election Day. The State Board of Elections (SBE) in Richmond invited each party to supply one observer to be present and interact with the leadership and staff of the SBE. A party could substitute for its observer over the course of the thirteen hours the polls were open, as well as the period before and after. I was the observer for the Democratic Party of Virginia. I usually arrived before the polls opened and departed only after the last votes were cast. I played this role for all general elections and several primary elections in this period. For a few elections, including the 2008 presidential primary, I began in that role and someone relieved me late in the day.

The role was tightly coordinated with the rest of the effort by my party to protect the vote. Before Election Day, I participated in the training and coordination meetings for precinct monitors and observers, as well as for the boiler room (a central, colocated group of expert lawyers who sifted through and followed up on information from monitors in the field, aggregated information, directed responses, etc.). I met the people, learned the procedures, and built a strong relationship with the boiler room and political teams. I also had access to the software program that showed in real time all the information that the precinct monitors or the boiler room personnel had input about individual incidents. I could sort the information by county, type of incident, assessed severity, time of occurrence, and other factors. My job was to escalate to the SBE or otherwise respond to requests for help at the SBE from the boiler-room leadership and to convey back information about what was happening at the SBE and around the state from the SBE's perspective. In addition—particularly the first few times I was there—the SBE established an open and transparent model that enabled the observers to do much more to address election issues.

In my first years in this role, SBE secretary Nancy Rodrigues invited both parties' observers to sit with her in her office, the hub of many of the SBE's Election Day activities. We were sometimes joined by SBE staff, SBE members, or a representative of the state attorney general. We were able to hear reports from staff about issues they were learning about and Secretary Rodrigues's telephone calls with county and city registrars and others. On some occasions, we were invited to participate in the conversation in a limited fashion. Many of the calls were put on speaker, and the secretary always disclosed who was in the room. If a legal issue required sensitive consultation with the Attorney General's office, or it was otherwise appropriate, we briefly stepped out. This was the gold standard. We could hear the secretary of the SBE discuss with jurisdictions their particular election issues and relevant voter calls and complaints, the status of issues, and next steps. Near the end of a call, Secretary Rodrigues would often turn to the observers to ask whether we had reports or descriptions of any other problems or issues in the jurisdiction that was on the phone or whether we knew other information about the issues they had discussed. To respond, I would look at the database reporting system that captured the up-to-date information submitted by our election monitoring volunteers and our boiler room or other information that had been highlighted for me to share with the relevant jurisdiction. Often, the county election officials agreed to look into a situation I raised if they did not already know about it and to call back the secretary with an update that I would be able to listen in on. For the most part, county officials seemed fine enough with this transparency.

Allowing the observers to engage with election officials at the SBE offices and across the Commonwealth in this way was a tremendously efficient way to identify and resolve issues and to ensure that all stakeholders had accurate and up-to-date information about the status of the election. This process built trust and provided a forum to share information and reduce misunderstanding and conflict. It even led to some cordial dialogue between the parties, with the party observers often agreeing how to address a thorny issue.

The SBE would also make statements to the press at certain scheduled times on Election Day to characterize for the public what was happening across Virginia. Shortly before doing so, it would often share a draft with the observers and allow the parties to provide some feedback, as the SBE was interested in making sure that the statement was accurate and wanted to know whether either party had a very different perspective from the SBE. Similarly, the SBE often shared with the observers draft guidance or updates it intended to send directly to the registrars during the day to address recurring questions or issues. Sometimes the SBE would consider suggestions from the observers, made openly in front of each other, about the language of the guidance. This was a way to make sure that the SBE would not unknowingly provide guidance that might be misunderstood and that a party would view as wrong or problematic. It enabled the SBE at least to consider other language and to become aware promptly of what might be in dispute. These opportunities to communicate about election issues across Virginia in a timely and effective manner—coupled with my close coordination with the boiler room—enabled everyone to be up to date, skip issues that already were addressed, and avoid inconsistencies. Sometimes, I would call a poll monitor directly, sometimes with the boiler room on the phone, to get more specific information or to be briefed on any new developments. It was crucial to have the most credible, complete, and up-to-date information available to share in conversations with registrars.

Other Virginia SBE secretaries, while cordial and professional, did not necessarily meet Secretary Rodrigues's gold standard in later years. Before one election, I objected strenuously to an SBE proposal to move observers to a different floor in the SBE offices, which would have severely reduced access to relevant SBE officials. In response, the proposal was modified to place us on the same floor as the secretary and much of the staff, but down the hall. This excluded the observers from most calls, reducing transparency and making the job tougher. That likely contributed to the Democratic Party filing a rare lawsuit one Election Day, based on sustained voter lines of two hours and more in certain jurisdictions. The SBE would not agree that lines longer than ninety minutes required action, such as an extension of polling hours or a different process to check in voters (e.g., splitting the polling books to create additional check-in lines), where other approaches were unavailable or unsuccessful at reducing the lines. On one Election Day when I was otherwise relegated to an office down the hall from the secretary, with some drama I came to the secretary's office and stood there holding my phone out. I outlined a proposal as it was conveyed to me by the Democratic Party's counsel, identifying what remedies would be acceptable for polling places still experiencing delays of similar magnitude as an alternative to filing a lawsuit. I waited as the SBE discussed the delays and the proposal and decided not to do what we requested. I told my colleagues the response and to go ahead and file suit. Such lawsuits rarely prevail in Virginia, and this suit met that common fate.

Virginia's 2008 Presidential Primary Election in Chesterfield County as I Saw It from the Virginia State Board of Elections

The fastest-paced Election Day that I experienced at the Virginia SBE was the 2008 presidential election. I stayed on duty the entire time, beginning before the polls opened, and I was exhausted by the end of the day. Turnout was high. There also were many volunteers monitoring the precincts, and at times the information flooded in. Practicing my own kind of emergency preparedness, I brought a laptop, an iPad, and a cell phone. I arranged to have access to the guest broadband service at the SBE and the ability to connect to different mobile carriers for each device. I researched which two carriers provided the best connections in that location. In addition, I brought an inkjet printer and paper. I realized that it was sometimes helpful to the SBE staff for me to provide a specific description of incidents in order to avoid miscommunication and to generate needed follow-up, particularly when we were not in the same room as the secretary and SBE staff.

While the presidential general elections in 2008 and 2012 were by far the busiest for me at the SBE, the most consequential from a voter protection standpoint turned out to be the 2008 presidential primaries. Of course, in a presidential primary, voters choose the candidate who will represent their party in the subsequent general election, and although multiple parties hold their primaries on the same day, the parties do not compete directly against one another. I was the Democratic Party observer at the SBE, stationed in Secretary Rodrigues's office as described above. While there, I learned of a number of problems. These plagued Democrats much more than the Republicans, given the historically high participation levels after Senators Barack Obama and Hillary Clinton, who were competing for the Democratic presidential nomination, campaigned in and prioritized Virginia, an important swing state.

Early on Primary Day, the SBE received phone complaints about delays and long lines in Chesterfield County—a county I did not know much about yet. It was located just below Richmond and in a different media market than the northern Virginia/Washington suburbs where I resided. Reports from observers and voters alike conveyed disturbing information about early-morning voting problems there.

Chesterfield County was a large, historically Republican, and mostly White county that was in the midst of change. The county's Democratic voting performance was substantially increasing, and the county was adding new multifamily housing and becoming more diverse. Chesterfield had reportedly been the only county in Virginia to have monitors assigned to it in 2004 by the US Department of Justice under the Voting Rights Act. This followed a series of complaints, including allegations about an intention to place armed guards at polling precincts. In 2006, the American Civil Liberties Union asked the Department of Justice to send monitors to Chesterfield County based on a litany of allegations about voter ID requirements; the handling of provisional ballots; and alleged abuse, such as requiring that voters provide social security numbers to obtain absentee ballots. I was not initially aware of these earlier allegations.

Secretary Rodrigues reached out to the general registrar in Chesterfield County to report the calls, to learn more about what was happening and whether the SBE could provide help. The registrar said that the wait that morning in a specific precinct under discussion was only fifteen minutes and not the forty-five minutes that one voter had reported to us. That local registrar was not very receptive to the SBE. As I listened in on that call, I was able to pass along additional reports of delays. I also noted that the registrar's statements were not consistent with what voters were telling us—so someone had to be wrong. I asked him if he would mind checking directly with the precinct involved and let Secretary Rodrigues know which information was correct. He said he would do that and later called back to say wait times there were from fifteen to forty-five minutes. This did not give us confidence in the process or in the accuracy of the reports we were receiving from that registrar.

The SBE received complaints directly from voters in several precincts and from other sources relating to Chesterfield County. The Democratic Party also received complaints about several Chesterfield County precincts from voters, poll observers, and local party officials. The press was becoming aware, too. All these reports concerned long waits for Democratic primary ballots and voters who were leaving crowded polling places without voting, with some saying they would try to return later. This information and high turnout across Virginia suggested major turnout still to come, as did national voter participation trends from primaries earlier that year. We raised with the Chesterfield County registrar the possibility of another major rush of voters around dinnertime and of a possible shortage of ballots. On a series of calls with the secretary, the registrar advised us that, notwithstanding the high morning turnout and the voters who said they would come back to vote later due to the long lines and delays, dinnertime would not be a busy voting time in Chesterfield County. He said that only the morning is a busy voting time in Chesterfield County and that his county did not need help. I urged that the county consider steps such as splitting poll books to enable more and faster check-in lines, as well as other steps to be ready for another busy period, all to no avail.

Failures by Chesterfield County Election Officials Deprived Voters of the Right to Vote

Another observer from my party relieved me just before the busy voting time at the end of the day. I subsequently learned that devastating problems arose when the voter rush that everyone (except the Chesterfield County registrar) had predicted actually materialized. Precincts in Chesterfield County ran low on ballots and sought more from the county registrar during the day, even as the registrar denied to the SBE, while I was listening in, that there was a problem. He refused offers of help from the SBE. Eventually, traffic and long distances made timely delivery from the county registrar's office of additional ballots they could find or print (they also had a printer equipment problem) difficult. Eventually, voter complaints made directly to the

SBE and information from Democratic Party observers clearly illuminated serious problems in Chesterfield County. While the secretary made a couple of the SBE's employees available earlier that day to help a precinct in a different county that had a problem and was grateful for the assistance, her offers to help Chesterfield County with its possible ballot shortage and other issues were refused. Nevertheless, the secretary determined that she had the authority to dispatch state troopers to deliver additional ballots to precincts in Chesterfield County that had none, and she did so. By then, the county's failure to share information had left little time for that to work, although state troopers succeeded in bringing more ballots to at least one precinct that ran out before the polls closed.

What happened in Chesterfield County was shocking and sad. The Chesterfield County registrar and electoral board stood by as numerous precincts ran out of Democratic ballots. Lines ballooned to hundreds of voters. Delays proliferated. Some older and disabled voters gave up. Some voting precinct officials who had continually requested additional ballots from the registrar during the day were frustrated. Finally, after long delays, county election officials asked precinct election officials to create Democratic primary ballots out of scrap paper. In turn, some precinct voting officials assured waiting voters that their scrap paper votes would count and that they could then leave without waiting for additional printed Democratic ballots. Many just left rather than cast votes on scrap paper that they feared would not count.

There was no consultation by the Chesterfield County registrar's office about voting on "scrap paper" with the SBE, with any Voting Rights Act enforcers (Virginia was subject to the Voting Rights Act), or even with a lawyer for Chesterfield County (although the chair of the local electoral board was a lawyer and reportedly was involved in the decision to allow this manner of voting). Finally, even though many left the long lines without voting due to the delays and confusion, and others left after hearing that scrap paper would be used for ballots, some 299 eligible voters stayed and cast their votes on scrap paper, writing down the name of their preferred candidate. All these scrap-paper ballots were ultimately determined not to meet the requirements of state law and the county could not count them. So, it is clear that no fewer than hundreds of voters were disenfranchised by the way election officials in Chesterfield County ran the election, including voters who did absolutely everything asked of them by the precinct election officials at their polling places. In fact, highly credible claims documented by affidavits suggest clearly that the number of disenfranchised Democratic primary voters in Chesterfield County totaled at least hundreds more given all the people who left polling places without voting, maybe considerably more than 1,000 voters.

The affidavits showed that voters left the long lines without voting for many reasons. For example, voters referred to jobs to which they could not be late and unaffordable economic costs associated with waiting, such as paying for extra child care if it was available. One voter estimated under oath that he saw 100 people leave the line in a single precinct. In other precincts, there was testimony that many more left without voting. One affiant saw at least ten cars enter a parking lot and, not finding any places to park, drive away. In affidavits, voters described having waited in cars as those with whom they had come to vote who were in better health, and better able to stand in line to vote, would do so. A spouse, neighbor, or friend would then call them to come in to vote when that person had made his or her way to the front of the line. Sometimes, however, even those individuals who did go in to save a spot in line never made it to the front of the line—meaning they had no chance to vote. Affidavits also described a lack of chairs and disabled parking at voting sites. One voter stated that she had to sit in another room and asked someone in line to come get her when they got close to the front of the line. Another woman who relied on an oxygen tank said in her affidavit that she had to leave without voting because of the long, disorderly lines as her oxygen came close to running out.

Of sixty-three voting precincts in Chesterfield County, nine ran out of Democratic ballots. Six of those nine, or two-thirds, were among the dozen precincts with the highest African American voting-age populations in Chesterfield County. Those six precincts accounted for most of the voters given irregular pieces of scrap paper to use as Democratic ballots. Apparently, in *at least* one precinct, voters in a long line were mostly African American. With the supply of Democratic ballots exhausted in that precinct, the precinct workers invited the Republicans to come forward out of line and vote, since there were enough Republican ballots available. A stream of White voters left the line, coming forward to the front, bypassing waiting and frustrated African American voters. What an extraordinarily disturbing scene.

To rebut the inference that it had conducted the election in a way that disproportionally harmed Black voters, Chesterfield County's lawyers responded in subsequent litigation that most of the affected precincts were majority White. However, the county was referring to the racial composition of *all* registered voters in a precinct, of course—not those who vote in a Democratic primary election. As is clear from data across the nation, African American voters disproportionately support Democrats. Most were voting in the Democratic primary in which voters were disenfranchised, not in the Republican primary that had enough ballots. This was reinforced by the affidavits describing the stream of White Republican voters bypassing African American voters waiting in line to vote in the Democratic primary.

This mess generated considerable outrage after it occurred. The county registrar alternated between apologizing, deflecting, and accusing. He was proud and sure of himself, of his expertise and judgment, and did not appreciate being questioned or criticized. As Primary Day unfolded, he denied problems were occurring, responded slowly, and insisted there would not be a rush of voters in the evening when he was asked early in the day to take measures to prepare for exactly that event in light of the severe problems that arose in the morning. In the days and weeks after the primary election, while occasionally acknowledging responsibility and apologizing for portions of what happened, he interspersed attacks and excuses and deflected responsibility.

The Aftermath of the Chesterfield County Mess—the Firm's Pro Bono Effort

I led a pro bono effort by our law firm to address the disastrous primary election in Chesterfield County. The associate who was my main colleague in the effort was a talented young lawyer named Elizabeth Gilbert. Often, there are no specific firsthand sworn statements in these circumstances. We sought to document exactly what happened to voters because of the decisions by Chesterfield County election officials. It took considerable effort, but we collected sworn statements from voters who personally encountered problems, including those who could not vote or who cast scrap-paper ballots that did not count. Our original plan was to build a clear and strong record of officials' mismanagement and voter disenfranchisement and leave it to the SBE to act on that record and protect voters by ensuring that Chesterfield County would change its ways—and hopefully its senior electoral leadership.

We obtained many sworn affidavits from voters who were harmed, and we were even able to obtain a few from election officers in the affected precincts, describing the county election officials' failure to provide additional ballots despite repeated requests these precinct officials made over many hours. The affidavits also described the county registrar's office telling precinct officials to use scrap paper to create ballots. Voters describe waiting in line for hours, including trying to do so with children present. One described doing so and then, at the end, being handed and then completing one of the 299 scrap-paper ballots that were not counted. The affidavits taken together describe witnessing hundreds of prospective voters leaving the lines either as they waited for ballots or learned they would only get scrap paper. Some voters with disabilities explained why the lines and confusion prevented them from voting. We provided many of these sworn statements to the Virginia SBE as part of its investigatory process. I spoke at the SBE hearing on the matter, describing the conversations I had with the Chesterfield County registrar on

Election Day while I was at the SBE as an observer, summarizing the affidavits, and explaining what they showed.

The SBE investigation concluded, among other things, that Chesterfield County: (1) "improperly assessed voter turnout" and appeared to have failed to thoughtfully distribute ballots; (2) failed to fully staff its precincts; (3) exacerbated problems by instructing poll workers not to "split the poll books" to allow more than one check-in line at each precinct; (4) "failed to promptly respond" to ballot shortages by waiting several hours to print more or to follow the approved procedure of photocopying ballots; and (5) failed to accept assistance from the State Board of Elections, which offered to provide additional poll workers and to print and distribute ballots.[3]

Although the SBE issued a highly informative, important, and critical report, it did not take or recommend any serious personnel changes and actions (which would have been difficult for the SBE to make happen). Neither were there any resignations by officials in Chesterfield County. Notwithstanding, the Chesterfield County registrar promptly stood up at the SBE meeting and said to the press and public that everyone should just ignore what he called the flawed conclusions contained in the SBE report. Along the same lines, one Chesterfield County Election Board member reportedly said earlier: "It really doesn't concern me about what the state board says."[4]

Those rejections by Chesterfield County election leaders of the SBE's findings and recommendations, coupled with their problematic actions and frequently combative statements on primary Election Day and thereafter, led us to conclude that the matter should not stop there. We availed ourselves of forums at the Department of Justice and the United States Congress to ensure that Chesterfield County would change its approach, respect voters, and properly administer the 2008 general election. Two major next steps were: the appearance of one of our pro bono clients before the Senate Judiciary Committee; and our filing of a complaint at the Department of Justice, citing the Voting Rights Act, various disabilities laws, and other relevant constitutional and statutory law. The complaint included the affidavits, newspaper reports about the comments by Chesterfield County election officials, an analysis of relevant law, and the investigative report from the SBE.

Senate Judiciary Committee Testimony

One of our pro bono clients, who had voted on scrap paper and had her vote discarded, accepted an invitation to testify publicly at a hearing of the Senate Judiciary Committee. The topic of the hearing was readiness for the 2008 general election. Committee staff expressed a desire to hear from at least one witness with a human story about voting problems, and that is exactly what they got.[5] We thought that her story was important to tell so that senators and the public would hear a true and compelling story from a real person who did everything asked of her—but who still was denied her right to vote. We interviewed her extensively and prepared a draft of her testimony based on what she told us. We incorporated her changes, and she practiced with us just before the hearing. We hoped that she would touch hearts as well as minds. Following is a summary of what she said.

Our client was an African American teacher who lived in Chesterfield County and taught middle school. She explained that she was not a public person, just someone who treasured the right to vote. As a child, she and other children in her family accompanied her grandmother to vote in Virginia. Her grandmother earned money by cleaning houses and had to clean extra houses to raise the money to pay the poll tax when voting time came around, because that was still the era of barriers like poll taxes in the South.

Our client had brought her second-grade son with her to the polling place to teach him how important voting is—the way her grandmother taught her. She wanted him to come out for this historic primary election for president, where the choices were an African American man and a woman, something that had never happened before. He had been learning about Susan B. Anthony and the suffrage movement in school, so this especially resonated with her as a teaching opportunity.

Her mother, who votes at the same precinct, told her there was already a line at 6:15 A.M. Our client first tried to vote at the polling place with her son in the morning, around 7:30 A.M., but the parking situation was terrible and the line was too long. She decided to try again later because her son had to go to school, and she had to get to work as a teacher at a different school. She came back to the polling place with her son around 5 P.M. Cars were parked all over, including on the grass. When she got inside, the line was incredibly long, maybe with 200 people, snaking out of the cafeteria and through the hallways, down toward classrooms. She and her son were fortunate because his basketball coach was behind them in line. With his help and that of another person, she tried to keep her son engaged, a young child who had already had a long day.

She knew others were less fortunate. She watched others leave without voting, including a mother with a daughter who had a disability. She listened to a woman in line near her explain that she had paid extra money to have her son stay late at day care so she could vote, but after an hour without voting and no clarity as to what was happening, that woman had to leave. She saw another woman who stood in line with the plan to get her disabled husband from the car to vote when she got close, but she had to leave without voting, since there was nowhere to sit and rest. She also watched Republican voters, mostly White, proceed to the front of the line because there were plenty of ballots for them—it was just Democratic ballots that ran out, and those voters happened to be disproportionately Black.

Still, she had no idea what was about to happen to her vote. After an hour and a half of confusion and uncertainty, election officials gave her and other voters pieces of scrap paper to use to vote—just torn-up, old-fashioned computer paper, green and with perforations—and her scrap-paper ballot would never count, notwithstanding that she was assured otherwise by her precinct voting officials.

She testified, sadly, that even her grandmother would have been surprised that her granddaughter lost her right to vote in 2008. Some of those listening in the hearing room shed a tear as she quietly told her story.

Optics/Strategic Considerations

We considered whether to file suit against Chesterfield County. We did not do so principally for two reasons.

First, one of our key objectives at that point was to protect our clients' voting rights by ensuring a fair and efficient 2008 general election in Chesterfield County. If we could not secure removal of the Chesterfield County registrar, then we thought the best thing would be to keep the pressure on by getting the Department of Justice to take important oversight action and to send monitors to Chesterfield County for the general election. We felt that our case for that relief was strong.

Second, ironically, we were concerned that if we filed suit in federal court and won—and we thought we would win—we would have the right to an award of attorneys' fees from Chesterfield County. These fees would be very substantial, as our law firm was devoting hundreds of hours of pro bono work to the project and large Washington firms charge high rates. A suit might also be expensive and time-consuming and might not provide timely and effective relief. Moreover, we were concerned that a lawsuit might unfairly be characterized as an attempt to malign the county and generate profit for big-city lawyers at the expense of county taxpayers. Those accusations would be wrong and unfair to our clients, all of whom were Chesterfield County residents and voters, and unfair to us as lawyers. We wanted to keep the spotlight on the county's failures and the steps needed for improvement. Fortunately, the firm was not pressing me to recover fees for our substantial pro bono investment.

Not surprisingly, the county disagreed with the complaint and arguments that we submitted to the Civil Rights Division of the US Department of Justice. In their responsive filing, they disputed some points and tried mightily to minimize others.[6] They defended the decision to use scrap-paper ballots that disenfranchised so many voters by pointing a finger elsewhere, saying that Virginia erred in not counting them. Nevertheless, even they acknowledged that there were major failings by Chesterfield County election officials: "There is no question that the Chesterfield County Registrar and the Chesterfield County Electoral Board miscalculated turnout on Primary Day 2008, were slow in reacting to the spike in turnout when it actually occurred, and that these miscalculations led to a shortage of ballots and overcrowding due to insufficient staffing at polling places."[7] The county also grudgingly acknowledged: "It is likely that the heavy turnout did make it more difficult for some handicapped and elderly voters to vote in comfort. However, we believe any such problems were isolated."[8] According to the county: "The problem was exacerbated because inadequate provisions were made for quickly distributing additional ballots to precincts which needed them late in the day." It also said: "We do not dispute that lines for voting in Chesterfield were extremely long in some voting precincts."[9]

The Department of Justice announced that it would send federal monitors to Chesterfield County for the 2008 general election. It was the only jurisdiction in Virginia to receive that designation.[10] The monitors attended. The 2008 general election went relatively smoothly in Chesterfield County and throughout Virginia. Our clients were protected. One very senior elected official in Virginia told me that the spotlight our pro bono efforts shined on Chesterfield County after the primary helped preparation for the general election not only in Chesterfield County but also throughout all of Virginia for the 2008 general election. He said that other election officials in Virginia watched these events and saw the pressure we had applied on Chesterfield County. He said that none of the others wanted to become "that guy" and that every time they had a choice as the general election approached, they chose to do more to be prepared rather than less.

Lessons Learned: Crisis Lawyering on Election Day

The events that transpired in Chesterfield County in 2008 led us to identify several important lessons. First: preparation and anticipation are crucial. Lawyers always need to be prepared. Because elections are sensitive, high-stakes exercises at the core of our democracy that arrive on schedule, serious, timely, and effective preparation is both possible and necessary. Also, because the "attack surface" is understood (e.g., voting machines, databases, voters' perceptions, etc.) and some of the flashpoints are as well (identifying and authenticating voters, student residency, long lines and delays, etc.), it is possible not only to anticipate problems but also to develop ways to avoid or solve them. Lawyers can anticipate disputes and should prepare strategies and tools in advance for dealing with them. In some instances, this involves working up a strategic playbook—which may also include exemplars or drafts of relevant court papers, press releases, and the like.

Second: although general preparation and anticipation are crucial in a crisis, it is also important to have a long-term focus on how to avoid an election crisis. This long-term focus may not always be the job of the same lawyer who would be called upon to respond to a crisis. It is vital, however, that someone maintain a long-term and year-round focus on risks that could jeopardize election fairness or worse. This includes focusing on choices relating to the purchase or retirement of election systems and voting machines, budgets and funding, staffing, the availability of early voting, voter eligibility, changes to polling locations, and related issues. Ideally, this is someone who has worked to ensure that we make the investments necessary to secure our elections and the sanctity of the vote.

Third: organization is crucial, including a process to obtain reliable and credible situational awareness. Developing situational awareness before, especially during, and after Election Day, and to be ready and able to use it promptly and effectively, is another important aspect of preparation. It is vital that we organize the ways we receive and update information to ensure that it is accurate to the greatest extent possible. This will help to minimize the misinformation and rumors that so often arise in high-pressure, high-stakes situations such as elections. Organization may include providing training in advance for volunteers and deploying them properly to polling places. It also may include a system to collect their input, as well as a boiler room (usually staffed by lawyers or others with substantial election experience) to serve as a point of contact and vet and prioritize reports and claims. It also includes having well-developed plans that include follow-up steps that can be implemented promptly. This may include having contact information for and an ability to reach key election and elected officials, the press, and others as needed. If the lawyer and the lawyer's team cannot reach the county registrar, a judge, or other official to highlight and resolve a problem or to obtain a needed determination, then the result may well be failure, because timing is essential.

Fourth: the timely communication of accurate information is important. This is also a part of what it means to be organized. If information is not conveyed effectively with enough consistency and granularity to be useful, then the crisis response will suffer, potentially lack reliability, and squander trust. As noted, I brought a laptop, an iPad, a cell phone and a printer to my Election Day work as an observer at the State Board of Elections, enabling me to see reports as they came in from my party's observers, follow up as necessary with the volunteers or with the boiler room for more detail, use email or texts to communicate and confirm information as needed, and print out certain reports and details for the SBE to provide to their staff for follow-up.

Fifth: solid and steady leadership is required. Planning and organization will not be enough if there is not enough leadership or sound management to act and make timely and effective decisions before, during, and after Election Day. In many crises, authority is unclear. This creates a risk that decision makers will be excessively cautious, fear overstepping their authority, feel disempowered to act, perceive that they will not be held accountable, or passively wait for more reliable information rather than act decisively. However, a worry on Election Day is that even if there is good leadership—and especially if there is not—an unprepared volunteer might represent the organization poorly and do real damage. That damage may come from unnecessarily alienating those who can help, destroying trust that has taken time and effort to develop, mischaracterizing and possibly overprioritizing a problem, and creating a distraction or possibly even a political problem. Good implementation of other elements of this list will help avoid this problem, such as having clear objectives, access to good training complete with clear dos and don'ts, and having a good organization and a good communications network in place. These will help avoid, spot, and address issues quickly.

Sixth: good judgment and a measure of passion are important as well. All sorts of walls may stand in front of the lawyer seeking to resolve an election crisis. Moreover, timely choices need to be made, because the list of problems is usually always long. Prioritizing problems based on the impact they can have is crucial. While not every problem warrants a conversation with the most senior officials during busy and scarce Election Day time, too much patience and deference can lead to mistakes being made. That certainly does not mean that a lawyer should be excused for behaving rashly, but it does mean that in many instances there should be a very limited time before inquiring again about the status of some problems, or providing additional detail, or considering other solutions and other approaches. Situational awareness is important and requires that lawyers collect sound information from volunteers and use that information properly. Whenever possible, it is important to maintain reasonable situational awareness of the status of problems and any efforts by election officials to address them. As discussed previously, one of the most effective Election Day experiences I ever had was when I was the Democratic Party's observer at Virginia's SBE on Election Day at a time when the SBE secretary allowed observers from both parties to sit with her in her office and listen to and sometimes participate in her phone calls. That gold standard unfortunately ended when the board secretary position was filled by the other party and the new official did not see the advantage of ensuring that level of transparency.

Seventh: related to the other elements above, it is critical to keep overall goals and timing in mind. Lawyers should be practical, effective, and sometimes creative. Often that means not resorting to litigating in the courts. Along these lines, we typically advise volunteer monitors at polling places to introduce themselves to the poll workers in the morning before the polls open and to bring a box of donuts to share with them. Courtesy, relationship-building, respect, and mutual trust can go a long way toward solving problems.

Lawyers can play a crucial role in helping to protect the precious right to vote and the integrity of our elections. While this may happen on Election Day, some lawyers do this many other days of the year as well.

Elections will never be free from the risk of crises, but crises are far more likely to occur—and cause more damage—in the absence of good preparation. Therefore, it is critical to make prudent decisions to manage risk and to apportion resources wisely. We should not compress voting into thirteen or fourteen hours on Election Day, save for limited absentee voting where a voter has a specified excuse. That is when we have the most pressure and the least time to assess and meet a challenge. It maximizes the chances that we will disenfranchise voters. We should allow voting over multiple days for any reason. We also need to focus on the big picture as well as the small. We cannot afford to be indifferent to the deficiencies in the capabilities, resources, and preparedness of any jurisdiction, because a whole state or nation can be affected by the outcome. Ultimately, a proactive approach is needed; crisis prevention is better than crisis management when it comes to Election Day lawyering.

NOTES

1 *Andrews v. Koch* (E.D.N.Y.), *consolidated with, Herron v. Koch*, 523 F. Supp. 167 (S.D.N.Y. 1981), *cert. denied*, 453 U.S. 946 (1981).
2 The program was focused narrowly on election protection and protecting the right to vote, not get-out-the-vote or other partisan programs.
3 VIRGINIA STATE BOARD OF ELECTIONS, REVIEW OF PRESIDENTIAL PRIMARY, FEBRUARY 12, 2008, IN CHESTERFIELD COUNTY 34–35 (May 23, 2008) (on file with author).
4 *Board of Elections Member Criticizes Some Democrats*, CHESTERFIELD OBSERVER (May 14, 2008).
5 U.S. Senate Judiciary Committee, Protecting the Right to Vote: Oversight of the Department of Justice's Preparations for the 2008 General Election (110th Congress, Sept. 9, 2008) (testimony of Keshia Anderson).
6 *See* Office of the County Attorney, Chesterfield County, Letter to U.S. Department of Justice (Aug. 7, 2008) (on file with author).
7 *Id.*, at 5–6.
8 *Id.*, at 7.
9 *Id.*, at 8.
10 U.S. Department of Justice, *Department of Justice to Monitor Polls in 23 States Across the Nation on Election Day* (Oct. 30, 2008).

PART III

Beyond Borders and Silos

12

Bordering on Crisis

Overcoming Multiagency Crisis Coordination Challenges

BRIAN WILSON AND NORA JOHNSON

Crisis lawyering, like whole-of-government collaboration, is best described through example. This chapter distills lessons from events that include cargo on a vessel that was reportedly spiked with a radioactive substance; an inbound ship with hundreds of migrants that potentially included members of a terrorist organization; a nongovernmental organization using a vessel to interfere with lawfully authorized fishing activities; and maritime drug trafficking involving multiple countries. These events, collectively, provide insight into the role of a lawyer in whole-of-government coordination, multilateral collaboration, and crisis[1] response.

Governments are frequently organized into agencies that have unique expertise to assess challenges and respond. These agencies may operate under separate chains of command, with separate authorities, budgets, and priorities. Threats, however, typically do not correspond with agency boundaries—or national borders—and thus governments are confronted with ensuring that information is shared and that responses are integrated among departments tasked with fundamentally different missions. Lawyers are involved in every aspect of the collaboration challenge, from information acquisition and information sharing to decisions and response activities.

An impressive level of attention has recently centered on coordination. In 2017, the United Nations Security Council adopted Resolution 2341, highlighting that collaboration is not a single-nation issue.[2] This measure called "upon Member States to explore ways to exchange relevant information and to cooperate actively in the prevention, protection, mitigation, preparedness, investigation, response to or recovery from terrorist attacks planned or committed against critical infrastructure."[3] Academia is also focusing on whole-of-government frameworks and crisis management, including the Simons Center for Interagency Cooperation;[4] William & Mary's Whole of Government Center of Excellence;[5] the College of Emergency Preparedness, Homeland Security and Cybersecurity, University of Albany, State University of New York;[6] and the Swedish National Defence College's National Center for Crisis Management, Research and Training.[7] Moreover, several states have developed frameworks to address maritime crisis response integration.

Overcoming investigative, crisis-response, and information-sharing challenges are certainly not new considerations, though contemporary threats are more complex. This complexity requires the early involvement of lawyers, who must be prepared to take on a variety of roles, codevelop solutions, and demonstrate collaborative leadership. Historical responses to events discussed in this chapter, the experience of the authors coordinating national level threat responses that required multiagency cooperation, as well as findings from a survey developed by the authors and administered to over 500 government officials from over 100 countries were distilled to develop the "Rules for Crisis Lawyering in a Multi-Agency Environment" presented at the end of this chapter.

A crisis may involve hundreds—potentially thousands—of decisions, some of which require immediate action. A key element of interagency alignment involves lawyers who are increasingly being called upon to advise in multiagency planning and crisis management.[8]

Emphasis on coordination,[9] information sharing, and crisis response is a positive governance development. This collaborative pivot, however, has not resulted in a universally accepted definition of whole-of-government coordination or even a general consensus on the terminology to be used. Fortunately, differences in lexicon have not impeded collaboration, as varied terms reflect varied national priorities and varied organizational structures. Thus, while different terms (and definitions) for national-level coordination exist— *whole-of-government, interagency, interministerial, and multiagency,* among others—a common element is that the construct synchronizes the actions of multiple agencies within a government.

The authors define the "interagency concept" as a construct that alters the governance status quo by providing a documented collaborative framework, formally identifying agencies involved in response activities, removing situational ambiguity, and overcoming information-sharing barriers to make a nation safer. That being said, the authors believe interagency concepts, including its elements, are best defined by individual states, as these constructs integrate multiple agencies within a government and are based on national priorities.

The emergence of whole-of-government maritime response frameworks, which generally began in 2005, expanded in the ensuing years to address integration challenges amid tremendous complexity. Some national-level processes operate under the principle of command and control with one person in charge, while others function under unity of effort, with required collaboration (though no ability to order another agency to take action); some direct information sharing across the government; and some focus on planning as well as response activities, with others focused on safety events while others primarily address security threats. Regardless of the model or focus, the development of interagency frameworks represents, in a way, "bold, persistent experimentation."[10] Countries that have adopted horizontal response frameworks (or offices) in a maritime context include:

— Australia: Maritime Border Command
— Brunei: National Maritime Coordination Centre
— Canada: Maritime Event Response Protocol
— Georgia: Joint Maritime Operations Center
— Indonesia: BAKAMLA
— Japan: Crisis Management Center
— Philippines: National Coast Watch Center
— Senegal: High Authority in Charge of Coordinating Maritime Safety, Maritime Security, and Marine Environnemental Pollution
— Thailand: Maritime Enforcement Coordinating Centre
— United States: Maritime Operational Threat Response Plan (MOTR) and the Global MOTR Coordination Center
— United Kingdom: National Maritime Information Centre

Though each process has different substantive elements, it is instructive to examine specific constructs to identify key principles and competencies of crisis lawyering. In the United States, the Maritime Operational Threat Response Plan was approved by the president in 2006 to align the interagency response to maritime threats. The MOTR process is used daily by the Departments of Defense, Homeland Security, Justice, and State, among others, to share information, identify courses of action, and agree on desired national outcomes. This plan was developed to address security threats that involve multiple agencies that operate under different chains of command, with different authorities and different responsibilities. Primary areas of coordination under the US whole-of-government maritime threat response process include drug trafficking, migrant interdiction, illegal fishing, and piracy.

In Canada, the Maritime Event Response Protocol (MERP) addresses both safety events and security threats. The MERP process brings together multiple agencies/entities to support an integrated Canadian approach to maritime challenges, as often no single federal department or agency has complete response responsibility. Moreover, Canada's multiagency approach reflects the government of Canada's approach to emergency management: whole-of-government, collaborative, and all hazards. MERP has effectively integrated multiple agencies in response activities and has similarly integrated agencies for pre-event planning.[11]

And, the United Kingdom's National Maritime Information Centre (NMIC) supports "cross-government efforts to monitor, evaluate and address threats to [UK] shipping worldwide, with special focus on activity in the UK Exclusive Economic Zone."[12]

Attorneys were essential in the development of collaborative information-sharing constructs and have remained integral contributors to their effective implementation as well as their enduring use. The authors were the primary drafters of the first international collaborative process to bridge whole-of-government maritime threat response processes: the Canadian-US MERP/MOTR Strategic Protocol, approved in 2012. This pioneering construct was developed to complement national-level action by enhancing binational communication and better positioning each nation to identify the full scope of threats, take appropriate response action, and minimize risk.

A noteworthy example of collaboration under MERP-MOTR involved the response to multiple vessels en route to Canada and the United States carrying possibly contaminated containers following a series of explosions that occurred at the Port of Tianjin, China, in 2015. The blast reportedly killed 173 and injured nearly 800 people, causing damage in excess of $1 billion.[13] More than 700 tons of sodium cyanide exploded, a substance so potent, "when dissolved or burned, it releases the highly poisonous gas hydrogen cyanide."[14] And "exposure to sodium cyanide—a white crystalline or granular power with a variety of industrial uses—can be 'rapidly fatal,' according the U.S. Centers for Disease Control and Prevention."[15]

Moreover, "The China Earthquake Networks Centre said the initial explosion . . . had a power equivalent of three tonnes of TNT detonating, while the second was the equivalent of 21 tonnes."[16] Area residents stated the blast "felt like an atomic bomb had hit."[17] With land-based rescue under way, questions surfaced regarding whether containers and ships berthed in, or near, the Port of Tianjin—the tenth-largest container facility in the world—at the time of the blast were transporting dangerous toxins?[18] The MERP/MOTR Strategic Protocol provided the platform to bilaterally examine urgent safety and health issues involving multiple agencies.

Sharing information across the border to determine the risk of contamination and response considerations represented MERP-MOTR priorities. More than 100 US and Canadian government officials (from approximately fifteen agencies/departments)—a remarkable array of expertise—simultaneously participated in Strategic Protocol coordination activities to assess the impact of, and response to, the Tianjin explosions on cargo subsequently loaded onto hundreds of ships.

Agency counselors, importantly, first had access to small group meetings that didn't necessarily include legal issues and were thus able to identify operative statutes, statutory obstacles, and possible courses of action. From examining emergency preparedness responsibilities, notice of arrival requirements, occupational safety and public health considerations, notice of hazardous conditions provisions, as well as laws regarding an affirmative obligation on masters to report an illness or death onboard inbound vessels, lawyers were essential to identifying effective decisions to an uncertain challenge.

The response to the Tianjin explosions also highlighted the value of, and need for, broader multilateral collaboration in circumstances that have the potential to cross geographic borders. *Were toxic chemicals on, or in, containers and did they represent a threat?* Government officials around the globe were assessing how to best approach this potential safety and security challenge, each with access to different information and using different risk methodologies. In a tightly coupled network like maritime shipping, taking a collective approach and sharing information can improve awareness, reduce duplication of testing, and decrease delays that could be associated to an independent approach requiring examination in multiple ports of call in various countries. The MERP/MOTR Strategic Protocol demonstrated the value of a framework—an agreement—before a crisis to support a networked response, ensure points of contact, and provide an ability to share legal, policy, and regulatory information. Notably, lawyers were involved in all discussions, evaluating the situation and developing courses of action.

The success of MERP-MOTR sparked the development of a subsequent multinational agreement (the "Strategic Arrangement"), also co-drafted by the authors, which included Australia, Canada, New Zealand, the United Kingdom, and the United States. Signed in 2016, the Strategic Arrangement supports the exchange of maritime safety and security information by connecting centers and national-level offices charged with whole-of-government responsibilities. The Strategic Arrangement created a networked approach to information sharing, collaboration, and maritime response actions. Lawyers were pivotal to the development of policy instruments/agreements that facilitated collaboration. By identifying and developing courses of action to share information and take action, attorneys clarified legal issues stemming from policy disagreements, encouraged discussions, and maintained focus on achieving the desired outcome.

To better assess requirements for developing and sustaining interagency crisis-management frameworks, the authors created a survey that included

twenty statements rated by Likert scale responses ranging from strongly disagree, disagree, neither disagree nor agree, agree, and strongly agree. The survey
sought to identify challenges to multiagency collaboration; sharing information; whether sufficient guidance and training exists; and, ultimately, to provide
recommendations. In approximately two years, more than 500 government officials from 100 countries participated in the survey. The survey results complement lessons learned from crisis response activities discussed below.

In 2010, a derelict cargo ship, *SUN SEA*, with 492 Sri Lankan migrants
arrived in Canadian waters, off the coast of British Columbia, after miracu-
lously completing its transit from the Gulf of Thailand through the Indian
and Pacific Oceans. Prior to arriving in Canada, the journey sparked media
interest and inquiries to a United States Coast Guard (USCG) office in Hawaii
regarding the scope of US search and rescue (SAR) obligations. Based exclusively on what was known at this point of the transit, the situation might not
have been considered a crisis. Considerations for the USCG included whether
to consult a staff attorney for what *might* be viewed as basic SAR questions or
to elevate the inquiry for higher-level action.

The *SUN SEA* transit fortunately did not require assistance at sea, and while
it concluded in Canada, a crisis was just beginning that would involve multiple organizations and nations to resolve. Questions about nonrefoulement,
protection of personal information, prosecution of smugglers, environmental
protection, and mooring/disposition of the vessel concluded with changes to
Canadian law. Collaborative issues identified in the response also sparked
the development of a binational, information-sharing protocol. In advance
of *SUN SEA*'s arrival, there was concern that passengers were infected with
contagions or gravely sick. The preliminary focus on health was dramatically
expanded when Public Safety Minister Vic Towes announced the Canadian
government believed *SUN SEA* also included "suspected human smugglers
and terrorists."[19] Safety considerations remained, prompting the Canadian
medical community, which subsequently published a report, to note early
challenges included uncertainty over *SUN SEA*'s arrival date and location.[20] A
lack of information to a known challenge triggered a "multi-faceted response
[involving] novel partnerships and plans."[21] Solely focused on the medical
considerations within Canada, the report further noted the "dynamic nature
of [the] event," a "pre-event duty to maintain secrecy versus [a] duty to no-
tify," the necessity of response "innovation," and the "importance of planning
and plan sharing."[22] The presentation candidly noted that lessons learned included the "need for more timely information"; the challenges of "involving
multiple internal and external stakeholders"; and managing "on site security"
and "media scrutiny."[23]

The *SUN SEA* affair required an approach that integrated security, law enforcement, health, regulatory, search and rescue, immigration, and diplomatic organizations. While several nations would have a role in this event, national-level coordination issues associated with events surrounding *SUN SEA* are emblematic of contemporary crisis lawyering: synchronizing the efforts of a dizzying array of government agencies, nations, and the private sector along with, at times, sensitive information that cannot be widely disseminated. The *SUN SEA* affair highlights the value—frequently the necessity—of a documented process to plan, share, and protect information across the whole of government with other nations, as well as to coordinate actions to develop solutions, integrate the private sector, address privacy requirements, and involve lawyers. Response communities are generally organized based on their distinct authorities and responsibilities. That makes sense for most events, as the mission for a search and rescue will involve considerations that are substantively different from a contagion, fuel spill, or criminal investigation. However, crisis responses generally don't fit within the parameters of a single community.

To better assess collaboration challenges, such as those that arose during the *SUN SEA* affair, government officials from over 100 countries were asked their opinion regarding the following statement: "The response to a significant security threat or event generally involves more than one agency or department." In this case, 98 percent agreed or strongly agreed. The exceedingly high positive response rate confirms that the contemporary response environment is multiagency, and for crisis lawyering this result also confirms an effective counselor must have awareness of partner agency authorities and capabilities. The crisis lawyer must readily establish what information is known among multiple organizations and what needs to be known (and who will be responsible) at the outset of a crisis; legal points of contact for participating agencies; the decision-making process; privacy requirements; what may be shared with other agencies; private-sector involvement; multinational, information-sharing practices; and policy, regulatory, and legal considerations. A crisis lawyer can support a multiagency response through the development of inclusive decision-making and information-exchange processes that respect departmental authorities and each agency's unique organizational culture. Undertaking such collaborative efforts requires an attorney to possess competencies along with legal knowledge; it requires skills, knowledge, and abilities related to trust building, role clarification, and solution development.[24] Building trust and a collaborative environment is not easily attainable.[25] Despite direction from a head of state to collaborate, personnel may have myopic agency interests or cultures that disfavor sharing information. Role clarification[26] can be an effective tool for the crisis lawyer to overcome parochialism that often exists during multiagency crisis responses, particularly in situations where jurisdictions, authorities, and capabilities overlap. A crisis lawyer is well placed to build, support, and document a common understanding of organizational mandates, jurisdictions, and accountabilities to support effective multiagency decision-making. This requires an ability to listen to others to understand and clarify overlapping or conflicting mandates, roles, authorities, or jurisdictions. Crisis management practitioners and counselors who know their role and the role of those in other organizations can use this knowledge to appropriately establish interagency response goals and settle impasses.

The response to the blast at the Port of Tianjin China and the SUN SEA affair also affirms that crisis situations often require collaborative planning, problem-solving, and decision-making to achieve the best outcomes possible. Information supports effective decision-making. Yet, of the 500-plus government official survey participants, 63 percent agreed or strongly agreed that information sharing is limited over concern of how other government agencies will protect or safeguard data. This survey result once again highlights the importance of developing trust between organizations and the need for documented information-sharing mechanisms. Participation by lawyers in the development of data collection and information-sharing mechanisms is therefore critical. Such instruments enable organizations to better understand, in advance of a crisis, what information can be shared with whom, whether restrictions exist that govern its use, and any protections that must be legally maintained. At the same time, effective response action demands that crisis lawyers, whenever possible, adopt a "need to share," rather than a "need to know," approach to information sharing.

Addressing a potential biological threat aboard the CSAV RIO PUEBLO, described below, was unfortunately chaotic, perhaps inevitably, because organizations were not conditioned—or even authorized—to share information, and no formal crisis-coordination process existed to support the exchange of information and align strategic courses of action. The first report was unsubstantiated, but extraordinary: a vessel approaching the United States was carrying one million lemons spiked with a radiological substance.[27] The ship's destination was the Port of New York/Newark, in close proximity to the largest concentration of people in the United States. The cargo was slated for delivery in New York and throughout the country, with the potential to cause devastating damage across thousands of miles.

All options involved some level of operational and legal risk: *Permit the RIO PUEBLO into port, permanently deny entry, or conduct offshore (or in port) inspections?* The threat was not yet confirmed, and the commercial ship was carrying other perishable cargo that, in addition to the fruit, was worth millions. Key details about the lemons were not initially known, as the first report of possible illicit activity was an anonymous email message.[28] In the first hours following receipt of the (anonymous) report that some cargo was contaminated with a biological substance, assumptions were made—*the existence of a national security threat*. This assumption regrettably remained unchanged. New information was discounted, and initial decisions as well as courses of action were left static.

Approximately forty local, state, and national agencies that normally operate under separate chains of command would participate in response activities.[29] Integration would be essential, however, because the search for toxins included agencies duplicating tests along with fumigation.[30] "Reportedly, disagreements erupted once the first-round tests indicated there was no imminent danger, with state and local officials insisting that the ship and its suspect containers be kept offshore until all risk of danger was eliminated and with US Customs officials arguing for towing the ship into port so that they could lay to rest the worst-case scenarios by using specialized equipment to detect any dispersal devices."[31] Six days of inspections by several agencies affirmed what was known following the first examination: no toxic chemicals were aboard CSAV *RIO PUEBLO*.[32] One million lemons valued at $70,000 were nevertheless destroyed, and millions of dollars' worth of other cargo was delayed, the cost of which was not calculated. Enforcement activities were estimated to cost $1.3 million.[33]

Officials involved in RIO PUEBLO were pressed to make decisions of higher precision with less information, under faster time constraints, in an environment of heightened public expectations and intense media (and social media) scrutiny. Diplomatic and legal considerations converged with safety and security. One newspaper framed the challenge as pitting "anti-terror tactics [with the] free flow of trade."[34] The *RIO PUEBLO* response led the World Shipping Council to call for the development of a pre-identified plan to deal with future similar contingencies. Other commentary—including criticism—soon followed. "The shipping industry, as well as some of the officials involved, question why the Coast Guard kept the ship at sea for a week, delaying delivery of millions of dollars worth of other merchandise. In Argentina . . . government officials are indignant they were not informed about the alleged threat until media reports of a Coast Guard news conference on Aug. 6. Shouldn't they be notified at once, they ask, of allegations that biological weapons are being deployed from their nation's ports?"[35]

Despite a botched response, "Lemongate," as it has been derisively called, has had enduring resonance.[36] The *RIO PUEBLO* affair highlighted that advice provided on unconfirmed, incomplete, or dated information is inherently flawed;

278 BRIAN WILSON AND NORA JOHNSON

and, separately, that the involvement of more agencies—more people—does not necessarily improve a response. A crisis lawyer can function most effectively with a documented process that has the full support of senior officials throughout an organization and with partner agencies. Support includes access to meetings and information, required participation in preliminary decision-making, and compulsory review (including, where appropriate, "legal clearance") prior to significant decisions. Pre-identified points of contact, availability 24/7, clearly defined triggers for notification, information exchange coordination, checklists (including scripts that guide discussions and encourage engagement from all organizations with equities, consistent agendas, and issue-specific response legal considerations), and documenting actions are all critical.

The authors recognize that a crisis involves scores of decisions, many of which require immediate action. Moreover, decisions may at times be required with incomplete information. That being said, awareness of the information required for effective response activities, collectively evaluating it for reliability, and sharing it appropriately are critical functions of any crisis lawyer. Providing counsel in this environment requires candidly acknowledging that one's own understanding of the issue may be incomplete and that information from additional sources may be necessary to assess the situation, accurately frame problems, identify interdependencies, and mitigate potential unintended consequences of decisions.

Responses to complex crises such as the *RIO PUEBLO*, however, often suffer from information-sharing barriers, both real and perceived. At times, a "hold close" approach is necessary to protect sensitive investigative information or intelligence. Yet, in the context of a national-level, multijurisdictional response such as *RIO PUEBLO*, which included the participation of more than three dozen organizations, focusing first on less sensitive information that could be shared may have increased understanding of interdependencies and reduced unintended (and adverse) impacts of the courses of action. A case in point is the *M/V NORDIC*. In 1991, the US Coast Guard sought to board a Honduran-flagged coastal freighter (*M/V NORDIC*) suspected of drug trafficking.[37] Though the USCG frequently conducts counterdrug operations, this specific response was judicially called "grossly deficient"[38] largely based on information-sharing failures. An extraordinary judicial opinion found the response included "considerable [US Government] confusion, miscommunication, and misinformation, some of which appears to be deliberate, or at least, perverse after the fact attempts at cosmetic restoration."[39]

Bram Coumou, *NORDIC*'s master, piloted the vessel from Colombia to the Caribbean Sea. Before arriving at its destination in Haiti, Bram, an American citizen, notified the USCG he suspected that illicit drugs were on his ship.[40]

Cargo was off-loaded from the *NORDIC* while docked at St. Marc, Haiti, in part with the cooperation and assistance of Coumou, the "only available crane operator."[41] After cocaine was discovered on *NORDIC*, the Haitian government requested that the United States waive jurisdiction over Coumou.[42] A US government interagency response process[43] that facilitated discussions arrived at decisions based on inaccurate information. The US government agreed with Haiti exercising jurisdiction over Coumou. Despite providing the information of illicit drug trafficking and extensively cooperating in the search of *NORDIC*, Coumou spent six months in a Haitian jail before he was acquitted at a trial in Haiti.

The US federal court opinion held that the decision to waive jurisdiction over Coumou was based on "reports and related memoranda" deemed to be "grossly deficient and inaccurate."[44] The ruling also stated: "The [Haitian prison] experience was a nightmare. During this time, he suffered from malnutrition, infections, and diseases, including bronchitis, pneumonia, kidney infection, chronic back pain, nerve disorder, fungal and eye infection, chronic diarrhea, dehydration, and marasmus, and he witnessed numerous atrocities, perpetrated both by Haitian officials and other prisoners, including beatings and torture, some of which ended in the death of the victim."[45]

Bram Coumou's civil proceeding asserted US government negligence, among other things, and requested damages for his arrest and confinement. The US Fifth Circuit Court of Appeals reversed the district judge's finding that the government was per se liable for personal injury and property damage, but it remanded the case "to determine whether the government's failure to convey information to Haitian authorities constituted a breach of its duty of reasonable care."[46] The court further held: "Even if the government is immune from tort suits with respect to its policy decision to search the *NORDIC* in Haiti and then accede to the Haitian request to exercise Haitian jurisdiction, it still had a duty to exercise reasonable care in carrying out that policy."[47] The response demonstrated that the existence of a response process does not guarantee an effective response, though the collaborative process used during the response to Coumou has since been refined by the United States and expanded to better support effective coordination and information exchange. The *NORDIC* affair also reinforces the need for the crisis lawyer to both have a questioning attitude and consider the entirety of the response spectrum (addressing "how does this event end") when initially framing issues and providing advice on courses of action. Involvement at every stage of the response, ensuring clarity on your role in the decision-making process, validating assumptions repeatedly, and actively seeking accurate, timely, and repeatedly updated information are equally important.

The challenges with validating and sharing information are not isolated to the *SUN SEA, RIO PUEBLO*, and *NORDIC* responses. In 2008, news coverage in Canada heralded sensational claims of piracy after the Royal Canadian Mounted Police boarded and seized a Sea Shepherd Conservation Society–controlled vessel adorned with skull and crossbones along with the names of vessels it had rammed or sunk. The Dutch-flagged research vessel, named after the Canadian author and eco-activist Farley Mowat, deployed to the Canadian coast to obstruct lawfully authorized seal-hunt activity.[48] Over the ensuing weeks, the crew willfully ignored orders to depart Canadian waters, jockeying back and forth between Canada's territorial sea and the Exclusive Economic Zone, claiming that navigational freedoms allowed such action. The vessel would "graze" a Canadian Coast Guard ship twice and come perilously close—within nine meters—to boats and people on ice floes, prompting seasoned fishers to fear for their lives.[49]

During the kinetic-response phase, no single department in Canada possessed sufficient authorities, mandates, resources, or information. Similar to the *SUN SEA*, this event occurred amid significant media interest and, at times, incomplete information. Planning, discussions, and legal consultations were occurring within safety, security, environmental, search and rescue, diplomatic, judicial, law enforcement, border, and military agencies—silos, to use an analogy—in support of their own internal mandates. These efforts led to the development of recommendations provided individually to senior agency officials. The complexity of the case, together with the sensitivity and social divisiveness of the issue, required whole-of-government integration.

The crisis received extensive media attention for weeks, with inaccurate assertions from the vessel's owner that the seizure of *FARLEY MOWAT* was an act of war.[50] In protest, the vessel's owner delivered to a courthouse 2,500 Canadian two-dollar coins to obtain the release of the master and first officer, stating "since they're going to board our vessel at gunpoint on the high seas and take all our property, they are pirates and we will give them a pirate ransom."[51] Media inquiries were constant, public responses from several ministers were necessary, and responding to calls from senior government officials for information became a predominant near-term action of those managing the crisis. The two arrested crewmembers were deported; following weeks of rhetoric in the press, the crisis appeared to have abated. Yet, the case would endure for another nine years.

Following the seizure of the *FARLEY MOWAT* in 2008, the vessel was later auctioned; however, after a failed bid, the Canadian government sold it for scrap in 2014 to help pay six years of docking fees. The new owner attempted to tow the vessel away for decommissioning. Unable to do so, he subsequently moved the vessel to a small community wharf, purportedly under the cover of darkness, abandoning it in a small community, taking up a quarter of the town's wharf space. In 2015, *FARLEY MOWAT* began to sink, adding $550,000 to government costs, as the Canadian Coast Guard was forced to deploy oil booms, refloat the vessel, and repeatedly pump polluted water out of the vessel to keep it afloat. A year later, the *FARLEY MOWAT* caught fire. The new owner repeatedly ignored court orders to move the vessel, resulting in imprisonment for contempt of court in 2016. Following a declaration that *FARLEY MOWAT* was "an imminent pollution threat to the environment," it was finally towed away.[52]

Inquiries that followed these events concluded that the response actions were reasonable and necessary as well as consistent with laws and regulations. Remediation, disposition, and vessel recovery costs related to the *FARLEY MOWAT* would ultimately exceed $1 million and consume judicial attention for more than a decade.[53] The lessons learned from the response inspired the development of a whole-of-government framework—specifically the MERP, which remains operative today—to better coordinate and integrate multilevel response structures to respond to threats by establishing the prerequisite triggers and communication procedures for initiating Canada's Response Protocol, setting forth the collaborative planning process to establish situational awareness, share information, develop options and plans, and conduct after-action reviews.[54]

It is not realistic to expect information to be seamlessly exchanged or for collaboration to flawlessly occur when those involved in a crisis are meeting one another for the first time during the event.[55] Rather, preparing whole-of-government crisis responders requires building familiarity with multiagency participants and established processes. Cultivating relationships and networks in advance of a crisis can help lawyers overcome collaboration challenges by providing more ready access to the information, expertise, and lobbying assistance from other organizations that is often required to build consensus around strategic courses of actions.

An integrated response to significant threats and events—particularly as examined in training and "live" as well as "tabletop" exercises—can assist a crisis lawyer. Such efforts can build confidence to work within a multiagency response environment, align expectations, and encourage the response to novel events that don't have preestablished plans. Frequent exercises (and training) also build proficiency in the use of documented collaborative process and trust. Yet, when survey participants were asked whether their organization provided adequate training with regard to whole-of-government collaboration (e.g., when to share information, who is authorized to share information, what decisions may fall within a whole-of-government framework, etc.), only 39 percent of respondents agreed or strongly agreed.

This survey result highlights a crucial whole-of-government crisis governance priority that is not currently being met: ensuring that officials, including crisis lawyers, are prepared, competent, and capable of operating within a multiagency environment. The authors recognize that responsibilities related to crisis management are frequently secondary tasks in relation to day-to-day assignments or are seen as separate functions done by others inside an organization. Regardless of misperceptions, a crisis often affects the entire organization. When emergency or crisis-management functions are not well understood or embraced, organizations suffer from so-called intervention bias, or the tendency to overreach and take on tasks for which an organization is ill equipped, and abdication bias, which unfortunately results in eschewing responsibility or blaming others.[56]

Further challenges arise when personnel who are assigned to work in a multiagency environment do not possess the requisite training, experience, knowledge, or skills[57] and are thus unable to effectively support the whole-of-government response. Developing training requirements (including the completion of these requirements in annual reviews), periodic exercises, and drafting interagency competencies all represent best practices to improve a multiagency crisis response. Attorneys, as well as senior government officials, have a critical role in training by prioritizing participation in training programs, exercises, and updating information-sharing processes as necessary.

In the context of training and exercises, a crisis lawyer can take on a role as an evaluator documenting and evaluating collective decisions and decision-making processes; evaluating the currency of joint plans and processes against changes in legislation, jurisprudence, good practice, policies, and relevant doctrine; and making recommendations to update plans and instruments to address risks, lessons learned, errors, and omissions. It is not uncommon for disagreements to surface regarding jurisdiction, authorities, roles, and responsibilities or information sharing during exercises. A crisis lawyer can work as a mediator or process facilitator to help resolve disagreements. Following exercises, a lawyer has an important role in supporting the development of after-action reports, updating doctrine, and revising training.

To support the development of whole-of-government national-level training and exercises, the authors developed "Rules for Crisis Lawyering in a Multi-Agency Response Environment." These rules were distilled from the firsthand experiences of the authors in drafting multilateral information sharing agreements, coordinating interagency responses, and analyzing findings from the survey of government officials. The rules seek to codify the authors' personal observations of requirements, processes, skills, knowledge, and attributes employed by effective lawyers operating in a multiagency crisis environment. They are not intended to serve as a holistic crisis-response framework or to supplant existing competencies of an attorney. They may be used to support professional development, training, and collaborative responses.

Rules for Crisis Lawyering in a Multi-Agency Response Environment

- Before a crisis, build, manage, and sustain credible, trust-based relationships with colleagues, senior ranking personnel, and other organizations. Know which organizations are—or should be—at the (decision-making) table and know who will be sitting in the chairs.
- Always have access to contact information for colleagues within your agency and in partner agencies (and ensure they will take your calls or respond to texts at any time of the day). As necessary, develop redundant communications systems and alternate IT/connectivity plans.
- Actively seek out newly reporting personnel in advance of a crisis to educate/discuss/familiarize on the information-sharing and decision-making processes.
- Develop and document processes and checklists for the response to threats/events, seek to improve them daily, and validate them annually.
- Seek out opportunities to plan, train, exercise, and work together in advance of a crisis. A collective response to significant threats and events—particularly as examined in training and exercises—can assist a crisis lawyer regarding how to align expectations, how to effectively improvise when faced with novel events that don't have preestablished plans, how to optimize application of disparate enabling authorities, how to work effectively within multiagency response environments, and how to feel more confident in a time-compressed, information-scarce environment.
- Approach crisis response with the expectation a significant threat/disaster will involve more than a single agency and possibly implicate several nations.
- Advocate to involve lawyers on all issues and ensure clarity on their role in the decision-making process.
- Integrate public affairs/media response communities soonest.
- Engage all relevant organizations, and remember that more people doesn't always equal a more effective response: focus on the information exchange and decision-making *process* and not the number of people.
- At the outset of a crisis, discuss "how does this event end?" A questioning attitude will support accurate issue framing throughout the entirety of the response spectrum.
- Create a safe environment in which to express diverse opinions, actively elicit input from diverse organizations, and reconcile divergent priorities and opinions.

- Collaboratively define issues and codevelop solutions to support aligned outcomes: demonstrating an inclusive approach to developing courses of action and forging consensus among those with differing views will improve understanding of interdependency and nonlinearity and will enable adaption as conditions and information change.
- Avoid creating new policy during the crisis-response phase.
- Disseminate information expeditiously, often, and as widely as possible under a documented process. Develop processes to support gathering, exchange, and analysis of information so that it can be understood by necessary audiences and accessible in a timely fashion.
- Know in advance what information can be shared and with whom, the existence of restrictions, and the protections that must be maintained. Apply discretion and judgment in dealing with sensitive issues and data.
- Know your role and the roles of others. Seek to understand the mandates, roles, authorities, jurisdictions of the various organizations that may be involved in the course of a response and the resources, knowledge, and skills they possess. Use of role clarification can overcome parochialism, solve impasses, and further develop trust between individuals and organizations, particularly in situations where jurisdictions, authorities, and capabilities may overlap.
- Speak as one voice during the response to significant events and threats and have a preidentified process for resolving disagreements.
- Demonstrate commitment, focus, and enthusiasm: self-management and professional conduct will support a collaborative practice model and assist in steering discussions/negotiations successfully through complex issues.
- Recognize contributions of all participants and reward those who have had an impact.
- Pay the price: effective crisis preparedness comes at a cost (time, resources, and training). Dedicated, neutral facilitators (who possess subject matter expertise) improve the decision-making process. Train personnel on coordination (and information exchange) processes and conduct exercises frequently, ensuring such efforts are documented and prioritized.

Conclusion

The events we have examined in this chapter underscore the notion that an effective crisis response requires both a networked approach and an attorney at all phases. The focus is no longer on a single organization or solely client based but instead requires a whole-of-government approach to achieve shared outcomes. In contrast to the traditional role of counsel, crisis lawyering promotes cohesion among participants while simultaneously protecting and supporting national positions. Results are not based singularly upon effectively pleading a case or identifying and interpreting judicial rulings/ statutes; results are achieved by using the law as an enabler to collaboratively address complex challenges.

The authors recognize that threats will evolve, and in this regard so too must organizations, collaborative processes, and the law. Response elements that will have enduring resonance, regardless of the threat, include the development of a documented whole-of-government process, transparency, training, senior leader support, integration of lawyers, trust, and the expeditious exchange of information within a government and, as appropriate, among nations (and the private sector).

An assumption in this chapter is that crisis lawyers will have specialized, technical knowledge in the domain(s) within which they are practicing. Yet, the case studies we examined in this chapter, along with survey results, reinforce the notion that, in a multiagency environment, understanding collaboration—including its limitations and opportunities—is also a key competency. Awareness of when information will be shared (and protected), what agencies could be involved in a response, and, more broadly, how a nation speaks with one voice is essential.

Crisis lawyering is "more than simply a matter of agenda setting."[58] In this chapter, we emphasized that the response to crises historically has involved uncertainty, urgency to act, as well as organizational risk and that it is now time to bring an additional consideration to the strategic response landscape: whole-of-government collaboration. A key element of interagency alignment involves lawyers who are increasingly being called on to advise in crisis situations. Awareness of lessons learned, best practices, and development of specialized competencies related to trust building, codevelopment of solutions and capabilities, role clarification, information sharing, and collaborative leadership is crucial for the crisis lawyer to effectively navigate the coordination obstacles in this operating environment.

NOTES

Brian Wilson is the Deputy Director, Global Maritime Operational Threat Response Coordination Center, US Coast Guard/US Department of Homeland Security, and Nora Johnson is the Director of the Office of Incident Management at Transport Canada. The views expressed are those of the authors and do not reflect the official policy or position of the U.S. Navy, U.S. Coast Guard, U.S. Department of Homeland Security, Transport Canada, or the Government of Canada.

1 There is not a single, universally recognized definition of a crisis. *See, e.g.,*
   THOMAS A. BIRKLAND, LESSONS OF DISASTER, POLICY CHANGE AFTER

CATASTROPHIC EVENTS (2007). Birkland noted a description of a crisis as a "situation faced by an individual, group or organization which they are unable to cope with by the use of normal routine procedures and in which stress is created by sudden change." *Id.*, at 5.

2   S.C. Res. 2341(2017).

3   *Id.* at ¶ 4.

4   The Arthur D. Simons Center for Interagency Cooperation conducts research, analysis, and publishes the *InterAgency Journal*; *see* ARTHUR D. SIMONS CENTER FOR INTERAGENCY COOPERATION, http://thesimonscenter.org.

5   William & Mary's program focuses on "complex national security and other public policy problems [to] support research into 'whole of government' solutions to these problems"; *see* WM & MARY NEW CNTR. FOR GOV., www.wm.edu.

6   SUNY Albany programs include an undergraduate major in Emergency Preparedness, Homeland Security, and Cybersecurity; *see College of Emergency Preparedness, Homeland Security and Cybersecurity*, SUNY ALBANY, www.albany.edu.

7   The Swedish Defence University's National Center for Crisis Management Research and Training (CRISMART), examines crisis management, preparedness, and response, focusing in part on the decision-making process; *See* CRISIS MANAGEMENT RESEARCH AND TRAINING (CRISMART), ETH ZURICH CTR. FOR SECURITY STUD., www.css.ethz.ch.

8   *See, e.g.*, United States et al., *Legal Support to Military Operations Joint Publication 1-04* (2016), www.jcs.mil: "Legal advisors actively participate in the entire planning process from joint intelligence preparation of the operational environment development, to mission analysis, to course of action (COA) development and recommendation, through execution." *Id.*, at ix.

9   Similar to challenges with defining interagency collaboration, defining the word "coordination" is also elusive. "Coordination can have many different meanings. The term is rarely defined." ARJEN BOIN ET AL., MANAGING HURRICANE KATRINA; LESSONS FROM A MEGACRISIS 167 (2019).

10 BIRKLAND, LESSONS OF DISASTER, 15 (citing U.S. president Franklin Roosevelt's statement in the 1930s regarding what would be necessary to effectively respond to the Great Depression, an unprecedented economic crisis.)

11 *See generally* Dr. Andrea Charron et. al., *'Left of Bang': NORAD's Maritime Warning Mission and North American Domain Awareness* 4–63 (2015), https://umanitoba.ca.

12 *United Kingdom, Maritime Annual Report*, DEP'T. OF TRANSP. (2017–2018), https://assets.publishing.service.gov.uk.

13 Caroline Mortimer, *Tianjin Explosion: Gigantic Crater Left by Chinese Factory Accident Revealed*, INDEPENDENT (2016), wwwindependent.co.uk.

14 *China Explosions: What We Know About What Happened in Tianjin*, BBC NEWS, (Aug. 17, 2015), www.bbc.com, (hereinafter *China Explosions*).

15 Tom Phillips, *Tianjin Blasts: Fears of Cyanide Pollution as Chinese Officials Lambasted*, GUARDIAN (Aug. 17, 2015), www.theguardian.com.

16 Mortimer, *Tianjin Explosion*.

17 *Id.*

18 Associated Press, *Tianjin Explosion: China Blast Disrupts World's 10th Largest Port*, INDIAN EXPRESS (Aug. 14, 2015), https://indianexpress.com.

19 Tamsyn Burgmann, *Terrorists or Civilians? MV Sun Sea passengers Face Scrutiny in Days Ahead*, WINNIPEG FREE PRESS (Aug. 13, 2010). *See also Sun Sea: Five Years Later*, CAN. COUNCIL FOR REFUGEES (Aug. 2015), https://ccrweb.ca/sites.

20 *Migrant Ships: A Multi-jurisdictional Approach to Planning & Response*, PUB. HEALTH AGENCY OF CAN.

21 *Id.*

22 *Id.*

23 *Id.*

24 *Civil Defence Emergency Management Competency Framework Technical Standard for the CDM Sector (TS02/09)*, N.Z. MINISTRY OF CIV. DEFENCE & EMERGENCY MGMT. (May 2011), www.civildefence.govt.nz (hereinafter "Civil Defence Emergency Management Competency Framework"); *The Canadian Inter-professional Health Collaborative: A National Inter-professional Competency Framework*, HER MAJESTY THE QUEEN IN RIGHT OF CAN. (2010), www.cihc.ca.

25 *See, e.g.*, BOIN ET AL., MANAGING HURRICANE KATRINA, 164–65 (showing a study of Hurricane Katrina noted the coordination challenge identified during the response to Hurricane Katrina: "A wide variety of citizens, officials, and organizations—many not hierarchically related to one another—must be enticed to work together under difficult conditions. The common goal is to make a number of critically important things happen: save lives, lessen suffering, deliver much-needed supplies, evacuate people, provide safety and security, and start the rebuilding.") *See also id.*, at 154–55 ("Officials at all levels seemed to be waiting for the disaster that fit their plans, rather than planning and building scalable capacities to meet [the crisis].").

26 Civil Defence Emergency Management Competency Framework.

27 Paul Blustein & Brian Byrnes, *Lemons Caught in a Homeland Security Squeeze*, WASH. POST (Sept. 10, 2004).

28 *Id.*

29 A study of an unrelated event, Hurricane Katrina, noted the varying approaches to threat response included: "A bottom-up approach assumes that much of the required cooperation will just happen in the initial phase: people tend to work together in response to a disaster. This is called 'emergency coordination' [and under this approach] there is no plan, no coordinator. It materializes seemingly without any steering, like an invisible hand." BOIN ET AL., MANAGING HURRICANE KATRINA, 80.

30 Blustein & Byrnes, *Lemons*.

31 *Id.*

32 *The FBI's Efforts to Protect the Nation's Seaports*, U.S. DEP'T OF JUST. OFF. OF THE INSPECTOR GEN. AUDIT DIV. (Mar. 2006).

33 Blustein & Byrnes, *Lemons*.

34 *Id*. The author led the article by asking "who would accuse innocent fruit of harboring weapons of mass destruction"?

35 *Id*.

36 *Id*.

37 *Id*.

38 *Coumou v. United States*, 107 F.3d 290 (5th Cir. 1997) ("The government was required to take reasonable care to see that Haitian officials learned of Coumou's cooperation. Its failure to transmit the information may have been the result of a breach of that duty.") .

39 *Id*. (citing to the district court finding).

40 *Id*.

41 *Id*.

42 *Id*.

43 *Id*., citing U.S. Presidential Directive-27 (PD-27), *Procedures for Dealing with Non-military Incidents* (Jan. 19, 1978). While PD-27 remains operative, U.S. interagency collaboration to maritime threats now occurs in in accordance with the MOTR Plan (2006).

44 107 F.3d at 294 (footnote omitted).

45 *Id*.

46 *Id*., at 296.

47 *Id*.

48 Mike Dembeck, *Fearing 'Pollution Threat,' Ottawa Steps in to Remove Notorious MV Farley Mowat*, GLOBE & MAIL (June 16, 2017), www.theglobeandmail.com.

49 *Id*.

50 *Id*.

51 Keith Doucette, *Farley Mowat Bails Out Crew and Namesake Ship*, GLOBE & MAIL (Apr. 27, 2018), www.theglobeandmail.com. The toonie coins "had to be counted twice" reportedly after court officials "lost track . . . and had to start over." *Id*. *See also Author Farley Mowat Bails Out Anti-sealing Protestors*, CBC NEWS (Apr. 14, 2008), www.cbc.ca.

52 Dembeck, *Fearing 'Pollution Threat.'*

53 *See Shelburne Celebrates Removal of MV Farley Mowat*, CBC News (July 27, 2017), www.cbc.ca4. *See also* Kathy Johnson, *Federal Court Orders MV Farley Mowat Owner to Pay Big Bucks for Pollution Cleanup in Shelburne Harbor*, SHELBOURNE COUNTY COAST GUARD (Feb. 7, 2019), www.thecoastguard.ca.

54 *See generally* Charron et. al., *'Left of Bang.'*

55 Birkland, LESSONS OF DISASTER, 5 ("The entire field of crisis management is devoted to the development of nonmormal procedures to nonroutine managerial problems"); *see id*. at 165–66 ("[T]here are very few novel problems and solutions").

56 *See* Tim Johnson, Crisis Leadership: how to Lead in Times of Crisis, Threat and Uncertainty 91 (2017).

57 *See generally* Eide Aslak et. al., *Key Challenges in Multi-Agency Collaboration During Large-Scale Emergency Management* (Jan. 2014).

58 Birkland, Lessons of Disaster, 29. The quote is in the context of postdisaster policy learning, although it is relevant to crisis lawyers. Regarding policy change, Birkland further stated: "Whether [postdisaster policy learning] seeks something more tangible than greater attention is the question [and a broader goal is the desire] to link attention to actual policy change." *Id.* at 11.

13

Legal Advice in Crisis Training for Government Lawyers

Perspectives from the United States and Sweden

ERIC K. STERN, BRAD KIESERMAN, TORKEL SCHLEGEL,
PER-ÅKE MÅRTENSSON, AND ELLA CARLBERG

As noted elsewhere in this volume, traditional forms of legal education in the United States and around the world have not always prepared lawyers well for the rigors of crisis management. In this chapter we will first describe a pioneering effort—and academic-practitioner partnership—between the Office of Chief Counsel of the US Federal Emergency Management Agency (FEMA) and a multidisciplinary team of university-based experts to develop usable and trainable knowledge and skills designed to improve the ability and performance of government lawyers under highly challenging conditions. The methodology, experience, and results—training designs and good practice models—of the FEMA Legal Advice in Crisis (AIC) project will be described below.

The positive results of FEMA's AIC project stimulated the posing of an additional question, namely: Are the challenges and good practices for *crisis lawyering* identified by US government leaders and high-performing US government lawyers unique to the United States context, or do they apply to a significant extent to other highly developed countries as well? This question was explored in the context of an ongoing and fruitful partnership with the Swedish Civil Contingencies Agency (MSB) and a parallel Swedish research and professional educational effort organized by Swedish Defense University.

The FEMA Advice in Crisis Project

As part of a broader constellation of efforts to improve the capacity of FEMA in the post–Hurricane Katrina context, FEMA leadership identified the uneven performance and impact of the lawyers at the FEMA Office of Chief Counsel (OCC) as a source of vulnerability in managing disasters under the legal and financial umbrella of the Stafford Disaster Relief and Emergency Assistance Act.[1] Seeking to better understand the legal advice needs of FEMA leaders and the secrets of success employed by a limited number of star disaster lawyers at the agency, FEMA's OCC partnered with a team of researchers based at the University of Virginia. OCC leadership and AIC researchers set out to explore effective and less effective forms of collaboration between leaders and lawyers in crises. Drawing on the crisis-management literature and more than sixty AIC interviews with senior leaders and lawyers at FEMA and other government agencies, as well as numerous group discussions, a number of key findings emerged.[2] These findings were used as the point of departure for developing a number of interactive training modules (to be described in more detail below) that were used to train roughly 180 lawyers from FEMA and partner agencies.

The project focused on the specific crisis-management context of disaster management (with a certain emphasis on the response and early recovery stages) and posed three central questions:

- What do leaders need from their lawyers in disasters?
- How can lawyers most effectively advise their leaders in disasters?
- How can leaders get the most out of their lawyers in such situations?

The first two of these questions (but not the third) will be discussed in this chapter.

Note that, as in other crisis contexts explored in this volume, disaster operations require high-level advice and decision-making processes to function under very difficult circumstances. As noted in the introduction to this volume, it is useful to conceptualize crises (including natural and anthropogenic disasters) in terms of three subjective criteria: threat, uncertainty, and urgency.[3]

What Do FEMA Leaders Need from Their Lawyers in Disasters?

The AIC research found that FEMA leaders want lawyers who will be loyal and trustworthy members of their teams, working effectively with other team members toward mission fulfillment. They want lawyers who can keep up with the rapid pace associated with the response and recovery phase of a disaster and who have the endurance to keep up that pace for weeks or months at a time, if necessary. They want lawyers who have a *can-do attitude* and who are willing to work creatively with the available legal authorities—such as those stemming from the Stafford Act—to enable rapid development and deployment of solutions to urgent humanitarian and administrative problems.

Crisis leaders do not want lawyers who are risk-averse and whose knee-jerk reaction is to say "no" in a climate of fast-paced crisis decision-making, where adaptation and innovation are essential to success. When identifying obstacles to a potential action, leaders want their lawyers to distinguish clearly between matters of habit ("the agency never does that"), guidelines, policy, and statutory prohibitions. Leaders and their lawyers can overcome some types of apparent obstacles more easily than others. Habits may be easier to change than policies, and policies are easier to change (or circumvent) than laws. Good leaders value integrity and judgment. Leaders want lawyers who are able to manage—rather than avoid or seek to completely ignore—risk and contribute to solving urgent crisis problems. However, when the legal risks are too great, they also want a lawyer who is willing and able to pull the emergency brake if the team is on a collision course with the law. As one seasoned federal coordinating officer put it in one of the FEMA AIC interviews, "I don't want my lawyer to keep me out of court. I want my lawyer to keep me out of jail."

An important finding from the AIC leader interviews was the validation of the so-called SALT performance standard (defined below) that came to be adopted by and widely accepted at FEMA OCC:

> SALT is a set of individual performance criteria linked to the FEMA Office of Chief Counsel (OCC) Mission Statement. OCC employees apply SALT to assess their legal advice, counsel, risk analysis, dispute resolution services and other assignments. Consistent application of SALT supports the OCC's mission accomplishment and reinforces the relationships necessary for our senior leaders and client-partners to feel confident in seeking and using OCC services as an integral part of their business processes. In every action and encounter, and in all the advice we provide, we are:
>
> *Solution-oriented*—Where others see obstacles, we focus on legally viable solutions and outcomes. We are open to the ideas of others and provide options, constructive alternatives and creative solutions to legal problems. We support continuous learning and collaborative environments that foster new ideas, understanding and better ways to execute FEMA's mission. We help resolve conflicts and eliminate needless barriers that interfere with the agency's efforts to achieve its mission. We assess what is valuable from current and past activity in our practice, document it and share with those who need to know.
>
> *Articulate*—We express our positions and explain law and policy in an organized, well-reasoned and persuasive manner, both orally and in writing. We use language that is appropriate to the client-partner, without use of undue "legalese" that might confuse or distort the message.
>
> *Legally Sufficient*—To the extent that operational conditions permit, we apply the aphorism "Salt away the facts, the law will keep." This means we aggressively develop the facts before applying the law to arrive at legal conclusions and options. When we render a legal opinion, in any form, we cite legal authorities

(using the Bluebook for all written work) to demonstrate that our opinion substantially satisfies applicable statutory, regulatory and federal executive branch requirements so that our client-partners and those who may later review our opinions understand our reasoning. We are professionally responsible and uphold our duties to our clients, courts and the legal profession.

Timely—We deliver advice and counsel on demand, where and when our client-partners need it, and aggressively anticipate issues and obstacles to mission accomplishment. By being proactive, responsive and accessible, we prevent problems. We meet the timelines required to support critical or urgent agency operations, and communicate with our clients to establish appropriately prioritized timelines for routine matters. To the extent that operations permit, we provide our colleagues with sufficient time in which to review, consult and coordinate on complex issues.[4]

Note that the often severe time pressure and resource constraints associated with disasters (and other forms of crisis situations) create recurring professional-quality dilemmas for crisis lawyers. Leaders will turn to lawyers for guidance in fast-paced, dynamic situations, and if lawyers do not provide input in a timely fashion, crucial decisions are likely to be made without the benefit of legal counsel. As a result, crisis lawyering involves coming to terms with providing opinions based on legal research/knowledge of the law that is good enough (as opposed to optimal) in relation to the situation, context, and operational tempo.

Based on a review of the literature and the extensive AIC project interviews described above, the AIC researchers were able to distill three good practice models informed by state-of-the-art thinking from the literature and gleaned from the skill set of a number of the best-performing and most experienced FEMA lawyers. The interview responses converged around three key secrets of success that are consistently employed by high-performing lawyers, namely: preparation, systematic holistic analysis, and social competence/group awareness.

The first model ("PREP") focuses on mission preparation and outlines measures lawyers could take to be better prepared for field deployment, enabling them to orient themselves rapidly in a disaster, its sociopolitical context, and the crisis team (e.g., the leadership of a FEMA Joint Field Office) and to prepare themselves to pull the emergency brake if legal, ethical, or other relevant redlines are about to be crossed. The second model ("SOAP") outlines a systematic procedure for producing and delivering substantive legal advice and for managing risk (informed by a holistic analysis of practical, legal, and ethical considerations) to leaders. The third model ("GAIN") explores the group context and the complex negotiation of role demands necessary to gain trust and influence and strike an appropriate balance between team play and the unique responsibilities of the lawyer in a crisis team. (See below for more detailed descriptions of the content of the models.)

Building on the AIC research, the above-mentioned practice models, and the SALT performance standard, a four-day training for the FEMA cadre of lawyers was developed and delivered in May 2011 in Charlottesville, Virginia. A second training was delivered the following year in Arlington, Virginia. In addition to lectures, briefings, and seminars, there were a number of interactive text- and video-based teaching case exercises. The exercises enabled the lawyers to practice their AIC skills and learn by doing and gave them an opportunity to discuss with their peers the difficulties specific to a crisis context. Several of the exercises involved role reversals designed to enhance the lawyers' appreciation of the responsibilities of others in the organization. In one exercise, FEMA lawyers played the role of leader and made a difficult judgment call under pressure in an ethically and legally complex crisis. In another, they played a public affairs officer and explained alleged irregularities in a disaster response to inquisitive journalists in the context of an "ambush" interview.

Good Practice Modules: A Closer Look

In this section we provide an overview of the good-practice models PREP and GAIN. In somewhat greater detail, the SOAP module (explicating a step-by-step approach for the production and delivery of substantive legal advice in crisis) will be explained.

PREP

Leaders and top lawyers at FEMA agree that a key prerequisite for success is being *prepared* for the rigors of practicing law in crisis or disaster environments.[5] The pace is fast, and disaster lawyers must hit the ground running. The following section outlines four key categories of preparation that may be helpful in improving the likelihood of successful performance. While they do not guarantee success, they clearly improve the odds. Furthermore, failure to prepare will stack the deck toward failure.

The following bullet points summarize some ways to prepare oneself for crisis operations and to pave the way for good collaborative relationships with colleagues (see also the GAIN model in the next section):

- *Prepare for availability and extended absence*: Two of the factors most emphasized by FEMA leaders and top-performing lawyers interviewed by AIC researchers are availability and commitment. Clients want lawyers to be readily available and prepared to commit to longer deployments as lawyer turnover is perceived to be disruptive.

- *Establish predeparture communication by phone and/or email with key team members and collaborators inside and outside of the organization.* This enables lawyers to connect with their clients, other team members, and partners at an early stage, by establishing relationships and providing communication links that can help to improve the lawyer's situational awareness going into an operative or other relevant crisis lawyering setting.
- *Meet and greet leaders* (e.g., a FEMA Federal Coordinating Officer) *and team broadly on arrival.* Lawyers should follow up their predeployment contacts, and complement these contacts with additional personnel introductions, once on site. By doing so, lawyers signal not only sociability but also approachability and willingness to be a part of the team.
- *Know your redlines.* In engineering, the term "redlines" refers to the maximum engine speed at which an engine or motor and its components are designed to operate without causing damage to the components themselves or other parts of the engine. For emergency management lawyers, "knowing your redlines" means having a clear understanding of ethical duties and the limits of the law and how these bounding factors might present themselves in a disaster setting, before providing advice in crisis.

Furthermore, the prospects for providing successful advice improve if lawyers do not wait for field deployment or first meetings of dedicated crisis/disaster teams at headquarters to begin mission reconnaissance. Once assigned, lawyers should immediately begin informing themselves about the situation, context, and role they will be assuming. Similarly, it is critical to gather/secure access to general and specialized legal resources on paper and/or in electronic form. This is particularly relevant for field deployments, but it can also facilitate the development of timely and legally sufficient advice at headquarters or in interagency environments. Effective crisis attorneys search and compile resources for anticipated issues involving, among others: authorities (for FEMA and collaborating agencies), regulations, guidelines, policy, opinions, precedents, new or recent initiatives (or changes in policy or guidance), as well as particularly relevant points of local law.

GAIN

Based on the collective experience of crisis leaders and some of their finest and most effective attorneys, AIC researchers developed the GAIN model, which identifies some of the key social-behavioral elements of advice in crisis.[6] The elements of GAIN include: Group Dynamics; Active Engagement; Individual Requirements; and Negotiation.

Group Dynamics: Much of the work of FEMA lawyers takes place in the context of groups or teams. Developing the ability to "read" those groups, and understand their culture and processes, can help lawyers identify opportunities and strategies to intervene in the right way, at the right time, for maximum impact. Groups are thought to change over time and exhibit different characteristics at different stages of maturity. Furthermore, groups exhibit different mixes of competitive/conflictual and collaborative tendencies that can impact positively or negatively (e.g., so-called groupthink) on information-sharing and group decision-making.[7]

Active Engagement: The AIC interviews generated numerous descriptions of lawyers who were marginalized or—in extreme cases—removed from their teams and sent home. Once again, the big challenge for lawyers is to find ways to engage as team players in order to bring their knowledge and judgment to bear to the benefit of the disaster-management effort. In some contexts and situations, according to leader and team preferences, lawyers may engage as technical experts drawing closely on core professional expertise. In others, lawyers may be expected to serve as "wise counsel," weighing in more broadly by drawing on their general/domain knowledge and problem-solving experience. Effectiveness and impact tend to be maximized through active listening, interacting with others in ways that build social capital and goodwill over time, developing understanding and empathy for other roles (leader, crisis communicator, technical expert, etc.) and picking one's battles.

Individual Requirements: While the attorney is generally part of a broader multiprofessional crisis team in FEMA settings (as in other crisis-management settings), attorneys may face cross-pressures and duties that are somewhat different than those of other players, not least in the government setting. Who is the client and to whom is the ultimate loyalty owed for the FEMA lawyer? FEMA leaders tend to want (1) their lawyers to be loyal and (2) leader-lawyer communications to be privileged (as in private-practice settings). However, in the government context, lawyers may have competing obligations to the law, to agency leadership and policy, to the Office of Chief Counsel, to professional ethical standards, and the like.[8] Team play must be balanced with living up to the individual requirements associated with the government attorney's role.

Negotiation: The term "negotiation"—in its various meanings—captures a number of modes of social interaction which are critical for crisis lawyering. First of all (to sum up the discussion above), lawyers must negotiate the complex social and political-administrative terrain in which they are embedded and operating in crisis. Second, lawyers can contribute to conflict resolution, consensus-building, and negotiating viable solutions within their crisis teams and between these teams and headquarters. Third, lawyers (including FEMA lawyers) are often involved in negotiations with outside partners and parties that are critical to the success of disaster response and recovery operations.

SOAP

SENSE-MAKING: The first step toward effective substantive advising in a disaster is to make sense of the situation (see the discussion of crisis leadership tasks in the introduction to this volume).[9] This may seem obvious, but it is a nontrivial and ongoing task as disaster and postdisaster contexts tend to be complex, dynamic, ambiguous, and uncertain. Just as one feels as if one is getting one's bearings and has a good understanding of the situation and problems to be faced by the team in which the lawyer is embedded, new developments will necessitate updating and rethinking. It is an iterative process, one that may require abandoning previously held views and priorities[10] as the operating picture evolves. While sense-making is in part an intuitive activity,[11] it can be facilitated and improved by using a set of core questions to challenge the environment and improve contextual and situational awareness. This is not only a way of combatting the phenomena of stress-induced tunnel vision and groupthink; it is also a good practice for lawyering and decision-making under more normal situations.

Asking the following questions can help lawyers (and leaders) better make sense of the situations facing them and improve performance in disasters and crises:

- Which values are at stake in this situation and for whom?[12]
- What are the key uncertainties in this situation (and how might information gathering, analysis, consultation, etc., reduce them)?
- What is the time frame for developing and delivering advice (which is in turn related to the client or team's time frame for action)? Are there ways of buying time without compromising the mission and public affairs messaging or otherwise delaying the work flow among the team?

Effective sense-making—a key part of problem solving—is facilitated by contextual awareness. A very common source of failure in disaster management (not to mention public policy writ large, business, and personal life) is building solutions around underdeveloped or inappropriate specifications of the problem[13] that neglect critical values and stakeholder interests.[14]

OPTIONS: In providing advice to leaders and other clients in disaster operations, lawyers will engage at different stages of the problem-solving process. In some cases, a decision maker will have a preferred option. For example, in one disaster in a remote Alaskan village, the Federal Coordinating Officer (FCO) strongly preferred partnering with voluntary agencies to leverage assistance resources to provide replacement housing. Accordingly, FEMA attorneys developed a transactional framework allowing the agency to provide funds for log-house kits for displaced households, which were constructed under the supervision of the Mennonite Disaster Service and furnished by Samaritan's Purse.

The attorney is likely to face questions of the following nature:

- Are we authorized (or can you find me the authority) to do X?
- Are we prohibited from doing X?
- What are the legal (and possibly ethical, practical, political, or other) risks associated with doing X?
- How can we manage the legal and other risks associated with doing X?
- Is there a better (e.g., faster, cheaper, more effective, and/or less risky) way than X to achieve the goal?
- What were the lessons learned the last time we did X?

Clients may also identify a short list of two or more options under serious consideration and ask for a relative analysis of the costs, risks, and/or benefits associated with them. If there is a single or limited number of favored options on the table, the attorney should follow the assessment process described below. In other situations—and especially if the lawyer is brought in to the process at an early stage—lawyers may be asked to be a part of the process of identifying or developing options. This may involve drawing upon historical/ organizational memory or the current set of procedures to help generate options, or it may entail a creative process of coming up with a novel approach. Obviously, the latter is more likely to be necessary when FEMA is facing a situation that is qualitatively or quantitatively different from those faced in the past and that have shaped the frame of reference and established action repertoire. It is crucial, in such circumstances, for the attorney to understand the delicate interface of law and policy and the need to work in partnership with program staff in developing novel approaches.[15] Failure to involve and integrate the subject-matter program experts can lead to perfectly legal plans on paper that are not executable on the ground. Program staff must have buy-in on the suggested solution, as they will actually have to execute the plan and deal with the consequences. Again, once an option or limited set of options has been produced, the lawyer should shift to assessment.

ASSESSMENT: The assessment process is critical to producing high-quality advice in crisis. While assessment should be seen as a broad process drawing on multiple perspectives in relation to the option(s) under examination, many lawyers focus explicitly on only one or two of these perspectives (and perhaps treat some of them in a more intuitive or explicit fashion). The best disaster lawyers, however, analyze options in a systematic and comprehensive fashion. This process draws on four dimensions and gives attorneys the ability to weigh and integrate the results of this process in the advice they give to their clients and teams. The key dimensions of assessment are: authorization, prohibition, risk, and judgment.

Let us begin with *authorization*. Does the option appear to be authorized by the Stafford Act or by supplementary authority? Disaster lawyers should keep in mind that Stafford was deliberately formulated to be a broad and flexible instrument and is subject to alternative and evolving opinions. The authorities available under Stafford may be interpreted broadly or narrowly, in part according to the policies and priorities set by FEMA's leadership (and the White House), as well as the zeitgeist of the times. While the Stafford Act tends to loom large in the assortment of authorities available to FEMA, it is critical to keep in mind that other supplementary authorities may be available and provide authorization for actions that clients deem necessary or useful in addressing the needs of responding organizations, survivors, and other parties. Should these authorities not be directly available to FEMA, at times they may be borrowed from other agencies through cooperative agreements. For example, FEMA assisted the United States Agency for International Development (USAID) with assets and personnel to support the response efforts after the 2010 Haiti earthquake. These assets included Mobile Emergency Response Support personnel and equipment, the Incident Management Assistance Team, and an Incident Response Vehicle to help establish communications for relief efforts on the ground and provide subject-matter expertise and technical support. These activities were undertaken pursuant to an Inter-Agency Agreement with USAID under the authorities of the Foreign Assistance Act of 1961. Part of being solution-oriented (and "getting to yes") is about being creative in developing (and arguing) defensible rationales for authorizing practically necessary action under extreme circumstances.

The next dimension of assessment is *prohibition*. Is there a specific legal or policy-based prohibition, and from what legal authority does it derive? Lawyers are likely to be particularly aware of and sensitive to such prohibitions when they involve potential infringements of fundamental rights and protections. When examining prohibitions and other forms of potentially prohibitive constraints, it is critical to distinguish between types of prohibitions and whether they stem from the United States Constitution, statutes (including appropriations law), regulations, executive orders, policies, tactical guidelines (e.g., a FEMA letter from the FEMA administrator), and/or past agency policies and/or practices. Note that lesser-order prohibitions (especially those stemming from a past agency policy) may well be amenable to change or dispensation in consultation with leaders within or outside of FEMA, especially if in tune with broader trends and shifts in policy and/or political and operational imperatives. Situational and contextual factors will determine the viability and appropriateness of such courses of action. *When communicating to clients that certain prohibitions appear to be insurmountable obstacles to a particular course of action, lawyers should be specific about the source and nature of those prohibitions.* It is important to work with the client on formulating a Plan B or C if the favored course of action appears impossible to implement. This is a central aspect of being "solution-oriented," as suggested by the SALT performance standards. It is also important to store these non-starter options for future reference in case there are calls for post-crisis legislative proposals.

The third dimension of assessment is *risk*. What are the legal (and other) risks associated with this option in relation to other alternative courses of action or inaction? Disaster management is fraught with risk, and disaster managers are aware and often willing to accept a degree of (and in extreme situations more than a little) risk. Many of the leaders interviewed strongly emphasized their desire to do the right thing despite potential legal exposure. Lawyers who seek to avoid legal risk completely will be perceived as obstacles to effective disaster management and are likely to be marginalized within their teams. Furthermore, legal risks must be weighed against other forms of risk (e.g., to life, property, FEMA's reputation, political viability, ethics in the broader sense of the word, etc.) when giving advice. The old adage "desperate times call for desperate measures" captures the balancing act that FEMA leaders are called upon to undertake when making crucial decisions during and in the aftermath of disasters.

When it is (or may be) necessary to embark on a course of action fraught with legal risk, part of the lawyer's task is to look for ways of managing or minimizing these risks. For example, contemporaneous documentation (not only of the legal opinion but also of the situational imperatives and deliberative process behind the measure in question) may help to protect the leaders and lawyers involved. Formulating a viable exit strategy should also be part of the implementation plan. What are the metrics? Are there objective standards in place? How will this be conveyed to the state, applicants, the public, and Congress?

Last but not least, it is imperative to exercise and apply *judgment* to the matter in question.[16] Leaders (and other clients) told the Advice in Crisis investigators of their strong motivations to do the right thing during and after disasters. Leaders of good character, judgment, and intention often have an intuitive sense of what needs to be done in critical situations like disasters. Bases for such normative determinations may have to do with meeting the urgent needs of survivors, preventing disproportionate direct or collateral damage, or living up to fundamental norms of fairness. As stated succinctly by one veteran disaster lawyer interviewed by the Advice in Crisis team: "Is this for the greater good?" As in other areas of the law, it is necessary to address that question in two ways:

- Is this for the greater good in this situation?
- Is this for the greater good in terms of the precedent it would set and/or the incentive structure it would create?[17]

One aspect of exercising judgment is knowing when to seek different perspectives, consult more experienced attorneys, or elevate a decision. Further complicating this exercise in judgment is the sense of urgency and attendant time compression associated with crises. Therefore, one important and recurring role decision makers will ask lawyers to play is helping to decide when "to ask permission" and when to seek "forgiveness." It is unlikely that the lawyer will have the time and information necessary to thoroughly consider all the potential options and consequences associated with a particular decision during crisis operations. Emergency management lawyers must come to the table knowledgeable along with a strong ethical compass and readily accessible network for technical "reachback" (e.g., to FEMA's OCC!). Without these capabilities, the lawyer will not be prepared to exercise and apply judgment effectively in crises. Finally, one of the most important dimensions of judgment is determining whether a particular solution is practically viable and can be implemented. While the lawyer may not be the only one around the table who can weigh in on the practicality or mechanics of implementation, lawyers may have highly relevant input to contribute on this point because of their legal expertise and general knowledge and experience. Disaster management, like politics, is the art of the possible.

PROVISION OF ADVICE: Once the previous steps have been completed, lawyers will need to communicate the advice produced to clients and/or to the disaster management teams in which they are embedded. Doing so effectively requires adapting and packaging the advice in ways that are appropriate to the situation and the context in which the advice is being given, as explored in the socio-behavioral (GAIN) dimension above. Consider the following factors:

- Situation: Is the work taking place under crisis-like conditions, and what is the time frame involved? How much pressure is on the disaster management team and its leaders?

- Organizational context: What is the nature of the organizational context (headquarters, regional office, Joint Field Office, etc.) and the local culture?
- Venue and form: Is it most appropriate to convey this advice to a leader or other client in a one-on-one situation, at a senior staff meeting, at an all-hands meeting (generally not!), at a meeting with state and local officials, or some other forum? Should one deliver an oral or a written opinion? If written, will an informal email message suffice, or is a more formal written document necessary?
- Risk picture: Generally speaking, it is better to package advice in terms of alternative levels of risk associated with the option(s) in question rather than as a binary black-and-white (i.e., "you can or cannot go forward with a particular course of action"). However, in cases characterized by unacceptably high levels of legal risk (and not least when compensating humanitarian imperatives are not part of the picture), wise leaders want their lawyers to be prepared to pull the emergency brake and express their objections in the strongest possible terms. Note that contemporaneous and comprehensive documentation is part of managing risk and likely to be of great value when difficult questions are subsequently asked—and criticism forthcoming—in the wake of the crisis or disaster.
- Leader/collaborator personalities: Clients vary greatly in their approach to processing information, open- versus closed-mindedness, big-picture versus detail orientation, familiarity/expertise with the relevant legal issues and modes of legal reasoning, ability to function in stressful environ-ments, and so on. The most effective disaster lawyers cultivate the ability to adapt to the personalities and leadership styles of their clients. Given the same problem and assessment of options, a lawyer might choose to do a three-minute nutshell brief to a big-picture and action-oriented leader but present the same material and results in a fifteen-minute briefing to a detail-oriented, reflective, and legally interested leader. In this sense, being articulate in the SALT sense described above is partly in relation to the person(s) to whom the advice is being delivered. As noted, provision of advice should be consistent with the SALT performance standards and be: Solution-oriented, Articulate, Legally Sufficient, and Timely.

Finally, lawyers can and often should play a role in developing or review-ing messaging/external affairs guidance pre- and post-decision. For example, in response to the devastating April 2011 tornados that struck Alabama and Mississippi, FEMA's OCC worked in conjunction with the White House, with FEMA leadership at headquarters and in the field, and with program staff on developing a streamlined private property debris removal plan called #OperationCleanSweep. OCC also assisted the external affairs and program staff on press releases and fact sheets. Furthermore, OCC engaged in gathering data for lessons learned from the project. Despite occasional tensions between lawyers and crisis communication professionals (such as public or external affairs officers) over balancing transparency, responsibility-taking (and protection of organizational brands), and limiting legal exposure when things have gone wrong, heedful interrelating among lawyers and communicators tends to pay significant dividends.

Swedish Civil Contingencies Agency/Swedish Defense University Crisis Legal Advisers Initiative

In this section we describe a parallel initiative that developed in Sweden in the period from roughly 2014 to 2019. The Swedish initiative had roots in several intersecting streams of activity. One was a large-scale European Union U 7th Framework Program (called "AniBioThreat") focusing on the challenges of coping with animal-borne diseases in the European context. One of the key findings of the project was a need to strengthen expert networks (including the legal dimension) in order to support leaders in crisis situations. This project led to the creation of a multiagency legal advisers network focusing on bioterrorism in 2012. A second key stream of activity was the ongoing societal security/homeland security (broadly defined to include emergency management) science and technology collaboration between the United States (Department of Homeland Security's Science and Technology Directorate) and Sweden (Swedish Civil Contingencies Agency). One of many collaborative projects and initiatives in this constellation was a project examining methods for better preparing strategic leaders (and their advisers) for the rigors of crisis management.[18] This work also served to highlight the need to prepare not only leaders but also key crisis management collaborators (such as legal advisers and crisis communication experts) to work together effectively under highly stressful conditions. Third, building on the AniBioThreat results and vivid experiences from major crisis events—such as the Swedish forest fires of 2014 as well as subsequent events such as the Ebola outbreak in West Africa, the migration crisis, and several incidents involving terrorism—there was growing awareness of the need to to prepare and better connect lawyers serving in national government agencies and regional governments. As a result, the chief of the legal division at the Swedish Civil Contingencies Agency (Torkel Schlegel) and other leaders in the government, legal, and crisis-management communities (e.g., Per-Åke Mårtensson) took steps to develop a broader network connecting legal advisers with potential roles in crisis and emergencies. These developments set the stage for exploring the relevance of the FEMA AIC concept to Sweden. Somewhat surprisingly for some, it turned out that the AIC methods addressed general issues of crisis lawyering that largely transcended the legal, cultural, and political-administrative differences between Sweden and the United States.

A series of scholar-practitioner workshops were held in Sweden to explore questions parallel to those that drove the AIC project. Swedish lawyers were brought together to discuss their experiences of working under crisis conditions, as well as to what extent traditional Swedish legal education prepared them for crisis lawyering. With the partial exception of specialized operational lawyers from the Swedish military and police, the consensus was that traditional legal education and legal career paths in Sweden did not adequately prepare lawyers to support leaders and contribute effectively to multidisciplinary teams in crisis situations. In addition, many of the Swedish lawyers found that the AIC framework not only provided guidance for crisis situations but also was conducive to improving lawyers' performance, problem-solving ability, and client relations in other situations where gaps between decision maker intentions and legal conclusions can emerge. Furthermore, it was noted that lawyers were often not included in crisis teams or crisis staff organizations—despite the fact that the work of these bodies often involve navigating complex legal issues.

Similarly, Swedish leaders and crisis communication experts were asked about their experience of working with lawyers in crises and emergencies and what they wanted and needed from their lawyers in such extreme situations. The results of the workshops were startlingly similar to the AIC findings. Leaders had mixed experiences in working with lawyers, and lawyers were perceived as potential liabilities as well as potential assets in crisis management teams. Swedish leaders wanted their lawyers to be prepared and have a deep and well-grounded understanding and awareness of the situation and leaders' concerns; to be convincing, accessible, and collaborative and social, creative, and flexible and able to keep up in fast-paced situations; to have the stamina to participate over the course of a prolonged operation or mission; to be able to tolerate uncertainty; to be able to cope with and manage risk; to be proactive, well-informed about the law and their organizations, loyal and trustworthy, competent, pragmatic, and problem-solving; and to be able to pull on the emergency brake if needed.

The key findings of the Swedish workshops were as follows:

- The quality of crisis legal services delivered to Swedish leaders varies considerably across lawyers and domains, and many government lawyers are ill-prepared and -equipped to cope with crisis conditions.
- Swedish government lawyers have a significant need for supplementary training to improve their ability to participate in crisis management efforts.

On the basis of these exploratory activities in 2015, the Swedish Civil Contingencies Agency asked the Swedish Defense University in late 2015 to collaborate in developing an interactive pilot Legal Advisors Course, targeting lawyers working in civilian agencies, the defense sector, and county governments. With active support from FEMA (which provided materials and expertise), a combined team of experts from the legal division of the Swedish Civil Contingencies Agency (authors Schlegel and Carlberg), and the Swedish Defense University (Stern, Mårtensson, and Marika Eriksson, an experienced practitioner of military operational law) developed a four-day Crisis Legal Advisors course culminating in a major scenario exercise.

In the initial delivery, FEMA AIC training materials were used extensively. Participants benefited greatly from remote participation by former chief counsel of FEMA Brad Kieserman (who gave a much-appreciated video briefing) and the presence of his Swedish counterpart Torkel Schlegel (who participated in the entire workshop). The feedback from the initial delivery was highly positive from the participants and the Swedish Civil Contingencies Agency. The SOAP and GAIN modules (briefly described above) were particularly well received. The original PREP module was perceived by some participants as more FEMA-specific and less relevant to participants who were unlikely to become involved in field deployments. Some participants expressed a strong preference for teaching materials in Swedish and portraying more familiar roles and agency contexts.

The course—which has consistently received rave reviews from participants—has been incrementally and iteratively revised from year to year. Additional teaching cases and exercise materials in Swedish and grounded in Swedish political-administrative settings have been developed, including an innovative multiprofessional exercise design in which cells of lawyers practice working in multiprofessional teams alongside seasoned crisis leaders and crisis communications professionals. The PREP module and associated activities have been reworked for greater relevance to those who may experience crises in their own offices or buildings across town. That being said, the crisis events of recent years (e.g., the large-scale wildfires in Sweden in 2018) have created a number of situations in which Swedish lawyers have been thrust into situations in which "field lawyering" in relatively remote locations at home and abroad have been required, reinforcing the relevance of the PREP module as originally formulated as well.

Partly stemming (as noted above) from the early work in building a crisis legal advisers' network, the Swedish Crisis Legal Advisors Course has over the course of five deliveries contributed to the further extension of such networks and the development of a broader community of practice and the institutionalization of good practices with regard to crisis lawyering in Sweden. For example, on October 26, 2016, the Swedish Association of County Boards (www.lansstyrelsen.se) created a mutual legal support network connecting lawyers from the various counties across the country. Tellingly, the coordinating group for the network (officially the Collaboration Group for Legal Support in Crisis) was code-named "Lst SALT," explicitly referencing the performance standards propagated in both the US and Swedish legal advice in crisis projects. The recent emphasis has been on revitalizing the Swedish Total Defense concept, civil defense, and active preparations for coping with a broad spectrum of potential crisis contingencies, including various forms of hybrid warfare and military hostilities.

Conclusions

Crises are tough tests of the ability of societies, organizations, and professionals to adapt to severe and highly stressful working conditions. Lawyers—not least government lawyers—have a key role to play in guiding crisis response and recovery. Crises place extraordinary demands on lawyers and on the leaders they serve and the other professionals with whom they need to collaborate. The FEMA project described above labeled the interaction between lawyers and decision makers in the context of disaster operations "Advice in Crisis." This is a phrase that can be interpreted in different ways. The more direct meaning focuses on the challenge of developing and communicating legal advice in extreme situations. The second interpretation refers to the loss of professional legitimacy that can occur when lawyers tasked to support crisis leaders and teams are not ready to provide the legal services so urgently needed to inform and guide decision-making and problem-solving in disasters and other forms of crisis. Such lawyers—who may be very capable in steady-state transactional or litigation settings—find themselves facing a crisis within a crisis as they fail to rise to the occasion and meet the expectations of their leaders and teammates.

In the first part of the chapter, we describe a good practice framework and in-service training approach designed to help lawyers succeed in crisis lawyering and avoid finding their advice (and their professional credibility) in crisis. However, while the US Legal Advice in Crisis project was well received by FEMA leadership and the Office of Chief Counsel and reportedly has had a lasting and positive impact,[19] it remained an open question as to what extent these findings and frameworks were relevant and potentially applicable outside of the FEMA context.

In the second part of the chapter, we describe an exploration of the relevance and deployment of a localized version of the Advice in Crisis framework in a non-US setting. Initially, there was some reason for skepticism regarding how well the framework would travel. Sweden has a very different legal framework (with roots in the Napoleonic Code), as well as very different political-administrative structures, cultures, and legal educational traditions compared to the United States. However, despite these important differences, the similarities in challenges facing leaders and lawyers in crisis proved more fundamental and—with significant adaptation and localized elaboration—the Swedish Crisis Legal Advisors' framework has proved helpful in improving the crisis preparedness of government agencies at national and regional levels and of more than a hundred government lawyers and counting.

While it would be risky to assume that the challenges facing U.S. and Swedish government lawyers and the tool kit of interactive instructional designs and good practices assembled via the US and Swedish Legal Advice in Crisis projects can be directly exported to other highly developed (and other) countries, the results of these pilot efforts do strongly suggest that further exploration, adaptation, and refinement of the AIC framework in other national or international organizational contexts is both warranted and promising.

Furthermore, the authors of this chapter also look forward with anticipation to comparing the results of the FEMA Advice in Crisis project and the Swedish Crisis Legal Advisors project with the findings of the other chapters in this volume exploring legal advice in crisis in a wide variety of other government-, corporate-, and nonprofit-sector settings.

NOTES

1 The following section draws heavily upon three previous FEMA AIC publications. Eric Stern et al., *Advice in Crisis: Leaders, Lawyers and the Art of Disaster Management*, in HOMELAND SECURITY HANDBOOK: STRATEGIC GUIDANCE FOR A COORDINATED APPROACH TO EFFECTIVE SECURITY AND EMERGENCY MANAGEMENT (David G. Kamien ed., 2012); Eric Stern et al., *Advice in Crises: Towards Best Practices for Providing Legal Advice Under Disaster Conditions*, FEMA DISASTER OPERATIONS LEGAL RESOURCE 53–56 (2011); Eric Stern et al., *How to Collaborate with Lawyers in Crisis*, EMERGENCY MANAGEMENT (2012), WWW.EMERGENCYMGMT.COM/TEMPLATES/GOV_PRINT_ARTICLE?ID=142351215. With regard to the sections on the FEMA AIC project, we would like to acknowledge very important contributions to the AIC effort by Gregory Saathoff, MD, Mary Ellen Martinet, Patrick Walsh, Adrian Sevier, Rachael Bralliar, Elisabeth Renieris, and Dr. Christopher Holstege. Thanks also to numerous colleagues at the Swedish Defense University, the Swedish Civil Contingencies Agency, the Swedish Armed Forces, the Swedish National Board of Health, and several Stockholm Region Fire and Rescue Services, among others.

2 For a full list of FEMA AIC interviews, *see* Stern et al., *Advice in Crises.*

3 Arjen Boin, Paul 't Hart, Eric Stern & Bengt Sundelius, The Politics of Crisis Management: Public Leadership under Pressure (2nd ed. 2017). For a detailed exploration of the implications of these conditions for crisis lawyering, *see* Stern et al., *Advice in Crisis.*

4 Stern et al., *How to Collaborate.*

5 The description of the model is drawn from *id.* at 716–18.

6 For a more detailed treatment of the GAIN module, *see id.* at 718–26.

7 *See, e.g.,* BEYOND GROUPTHINK (Paul 't Hart, Eric K. Stern & Bengt Sundelius eds., 1997); CASS R. SUNSTEIN & REID HASTIE, WISER: GETTING BEYOND GROUPTHINK TO MAKE GROUPS SMARTER (2014).

8 *See* Gary J. Edles, *Assessing Who Is the Client in the Government Context,* 10 FALL ADMIN. & REG L. NEWS 31 (2005); P.E. Salking, *Beware: What You Say to Your (Government) Lawyer May Be Held against You—The Erosion of Government Attorney-Client Confidentiality,* 35 URB. L. 283 (2003).

9 *See* Stern et al., *How to Collaborate,* 726–32.

10 *Cf.* Ben W. Heineman Jr., *Lawyers as Leaders,* 116 YALE L.J. 266–71 (2007).

11 *See infra,* the discussion of GAIN above; *cf.* JOHN R. BOYD, DESTRUCTION AND CREATION (1976).

12 MALCOM GLADWELL, BLINK: THE POWER OF THINKING WITHOUT THINKING (2005).

13 IAN I. MISTRO & ABRAHAM SILVERS, DIRTY ROTTEN STRATEGIES: HOW WE TRICK OURSELVES & OTHERS INTO SOLVING THE WRONG PROBLEMS PRECISELY (2010).

14 RALPH L. KEENEY, VALUE-FOCUSED THINKING: A PATH TO CREATIVE DECISION MAKING (1992); Ian I. Mitroff & James R. Emshoff, *On Strategic Assumption-Making: A Dialectical Approach to Policy and Planning,* 4 ACADEMY OF MGMT. REV. 1–12 (1979).

15 Henry Mintzberg et al., *The Structure of Unstructured Decision Processes,* 21 ADMIN. SCI. QUARTERLY 246–75 (1976).

16 STANLEY A. RENSHON & DEBORAH W. LARSON, GOOD JUDGMENT IN FOREIGN POLICY: THEORY & APPLICATION (2003).

17 WARD FARSNWORTH, THE LEGAL ANALYST: A TOOLKIT FOR THIKNING ABOUT THE LAW (2007).

18 Eric Stern, *Designing Crisis Management Training and Exercises for Strategic Leaders* (2014), www.diva-portal.org.

19 *See e.g.,* remarks by Tom Balint, FEMA Associate Chief Counsel for Resilience-Preparedness, at University of Albany, Albany Law, "Crisis Lawyering" Panel, October 2018.

PART IV

Educating and Skill-Building

14

Call Air Traffic Control!

Confronting Crisis as Lawyers and Teachers

MUNEER I. AHMAD AND MICHAEL J. WISHNIE

Shortly after 10 P.M. on Friday, January 27, 2017, one week after the inauguration of US president Donald Trump, two former students called one of us to
report that their client was being detained at John F. Kennedy International
Airport in New York and that they were thinking about filing an emergency
lawsuit. That man, Hameed Khalid Darweesh, was an Iraqi interpreter and
engineer who, for approximately a decade, performed valuable work for the
US government, including as an interpreter for the 101st Airborne Division
in Baghdad and Mosul and as a project engineer for both the US government
and US contractors. On the basis of this work, he received an Iraqi Special
Immigrant Visa, designed especially for people like Mr. Darweesh who, by
virtue of their work for the US government, are at grave and special risk for
violence. We later learned that a second client, Haider Sameer Abdulkhaleq
Alshawi, was also being detained at the same airport, despite having been
granted a visa to join his wife and children; they had received refugee status
due to their family's association with the US military.

The detention of Mr. Darweesh and Mr. Alshawi by US Customs and Border
Protection (CBP) officials at JFK was based solely on an executive order issued
by the president late that Friday afternoon—what would later come to be known
as the Trump administration's first Muslim Ban. The order created chaos across
the country and around the world—separating families, keeping students from
returning to school, and placing people like Mr. Darweesh and Mr. Alshawi in
danger not only of deportation but also of return to their deaths. That night,
students and faculty in the clinic we teach at Yale Law School worked alongside lawyers from the International Refugee Assistance Project, the National
Immigration Law Center, and the ACLU Immigrants' Rights Project to draft
and file an emergency lawsuit. Just after 5:30 A.M. the next day—approximately
seven hours after we received that Friday night call—we filed a nationwide class
action challenging the government's action. By 8 P.M. that evening, we had
obtained the first nationwide injunction against the Muslim Ban.

While the Muslim Ban presented uniquely exigent circumstances in a tumultuous political moment, immigration lawyers long have been familiar with crisis. Particularly for those defending clients against deportation, exigency is a recurring, if episodic, feature of practice. For people seeking asylum, refugee status, or other legal forms of protection against persecution, the stakes often literally are life or death. Likewise, for immigrants facing imminent "removal"—an anodyne legal phrase that frequently denotes permanent separation from one's children, spouse, community, or livelihood—the consequences often are devastating. This was true under the Barack Obama administration, as well as administrations of both political parties before it. But the election of Donald Trump—who has made the dehumanization of immigrants a centerpiece of his presidency—rendered immigration newly and relentlessly rife with crisis. Since Trump's inauguration, the administration has rolled out countless new enforcement policies and practices, forcibly separated parents from their children, terminated legal protections for millions of people, mounted a full-scale assault on refugees and asylum-seekers, and created *in terrorem* effects for immigrants and communities of color through persistent racialization and demonization of refugees and immigrants. As a result, the imperative for time-sensitive, high-stakes lawyering in the immigration space has never been greater.

While the full expression of Trump's attack on immigrants is manifest in scores of actions and policies, in this chapter we turn back the clock to the first days, weeks, and months of the administration and examine the lawyering in which we and our students engaged in two crises: the overnight challenge to the original Muslim Ban, and the first few days of the intensive representation of a woman who sought sanctuary from deportation in a New Haven, Connecticut, church—the first person to do so in our state. We highlight these two cases in order to demonstrate the different forms that crisis lawyering in the same practice area can take—from a class-action lawsuit challenging national policy, to the multipronged defense of a local resident—and the commonalities that exist across them. In so doing, we aspire to give further definition to what constitutes "crisis lawyering" and to reflect on lessons that may be useful not only for lawyers or clinical teachers but for other fields as well.

Many occupations demand the exercise of judgment, skill, and collaboration so as to address urgent problems under significant time pressure. For some lawyers, this is true on a regular basis. For many teachers—and certainly those teaching at a university level—these circumstances are probably less common. We are clinical professors of law, which means that we are both lawyers and teachers. We teach full-time at a law school, but in our classes we do not deliver lectures; instead, we lead seminars and supervise law students representing real clients with real legal problems in courts, before legislatures and agencies, and in other settings in which lawyers practice. Like medical students whose training includes treating real patients in a teaching hospital, our students earn grades and course credit by representing clients, without pay, under our supervision. For years, we have cotaught a clinical course at Yale Law School in which students represent indigent immigrants facing deportation, among other matters.

We undertook our work on the first Muslim Ban and the sanctuary case while teaching this course. Because law clinics such as ours are committed to the dual goals of client service and student learning, crisis lawyering in a clinical context poses unique challenges and special opportunities. Ordinary precepts of clinical legal education, which seek to foreground the work of students over that of experienced attorneys, are placed under considerable stress. At the same time, crisis lawyering can illuminate a broader set of pedagogical commitments and cultivate students' abilities to engage in alternative lawyering modalities. We believe this to be important both because of the prevalence of crisis in the current moment and because crises of one form or another are endemic to nearly every form of social justice lawyering. Teaching the next generation of lawyers how to lawyer in crisis is, therefore, an essential element of the long-term struggles in which we are now engaged.

Although our reflections on these lawyering experiences center on the clinical context, we believe that many of them will be fruitful for crisis lawyering in all practice settings. For example, we identify ways in which the structure of our practice enabled us to work nimbly and effectively in crisis—but also how it constrained us. Crisis lawyering, then, can help to illuminate the architecture of one's practice, account for its strengths, and suggest directions for future development. We also discuss how lawyering in crisis can shed light on dominant, regressive, and often invisible practices that characterized our non–crisis lawyering as well. We therefore argue that crisis lawyering can serve as a stress test for one's lawyering generally, an opportunity to measure one's practices against one's values, and to take appropriate steps toward achieving a greater congruence between them.

Law clinics can have a laboratory quality, melding experimental practice with observation and learning. They require a deep commitment to critical reflection so as to capture insights about successful practice for future application. And they require a deep humility to both see and articulate the ways in which our practice falls short. It is in this spirit of action and learning that we enter this conversation on crisis lawyering.

We do so even as our engagement in and learning from crisis lawyering continues in the COVID-19 era. Starting in March 2020, our clinic began to represent individuals in immigration detention in order to secure their release because of the mortal threat of COVID-19 in the congregate environment of jails and prisons. This has included litigating federal habeas corpus petitions for nearly a dozen individuals, as well as cocounseling class-action litigation on behalf of 150 persons held in immigration detention at the most notorious facility in New England in a suit that reduced the immigration population by two-thirds and became a model for similar suits around the country. In addition, our students helped a local union to establish and staff an unemployment insurance application and technical assistance hotline in Connecticut following the sudden layoff of thousands of its members. One of us has also worked with students to represent incarcerated veterans in habeas petitions seeking their release, develop FAQs on access to federal and state veterans' benefits during the COVID-19 crisis, and engage in emergency political advocacy for incarcerated veterans. As this crisis has unfolded, our learnings from the two cases discussed in this chapter deeply informed our current practice. Indeed, the current conditions, and the extraordinary hardship they have created for millions of people, have reinforced for us the imperative to prepare future generations of social justice lawyers for crisis as an essential component of their practice.

Crisis Lawyering in a Clinical Setting

Modern law clinics originated as a reform movement in legal education born out of the progressive student activism of the 1960s. As the civil rights movement sharpened demands for racial and economic justice, advocates for President Lyndon Johnson's War on Poverty succeeded in securing federal funding for legal services for the poor, based on an understanding that law reform, in addition to traditional legal aid, was a necessary component of the antipoverty agenda. In this environment, students agitated for law schools to make their curricula more responsive to the newly articulated needs of poor people, and a first generation of clinicians brought client service into the mainstream of legal education. What began as a small-scale effort by local practitioners evolved into the most significant transformation in legal education since the advent of the Langdellian case method in the late nineteenth century. Rather than utilize appellate cases as the principal basis for teaching law, clinical legal education elaborated a curriculum around the firsthand experience of students representing clients. This included the integration of legal doctrine, lawyering skills, professional responsibility, and critical analysis of legal systems and theories. From its earliest days, then, the pedagogical and social justice missions of clinical legal education were inextricable. Today, the American Bar Association, which accredits US law schools, mandates that law schools require each student to earn at least six credits in "experiential" classes before graduation. Clinics are thus a feature of nearly every law school in the United States, although they vary significantly in scale, structure, and ambition.

As clinical legal education matured, its adherents developed an increasingly robust set of pedagogical practices and an associated body of scholarship. As is often the case with innovations, a set of experimental practices hardened into orthodoxies. Two hallmark features animate most every clinical program. The first is a commitment to placing students in professional role as lawyers representing real-life clients and endowing them with the primary decision-making responsibility that comes from occupying such a role. To the maximum extent possible, students are positioned as lawyers out in front, rather than as interns merely assisting faculty. From this axiom of clinical legal education flow a number of other pedagogical commitments. For example, the dominant model privileges the lawyer-client relationship as a principal focus of the lawyering experience. It also favors "small" cases, typically involving a single client with a discrete legal need, which enable a student to participate in the full life cycle of a case—client interviewing and counseling, fact investigation, development of a case theory, negotiation, briefing, and trial before an adjudicator—in the course of a semester or academic year. Such an approach implicitly reflects a traditional vision of lawyering, one that is as court-focused as it is client-oriented, without meaningful engagement in other modes of persuasion, such as media advocacy, legislative and regulatory advocacy, and organizing. For many clinicians, this may reflect a combination of pedagogical preference, normative vision, and institutional imperative; the high demand for clinical opportunities and perceived expense of operating a clinic (as opposed to a conventional classroom) mean that students are often limited to one or two semesters in a clinic, often as a capstone experience in their last year of law school.

The second hallmark feature is to pair lawyering activity with persistent, structured practices of critical reflection. This is fundamental for teaching students to recognize complexity, contingency, and the reasons for their successes and failures so that they can not only appraise their work retrospectively but also derive insight for future application. Teaching students to "learn how to learn from experience" is central to many clinics. But critical reflection is, by necessity, a slow and often loosely directed process. It works best when the pace of lawyering allows students and faculty to step back from the moment-to-moment and day-to-day decision-making in order to evaluate context, consider alternatives, narrate histories, and engage with theory. It is as much an imaginative enterprise as an analytical one. For these reasons, many clinicians have concluded that the imperative for critical reflection counsels not only small cases but also slow cases.

Because law students are novices, and the clinical approach typically places primary responsibility for a real client in their hands, it follows that the model contemplates students making mistakes. The cliché of learning from our mistakes is baked in and activated by the central clinical practice of critical reflection. This is further reason for the clinical model to prefer smaller cases, lower-profile cases, and cases that operate outside of the glare of local or even national attention.

The clinic we coteach, the Worker & Immigrant Rights Advocacy Clinic (WIRAC), adheres to some of these traditional clinical practices but routinely departs from others. For example, our docket typically features a number of individual client representations, including in immigration court proceedings, which approximate the paradigmatic clinical experience of students taking a client's case from beginning to end, and engaging in a set of traditional lawyering activities, over the course of one or two semesters. More often than not, however, our individual client representation is not so readily cabined. Instead, in a case that begins in immigration court, we may initiate parallel habeas corpus proceedings, Freedom of Information Act litigation, or a damages action in federal court; engage federal or state actors in policy advocacy; collaborate with the community groups from whom we accept case referrals in mobilizing support for our client; or pursue media and communications strategies. Because current immigration laws are harsh and unjust, and because we often take difficult cases that other lawyers have turned down or on referral from community groups pressing for legal assistance, we and our students often conclude that we have no choice but to expand our strategies beyond immigration court. Such multifaceted lawyering helps to blur the line between individual representation and impact litigation, or between "big" cases and "small" cases; the lawyering methodology treats each case as big, and each case as potentially impactful. This approach invariably extends beyond a single academic year, requires new students to join existing matters rather than initiating representation themselves, and arguably decenters the lawyer-client relationship as the central site for student learning while introducing a different set of lawyering skills and approaches to the traditional clinical model.

In addition to this robust form of individual client representation, we engage in a small number of cases that more closely fit the model of impact litigation and therefore deviate even more significantly from the traditional clinical model. In recent years, this has included a multistate class action to challenge prolonged immigration detention, actions for money damages arising out of immigration raids and conditions of immigration detention, and the first lawsuit in the country to challenge the Trump administration's termination of the Deferred Action for Childhood Arrivals (DACA) program.

Three structural features of our program facilitate such a heterogeneous and unconventional clinical docket. First, our students are able to begin taking a clinic in the second semester of their first year of law school. Second, students may continue to take the same clinic for subsequent semesters, and some will elect to do so for a total of five semesters. And third, as clinicians, we have the institutional and financial support to undertake ambitious litigation and nonlitigation projects. As faculty in the clinic, we and our colleagues have elected to take advantage of these circumstances in order to advance a model of multifaceted lawyering that strives to be responsive to community priorities, even when those push us into accepting the hardest cases or entering unfamiliar practice areas. Taken together, these institutional features enable the clinic to engage in longitudinal lawyering and the students to engage in longitudinal learning. The comparatively longer tenure of students in the clinic deepens their own knowledge, skills, and strategic judgment and also helps to deepen the institutional competencies of the clinic as a whole.

It is against this backdrop that we turn to discuss crisis lawyering. We do so mindful that our program design, financial support, and elite institutional status make possible a scale and complexity of work that is not available in every law clinic. At the same time, everyone, everywhere operates within some form of institutional constraint. An emergency can disrupt clinical practices in even the most traditional of programs. A crisis can narrow or eliminate student preparation, compel an instructor to displace the underprepared student by performing the lawyering activity so as to protect the client's interest, and when the emergency is prolonged, delay the opportunity for reflection. But like all experiences, and despite its limitations, a crisis can be a teaching opportunity as well. And to the extent the student intends to become a lawyer whose practice includes crisis-response, a crisis can be a critically important learning moment. One challenge of crisis lawyering, then, is to determine how to both work within and push against institutional constraints when exigent circumstances require, so as to seize the potential for student learning amidst an emergency.

Stories from the Field

One theme of this chapter is that crisis lawyering is a feature, not a bug, of many law practices. Clinicians who aim to help law students develop legal competencies essential to a successful twenty-first-century law practice therefore may wish to prepare students for lawyering emergencies and the skills and strategies necessary to navigate them on behalf of clients. And because lawyering crises are endogenous to so much legal work, the skills and strategies specific to this practice setting warrant special scrutiny. Before turning to lessons learned from crisis lawyering with law students, we present two brief case histories, one involving emergency structural reform litigation, and the other an emergency individual client representation. Both involve immigration and civil rights matters, as well as lawyering inside and outside of the courtroom.

The Muslim Ban

In the first days of the Trump administration, there had been talk of the government imposing a Muslim Ban, but when it went into effect on January 27, 2017, it nonetheless caught the nation by surprise. Indeed, the policy was not announced before it was implemented. Instead, it became known only when family members, friends, and lawyers awaiting the arrival of immigrants from affected countries discovered that these individuals were being detained. As word spread of detentions at airports across the country, the scale and human cost of the policy came into view.

The phone call we received that evening, just after 10 P.M., came from Becca Heller, a former clinic student and the executive director of the International Refugee Assistance Project (IRAP), and Justin Cox, also a former clinic student then working at the National Immigration Law Center (NILC). They reported that one, and then two, of their Iraqi clients were being detained at JFK Airport on the basis of the Muslim Ban and were facing the prospect of return to Iraq. Both clients possessed valid visas granted based on the likelihood that, by virtue of their work and association with the US military, their lives were at risk if they stayed in Iraq. As we would later learn, hundreds of people faced similar circumstances that evening, and tens of thousands of others were likely to be barred from the country soon thereafter.

While the contours of "crisis lawyering" may be contested, it was clear to us on that Friday night that we were confronting a crisis. Prior to his election, Donald Trump had made his animus toward Muslims clear, promising a "total and complete shutdown" of Muslims entering the United States. This was one part of candidate Trump's project to make a broad and consistent assault on immigrants and refugees a centerpiece of his campaign, which also included his reference to Mexican immigrants as murderers and rapists, as well as his repeated equation of Syrian refugees with terrorists. Within the first days of his presidency, he issued three executive orders on immigration. The first promised a host of changes in interior enforcement, including an intention to hire additional Immigration and Customs Enforcement (ICE) officers and to cut funding to so-called sanctuary cities. The second concerned border security and expressed a commitment to expanded use of detention at the US-Mexico border and the building of the long-promised border wall. The third and final executive order was the Muslim Ban. But unlike the first two orders—which announced broad shifts in immigration policy that would take months or years to execute—the Muslim Ban was implemented the day it became public, with visibly harmful effects. Indeed, the Muslim Ban was the first policy of the new Trump administration to produce such observable material change. Families were split apart, refugees were threatened with return to their deaths, and chaos broke out at airports across the country. A new, radical, and devastating policy was unfolding in real time.

The breadth and severity of the new policy came into focus only as it was being enforced in airports across the country that Friday night. The executive order became public only after enforcement had begun. It suspended entry of immigrants from seven Muslim-majority countries—Iran, Iraq, Libya, Somalia, Sudan, Syria, and Yemen; indefinitely suspended entry of Syrian refugees as "detrimental to the interests of the United States"; imposed a 120-day moratorium on the refugee resettlement program as a whole; and reduced the annual cap on refugee admissions from 110,000 to 50,000. On its face, the order applied to lawful permanent residents (green card holders) as well as temporary visitors. In practice, immigration officials were also barring entry of dual citizens.

Returning to that Friday night phone call, we recognized the opportunity and imperative for action and also understood that this was the leading edge of a broad assault on immigrants.[1] At 10:46 P.M., one of us emailed the entire WIRAC class—a group of approximately thirty students[2]—with the subject line "EMERGENCY—IRAQI REFUGEE TRAPPED AT JFK, NEED TWO-PAGE HABEAS PETITION DRAFTED AND FILED IN EDNY."[3] (A habeas petition, or petition for the writ of habeas corpus, is a procedure with deep roots in Anglo-American law for challenging the legality of the detention of an individual in government custody.) We also spoke with colleagues from NILC and the ACLU, a number of whom were former colleagues and clinic students.[4] Within a matter of minutes, a half-dozen current students began responding. Shortly after 11 P.M., we convened a conference call between WIRAC, IRAP, NILC, and the ACLU, during which we discussed the facts that were known to us, possible legal claims, and overall strategy. We also agreed on a timeline, determined by the flight schedule from JFK: a quick internet search told us that flights to Europe, through which our JFK clients had traveled, would not resume until 6 A.M. We therefore set a target of 5 A.M. to file our complaint, giving us about five hours from the time we all hung up the phone.

In the course of our late-night conference call, and a second one held around 2 A.M., the ambition of our project expanded significantly: from the two-page habeas contemplated in the subject line of the first email message sent to our students, to a nationwide class action on behalf of all individuals who had been or would be denied entry to the United States on the basis of the executive order. In the latter call, lawyers, teachers, and students debated whether to seek relief for a narrow class of persons detained only at JFK; a broader class, such as those detained at airports within New York State or the relevant judicial district; or even a nationwide class of all persons at all airports in the country. On the one hand, class-action litigation would invite many additional legal problems for us, beyond the already difficult legal challenge to the executive order itself. In other words, if we filed a broad class action seeking relief for people stranded in airports around the country, there was a real danger that the government could raise ancillary procedural and technical objections to the proposed class action that might delay or derail relief for Mr. Darweesh and Mr. Alshawi personally. On the other hand, defendants in class-action litigation frequently grant relief to named plaintiffs in order to moot out a case, so it might be that the likelihood of relief for Mr. Darweesh and Mr. Alshawi *increased* if we filed a large class action under his name. Moreover, as a number of students emphasized, no other lawyers were in a position to seek relief for the hundreds or thousands of unknown Muslim refugees and other travelers flying in the night skies or already stranded at a US airport. If we did not request broad relief, thousands of people might be returned to persecution or death. Persuaded by the students, one of us expressed a willingness to sign his name to a complaint for a nationwide class, and the other lawyers came to agree.

Our work plan therefore consisted of researching and drafting both a complaint for classwide habeas corpus relief and a motion for class certification. Students worked on the habeas petition and the class certification brief, under the supervision of three supervising attorneys from WIRAC[5] and in collaboration with attorneys from IRAP, NILC, and IRP. Some attorneys, including the two of us, drafted portions of the documents directly. Email and text messages and phone calls continued throughout the night, as everyone worked from their respective homes across the country. Ultimately, we produced a twenty-page complaint alleging that the executive order violated multiple statutes and constitutional protections, plus a twelve-page motion for class certification. The documents were far from perfect. There were typos and formatting errors, and one of our names was left off the signature block. But at 5:32 A.M., we filed both documents—warts and all—electronically with the US District Court for the Eastern District of New York and emailed a service copy to the United States Attorney in Brooklyn. *Darweesh v. Trump* became the first lawsuit in the country to challenge the Muslim Ban.

As day broke on Saturday, January 28, the chaos wrought by the Muslim Ban came into view. Television, the internet, and social media showed distraught friends and family members at airports waiting for their detained loved ones. Volunteer lawyers working with IRAP or other organizations, or operating on their own, took up residence in airport terminals to offer legal advice. And throughout the day, local grassroots organizations and spontaneous social media posts encouraged thousands of people to descend at airports across the country to protest the Muslim Ban, producing now-iconic images of resistance to the ban and to the Trump administration more generally. At Yale Law School, more and more WIRAC students joined the effort, taking over the clinic work spaces in the basement of the building and setting up war rooms in two conference rooms.

Around noon, we got word that the government was releasing our first named plaintiff, Mr. Darweesh, but to our knowledge Mr. Alshawi remained detained. While we expected his release as well in a government stratagem to moot our case and were heartened that the lawsuit was already having success, we remained committed to our putative class. It soon dawned on us that the filing of our complaint, early on a Saturday morning, was only the first step to trying to stop the Muslim Ban. We needed to get in front of a judge. But because it was Saturday, the courthouse in Brooklyn was closed. Other attorneys on the team learned the identity of the emergency "duty judge" on call in Brooklyn that weekend (judges deal with crises also), and we sought to contact her chambers. We soon learned that the duty judge would not take up the case unless we filed a third document requesting emergency relief.

And so that morning students broke into teams. One team worked on a motion for injunctive relief—what we styled as an "Emergency Motion for Stay of Removal." A second team worked to develop a template habeas corpus petition that lawyers–including a number of clinic alumni who were now rushing to airports everywhere—could use in individual cases across the country. And a third student team began to respond to a flood of press inquiries, including speaking on a national press call with dozens of reporters, and to brief Muslim, Arab, and South Asian community groups and other allies about the lawsuit. Shortly after 4 P.M., we filed our motion for injunctive relief—the third complex document in a sixteen-hour period. Soon thereafter, we called the court and, somewhat to our surprise, someone picked up. We advised the court of our lawsuit and our motion, and the voice on the other end of the line said the court had seen both. We then said we wanted a hearing before a judge, and the clerk asked when. We asked that it be held at 7 P.M., and the court agreed.

With less than three hours before the hearing, we scrambled to figure out how to cover it. One of us was in New Haven and was not admitted to practice before the court in which we filed, while the other, although properly admitted in the court, was in Boston and unable to reach the Brooklyn courthouse in time. Our students would not be able to appear absent a motion for student appearance; even assuming we had filed such a motion, we would not have had adequate time to prepare any student practitioner, particularly given the high-stakes nature of the case. We ultimately asked Lee Gelernt, a talented and experienced attorney from the ACLU who was based in New York and with whom both of us had worked for many years, to handle the hearing. In the meantime, we coordinated with the US Marshal's Office to ensure that the hearing would be open to the public, notwithstanding the weekend timetable, and with organizers on the ground at JFK Airport redirecting protestors to the federal courthouse in Brooklyn. "The courtroom is open to the public," we were told. And so, we worked to ensure that the public was there.

By seven o'clock that evening, a massive crowd converged on Cadman Plaza. When the duty judge for that weekend, Ann Donnelly, took the bench for a remarkable Saturday night hearing, the courtroom was full to capacity, and the hundreds who were not able to enter remained outside the building protesting. For those of us not present, we sat by our phones waiting anxiously for updates. The hearing itself was brief. The judge immediately homed in on the risk of irreparable harm if members of our class were removed, as we had argued in our papers, an argument that the government struggled to refute. Gelernt represented to the court a report he had received that the government was threatening to return a detained individual to Syria that evening. The judge then addressed the government attorneys: "Apparently, there is somebody who they're putting on a plane—what do you think about that—back to Syria? Irreparable harm?" Less than twenty minutes into the hearing, Judge Donnelly announced her decision from the bench—"The stay is granted"—and signed the proposed order that our students had drafted, finding a likelihood of success that the motion to certify a nationwide class would be granted and that plaintiffs would prevail on the merits. Back in New Haven, in Boston, and around the country, we received text messages from our cocounsel in the courtroom that the government was barred from removing anyone from the country on the basis of the executive order.

The moment we received this news was one of indescribable elation. Less than twenty-four hours earlier, we had embarked on what felt like an impossible task and did so knowing that the legal arguments were difficult, time was against us, and the chances of success—at least in our estimation—were low. And then, with startling alacrity, a federal court had enjoined the first major action undertaken by the Trump administration and had done so on the basis of our students' work. Over the course of our careers, each of us had been accustomed to uphill battles in which success came, if it came at all, after years, not hours, of struggle. The scale and aberrational nature of this victory was arresting.

Even as the homepage of the *New York Times* announced the court victory, our euphoria quickly dissolved under the weight of circumstances on the ground. Just as the mere filing of the lawsuit was not enough to secure judicial action, the issuance of a judicial order was not enough to ensure compliance. At our war room at the law school, students were fielding calls from attorneys across the country whose clients were still facing removal on the basis of the executive order. The US Attorney's Office in Brooklyn assured us that the order was being implemented, but lawyers in airports reported otherwise; their clients were still being told that they would be removed imminently. Omar Jadwat, an ACLU lawyer in Judge Donnelly's courtroom and the former clinic student of one of us, took pictures of the court order on his phone and emailed them out to advocates, leading lawyers to hold up their own phones to Customs and Border Protection officers in order to convince them that a federal court had barred the removal of the lawyers' clients. Not confident that the government would timely communicate the order to its own officials, one of us emailed a photograph of the order to the director of CBP, with this subject line: "URGENT: NATIONWIDE INJUNCTION HALTING REMOVALS PURSUANT TO EXECUTIVE ORDER."[6]

Sometime after 11 P.M., hours after Judge Donnelly had issued her order, we received word that the government had forced an Iranian Fulbright scholar onto a plane at JFK with the intention of returning her to Iran. From onboard the plane, she was in touch by phone with a cousin, who was with a lawyer inside the airport. One of us had an open line with the cousin and lawyer while speaking with the US Attorney's Office on another phone. As the plane pulled away from the gate, the government lawyer insisted that the individual was not being removed. The situation became increasingly desperate as the individual reported that the plane was taxiing down the runway. Inside our war room, students worked the phones. One tried to reach CBP at JFK, to no avail. Another contacted the carrier in Europe in an attempt to stop the plane. "Call air traffic control!" one of us finally suggested, prompting a first-year student, who had been in the clinic for all of two weeks, to instead track down a phone number for the Port Authority of New York and New Jersey police. He reached a live person, talked his way up to a supervisor, and then insisted that a federal court order prohibited the plane from taking off. The supervisor said he would call the control tower and told the student to hold.

We all waited, hearts pounding. Moments later, the student announced, "The plane is going back to the gate!" A couple of minutes later, the individual on the plane reported to her cousin that the plane was indeed turning around. A cheer went up in the room as we all marveled that a first-year law student had turned around an airplane taxiing toward takeoff.

That same day, and in subsequent days, dozens of new lawsuits challenging the Muslim Ban were filed, many of them individual habeas suits that used the templates that our students had developed. On the Monday following Judge Donnelly's order, the *Darweesh* case was transferred to another judge in Brooklyn, pursuant to the court's random-assignment system. The new judge had a different view of the case and, in an initial status conference, expressed significant doubt about the strength of our legal claims. But by then, other federal judges across the country had issued their own injunctions, and litigation on the merits of the executive order began in earnest. Our clinic's work continued at a rapid pace for an additional couple of weeks, including further court appearances, negotiations with the government, and media advocacy. Students were able to participate in some of these activities, such as media advocacy and judicial settlement talks, but not others. Notably, the court denied our motion for student appearances, and delayed ruling on a motion to reconsider, which ensured that we as supervisors and our cocounsel were the only ones with speaking roles in court.

Within a matter of weeks, our case was overtaken by other cases, and as more and more lawyers flooded in and new developments arose, we chose to recede into the background. Over the next few months, the original executive order would be replaced by a second, narrower executive order, which itself superseded by a still narrower presidential proclamation. Challenges to that proclamation—the third Muslim Ban—were eventually heard and rejected by the United States Supreme Court. We did not reach a final settlement of our case until early September 2017, but the bulk of our work was done in just the first few, intense hours and days.

Nury Chavarria

In the months after President Trump's inauguration, US Immigration and Customs Enforcement made numerous dramatic changes to its enforcement practices, with catastrophic results for millions of people around the country. Executive actions such as imposition of the first Muslim Ban had immediate, dramatic consequences, but other changes were less visible. For instance, in the years before 2017, many local ICE offices had entered "orders of supervision" for thousands of immigrants. Similar to an order of probation or parole in the criminal justice system, these arrangements allowed a person ordered removed to live and work at liberty in the community, provided the person checked in regularly with ICE and did not commit any criminal offenses. Under the new Trump administration, however, when people arrived for their regular ICE check-ins, officers began revoking these orders of supervision and directing people to leave the country promptly, at their own expense, or else face arrest and forcible deportation. In addition, when people ordered to depart began filing emergency motions to reopen their old deportation cases—often with a new attorney or based on changed country conditions—ICE no longer agreed to temporary stays to allow the immigration courts to adjudicate these motions.

In other words, rather than undertake time-intensive investigations to arrest and deport persons with serious criminal records or who posed a national security threat and who were in hiding, ICE agents could sit at their desks, wait for the least dangerous, lowest priority people to arrive for a check-in, arrest them, revoke their order of supervision, and then deny a temporary stay even when the person pursued a meritorious emergency motion in court. In response, immigrants and advocates around the country began testing resistance strategies. One approach was reflected in the decision by some people to seek sanctuary in a local religious institution, in the hope that ICE would not undertake an enforcement action at these houses of worship.

On July 20, 2017, six months to the day after Trump's inauguration, a woman named Nury Chavarria became the first person to seek sanctuary in Connecticut. A native of Guatemala, Ms. Chavarria had entered the United States unlawfully when she was nineteen, applied for political asylum, and been denied. She remained in the country, however, and by summer 2017 had lived in the United States for nearly twenty-five years, now the mother of four US citizen children, ages nine to twenty-one, the oldest of whom has cerebral palsy. With the assistance of her attorney, Glenn Formica, for many years Ms. Chavarria had lived and worked openly while checking in regularly with ICE as requested. At a summer 2017 check-in, however, ICE ordered her to return to Guatemala by July 20. She planned to comply, but at around noon that Thursday, she and community supporters instead met in New Haven with religious leaders from whom she requested sanctuary. Pastor Hector Luis Otero agreed, and she took up emergency residence in the church he leads, Iglesia de Dios. She was the thirteenth person in the United States to have sought sanctuary since the Trump administration had taken office. Over the course of the day, members of the church held a prayer vigil, and community supporters led by Kica Matos, Ana María Rivera Forastieri, Alok Bhatt, and members of the Connecticut Immigrant Rights Alliance and Unidad Latina en Acción assisted Ms. Chavarria in managing intense media interest, visits from elected officials, and a rally of supporters in front of the church. That evening, one of us forwarded an article in the *New Haven Register* on the developments to the clinic listserv, which includes all term-time and summer students and supervisors.

At first, Ms. Chavarria's attorney was outraged at her choice to seek sanctuary. "I stormed into the church, profane and boorish, worrying how I'd ever get my client out of there past what I thought were crazy radicals," Formica later told the *New York Times*. But that afternoon and evening, as Formica listened to his client and her allies, "I did a 180 on sanctuary right there." The next morning, a Friday, Formica called and emailed one of us. His email message was empty; the subject line read simply "It's Glenn Formica I need you."[7]

As a general rule, law school clinics do not take on new matters in late July, when regular students are away and summer coverage arrangements, often tenuous, are typically strained. In our clinic and many others at Yale Law School, we rely on a handful of summer interns to work full-time covering client matters that perhaps thirty students might handle on a part-time basis during the school year. In the summer of 2017, five students worked full-time in WIRAC, and they were fully engaged managing the existing docket in late July. Nevertheless, soon after speaking with Formica that Friday morning, one of us wrote the clinic listserv with a synopsis of the case, possible next steps, and a request for volunteers. Several summer students responded immediately, as did one term-time student, and before long all five summer students, one term-time student, and a summer student from another clinic were all working on the case.

That afternoon, one of us, together with the WIRAC clinical fellow Ruben Loyo and several summer students, went to the Iglesia de Dios to meet with Ms. Chavarria and conduct an initial interview. Her father, who had come to the United States even earlier than Ms. Chavarria, soon arrived, and we divided into two teams to speak separately with Ms. Chavarria and her father. By the evening, we decided to undertake the representation, which came to involve one of us, Mr. Loyo, and professor Marisol Orihuela, another codirector of the clinic, jointly supervising the six summer students and one term-time student.

Over the next several days, the students and supervisors worked day and night to undertake a substantial fact investigation, including interviews with Ms. Chavarria and some of her family members as well as detailed research into country conditions and efforts to obtain records from Guatemala and files from her first immigration attorney, back in the 1990s. The team also arranged for visits to the church by potential expert witnesses, and one supervisor coordinated efforts of a range of local officials to provide further support for the emergency motions to be filed on Ms. Chavarria's behalf. Supervisors and students consulted with attorneys around the country who had handled cases involving Guatemalan asylum-seekers; lawyers at the Asylum Seeker Advocacy Project (ASAP) at the Urban Justice Center, a new organization founded by four WIRAC alumnae, provided especially critical assistance. This emergency fact investigation yielded two new theories of relief that Ms. Chavarria had not previously pursued.[8]

In addition, over the weekend one of us asked senior legislative staff, and eventually Senator Richard Blumenthal (D-CT) personally, to introduce a private bill for the benefit of Ms. Chavarria. For many years, immigration officials had a practice of granting a temporary stay of deportation upon the filing of a private bill, so as to afford Congress time to consider the legislation. In May 2017, however, the Trump administration had suspended this long-standing courtesy to members of Congress. Senator Blumenthal, moreover, had not previously sponsored many such bills. He nevertheless agreed to do so for Ms. Chavarria and, on an emergency basis, filed the proposed bill on the following Tuesday, July 25. Because ICE would no longer grant a temporary stay, Ms. Chavarria turned to the Immigration Court, and the pendency of the private bill became a third ground on which Ms. Chavarria sought an emergency stay.

Together, the students and supervisors researched and drafted a motion to reopen Ms. Chavarria's case and an emergency motion to stay her removal, with supporting briefs, declarations, and exhibits; proofread, cite-checked, authenticated, and assembled all the materials; and filed both motions at the Immigration Court in Hartford on Wednesday morning, July 26, fewer than five days after accepting the representation on Friday evening. Given the risk that ICE might arrive at any time to arrest and deport Ms. Chavarria, the three supervisors joined personally in the research and drafting, engagement with experts, communications with the client, and fact development. The supervisors were also substantially more directive than usual in their edits and comments on student work, at times drafting or redrafting entire sections of a brief or a declaration. In all, the motions advanced multiple new arguments for relief, each developed essentially from scratch over the weekend, and some of which contained multiple alternate theories. The filings themselves were also substantial, including two briefs that together exceeded sixty pages, four declarations, and an additional twenty-six exhibits.

Within hours, the immigration judge granted the emergency stay motion. That evening, Ms. Chavarria emerged from the church and announced to a scrum of media that, protected by the court's stay, she was going home to her children. Joyful community allies, religious leaders, and elected officials celebrated the swift action that had, for the time being, turned back ICE and preserved a family. A clinical supervisor rather than a student spoke at the press conference. ICE has not sought to re-detain Ms. Chavarria since July 2017, and as a result she has returned to working and raising her children during the pendency of her case, which has slowed to a more routine pace.

The four and a half days from when the clinic accepted Ms. Chavarria's case to the filing of emergency motions, and the twenty-two hours from Friday night to Saturday night when the clinic helped secure a temporary restraining order in *Darweesh*, represent dramatic, high-profile examples of crisis lawyering in a clinical setting. Crisis lawyering is not uncommon in certain law practices, and neither, therefore, is crisis lawyering in a clinical setting. In our small clinic alone, for instance, one or both of us has supervised students providing emergency representation to thirty persons arrested by ICE in a summer raid in New Haven; multiple individuals in last-minute applications to the Board of Immigration Appeals or the US Court of Appeals for the Second Circuit, including for clients who have been within hours of physical removal; and traumatized children forcibly separated from their parents at the southern border and detained in Connecticut. We turn now to exploring some lessons learned from our experience of crisis lawyering in a clinical setting, which we believe have application to both extraordinary and common crises.

Reflections on Crisis Lawyering in a Clinical Setting

Lessons for Clinical Pedagogy

Among the core principles of contemporary clinical pedagogy is a commitment to teaching students to "plan, do, reflect" in everything they undertake. Underlying this commitment is the belief that, above all, clinical faculty must instruct students how to learn from experience, so that they may constantly refine and develop their lawyering competencies over a lifetime of practice. To emphasize the point, clinicians may caution students against the counterexample of the lawyer who questions a witness or counsels a client the same way in her last year of practice as she did in her first, never having reflected on her own methods to improve them. Of course, lawyering also involves a significant amount of spontaneity and improvisation, which no amount of planning can avoid. Nevertheless, it is fair to ask: Does crisis lawyering preclude teaching students how to learn from experience?

We conclude that it does not. As with all pedagogical choices, engaging in crisis lawyering involves tradeoffs. To be sure, crisis lawyering necessarily compresses the planning and doing of lawyering tasks and, depending how long the crisis continues, may delay the opportunity for the structured reflection that is critical to learning. Still, our experience persuades us that crisis lawyering affords learning and service opportunities not otherwise available and is compatible with clinical teaching goals.

To begin, we emphasize a point made earlier: representation of clients necessarily involves coping with unanticipated emergencies, some of which require a form of crisis intervention by the lawyer. In other words, lawyering *is* crisis lawyering. That is true in individual representation of clients facing eviction, contesting a divorce, resisting deportation, defending against criminal or juvenile offense charges, and countless other settings. It is also true in the representation of grassroots organizations in legislative or regulatory advocacy, communications, and even strategic planning. For generations, clinical instructors have not declined representation in these sorts of matters merely because there are sometimes client emergencies. To the contrary, this is the heart of clinical practice. At the same time, we recognize that some forms of representation, such as the *Darweesh* and *Chavarria* litigation, constitute extreme versions of emergency. We have taken a few lessons from our experience supervising students in crisis lawyering, in both its more generic and more exotic forms.

First, in the planning phase, supervisors will at times have no choice but to be more directive than usual (we say "than usual" in recognition that supervisors already locate themselves along a spectrum of directedness). With less time for open-ended discussion, exchange of written drafts, exploratory research by students, and the like, a supervisor likely will have to terminate discussion, request a decision, or even propose a decision directly. In written documents, a supervisor likely will have to be more directive in comments, foregoing the usual practice of inviting further research or reflection by a student. And in preparing a student for a performative moment during a crisis, whether in court, before the media, or otherwise, a supervisor may also need to be more directive than usual, specifically discouraging certain approaches or suggesting particular language and strategies. In our practice, one example of this included the comparatively directive instructions provided to the student who handled the nationwide press call midday Saturday in *Darweesh*, hours after we had filed suit and less than 24 hours since we had accepted the representation. Similarly, at times, the supervisor may have to step in and draft documents or portions of documents directly, as we did in both *Darweesh* and *Chavarria*. Direct drafting by supervisors is not our usual clinical practice, of course, but at times of crisis it can be necessary to protect the client's interest.

Departing from our usual level of directedness is not a step we take lightly, and we are conscious of the educational opportunities that are lost. We think these are balanced to some extent, however, by the modeling that we provide instead (modeling that we do not usually offer our students). For instance, the shift in our own supervision style in times of crisis demonstrates a flexibility and adaptability in our teaching practices, as well as a willingness to subordinate our own preferences to the client's interest. Students observe us exit our own teaching comfort zones, at least for the duration of the crisis. In crisis moments in which more than one supervisor is involved—which is the norm, in our experience—students will also observe clinicians debating more directly with each other than usual and even challenging or criticizing each other's approaches. Like watching one's parents argue, this can be both thrilling and alarming. Because even cosupervisors tend to coordinate their feedback in the planning phase, the direct observation of clinical supervisors debating urgent, time-sensitive questions in real time can be illuminating for students. To be clear: We do not contend that the benefits of temporarily abandoning a nondirective approach to the planning process outweigh the costs, only that there are some benefits; the calculation involves not merely the loss of student agency.

Second, in the execution phase of clinical work during a crisis, instructors likewise may have no choice but to conduct the representation themselves. In *Darweesh*, the initial court appearances were handled by attorneys, not students, contrary to our strong practice; this was because of the limited amount of time to prepare, as well as the initial reluctance of the court to permit law-student appearances, not because of the high stakes in the case.[9] In the *Chavarria* matter, a supervisor rather than a student spoke at the snap press conference held upon our client's securing an emergency stay and leaving sanctuary to return to her family. Over the course of our careers and hundreds of different matters, on a handful of occasions circumstances of crisis have required each of us to step in to execute a lawyering task that we would, in ordinary conditions, require a student to perform.

As when supervisors take a more directive approach in the planning phase, a supervisor who steps in to execute the lawyering task in the "doing" phase deprives a student of the opportunity to perform the legal task (and then reflect later on that performance). At the same time, there are some modest benefits that can result. For one thing, students seem to relish the experience of observing a supervisor perform, not least because it thrusts the student into the role of providing constructive feedback to the professor. For another, the supervisor is reminded, often powerfully, of just how difficult it is to undertake the lawyering activities in which we coach our students but that many clinicians have not themselves done in some years. The butterflies, anticipation, sleeplessness, and concern are a humbling and physical reminder of sensations the students experience every day in our clinic but that we ourselves may not have suffered for decades.

Finally, that supervisors are available to step in on occasion in crisis lawyering situations, and then step back when the crisis subsides, allows us to undertake a wider range of matters than would be possible if we insisted on representing only clients in cases where the risk of a crisis was minimized. In *Darweesh*, students expanded their role after the initial crisis passed, drafting motions and settlement plans, participating in court conferences, and dealing directly with government attorneys and the media. In *Chavarria*, after the initial stay was secured, students undertook the substantive briefing on the case and all related motions, conducted court hearings, and otherwise litigated the matter as any other in a clinical setting. Had supervisors been unwilling to participate directly in the litigation for the brief, initial period of crisis, however, we would have declined the representation entirely.

As the *Darweesh* and *Chavarria* cases demonstrate, fast-moving, high-profile matters can have important service and pedagogical advantages. When IRAP and NILC reached out to us regarding the Muslim Ban, we recognized the opportunity not only to address an urgent matter of public importance but also for our students to do so as well. If the early days of the Trump administration left many feeling helpless, the litigation provided an important occasion for students to both witness and participate in the enactment of the lawyer's role in moments of national crisis. While we are wary of valorizing the legal profession, our participation in the Muslim Ban litigation highlighted the unique societal role that lawyers can at times play. Likewise, our involvement in the *Chavarria* case illustrated the special force that legal intervention can have to support an existing community mobilization and to resolve crises.

But our students' learning was not limited to an abstract reflection on a professional role. Rather, they experienced firsthand the immersive and messy processes of high-stakes lawyering against the clock and amid community and national struggles. The exigent circumstances forced the students to accelerate their research and writing, as well as to engage in greater risk-taking and risk tolerance than a more deliberately paced case might require. It may be that the courage and improvisational actions of our clients in confronting overwhelming state power also inspired a resourcefulness in their legal teams. Certainly, the legal theories crafted in each case were novel, untested, and arguably underdeveloped. But the time imperatives of each case demanded action, even if the action was imperfect. The students thus learned another mode of lawyering and an associated set of skills beyond those that the prototypical clinical representation might afford. In this way, then, crisis lawyering can help to expand the set of competencies we understand lawyering to require and support a vision of multiple modalities of lawyering rather than a single, dogmatic view of lawyering skills.

In our experience, the final stage of clinical pedagogy—reflection—is the least threatened by crisis lawyering. If a crisis were to persist for days or weeks, it might delay the opportunity for meaningful reflection beyond the point of usefulness. That has not been our experience, however. The initial crisis in *Darweesh* subsided after the initial twenty-four to forty-eight hours, once the federal district court entered a nationwide order temporarily enjoining the original Muslim Ban and liberating thousands of travelers trapped in airports around the country. The litigation continued and was overtaken by other cases filed by other lawyers in other jurisdictions, but the initial all-nighter pace diminished almost immediately, allowing time for collective and structured reflection by students and supervisors within days, then continuing for weeks and even months. We made a number of internal mistakes in the first rush of activity, and as discussed below, students and supervisors spent months analyzing those choices, especially some of the ways in which gender bias influenced collaboration within the large team of students and among supervisors. In *Chavarria*, there similarly was no shortage of opportunities to reflect on our actions in the days and weeks after our client was freed from sanctuary. Ensuring time for structured reflection is the heart of clinical supervision, and in our experience, crisis lawyering may slightly delay, but need not displace, that critical activity.

Relationships Between Longitudinal, Non–Crisis Lawyering and Latitudinal, Crisis Lawyering

In time-exigent circumstances, one necessarily draws upon repositories of knowledge and habits of practice built up through prior, often nonexigent experience. Such was the case in *Darweesh* and *Chavarria*. With respect to *Darweesh*, for example, we and our students had represented detained immigrants in habeas proceedings, including habeas class actions, for a number of years. Because of our atypical curricular model, which permits students to be enrolled in a clinic throughout most of their law school career, some of the students who jumped suddenly into the Muslim Ban work had already worked on habeas matters and researched and drafted motions for class certification and injunctive relief. With respect to *Chavarria*, we had many years of experience representing individual immigrants who appeared to be out of legal options, and we had developed an expertise in using a seemingly mundane procedural device—a motion to reopen—to prevent the destructive impact of deportation. Likewise, we had preexisting, deep relationships with community leaders, elected officials, and the media, whom we could quickly recruit and engage in support of the legal campaign for Ms. Chavarria. Thus, we possessed relevant institutional knowledge, expertise, and relationships. And because they were held not only by the faculty but also by some (but, importantly, not all) of our students, we were able to access them readily. Just as we had template documents to draw from, we had mental schema, legal heuristics, and social networks on which we could rely.

To put this another way: our longitudinal, non-crisis lawyering enabled us to engage in latitudinal, crisis lawyering. Our longstanding practices and pedagogy equipped us with the substantive knowledge, core lawyering skills, and a spirit of creative, aggressive, and tenacious lawyering to address the unique challenges of the Muslim Ban and the imminent deportation of Ms. Chavarria within the time constraints of each case. Although we had not in any conscious way anticipated these crises, we were in fact prepared for them.

Importantly, such preparedness was as much a function of the clinic culture we have cultivated over the past many years as the doctrinal and practice expertise we had developed. The clinic has a reputation for demanding work. Whether in individual cases, group representations, or "impact" cases, generations of clinic students and faculty have established a record of intensive and ambitious lawyering, of taking on matters that many other law practices or law clinics typically would not, and of frequently achieving unlikely successes. As instructors, we have attempted to foster a deep commitment to collaboration—and indeed to fun—as essential elements of our work. At its best, the clinic has enjoyed a can-do spirit built upon individual dedication, deep camaraderie, an appetite for risk-taking, and a shared vision of justice. These sensibilities—what we collectively understand as the culture of the clinic—were essential resources for our work in *Darweesh* and *Chavarria*. Indeed, they were prerequisites; they could not be established in the first instance when these crises emerged.

We have also made conscious efforts to integrate current students into larger networks of lawyers and advocates, locally in New Haven and around Connecticut, as well as nationally. And we have treasured the frequent opportunities to collaborate with former students, including clinic alumni at IRAP, NILC, and the ACLU in *Darweesh* and at ASAP in *Chavarria*. Our investment in networks of colleagues and allies is not merely transactional, of course, but nourishes our own professional relationships and work while introducing newer students to longtime coconspirators. Neither is the investment in networks limited to clinic alumni; many of our most frequent collaborators have no particular relationship to Yale Law School. We have found a special joy in these connections and in the mutual support we provide to and receive from colleagues far from New Haven. In times of crisis, there is an asymmetry in the ability of clinical supervisors and students to draw support from these networks—supervisors are more senior and inevitably have developed more relationships, whereas students are transient and new to legal practice. But we have found that students, once invited into a supervisor's existing relationships, are consistently effective in mobilizing networks and allies in support of a client in crisis.

Just as this past-as-prologue account demonstrates the ways in which our clinic was well-situated to step into the specific crises, it predicts the inevitability of blind spots. In *Darweesh*, by virtue of our past experience, it was readily apparent that a writ of habeas corpus was the appropriate procedural mechanism for representing currently detained individuals and that a class action was the right method for the representation of a group of individuals with shared characteristics but whose exact numbers and identities were unknown to us. Similarly, our and our cocounsel's expertise with asylum and refugee law led us to focus our legal claims on the rights of refugees and asylum-seekers. However, our lack of significant prior experience with religious discrimination cases led us to give only cursory treatment to that critical dimension of the Muslim Ban. Although we included in the complaint a claim that the executive order violated the US Constitution because it was substantially motivated by animus toward Muslims and had a disparate impact on them, this was one of the last legal claims made in the complaint. Lacking expertise in religious discrimination claims, or the time to consult with experts in that field, we defaulted to claims within our wheelhouse, somewhat mechanically extending the framework of national-origin discrimination to religion. We did not include more robust claims, such as under the Establishment Clause or the Religious Freedom Restoration Act. These would become the central claims of subsequent challenges to the Muslim Ban, its second and third iterations, and the litigation before the Supreme Court.

Arguably, our doctrinal blind spots reflected a broader misapprehension of what was unfolding on that Friday evening. That legal claims regarding refugees and asylum-seekers predominated, in both number and order of presentation, over the single claim related to religious discrimination suggests a narrative understanding of the case as being, at base, a Refugee Ban rather than a Muslim Ban. Indeed, we did not recite candidate Trump's repeated statements about wanting to impose a Muslim Ban and did not focus on the elements of the executive order that indicated a targeting of Muslims

CALL AIR TRAFFIC CONTROL! | 335

(e.g., the selection of only Muslim-majority countries, multiple references to honor killings), and religious discrimination is not mentioned at all in the introductory paragraphs of the complaint. Even in the first days of the litigation, we were inconsistent in describing the executive order. Our first press release referred to "Trump's Order Banning Refugees," though we and our cocounsel later embraced the Muslim Ban language and narrative. Looking back, it seems curious that we failed to center religious discrimination at the outset, not least because one of us is Muslim. But collectively, our predominant framework was one of immigrant and refugee rights, and our passing treatment of religion mirrored the relationship of anti-Muslim discrimination to immigrant rights advocacy more generally.

Although each of us had represented Muslims in the aftermath of September 11, we had rarely represented Muslim individuals or communities in WIRAC. Our reflections on the *Darweesh* litigation helped us to see this as an important gap in our work and led us to affirmatively seek out Muslim clients. Thus, one outcome of our crisis lawyering on behalf of Muslim clients in *Darweesh* has been for us to incorporate non-crisis representation of Muslim individuals and organizations into our longitudinal model.

Lessons for Case Selection

Clinical instructors have long debated, without resolution, whether it is better to teach students to lawyer on "small" cases—typically involving some form of summary process without discovery (such as eviction defense or political asylum cases) and a one-semester time horizon (such as misdemeanor charges)—or "big" cases that may last longer than one semester and involve greater legal, factual, or procedural complexity (such as federal employment discrimination or prisoner's rights cases). Collectively, we have supervised students in clinical programs for more than thirty years, and we have generally resisted the "big versus small case" argument because we perceive pedagogical value in all manner of cases.

In fact, in our clinics, we require students to handle both what some would consider small cases, such as an individual removal defense proceeding or veteran's disability benefits application, and large cases, such as complex civil rights and class-action suits. We do not build our docket around strategic litigation, but we do not hesitate to undertake bold or creative matters either; our primary goal on intake is to surrender the decision about how best to allocate our scarce representational resources to the communities we serve, organized through their own grassroots groups, labor unions, and faith organizations. Because these groups sometimes prioritize representation of individual members (such as in wage-and-hour litigation or removal defense) around whom the groups are organizing, and at other times ask that our clinics represent the organization itself (often in legislative or regulatory advocacy or in strategic planning), we end up with a mix of matters. Our secondary goal on intake is to accommodate diverse and varying student preferences for certain kinds of matters or to engage with particular organizations, communities, and issues. We hold a tertiary goal of representing underserved communities and addressing unexpressed legal needs—for example, by aspiring to racial, ethnic, and gender diversity in our client population and by serving constituencies such as detained clients for whom grassroots organization is difficult if not impossible. The result is consistently an inconsistent array of cases of all sizes and shapes, but frequently they are ones that call on the students to engage in risk-taking and multipronged advocacy in collaboration with community mobilizations.

From the perspective of crisis lawyering, we observe that emergencies are more common in so-called small cases involving individual client representation. Many of our clients lead precarious lives: they are struggling with poverty, constrained by undocumented status, stigmatized by criminal history and mental health or other disabilities, suffering personal trauma, or confronting daily the burdens of racial and other prejudices. These circumstances regularly result in sudden challenges in our clients' lives—from unexpected homelessness to an encounter with law enforcement that risks deportation— which in turn require emergency legal interventions. These lawyering crises also arise in complex litigation, but in our practice they have been infrequent.

A desire to minimize crisis lawyering might then lead a clinical supervisor, counterintuitively, to *prefer* complex, multi-year litigation over the exigencies, and regular emergencies, of a housing, immigration, or family law practice. Yet these practice areas are far more dominant in clinical education than are cases such as *Darweesh* or *Chavarria*. If anything, we suspect that our occasional involvement in large-scale, high-stakes, high-profile cases renders our practice less likely to involve crisis lawyering than, say, a busy housing or family law practice.

Crisis Lawyering as Stress Test

Our experience suggests that crisis lawyering may function as a sort of stress test of equitable collaboration practices. In times of felt pressure, individuals working in groups may default to baseline, often regressive, practices. These can be corrosive, but the stress test of crisis lawyering may also reveal uncomfortable aspects of one's lawyering practice that are otherwise masked. Such exposure may, in turn, give rise to opportunity for critical reflection and reform.

Our experience in *Darweesh* is particularly instructive. Although our work there with our partners and clients was wildly successful by many measures, our individual and collective practices were not without their problems. It was hard to ignore, for example, that it was a senior, white male, non-Muslim ACLU lawyer who stood up in court to speak. We were the ones who asked him to present argument, and we recognized that he was the most experienced attorney among cocounsel and a superb courtroom lawyer. We were also grateful for his willingness to shoulder the stress and challenge of representing the *Darweesh* plaintiffs at an extraordinary Saturday night hearing with no meaningful time to prepare. The resulting media coverage naturally highlighted his role, however, while obscuring that a diverse group of young students—women and men working overnight in our basement clinic space—had done much of the heavy lifting to file the lawsuit about discrimination against Muslims and refugees. Moreover, we found that in those first days of the case—when students and faculty alike were working until all hours creating work product on incredibly tight timelines in a case being closely watched at the national level—work distribution within the clinic began to assume gendered and racialized patterns. Who did the administrative work and who did the complex legal research? Who managed amicus briefs and who took the lead in drafting the merits briefing? We neither had nor made time in the moment to raise or confront these questions.

Patterns of social exclusion tend to replicate themselves, even in progressive spaces. Indeed, we should not be surprised when that happens. We are mindful that similar dynamics played out in our clinical program a generation prior, when students (including one of us) and faculty litigated on behalf of Haitian refugees interned at Guantánamo Bay. If, as we believe, exclusion is the result of structural forces, then we should not expect that individual goodwill, or the mere passage of time, will be sufficient to overcome those forces. Rather, it takes consistent and intentional practices, a willingness to engage in self-critique, and a commitment to trying new approaches. And in the absence of intentional practice, we should expect socially regressive practices to manifest.

But if crisis lawyering helps to reveal these practices, we should be honest in recognizing that even in times of non–crisis lawyering, our conversations about race, gender, and privilege tend to be impoverished, we tend to avoid them because they are difficult, and, as a result, the barriers to entry of such conversations remain high. Crisis lawyering in *Darweesh* illuminated and exacerbated these dynamics, but it did not create them. In the aftermath of our work on the case, our students initiated a deep—and at times painful—set of conversations around gender dynamics in our clinic. Over a period of months, we reflected on our classroom and lawyering culture, our individual roles, and our normative vision for an equitable learning and practice environment. We adopted some changes in our collective practices, incorporated an explicit focus on gender into our classroom discussion of collaboration, and have tried to normalize gender as a constant and visible topic for examination and action. This is an ongoing and imperfect endeavor whose origins are in crisis but whose object is the routine study and practice of law.

Conclusion

From the Muslim Ban to the threatened deportation of Nury Chavarria to the extraordinary challenges now posed by COVID-19, our experiences in lawyering during a crisis persuade us that we cannot avoid the stress, improvisation, and errors that necessarily attend such work. Nor should we. We do best when we hold to our commitment to engage in critical reflection (even if the reflection must be deferred) and when we trust in each other and our networks and relationships. We try to remain vigilant to the ways in which emergencies can stress-test our routine practices and reveal less visible or corrosive practices. And when at a loss to divine any way forward for our clients, we still repeat to each other: "Call air traffic control!"

NOTES

1 IRAP knew that the president was likely to issue the executive order and had encouraged its clients around the world who were authorized to travel to the United States to do so immediately. Ms. Heller had been in touch with one of us earlier that week for referrals to prepare emergency local legal assistance to a handful of IRAP clients scheduled to arrive in various airports in the days before the executive order was issued. Individual counsel for Mr. Darweesh was at JFK, as were IRAP lawyers for other of their clients.

2 Over the course of the litigation, nearly every student in the clinic worked on some aspect of the case, including: Tiffany Bailey, Will Bloom, Adam Bradlow, Jordan Cohen, Catherine Chen, David Chen, Charles Du, Susanna Evarts, Bertolain Elysee, Natalia (Nazarewicz) Friedlander, Katherine Haas, Amit Jain, Clare Kane, Healy Ko, Aaron Korthuis, Andie Levien, Carolyn Lipp, Zachary-John Manfredi, Melissa Marichal, Adán Martinez, Joseph Meyers, My Khanh Ngo, Carolyn O'Connor, Megha Ram, Victoria Roeck, Thomas Scott-Railton, Yusuf Saei, Nancy Yun Tang, Emily Villano, Rachel Wilf-Townsend, Liz Willis, and Ricky Zacharias.

3 Email from Michael Wishnie (Jan. 27, 2019) (copy on file with authors).

4 In addition to Justin Cox and Becca Heller, our former students included Stephen Poellot at IRAP, and Omar Jadwat and Cody Wofsy at the ACLU. An even larger

number of former students engaged in other forms of advocacy regarding the Muslim Ban, from filing amicus briefs in *Darweesh*, to volunteering at airports across the country, to initiating their own litigation directly challenging the ban and its subsequent iterations. These included Sameer Ahmed, Amanda Aikman, Caitlin Bellis, Alina Das, Kate Huddleston, Ana Muñoz, Paul Hughes, Aadhithi Padmanabhan, Simon Sandoval-Moshenberg, Swapna Reddy, Yaman Salahi, Anjana Samant, and Sirine Shebaya.

5 In addition to the two of us, Elora Mukherjee, a clinical professor at Columbia Law School who c-taught the clinic with us that year, supervised the matter from that first night onward. Our colleague professor Marisol Orihuela joined the supervision the following day.

6 Email from Muneer Ahmad (Jan. 27, 2019) (copy on file with authors).

7 Email to Michael Wishnie, July 21, 2017, 10:07 A.M. (in possession of authors).

8 The summer students were Laika Abdulali, Rana Ayazi, Jessica Cisneros, Ana Islas, Yusuf Saei (a term-time student working in WIRAC that summer), and Cameron Sheldon, and the term-time student was David Chen. The recent clinic alumnae who founded ASAP, the organization that provided key assistance in the first few days of the representation, were Conchita Cruz, Swapna Reddy, Dorothy Tegeler, and Liz Willis.

9 We have supervised students in a number of high-stakes matters. In these, students have handled trial and appellate arguments, including in major suits before the Connecticut Supreme Court (twice), U.S. Court of Appeals for Veterans Claims *en banc* (twice), and the U.S. Courts of Appeals (four times in 2019 alone). To mention a recent example, in January 2019, the Second Circuit held oral argument in consolidated cases challenging termination of the DACA program. A third-year student presented the principal argument in one of the two consolidated cases, before a full courtroom and overflow room, while broadcast on C-SPAN.

15

Leveraging Lawyers' Strengths and Training Them to Support Team Problem-Solving Under Crisis Conditions

SCOTT WESTFAHL

In . . . a [crisis] situation, professionals often perceive the lawyer who gets in the way of timely action as an obstacle to dealing with the event. Attorneys may find themselves literally locked out of emergency operations centers unless they have taken the pains to become a part of the team during the early stages of emergency management.
—anonymous senior crisis leadership practitioner

I don't want my lawyer to keep me out of court; I want my lawyer to keep me out of jail.
—anonymous Federal Coordinating Officer at FEMA

Crisis situations typically present significant legal and ethical challenges. Lawyers often play a critical role in sorting, analyzing, and proactively addressing these challenges. Their legal training and expertise provide them with powerful capabilities to help lead in a crisis and to provide critical input. However, some of their learned behaviors and tendencies may create significant impediments to successful crisis resolution. In the context of the groundbreaking meta-leadership model developed jointly by scholars at the Harvard School of Public Health and Kennedy School of Government,[1] I will discuss how lawyers can successfully cultivate and leverage their skills, experience, and problem-solving abilities to help lead in a crisis. I also offer suggestions as to how to train lawyers to improve their awareness of, and help to mitigate against, counterproductive activities and reactions that they may exhibit when under stress in a crisis.

The Meta-leadership Model

Developed in the wake of September 11, the groundbreaking meta-leadership model for crisis leadership is based on an extensive survey of international leadership experience of both failures and successes. It integrates and translates leadership analysis, practice, and scholarship into five dimensions of leadership practice. Put simply, the first two dimensions are a leader's (1) self-awareness and (2) accurate perception and diagnosis of the crisis situation. Note that the heavy emphasis on situational awareness and problem diagnosis in that framework runs parallel to the central role of "sensemaking" in the FEMA Advice in Crisis perspective described in chapter 13 by Eric K. Stern and his cocontributors in this volume.[2] The other three are a leader's ability to lead "down" by energizing and leveraging followers in teams and via hierarchical organizational lines of authority; "up" by effectively managing, supporting, and advising those in charge; and "across" by leading across organizations/organizational peer units and integrating and accounting for the perspectives of key stakeholders. Leading across poses a challenge of creating unity of effort in crisis—without having unity of "command." Doing so requires drawing upon an alternative toolbox of leadership soft skills such as persuasion, negotiation, facilitation, and consensus-building. This framework will be referenced as a point of departure for reflecting on lawyers' typical strengths and challenges when operating in a crisis.

The Upside: Common Learned and Natural Strengths of Lawyers in a Crisis

While some traits and learned behaviors of lawyers can inhibit them from contributing most productively in a crisis, the good news is that they commonly bring many positive strengths to the crisis leadership table. Some of those strengths seem to be inherent in the "lawyer personality," and others are shaped over time by legal education and practice settings that select for and reward certain characteristics and behaviors over others. The danger of this analysis, of course, is stereotyping and applying broad generalizations to a very large, diverse group of people. Nonetheless, significant analyses by scholars of the legal profession, and observations by experts in the crisis leadership field, support the necessity of this discussion and framework.

Strengths Inherent in the Lawyer Personality

In training senior law firm leaders and in-house counsel about leadership at Harvard Law School Executive Education, we directly address the implications of common personality traits among lawyers. Using a framework drawn from motivational psychology and a related "personal values questionnaire,"[3] we have, by engaging with thousands of lawyers, confirmed that the great majority of top lawyers are motivated primarily by a high need for achievement. That need drives lawyers to seek autonomy, competition, and, above all, challenging tasks into which they put a tremendous amount of focused energy. They want to understand the rules and parameters of a situation or challenge and then want to go off to work on it alone to produce what they believe to be a perfect work product. In working on a challenge, they can become captive to their high need for achievement, meaning that it is hard to pull them out of their task and to expect them to do anything other than the articulated task at hand. Thus, it becomes critical to frame their tasks broadly to encompass the full range of contributions expected of them.

The high need for achievement drive is a critical lens through which to view lawyers' crisis-related personality strengths because it explains much of their natural working style in a crisis. They have an incredible ability to focus and work through all aspects of a difficult problem. Additionally, in part due to their competitive nature, they have a natural orientation toward learning and gathering additional information—an inherent curiosity—that can contribute importantly to analyzing a complex situation.

Legal Education and Practice Effects

My colleague David Wilkins and I have written extensively about lawyer development and how traditional legal education is increasingly out of step with the market for legal services and what effective lawyering now and, more importantly, in the future will require.[4] We have been very careful to acknowledge, however, that traditional models of legal education and lawyer development within the early years of corporate legal practice produce significant, highly relevant benefits. Law schools have seen their mission as teaching law students how to "think like lawyers," which traditionally has meant to instill in lawyers a passion for and dedication to the highest level of analytical rigor when considering a problem.

At its core, legal analytical rigor is the ability to view a problem from all conceivable angles and then articulate and persuade effectively on behalf of any stakeholder affected by the problem. This approach requires lawyers to sort through a mass of data and potentially misleading information to discern the facts and evidence that most effectively supports a particular stakeholder's viewpoint. No stone is left unturned, and "negative facts"—the absence of confirming evidence—are treated with due respect and attention as much as directly confirming "actual facts" and evidence. Among all positive lawyer traits, this ability can often in a crisis start to look like a superhero's superpower–with great force, lawyers work the problem to cut through the noise and misdirection inherent in a crisis to identify the "real" problem and potential ways through it.

Additionally, traditional legal education and corporate lawyer development greatly enhance lawyers' communication and persuasion/advocacy skills. Because so much of crisis leadership can depend on effective communication to multiple stakeholders with often competing agendas, these skills can be highly useful.[5] As much as it can sometimes inhibit learning through intimidation, the US law school classroom's Socratic approach requires law students to critically analyze and communicate complex problems and ideas on the spot in the context of a broader, conceptual discussion of legal, ethical, and societal norms. Sound familiar? Arguably, no other general model of professional education prepares students *more* effectively to lead in a crisis, given that a critical pillar of crisis leadership is the ability to communicate effectively under great pressure and stress. Law school training in that sense might be compared to the legendary stories of how Tiger Woods's father, Earl, trained his young son to putt and make golf shots under pressure by standing behind him making noises and creating distractions. Lawyers in training are building the muscle memory of crisis communication and response.

The rigors of legal practice also contribute to lawyers' ability to function in a crisis. Whether in private practice or public sector/government legal positions, high-need-for-achievement lawyers typically work very, very hard under a great deal of stress, managing multiple projects at once and holding themselves accountable to a very high standard of analytical and work product accountability. Their self-motivated, competitive drive for perfection ensures that they do not give up when facing a challenge and don't lose their focus when others might. Lawyers are often the reliable team members who responsibly perform assigned tasks and help keep the crisis team focused on timelines, deliverables, and end goals.

Finally, traditional legal education's emphasis on the dispassionate consideration of facts and positions provides lawyers with a mind-set that can be particularly helpful in a crisis. As the temperature rises and a crisis triggers significant and varied emotional responses from stakeholders, legal training helps lawyers to step back and more calmly assess what is happening. They are trained first to listen and then to sort facts from emotion, to analyze the situation and suggest options. By slowing down the process, lawyers can help mitigate against the knee-jerk, emotional responses and actions or inactions that can add fuel to the fire in a crisis.

A recent conversation with the general counsel (GC) of a global professional firm illustrates an extreme example of how this works. The CEO of the firm called the GC into her office to demand the immediate, "perp-walk" firing of a senior executive with whom the CEO was very upset. The CEO wanted to ignore the required due process and investigation and all of the negative ramifications of such an action. Brilliantly, instead of trying to push back against the CEO's strong emotional affect, the GC immediately "pulled a Frank Underwood"[6] and told the CEO he would immediately call police as well as building security and march the senior executive out of the office, shut off all computer access, and have staff pack up and send the personal contents of the executive's office for delivery to his home that afternoon. As the GC started to pick up the telephone, pretending to call the police, the CEO quickly backed down and suggested that the GC begin the necessary due process and investigation instead! The GC's legal training and finely tuned skills of persuasion and influence helped the firm avoid truly significant legal risk.

Meta-leadership Model Benefits

The above-described personality traits of lawyers and attributes of the traditional lawyer development model prepare lawyers to contribute significantly to effective meta-leadership in a crisis. There are some other benefits that we should mention.

SELF-AWARENESS. First, with respect to the dimension of self-awareness and self-regulation, effective meta-leadership most importantly requires a leader to mitigate against the "amygdala hijack" that often freezes leaders in a primal fight, flight, or freeze mode.[7] The model posits that leaders need to be able to move from the "emotional basement" of that initial, stress-induced activation of the amygdalae to the "middle" of the brain where prefrontal cortex, higher-level, complex, rational reasoning can occur. Legal training instills in lawyers an autoresponse toward dispassionate, critical thinking, and the rigors of legal practice build significant muscle memory that they can leverage to be the actors in a crisis who keep calm, keep thinking, and move a team toward rational consideration of the situation and more effective decision-making. For example, former president Barack Obama's legal training likely helped him to achieve his ability to be seen as the "cool" head in a crisis, rarely to be rattled, even though he has also faced significant criticism for just that virtue.[8]

ACCURATE DIAGNOSIS OF THE CRISIS. The second dimension of meta-leadership requires an "evidence-based, clear and actionable description of what is occurring" and "the ability to convey it to others."[9] Legal analytical rigor is ideally suited to provide the former, whereas legal advocacy and communication training is extremely useful for the latter. In simulation-based training of lawyers and law students, we have noted their extraordinary ability to adopt the viewpoint of a stakeholder, thoroughly explore it, and then passionately and effectively advocate for that viewpoint. To fully leverage their training, lawyers in a crisis should be tasked with broadly identifying stakeholders, rigorously analyzing their perspectives, and synthesizing that data and information into an actionable understanding of the situation.

MANAGING UP. Meta-leadership fails without effective managing "up," which involves effectively working with and influencing those to whom leaders are accountable.[10] This is a particular strength of lawyers because, through their legal training and practice, lawyers internalize a deep desire to serve their clients by listening to them, advocating for them, advising them, and protecting them against obvious and potential risks. They are trained to maintain a dispassionate, level-headed demeanor and approach and also to present hard truths to their clients when needed—all of which closely align with this dimension of the meta-leadership model. Good lawyers are also adept at serving clients with widely varying temperaments and working styles, a critical skill of the meta-leader.

MANAGING ACROSS. To be effective, a meta-leader must "influence, engage, and unify" many different stakeholders to "create unity of effort."[11] Meta-leadership benefits greatly if "cross-system linkages" can be built in advance, in part through formal agreements. It is clear that lawyers, given their impressive commercial success in the corporate deal space, are particularly well trained and well suited to the tasks of working with stakeholders to identify collaboration opportunities and then drafting formal agreements to codify those opportunities and provide a clear, helpful roadmap for action when certain events occur. Engaging legal counsel in such efforts in advance of crises would be highly beneficial to the goal of "managing across" and ensuring the likelihood of stakeholder cooperation.

The Downside: Potential Blind Spots That Impede Lawyers' Ability to Add Value in a Crisis

The learned and naturally occurring strengths that lawyers bring to a crisis are unfortunately also often paired with several important potential blind spots. It is important for lawyers to become self-aware about these blind spots and for those working with lawyers in a crisis also to be able to identify and mitigate them.

Teamwork

As helpful as it is that high-need-for-achievement lawyers love challenging tasks and attack them with incredible analytical rigor, their desire for autonomy can hinder the highly collaborative, multi-input, multi-stakeholder, inclusive process that effective crisis leadership can require. We observe this phenomenon as early as first year of law school. One Harvard faculty member who teaches at both Harvard Business School and Harvard Law School notes that, when he gives students a team-based assignment, business-school students get together in their teams and work out the problem in the same room to produce their best team answer. By contrast, his law students meet quickly after class, divide up the project, go back to their individual dorm rooms or apartments to work on their parts, and then assign one team member the task of integrating all of the various pieces of the assignment. Without any intervention, law students' method of working in teams leaves a lot to be desired! When I share this anecdote with practicing lawyers in our Harvard Law School Executive Education leadership programs, they sheepishly laugh and admit that is how they used to work, too.

Because traditional legal education requires little or no teamwork and rarely if ever provides any deeper guidance about how to work in teams,[12] lawyers enter the profession underprepared for collaborative work, even though their clients are increasingly demanding it.[13] Extensive experience and interviews with practicing lawyers in both private practice and the public sector confirm that the great majority of lawyer "teams" working on projects are not actually what other professions would consider to be teams. Rather, they are hierarchical, loose working groups where a senior person controls client contact, a midlevel "quarterback" person communicates up and down the chain, and individual contributors perform various tasks with little or no contact with each other or the broader purpose of the team's effort. There is no team launch or kickoff, there are few if any team meetings, information is shared loosely on a need-to-know, hierarchical basis, and the teams rarely if ever meet during or after the project to share lessons learned or any ideas about how to work more effectively together. By contrast, consulting, accounting, engineering, and military teams all employ team protocols and processes—some quite formal—to ensure team alignment, efficiency, and engagement.

So where does this leave us? Crisis team members may falsely assume that lawyers participating on the crisis team know how to work in a team effectively. This can lead to great disappointment or frustration when the autonomy-seeking lawyer fails to communicate or share information effectively with other team members and/or does not understand that a team effort, especially with a diverse team, provides a better solution by leveraging team members' individual and collective strengths. Other potential lawyer blind spots compound these issues, as illustrated below.

Low Resilience and Sociability

Personality assessments of lawyers suggest strongly that lawyers are lower on the scale of resilience and sociability traits compared to other professionals.[14] We see evidence of those findings through many reports of lawyers being particularly thin-skinned and defensive when receiving criticism and constructive feedback. More quickly and more aggressively, they become defensive. Rather than listen and learn, their natural instinct is to justify their action(s) or inaction(s) and even attack (actively or passively) the person offering the criticism. Exacerbating this effect is the fact that legal training has finely honed their ability to defend, justify, persuade, and even attack. Clearly, this can be dysfunctional in a crisis environment where the team requires each team member to be fully engaged, share openly, and stay focused on the challenge at hand rather than the egos in the room.

Skepticism and the Pessimistic Explanatory Style of Lawyers

Psychologists studying lawyers are concerned that lawyers have a higher degree of skepticism compared to other professionals.[15] The founder of positive psychology, Dr. Martin Seligmann, has artfully described how lawyers are highly selected and paid/rewarded for their uniquely powerful, pessimistic perspective.[16] As a simple example, a transactional/deal lawyer must anticipate in advance all the things that could go wrong with the deal and then structure the deal's legal documents to account for all potential negative events that might occur down the road. Lawyers are often deliberately positioned to play the devil's advocate role and/or to be the guardian against undue business, ethical, and existential risk. In-house counsel, for example, are given the unenviable role of enabling the business but also guarding against and saying "no" to their business partners, who may propose that the business engage in unwise/unethical/potentially illegal conduct. High-need-for-achievement lawyers will take risks but only *realistic* risks, which can sometimes frustrate company executives whose risk tolerance is much greater and indeed highly incentivized by their reward/compensation structures.

The ramifications of this for crisis teams are at times profound, including:

- Lawyers may impede effective crisis brainstorming by too quickly and too negatively shooting down presented ideas. The best brainstorming requires a broadening of options *before* that narrowing and critical thinking is applied.[17]

- When lawyers encounter push-back or even mild criticism from crisis team members, their egos may be more bruised than other team members realize and lawyers' defensive/unhelpful emotional responses to criticism may confuse the team at best and completely undermine it at worst.
- Lawyers may shut down their own creative contributions to crisis resolution by preconceiving their role too narrowly. They are incredibly smart and have great potential to offer out-of-the-box ideas. Yet if they perceive that their only role is to mitigate risk, those contributions will be lost.

Risk Aversion

As noted above, high-need-for-achievement lawyers have a high degree of risk aversion and compound that when they are either (1) positioned only to play the role of devil's advocate/skeptic or (2) adopt that posture on the crisis team themselves. In addition to undermining brainstorming and the lawyer's ability to contribute creatively to team problem-solving, risk aversion results in an agent-versus-principal issue. Lawyers on a crisis team are often required to make the call on a key issue and to act. Legal training and their natural risk aversion may leave them paralyzed, however, for several reasons. First, legal training emphasizes the gathering of *all* facts and information and deep analysis of every possible avenue or potentiality. Yet all important decisions in a crisis are by definition made with incomplete information. The question is when to stop the analysis and decide, and lawyers may be prone to over-analysis and then paralysis at critical times. Second, legal training emphasizes the consideration of a problem from all possible angles. A lawyer's answer to a legal question often begins with the phrase, "Well, on the one hand . . ." and a common joke among lawyers' business partners is that they are dealing with the "one-handed" lawyer who presents options but is incapable of making a recommendation. Lawyers' natural risk aversion compounds this problem, of course, as making a recommendation requires the lawyer to assume some element of risk for the course he or she recommends. As a result, lawyers may opt for "safer" solutions than optimal when leading in a crisis.[18]

The Advocacy Trap

Lawyers are trained to be black belts in advocacy, but that is sometimes dysfunctional on a crisis team. Optimal team decision-making requires that potential solutions be thoroughly vetted, which lawyers can do very well if they have no ego invested in the analysis. The problem arises when a well-trained, persuasive lawyer out-advocates others on the crisis team and puts "winning" the discussion ahead of finding the optimal solution. Worse, if the low resilience, thin-skinned lawyer "loses" the discussion, he or she may unproductively disengage from the crisis team for a while to heal a bruised ego. It becomes imperative for the lawyer to be self-aware and to help create a team environment that leverages the proven benefits of psychological safety and inclusion.

Meta-leadership Model Concerns

While we have noted that lawyer personality traits and legal training and experience can enhance the exercise of meta-leadership in a crisis, so too can they have significant negative effects.

SELF-AWARENESS. This is a foundational element of meta-leadership, but unfortunately, in our observation and experience, lawyers are among the least self-reflective professionals. First, legal training establishes a culture of always putting the client first rather than investing time in one's own reflective processes or growth. It is only recently that leadership development for lawyers has become an accepted practice, and even then, in most legal organizations, leadership development is much more limited than in comparable professional organizations. Second, because very few law schools or legal employers train lawyers to work in teams and lawyers are rarely assessed on their EQ skills, they may have a less-developed "understanding of the impact that personality, experience, culture, emotional expression and character have on others," which is fundamental to the meta-leadership model.[19]

ACCURATE DIAGNOSIS OF THE CRISIS. The concern here is that legal training in analytical rigor may lead lawyers to insist on overanalysis of all facts in a crisis. In the meta-leadership model, "a quick assessment that is close to the mark and moves the process forward is better than a slow though more accurate one that comes too late to make a difference."[20] Among those who criticized lawyer and President Barack Obama's crisis leadership style, many cited frustrations with his very deliberate, slow-paced (in their view) fact-finding.

LEADING THE BASE. The meta-leadership model suggests that effective leaders need to develop "strong, smart, capable followers not seen as [a] threat but rather as a valuable asset."[21] Leaders must be committed to leadership development and the empowerment of their followers. In our experience with leadership training for lawyers, we encounter several barriers here. First, lawyers trained to err on the side of perfectionism tend to delegate poorly. Rather than employ a "highest and best use of my time" test, they decide whether they can do something better than their subordinate and, if so, decide not to delegate.

Implications for Improving Lawyers' Ability to Add Value in a Crisis

There are many ways that the legal profession and the crisis leadership world can collaborate to improve lawyers' ability to add value in a crisis.

BUILDING LAWYER SELF-AWARENESS. Most critical is for legal academia and organizations to help lawyers become more self-aware of their potential blind spots related to crisis leadership. Helping lawyers to name and understand these learned and natural proclivities can build their muscle memory to recognize and mitigate against them in a crisis. Law schools and legal organizations should provide training related to lawyer personality and leadership and consider those equally important to the provision of training related to substantive legal topics.[22] Intensive executive education leadership programs modeled after traditional business school leadership programs can provide a forum for such training for practicing lawyers.[23] One of the most effective methods we have applied is using business school–style cases and simulations with groups of lawyers to illustrate how lawyer personality traits can impede effective decision-making in a crisis, for example.

WORKING IN TEAMS. More particularly, law students and practicing lawyers should be introduced to research, tools, and experiences that significantly enhance their ability to work more effectively in teams, particularly in a crisis where effective team communication and leveraging diverse team member's strengths becomes critically important. Using an adaptive leadership model based on the work of Harvard Kennedy School professor Ron Heifetz, we ask small groups of lawyers to form and name their own law firms and then work as an executive committee to make difficult decisions in three separate, challenging scenarios. We observe participants' deliberations and interactions and help them to understand how their natural and/or learned personality traits impact their ability to work together effectively. In particular, we focus on how lawyers tend to become thin-skinned and defensive when challenged and/or move too quickly to advocacy mode, which can introduce destructive power dynamics into the team's deliberations.

Within law schools, requiring significantly more team-based projects would be a very helpful start, provided that students would be introduced to and taught to apply basic team tools and processes. Team launches, team feedback, and team reflection tools are common across many professions but almost never applied in the legal profession. In the team-based courses I teach, students overwhelmingly report better results and higher satisfaction with their team experiences when we require them to learn and apply team-related tools and processes.

MIND-SET SHIFTING. The growth of mindfulness and resilience training for professionals—including lawyers—is a step forward toward helping lawyers adopt a more positive, growth-oriented mind-set.[24] This does not mean that lawyers should no longer play the role of skeptic or devil's advocate (for which they are often highly valued). Rather, lawyers need to become aware of the particular mind-set and approach they should bring to different roles they are playing. Crisis teams should clarify—and potentially broaden—their understanding of their expectations of lawyers on their teams. The "SALT" model adopted by FEMA's lawyers under the leadership of former FEMA general counsel Brad Kieserman is a great example of setting such expectations to leverage lawyers' strengths fully on a crisis team.

DESIGN THINKING AS A PROBLEM-SOLVING TOOL. As design thinking–based problem solving has moved from the world of products to the world of services, there is increasing interest among lawyers in how to apply design thinking to solve particularly tricky problems they encounter. For several years, I have taught design thinking approaches to law students and practicing lawyers and believe that it has a lot of potential to help lawyers function more effectively during a crisis. Design thinking–based problem-solving requires progression through five stages: empathy, problem definition, ideation, prototyping, and testing. Learning how to progress through these stages can enhance lawyers' crisis leadership capabilities, as follows:

- *Empathy*. Designers develop empathy by observation and open-ended questioning of a broad group of stakeholders, particularly focused on "extreme" users or people who love or hate a particular product or service. Lawyers become better listeners when practicing these skills, and they also learn how to interview in a much less biased way—a critical skill to have when gathering facts in a crisis.
- *Problem definition*. Too often, lawyers feel a need to show immediately that they are the smartest people in the room. As a result, we find that they sometimes jump too quickly to believing they understand a problem without fully exploring it. Designers spend most of their time at the problem-definition stage to ensure that they are not designing a hammer looking for a nail that doesn't exist. Having conducted numerous design sprints, hackathons, and workshops with lawyers, I have observed that helping them to seek broader context and center their problem definition in empathy for an end user or client helps them to define the problem(s) at hand much more effectively. I believe this stage of design thinking training can help lawyers in a crisis to think more holistically about the problem(s) at hand rather than viewing a crisis solely through a narrow, technical legal lens.

- *Ideation*. The ideation phase of design thinking requires creativity and an ability to brainstorm and build on teammates' ideas. Lawyers' natural and trained proclivity is to hear an idea and immediately start to attack it from all angles to test its merits. Designers first broaden their lens of potential solutions by deliberately including "wild" ideas in the mix before they start to narrow toward a solution set. In my experience in helping lawyers to follow brainstorming guidelines, I have been encouraged that, with prompts and structure, lawyers can generate ideas that are truly creative and interesting (and on par with those that designers themselves might develop).
- *Prototyping*. Legal education drills into lawyers' mind-sets the need to be perfect the first time. There can be no typos missed and no citation in error when you submit a brief to a court; neither can there be a misplaced comma in a term sheet that might dramatically alter the economics of a deal. Yet what designers do is decidedly different. Once a hypothesis is developed from research and brainstorming surfaces possible approaches, designers start prototyping quickly and roughly to be able to start testing whether they are on the right track. This notion of "failing quickly" and then learning is antithetical to the way lawyers are trained and the way we practice law or run legal organizations. Far too often, after a "pilot" approach at a law firm fails to meet all objectives, partners are much more resistant to piloting similar approaches in the future. It is not uncommon to hear law firm administrative professionals complain about partners urging them to "do something really innovative" and then continue on by asking "what are all the other firms doing?" Training lawyers to prototype quickly is quite a stretch for them at first, but success is possible if metrics are established in advance to measure learning rather than whether a prototype perfectly addresses the client's pain points. Putting lawyers in design teams and closely coaching them through their uneasiness with prototyping can produce surprisingly creative results.
- *Testing*. As prototypes are developed and testing is required, it is important to guide lawyers about how to measure success and how to capture related learning. Helping lawyers to develop those metrics themselves in a design simulation embeds the learning much more successfully than imposing it on them, as learning from failure needs to become a cultural norm rather than a mandatory duty. By analogy, General John Kelly relates how the US Marines have become more successful by changing the way they evaluate Marines as leaders. Traditionally, Marines have been trained to have a bias toward action and were evaluated on whether they took initiative and what results they achieved. It was career-limiting for a Marine to receive an after-action evaluation of "good initiative, bad judgment." Today, the Ma-

rines retain their bias toward action but focus on learning from mistakes. Thus, the after-action review instead would say "good initiative, what did we learn from it?"

LEADERSHIP DEVELOPMENT. As my colleague David Wilkins and I have strenuously argued, lawyer development at law schools and in legal organizations needs to include the education of lawyers across a much broader spectrum of leadership and professional skills. To prepare lawyers to add more value in a crisis, lawyer development must include training, tools, and experiences that help them to listen, give and receive feedback, communicate, facilitate, negotiate, analyze, think creatively and innovatively, and exercise judgment and to apply both legal and ethical frameworks in the broader context of a crisis. It is a hopeful sign that more law schools are initiating leadership training for law students, using simulations and cases drawn from real-life experiences. Executive education leadership programs across the arc of a lawyer's career can also positively affect their ability to add value during a crisis. Several of the case studies developed by Harvard Law School Executive Education directly address leadership in a crisis, including cases that consider the role of in-house lawyers involved in the General Motors ignition switch recall; having difficult conversations with a company's board during a crisis; managing a law firm successfully through a global financial crisis; and applying principles of adaptive leadership to meet new challenges. Some cases have also been developed for training law students and younger law firm associates, such as a case that asks students to play the role of an in-house lawyer who needs to deal with a product recall resulting from lead paint being found on toys; or a case about a mid-level associate at a law firm whose career and personal life may be unraveling due to passivity and false assumptions. Such cases help lawyers to build important perspective-taking and leadership skills, all of which are helpful in a crisis.

Finally, it is important that lawyers' learned and natural strengths and potential blind spots be on the radar and visible to leaders and crisis team members who are not lawyers.[25] This effort to unpack the world of crisis lawyering is a very important first step toward raising awareness and starting a productive dialogue that will have benefits across the broad field of crisis leadership.

Conclusion

While legal education and training provide lawyers with important critical skills for leadership in a crisis, lawyers also have blind spots and areas of relative deficiency that can derail effective crisis leadership. In the context of the meta-leadership model, we can greatly appreciate that lawyers have certain core skills that can be leveraged effectively to build situational awareness and an accurate diagnosis of a crisis, as well as to "manage up" and "manage across" particularly well. It is important, though, to understand that lawyers may fail to contribute to meta-leadership in a crisis due to their reluctance to self-reflect, their desire for perfection through endless deliberation, and their relative inability to work well in teams. Legal academic education and executive education for practicing lawyers provide avenues through which lawyers can build critical skills for working well in a crisis, and training lawyers in a design thinking–based problem solving is particularly promising in that regard.

NOTES

Epigraphs from Eric Stern et al., *Advice in Crisis: Leaders, Lawyers and the Art of Disaster Management, in* HOMELAND SECURITY HANDBOOK: STRATEGIC GUIDANCE FOR A COORDINATED APPROACH TO EFFECTIVE SECURITY AND EMERGENCY MANAGEMENT 715 (David J. Kamien ed., 2nd ed. 2012).

1 Dr. Leonard J. Marcus et al., *Crisis Preparedness & Crisis Response, in* HOMELAND SECURITY HANDBOOK: STRATEGIC GUIDANCE FOR A COORDINATED APPROACH TO EFFECTIVE SECURITY AND EMERGENCY MANAGEMENT 679–709 (David G. Kamien ed., 2nd ed. 2012). *See also,* LEONARD J. MARCUS ET AL., YOU'RE IT: CRISIS, CHANGE, AND HOW TO LEAD WHEN IT MATTERS MOST (2019).

2 *See* ARJEN BOIN ET AL., THE POLITICS OF CRISIS MANAGEMENT: PUBLIC LEADERSHIP UNDER PRESSURE (2005).

3 This assessment is drawn from the work of David C. McClelland in *The Achieving Society. See* DAVID C. MCCLELLAND, THE ACHIEVING SOCIETY (1961).

4 *See* Scott A. Westfahl & David B. Wilkins, *The Leadership Imperative: A Collaborative Approach to Professional Development in the Global Age of More for Less,* 69 STAN. L. REV. 1667 (2017).

5 ANDREW J. DUBRIN, HANDBOOK OF RESEARCH ON CRISIS LEADERSHIP IN ORGANIZATIONS 8–10 (2013); Leslie DeChurch et al., *A Historic Analysis of Leadership in Mission Critical Multiteam Environments,* 22 LEADERSHIP Q. 162 (2011).

6 From the Netflix series *House of Cards.*

7 Marcus et al., *Crisis Preparedness,* 687.

8 *See, e.g.,* BOIN ET AL., THE POLITICS OF CRISIS MANAGEMENT (discussing the critical importance of empathy in crisis leadership and crisis lawyering); Stern et al., chapter 13 in this volume.

9 BOIN ET AL., THE POLITICS OF CRISIS MANAGEMENT, 689.

10 *Id.* at 694.

11 *Id.* at 697.

12 *See* Westfahl & Wilkins, *The Leadership Imperative.* The author of this chapter is currently developing a new, team-based leadership course for first-year students

at Harvard Law School and is incorporating specific teaching, tools, and frameworks to help law students work more effectively in teams.

13 HEIDI K. GARDNER, SMART COLLABORATION: HOW PROFESSIONALS AND THEIR FIRMS SUCCEED BY BREAKING DOWN SILOS (2016).

14 Larry Richard, *Leadership Competencies in Law*, in LAW AND LEADERSHIP: INTEGRATING LEADERSHIP STUDIES INTO THE LAW SCHOOL CURRICULUM 35 (Paula Monopoli & Susan McCarty eds., 2013); Larry Richard, *Herding Cats: The Lawyer Personality Revealed*, 29 REP. TO LEGAL MGMT. 1 (2002); Larry Richard & Lisa Rohrer, *A Breed Apart?*, THE AMERICAN LAWYER 43–44 (July 1, 2011).

15 RICHARD, *Leadership Competencies*; Richard, *Herding Cats*.

16 MARTIN E. P. SELIGMAN, AUTHENTIC HAPPINESS: USING THE NEW POSITIVE PSYCHOLOGY TO REALIZE YOUR POTENTIAL FOR LASTING FULFILLMENT (2002).

17 *Brainstorming*, IDEO, www.ideou.com; *Brainstorm Rules*, DESIGN KIT, www.designkit.com.

18 *See* Stern et al., *Advice in Crisis*, 729–31, for a helpful discussion about how lawyers in a crisis view risk and how, ideally, lawyers should be trained to understand that "legal risks must be weighed against other forms of risk" and that "[l]awyers who seek to avoid legal risk completely will be perceived as obstacles to effective disaster management and are likely to be marginalized within their teams."

19 Marcus et al., *Crisis Preparedness*, 686.

20 *Id.* at 690.

21 *Id.* at 693.

22 As noted above, the author of this chapter has developed a new leadership course for first-year Harvard Law School students that includes such training.

23 For a thorough discussion of the lawyer executive education model, *see* Scott Westfahl, *Learning to Lead: Perspective on Bridging the Lawyer Leadership Gap*, in LEADERSHIP FOR LAWYERS 163–74 (Heidi K. Gardner & Rebecca Normand-Hochman eds., 2nd ed. 2019).

24 See the materials on lawyers and resilience and lawyers and well-being at www.pauladavislaack.com.

25 In our leadership programs for senior law-firm leaders and general counsel at Harvard Law School, we routinely and emphatically remind participants not to use the term "nonlawyers" to refer to the professionals without a law degree with whom they are working. The term is pejorative and often leads to resentment among professionals with whom lawyers need to collaborate!

Stay Calm and Carry On

How to Stay on Point When in a Crisis

JAY SULLIVAN

Arguably, there is no greater danger than to get between a parent and their child. If that parent is a female grizzly bear, run. Fast. But if the child is your client who has sought refuge in a crisis shelter, stand your ground. It won't be easy, and the claws from the other side will be just as sharp, but it's your job.

From 1989 to 1991, I was in-house counsel at a crisis shelter for runaway and homeless youth in New York City. Kids came to the agency for reasons both desperate and disparate. While most were homeless because they outgrew the city's foster care system, many had fled homes that were abusive or so dysfunctional that the teenager decided she might be safer looking for shelter elsewhere. Occasionally, kids came from loving, supportive families struggling to deal with the teenager's mental health or substance abuse challenges. We never knew what difficulty might walk through the door. Regardless, as the legal team, we needed to know and protect the child's rights while also protecting the child. When I teach negotiation skills at law firms, part of my job is to help lawyers recognize that if you go for the jugular, you can destroy a client's possibly ongoing relationship with the other party. When the other party is a child's parent, there is more at stake—and more finesse to the discussion.

As lawyers, we are bound not only by a code of ethics but also by the law itself. At the time I worked for this population, New York's Runaway and Homeless Youth Act[1] allowed any teenager over the age of sixteen to seek protection at a shelter for up to thirty days *against his or her parent's permission.* This allowed time for the family situation to stabilize and for others to intercede to help assess whether the youth should return home.

Our shelter was a massive building on the corner of 41st Street and 10th Avenue, at the entrance to the Lincoln Tunnel. Regularly, parents of a youth in our care would arrive and demand to see their child. If the child asserted his right to not speak with his parents, I would meet with the parents outside of the building. Whether it was late on a cold December afternoon, or high noon on a hot August day, we'd stand on the sidewalk on 41st Street—with a backdrop of traffic whirring, sirens blaring, and occasional pedestrians walking by. There, I'd inform them that their son or daughter did not wish to speak with them right now. The conversation usually went like this:

ME: I'm here to help reunite you with your son. John doesn't want to speak with you right now, and under the law, he's entitled to do that. Would it be helpful if we sat down on the bench over here and discussed what we can do today?

PARENT: No! Give me my son!

ME: I understand it must be very frustrating to not be able to speak with him right now. I certainly would be upset if someone kept me from speaking with my child. John is asserting his right to stay in the shelter at this point, and we need to honor that right. Would it be helpful if we discussed what we can do today?

PARENT: No. Give me my son. [Sometimes accompanied by expletives and fingers jabbing in the air.]

ME: That's not going to happen today. The law allows your son to refuse to speak with you right now. If we sit down and talk, we can discuss what we can accomplish today. Would that be helpful to you?

PARENT: No.

ME: Then what would be helpful to you?

PARENT: It would be helpful if you gave me my son.

ME: I understand you want to see your son. That's not going to happen today. I would be glad to discuss what we can accomplish. Would that be helpful?

Surprisingly, at that point, the conversation usually changed. After a few more rounds of "No," the parents would eventually sit down and talk. While it sounded like a very free-form conversation, the process worked because of a few key elements:

I delivered a clear, consistent message: They were not going to speak with John today.

I bolstered my position by referencing the law.

I validated the emotion in the situation.

I offered them control of the conversation.

I stayed calm and didn't get defensive or angry: I knew they themselves were in crisis as much as their child was.

I dealt with this scenario about once a month. While the parties involved were individuals, the issues were as significant to them as any faced by governments over arms negotiations gone awry or large corporate entities up against a recall or scandal.

The same five elements are important when advising a client in crisis. Lawyers guide their clients through a variety of crises. Often, the client is unable or would be ill-advised to speak for herself. Whether that client is a minor or a major corporation, the skills involved in protecting them remain the same. The client needs a clear, consistent message from their attorney, as well as an example of how poorly the situation may wind up if the client does not heed the advice. You have to acknowledge and address the client's emotions and give them control because, ultimately, they will decide on the course of action. Finally, you'll remain calm rather than heighten the tension. For instance:

> Mr. President, it's important that you do not testify before the Special Counsel. The Special Counsel will ask many challenging questions and any slip up could result in a perjury charge and possible jail time. I know this is a witch hunt and you are being treated unfairly. There is no "witch hunt exemption" in the perjury law, so regardless, you could be prosecuted if your story isn't 100 percent accurate. Ultimately, it's your decision. Remember that the judge or potential jury will unlikely be part of your base. I'm glad to walk you through this analysis as many times as it takes and to answer any questions you may have.

In this chapter, you will learn how to manage a crisis in the moment. You'll learn to:

1. Hone a clear and succinct message.
2. Support your message through stories or by leveraging authority.
3. Address the emotion expressed by others.
4. Offer the other person a semblance of control.
5. Control your own emotions when challenged.
6. Stay focused in the face of a myriad of distractions.

You will also learn to use the same skills to heighten the sense of urgency in others when that emotional response will help your position.

While some other chapters in this volume focus on theory, this chapter focuses on action; the physical things negotiators and lawyers can do and say—or avoid doing and saying—that will allow you to have more impact as you manage your way through a crisis.

I'll be drawing on both my nine years of experience as a lawyer and my twenty years of experience helping lawyers and other business professionals communicate more effectively with clients, the courts of law and public opinion, and regulators. The points shared are simple and straightforward. The tricky part is using them consistently in the fast-flowing and chaotic atmosphere of a crisis.

Crises come in many forms. An effective response will depend on context.

Is your client "in crisis," meaning they are in such a heightened state of urgency that they can't think clearly and are likely to say or do (or Tweet) something they shouldn't?

Is your client accustomed to dealing with challenging circumstances, and they need your guidance around how to handle what to them is simply "today's" crisis?

Are you responding to a crisis "manufactured" by a party with a narrow agenda?

Are you the party with the narrow agenda trying to create an element of conflict that best promotes your agenda?

In the first three scenarios, you are trying to deescalate the situation. In the final scenario, your cause is better served by promoting conflict.

Regardless of the scenario, the factors anyone should consider are the same. In this chapter, we'll focus on the steps you need to take regardless of the context for the crisis. I'll discuss each element from the perspective of deescalating the crisis. At the end of each, I'll share how to manage your approach where your cause is better served if you heighten tensions, because occasionally that will be your role in the discussion.

Hone a Clear and Succinct Message

You can't guide people through a crisis if you don't know the path to the exits. Therefore, you need to understand your own position well and articulate it clearly for an audience that is less familiar with the facts than you are. A clear message has five key components:

- It's short. Keep your core message to ten words or less in length.
- It's simple. Keep the vocabulary as straightforward as possible and minimize any jargon. (I'll talk later about language choice as a means of guiding the conversation.)
- It's upbeat. Focus on how to resolve the conflict rather than dwelling on the problem.
- It's framed as a benefit. The listener (i.e., the person you are addressing) should be able to understand the benefit to them immediately.
- It's repeatable. You'll have to say it several times in the same way for the other party to hear it clearly.

Keep It Short

The longer the message, the harder it will be for someone to hear it, understand it, and convey it to someone else clearly and simply. Ten words is about the most anyone can hear and repeat easily.

Keep It Simple

In addition to being short, the message should be delivered with simple language.

At work, we all spend more time talking to other people who do what we do and less time talking to people who do something else. Medical professionals spend more time talking to other medical professionals, accountants spend more time talking to other accountants, and so on.

As a result, we all get sucked into using jargon particular to our roles at work. The extra difficulty for us as attorneys is that our field is so varied, and our work is often so specialized, that we frequently cannot even understand each other if we don't challenge or rethink our own jargon. Jargon can get in the way. If you're talking to someone familiar with both the situation and the legal aspects of an issue, jargon speeds up comprehension. If the person is less familiar with either the situation or the issues, however, jargon inhibits comprehension. If, for example, you are outside counsel guiding your client's "GC" (general counsel) through an "M&A" (merger-acquisition) deal and you nonchalantly reference "backward integration," "the Bootstrap Effect," "Greenmail," or the "Lobster Trap," you run the risk of confusing the client, particularly if the GC comes from a tax or "RE" (real estate) background. (And realize that, to some, "GC," "M&A," and "RE" might also be jargon.) Avoid jargon because it has a high risk of slowing down the conversation.

To remind yourself to keep the message short and the language simple, think:

"Mr. Gorbachev, tear down this wall."
"No new taxes."
"There was no collusion."

The veracity of messages is also important. You'll want to avoid messages that themselves become the new crisis. We have all had moments where we made a statement and immediately said to ourselves, "Wow. That sounded so much better in my head than it did out loud." Often it wasn't just a word choice; it was the substance of what we conveyed. For most of us, that happens in an innocuous situation, such as responding to a spouse asking, "Do you mind if my mother comes to stay for a few days?" But if we are representing a client in a public situation, we have to manage our language and message more carefully.

Early in the Donald Trump administration, a White House spokesperson said the White House was relying on "alternative facts" when they rebutted easily proven data regarding the size of the crowd at the inauguration. She repeated the phrase throughout the on-air interview. "Alternative facts" became the next day's crisis and has become a punchline of sorts.

This problem is easy to avoid. Your message should make sense on its face.

Keep It Upbeat and Focused on the Benefit to the Listener

"We will decide as soon as we get the data" and "We won't decide until we get the data" both convey the same content: data first, decision second. However, the first phrasing—in the positive versus the negative—suggests we are trying to be proactive. We're eager to comply with a request. We want to move things forward. We just need information to move forward in the right direction. The second, negatively phrased statement can be heard as evasive, reticent, or timid.

When I spoke to parents on the sidewalk of 41st Street, I tried to always couple "You won't be talking to John today" with "Let's talk about how we can fix this."

Every corporate lawyer has had to tell his or her client at some point, "You can't do that." More successful lawyers phrase the entire conversation as: "Let's discuss options for getting there." The lawyer will include the client's preferred option in the list but bury it at the bottom.

Repeat It Often

For a message to work, the other party must hear it clearly and *recognize it* as the message. The first time you say something, no one hears it. The second time you say it, it sounds vaguely familiar from somewhere. The third time you say it, the listener finally hears it as the message you are trying to deliver. This is true even if you start by saying, "The main thing I want you to know is X." Repeating your message reinforces to the audience that this is the key takeaway.

The essence of being a good communicator is to think about how the listener needs to use your information. Always ask yourself:

Why is she reading my email?

Why is he attending this meeting?

What are they hoping to get from this presentation?

The more you consider your audience's needs in the moment, the more effective you will be as a communicator—especially in a crisis.

Very often, your audience will need to repeat your message to someone else so that the third person can make the decision. If the listener didn't hear your message clearly, she can't repeat it to that decision maker. She'll invariably deliver a twisted version of the message, not intentionally but because she didn't hear your main point *as the message.*

Staying on message is also the best way to deal with other voices that want to twist your central idea for their own purposes. You've chosen language that advances the agenda you want and frames the discussion to meet your needs. Having a short, sensible message that you can repeat easily and that will stay with the audience is your best defense to that offense.

Keeping your message short also helps you circle back to it when you are responding to questions. If possible and appropriate, it's best to wrap up your answers to questions with ". . . and that's why [message]" whenever you can.

You can easily ground your thoughts if you have a clear central idea. Routinely, when speaking to a high-stakes audience, such as the press or a large swath of the public, we can get flustered and lose our train of thought. Having a clear, concise point helps us get out of the weeds and return from a tangent to get back on course.

Your choice of language will increase or decrease the crisis. Sometimes, depending on your goal in a debate, you may want to escalate the sense of crisis. Doing so involves the right word selection. If you want people to pay stronger attention to your information, frame it in terms of how it impacts an individual rather than as a data point.

Nobel prize–winning economist Daniel Kahneman, in his 2011 book *Thinking, Fast and Slow*, shares how framing an issue can determine the audience's reaction to it.[2] If you are trying to downplay an issue, frame it purely as a number, which doesn't engage an audience emotionally. Saying "The vaccine carries a 0.001 percent risk of disability" does not elicit the same level of concern as saying "One child in every 100,000 will be permanently disabled by the vaccine." The second framing of the issue causes individuals to immediately think of that one child and creates a heightened level of concern. Speaking in terms of relative frequency of a rare occurrence makes the event seem more likely than speaking of it in terms of absolute probability. You can use your word choice to promote the use of vaccines by talking about numbers or discourage it by creating a sense of crisis.

The same approach will be employed against you by the media, depending on whether they support your position or object to it. Go on CNN's website and scroll down the column of headline banners. At least one or two will read, "John Doe *Breaks His Silence* about X." "Breaks his silence" suggests he has been dodging questions, holding back, or somehow prevented from speaking until now. The tone creates a sense of urgency—I am suddenly curious to read what John Doe has to say, even though I wasn't aware I had been interested before seeing that headline. It also creates a sense of scarcity; apparently, someone's been depriving me of John Doe's thoughts until now. It's basic economics that scarcity increases the value of things, even if those things are the opinions of someone we don't know.

If you are representing a client and want their thoughts noticed in a crowded, frenetic news cycle, have your client "break their silence." It's more interesting than you "issuing a press release."

The same is true when your client "speaks out," rather than just "speaks." "Speaking" isn't particularly challenging for most people and isn't noteworthy. "Speaking *out*" suggests taking a stand, perhaps at some personal or professional risk, even though, technically, it's just speaking.

Media outlets that want to help get your message out will use the "breaking his silence" or "speaks out" approach even if you don't position your information that way.

The flip side is when your client has been screaming from the mountaintops but to a press that is hostile to their position. In that case, the media will instead use "finally comments on" to describe any statement you issue, even if you comment on an issue within a reasonable time frame.

In both cases, the media are trying to redirect the audience's attention away from the *substantive issue* and toward *your client's responsiveness* to the issue. If the media's behavior is in your favor, run with it. If their positioning makes your job more challenging, respond to the comment calmly. Assert that you have responded timely and reiterate your message.

Back Up Your Message with Substance

A message itself is a conclusion. In fact, sometimes it's just an opinion. It carries weight because of the clout of the person saying it or because of the data behind it. You can "prove" a message in two ways: by sharing evidence, or by referencing an authority.

Share Evidence to Bolster Your Message

Evidence to support your message comes in the forms of stories, anecdotes, facts, examples, and statistics. When a client is experiencing a crisis, you need evidence that everything will work out—both when speaking to the client and when speaking on the client's behalf to other parties.

Stories and their shorter cousins, anecdotes, resonate with all of us.[3] Before widespread literacy, the history of cultures was captured in their stories. When you tell the story of what happened to your client, or what happened because of your client's actions, think in terms of how the story will impact the listener's senses. Listeners need to experience a story; we experience events through our senses. Is there a way to tell your client's story that will transport the listener to the moment? What would they see if they had been there? What would they hear, smell, touch, or taste? The more vividly you can anchor the story with sensory elements, the more it will impact the listener.

Stories have a structure—a beginning, a middle, and an end. The beginning usually positions the events in time or place.

"On a cold evening, two years ago, just before Thanksgiving . . ." evokes an image more than "On November 17, 2016. . . ."

Avoid being overly dramatic with lines like "It was a dark and stormy night" unless you want to be compared to Snoopy.

All stories end with a line that tells you the story is over. Aesop's Fables, from ancient Greece, all end with "and the moral of the story is. . . ." They hit you over the head with the message and tell you the events are concluded. Fairy tales end with ". . . and they all lived happily ever after" to accomplish the same goals.

"That's why you must acquit" or "So, again, my client is cooperating fully with the government in this investigation" tells the audience you've finished with your story.

The middle will vary in length and in subtle ways based on your needs in the moment. Which details you include and the way you describe them might change depending on the audience.

Stories don't need to be long or elaborate—usually, shorter is better.

An *example* is different from a *story.* Think of stories as "past tense" and examples as "future tense." An example could be posing a hypothetical or creating an image of what *would happen* in the future if the client took certain action. Examples can create powerful images for audiences. However, talking about the future usually requires making allowances for numerous variables. The further you get from the known facts when creating an example of future impact, the less powerful your example becomes.

Facts are data points, such as the number of votes cast for a candidate in an election, the number of people poisoned by an E. coli outbreak, and the number of gallons of oil leaked from a tanker. It should be hard for someone to contest them. The tricky part with facts is how they are put into context. After the financial collapse in 2008, I worked with countless clients on presentations where they had to share dismal performance numbers with their boards. They needed to present numbers in context. Many of the presentations sounded akin to: "We lost $500 million last quarter, which is good news because we had anticipated losing $800 million."

What sounds like *bad* news on its face is *good* news when put in context.

Statistics are amalgamations of data points that allow you to bolster an argument. Stats are powerful tools, but when using them to defend a client in crisis, be prepared. An experienced challenger will ask the underlying questions that might undermine the value of the stats. There's a quote usually attributed to British prime minister Benjamin Disraeli: "There are three kinds of lies: lies, damned lies, and statistics." Statistics can be used and manipulated to support just about any premise. Every large law firm tries to market itself as "the biggest and the best." The devil is in how they qualify the statistics. "We're the biggest and the best . . . at M&A in telecom, in New York, on Tuesdays." The validity of stats lies in the qualifications.

Let's pull the ideas of stories and statistics together. There's a great quote that a senior leader used in a moment of crisis. "One death is a tragedy. A million deaths is a statistic." He knew the story of one person's struggle and ultimate loss tugged at heartstrings and left a powerful impression, and also that statistics are so overwhelming they seem more like reference points. It's a powerful lesson to learn about bolstering your message. Now comes the context. The quote was, of course, by Joseph Stalin, who said it to *dismiss* concerns that his massacre of his own people would provoke outrage. Lesson learned.

Whether to use a story, an example, or a statistic will be driven by two elements: What's the most dramatic and readily available to you, and what is your client's bent—intellect or emotion? First, in any given situation, you may not have an easily packaged story that proves your point, references something with which your client is familiar, and provokes a strong reaction. You may need to find a statistic that will work instead. In other cases, the opposite will be true—statistics may not support your argument as well as one very dramatic, recent, high-profile example. Use what you've got.

Second, if you know your client well, you'll have a sense of whether that person will be more persuaded by a story that pulls at emotions or echoes quantitative analysis of a situation. If your client is more persuaded by emotion, and you have a dramatic story available that supports your point, leverage that. If your client has a more intellectual bent, be ready with the statistics, assuming there are some at your disposal.

How do stories and similar devices come into play during a crisis? Let's look at the various contexts.

If you are dealing with a client in crisis, a story or an example of how others overcame similar challenges can help calm your client. Similarly, if your client is insisting on taking a course of action you think will lead to disaster, a story of similar results can help them see the folly of their ways.

If you are speaking on behalf of your client who is under attack, you'll use statistics to blunt the scope of the matter, as mentioned above in the section on messaging, or tell stories that divert the focus of the conversation. When you frame your situation in comparison to a well-known event, you start to control the narrative. If you represent a family whose teenager has been shot by the police, you heighten the sense of crisis by saying, "It's *Ferguson* all over again." The #MeToo and Black Lives Matter movements are examples of strength in numbers and in comparison. Regardless of the type or extent of harassment or abuse someone has suffered, by attaching the #MeToo characterization to their story, they are now included in the world of longtime, systemic, often violent victimization. The plural "Lives" in Black Lives Matter ties a single event to a greater, horrific whole.

Here, too, the language you choose is important. Let's say your client is a large, global company accused of covering up the evidence of its faulty widgets. The press will immediately dub the situation "Widget-gate" to draw parallels to the Watergate coverup and to heighten the sense of crisis. In this case, your goal is to reframe your challenge to minimize the perceived scope and lessen the severity. When they call it "Widget-gate," you politely draw a clear distinction and refer to the "simple procedural inquiry" with which you are "fully cooperating." Tone remains important as well. Responding to allegations of "Widget-gate" with "WITCH HUNT!" won't help you much in the long run.

Leverage Authority

Your main authority in some instances will come from your own status. (Think of every exasperated parent's fallback argument: "Because I said so!") Between college and law school, I spent two years teaching English at a high school in Kingston, Jamaica. In addition, I lived at and helped run a nearby orphanage. I was barely older than some of my students and was often overwhelmed by the needs of the boys at the orphanage. But at school, I had the imprimatur of "teacher," and at the orphanage I was a de facto authority figure. Both gave me status, which gave me authority. As the attorney of record in a matter, as the policy director of whatever agency you serve, or as the assistant district attorney, you have inherent clout. (Of note: the above example of teaching and working at the orphanage is less than eighty words. Anecdotes don't have to be long to accomplish the goal.)

The other authority you can leverage is your own command of the facts and the law. There is no substitute for being prepared. Many lawyers and other professionals can bluff well. But even they come across with even greater confidence when *they know* they know their stuff.

Referencing a statute, citing a detail the rest of the audience doesn't know, or quoting an authority on the topic can enhance your credibility in the moment, and communicating in a crisis is all about getting from one moment to the next. When I was dealing with both teenagers and parents who were in crisis, I had the benefit of knowing the law. I was a relatively new attorney, so I didn't know *a lot* of law, but I knew what I needed to know, and I knew more than the other person. When dealing with clients in crisis, it helped me give them confidence. When dealing with other parties, it let me speak with confidence in the face of confrontation.

Sometimes a blanket statement such as "Studies have shown that . . ." will bolster your position, whether you're trying to decrease or heighten the sense of urgency.

To see how many of these elements converge, consider the case of the awful murder of Mollie Tibbetts in Iowa and the thoughtful, beautiful, passionate, and compassionate letter from her father. Mollie was killed by a Hispanic, undocumented man. The senseless crime was used by some to try to galvanize support for tougher immigration laws. As threats were made against the local Hispanic population, Mr. Tibbetts wrote a letter for the local paper to deescalate the crisis. As the father of the victim, Mr. Tibbets has ultimate clout when speaking out. His message was delivered with calm, dignity, and directness. He even used occasional humor, which always cuts through the anger that often imbues a crisis with sincerity. Most important, he spoke from the heart. He seemed to be channeling his daughter's spirit in his message rather than a lawyer's carefully crafted statement, but it's something from which anyone—lawyer or not—can learn about how to react in a crisis.

Address the Emotion

Communicating during a crisis is complicated because, in a crisis, the emotions of those involved are by definition heightened. It's important to address those emotions before dealing with the facts. Every attorney on the losing side of a case, on the steps of the courthouse, acknowledges, "Of course, we're disappointed. But we will be appealing." They address that emotions are involved. When leaders of the US Federal Emergency Management Agency stand before the microphones after a flood, fire, tornado, or other disaster, they don't rattle off statistics. They begin by acknowledging that they are working in communities that are in pain, that are suffering, and that need help and reassurance. For most people, emotions are stronger than reason. If you don't deal with the emotion, the other person can't hear or process the rational argument that actually fixes the problem.

There are three steps to addressing emotion in a conversation.

First, name the emotion. In professional contexts emotions are often considered illegitimate:

This is work.
This is business.
I should not bring emotions to the workplace.

That's ridiculous. People get emotional all the time at work. They are happy when things are going well. They are upset and stressed when deadlines are missed or budgets are exceeded.

Emotions are especially an issue when your clients are in crisis. They themselves are in the news. Their neighbors know they work for Enron or the other corporate pariah of the moment. When the economy collapsed in 2008, some of the companies that were expected to receive a bailout told their employees not to carry any bags or wear any garments that identified them as associated with the company, at least until the crisis abated.

We can't ignore that emotions are involved in all aspects of our lives. When we name the emotion, we give it credibility. In a way, we give it the respect it deserves:

I know you are frustrated.
I understand your doubt.
I hear your skepticism.

When we name the emotion, we let the other person know that we understand that this issue isn't just about facts—it's about feelings. This puts the technical issue in perspective. Naming the emotion also allows you to manage this aspect of the conversation, meaning you get to decide, in subtle ways, what emotion is being addressed. Your job when helping a client through a crisis is to deescalate the crisis. To that end, there's one emotion you should avoid naming. When someone is angry, don't say, "I know you're angry." It's been my experience that line will elicit one of two responses:

RESPONSE #1:
"Damn right, I'm angry! I'm pissed."

Now you've elevated the tension and made your job more difficult.

RESPONSE #2:
"I'm not angry! I'm not angry!" said defiantly and angrily.

Once someone has denied the obvious emotion they feel, you can't address it, and it becomes the undercurrent that colors the rest of the conversation.

If you are struggling to identify the emotion in the situation, or if the other person is genuinely angry, reframe their emotion as "concern." "Concern" is a great catch-all for emotions. In general, people don't enjoy feeling angry. It's a painful emotion, and it's exhausting. When you reframe "anger" as "concern," people often feel a sense of relief. You're helping them deal with this uncomfortable emotion by showing them they are rightfully "concerned" about the issue. A few people will push back and say, "I'm not *concerned*! I'm furious!" But most will opt for feeling "concerned." By the way, I understand your concern that this might seem like manipulating people's emotions. In fact, you're helping them manage their emotions so you can deal with the underlying problem.

Second, relate to the person. If emotions are in fact legitimate, it's appropriate that you, as another human being, should feel them too. Therefore, take a moment to close the gap between you and your audience—whether it's your client or a more public setting—and accept the emotions as understandable.

Try simple statements like "I, too, would feel this way if I were you" or "I thought so as well when I first heard this news."

You'll then create the needed space to resolve the emotion by offering a way out.

"I thought so as well, until I learned about X." You proffer more information as the key to how you overcame the anxiety you felt, akin to what the audience feels now.

When you relate to the other person, do so only if you can do so sincerely. If there's no way you can identify with what the other person is expressing, don't try it. You will both be, and appear, disingenuous. That will undermine your credibility.

Third, leave out "But" or "However" after acknowledging the other person's emotions or the mood of the public at large. "But" and "However" have a magical way of destroying all the goodwill you created when you named the emotion and identified with the person experiencing that emotion. Those words undermine the value of what came beforehand.

If I say to you "I know you're frustrated with this situation. However, . . ." I run the risk of sounding dismissive. The message conveyed is "I don't really care." When I go to walk downstairs dressed for an event and my wife says, "Honey, that's a really nice tie, but . . ." it doesn't matter what's coming next. I'm changing my tie.

Avoiding "but" and "however" are especially important when apologizing, and they aren't the only way that people qualify their contrition. In a corporate setting, leaders apologize only when it's been made clear that they have offended wide swaths of people. When the apology is framed as "*If I have offended anyone*, I am sorry," it comes across as tone-deaf. Are you not aware that you have offended someone? Is there any doubt as to your misstep?

On September 13, 2018, my wife, Mary, took my Jeep into the dealership for a routine service check. The dealership changed the oil, rotated the tires, and checked the brakes. A few hours later, Mary picked up the Jeep. Five minutes into the drive home, she felt the car shake violently, so she slowed down moments before the front driver's-side wheel came off the car, shot across a lane of oncoming traffic, and landed in a reservoir. Mary, an excellent driver, managed to maintain control of the Jeep and pull to the side of the road to safety. What could have been a tragedy was reduced to a harrowing story of survival.

When the tow truck brought Mary back to the dealership so she could get a replacement vehicle, the young, somewhat panicked attendant efficiently completed the paperwork for the loaner car but acknowledged what had happened by simply saying, "Yeah. I heard"—which didn't go over well with Mary.

The next day, the service manager at the dealership called. He apologized profusely, expressed his understanding of how serious the incident was, and took full responsibility. Had he not addressed the emotion in the situation, my subsequent discussions with the dealership would have been very different. (For instance, I would be mentioning the name of the dealership in this book.) From a customer service perspective, the service manager did the right thing. What about from a legal liability perspective?

The service manager knew no one had been hurt. Had someone been injured in the incident, creating the very real threat of a lawsuit, should he have taken a different course of action? Some lawyers would advocate that, had someone been injured, the dealership should refer any questions or comments to their attorneys and not speak directly with the injured parties. In this case—a tire falling off a car shortly after the tires were rotated—there was such a clear indication of liability that it's unlikely that an acknowledgement or denial of guilt would impact the outcome of a lawsuit. In other cases, where liability isn't as obvious on its face, what should a lawyer do? Short answer: talk to your client. Is there an ongoing relationship between the parties involved? Is there a base level of trust? Would an apology and an acknowledgement of responsibility heighten that sense of trust and thereby decrease the likelihood of a lawsuit?

Studies have shown that if doctors apologize for mistakes, they decrease the chance of a medical malpractice claim.[4] Strong doctor-patient relationships are built on trust. Patients are invested in the relationship. In general, we all accept that people make mistakes. When someone we trust makes a mistake, we forgive and move on. If there is no trust, or simply no relationship, we're less likely to be forgiving. As attorneys, it's important for us to understand human dynamics in general, as well as the relationship between our client and the other party in a conflict in order to guide the client appropriately.

When I worked with teenagers in crisis, I routinely saw young adults decide to return to family situations that were unhealthy. Sometimes, I knew they were choosing the lesser of two evils—returning to a family situation that was unsupportive but tolerable, or going into foster care, with its inherent uncertainty. ("The devil you know. . . .") But often, understanding their choice was a matter of being less strategic and more sympathetic. Everyone, no matter what his upbringing or life situation, understands that the desired human experience is to grow up in a safe, loving, nurturing family. Just because a teenager's life experience hasn't provided him with that situation doesn't mean that person has given up hope on finding that. *Hope* on the part of our clients sometimes gets in the way of them hearing our sound legal advice. We need to be aware of the emotion underlying our clients' decisions and address those emotions in order to give our clients sound advice.

Emotions don't come into play only with teenage clients. Let's say your corporate client is facing bad press because of a product malfunction, the bad actions of a corporate executive, or the unanticipated consequences of its advertising campaign. The general counsel or chief communications officer who contacts you has spent the last few hours being yelled at by everyone in the C-suite and dodging calls from the press. They are stressed. Stress is an emotion. You have to be the sympathetic ear, the steady voice, the strategic counselor—in that order.

Let's say you are counsel to the mayor of Atlanta in mid-2020, as violent protests erupt as a result of the police killing of George Floyd. You might advise your client to address the protests rather than the police brutality that led to the violence, to leverage her platform as the city's ultimate "law and order" authority figure. But to restore order, Mayor Keisha Lance Bottoms spoke from the heart, not the handbook. She addressed other parents of young Black men with sympathy and understanding and equal fury. Addressing the emotion in the situation first allowed her to address the strife in the city with strength. Addressing only the protests and not the underlying emotion would have only exacerbated the situation, not deescalated it. That's why understanding your client and their relationship to the audience is essential to navigate the crisis and determine how liability from a legal perspective fits into liability from a reputational perspective.

Offer the Other Person a Semblance of Control over the Conversation

People don't like to be "talked at," especially when they are in an emotional state. If, after acknowledging the emotion in the situation, you say to someone "Let me tell you why that's not the case" or "Here's why we did things that way," you're talking before they may be ready to hear you. You run the risk of coming across as controlling and pushy. Instead, offer the other person options. People feel helpless and frustrated when they feel they don't have control over a situation.

The parents I would deal with out on the sidewalk often felt as vulnerable as their child when he or she ran away from home. Now, in addition to any other chaos in their lives, they were threatened with someone—the state, a child-care agency, me—interfering in their relationship with their own child. To help them calm down, I needed to give them some semblance of control in the moment. I couldn't give them control over the *situation*, but I could give them control over the *conversation*.

If instead you ask, "Would it be helpful if I explain how we got to this point?" then the other person gets to make a decision. Making decisions implicitly puts us in charge in the moment. If the other person says, "Yes, that would be helpful," you can now explain the situation. If he says, "No, that's not helpful," you respond with, "What would be helpful for you to know?" Again, you're not giving up control of the situation, only the conversation.

Sometimes you have to run through this conversation loop a few times for the person to start calming down. Eventually, the other person hears your message and begins to focus on what can be accomplished.

This process works well not only when you are dealing with an individual experiencing a private crisis but also when you are addressing the press in the midst of a public crisis. When you are addressing the media, you're not addressing the reporters in the room; you're addressing the audience they reach. While you don't have control over how they eventually share your message, you'll have the best outcome if you still follow the process outlined above. Name the emotion. Relate to the audience if appropriate. Avoid "but," "however," and any other words or phrases that qualify the integrity of the emotion. In the case of a press conference, it's not appropriate to ask permission before you explain the situation. Instead, you can begin by stating, "I think it may be helpful to you if I explain the following." Then provide your response. This has a more open tone than saying, "What I want you to know is. . . ." You come across as trying to facilitate a solution rather than push an agenda. In almost all cases, it's best to avoid "What I want to tell you is. . . ."

The other word to avoid in a crisis is, "Look. . . ." "Look" has become the go-to beginning of many statements and is usually delivered with a tone that says "Shut up and let me talk," and it is often accompanied by the condescending finger-jab. Listen to any of the panel discussions on FOX, CNN, or MSNBC. As the moderator goes around the horn asking for input, more than half the time the speaker starts with "Look . . ." which creates an antagonistic tone and suggests everyone is at battle. If your goal is to come across as a reasoned professional who aims to move the discussion forward, you want to decrease the tension, not heighten the anxiety.

I have referenced throughout this chapter my conversations with the parents of my client, the teenager at the shelter. In those conversations, I was speaking as an attorney directly with the "opposing side" in a conflict. You could argue that I should have told the parents, "Go get an attorney and I'll speak with that person, but not directly with you." That would simply never have happened, and it's where reality and the suggested legal structure collide. Every lawyer is actually a "lawyer/something else," with the "something else" determined by her or his area of practice:

Lawyer/Social Worker
Lawyer/Marriage Counselor
Lawyer/Family Therapist
Lawyer/Claims Adjuster
Lawyer/Corporate Raider
Lawyer/Scientist

When I worked at the shelter, I was a lawyer/social worker, representing a client who usually wanted some kind of family reunification. When I practiced insurance law, I was a lawyer/claims adjuster, albeit on a large scale for multimillion-dollar professional liability claims. Even in that situation, I had to keep in mind the relationship of the parties and that the way I handled the conversation could impact the ongoing business between my client and the other party.

It's not just a matter of picking one of two hats to wear in a given situation. Our role exists on a spectrum, with a bit of both roles at play in every conversation. One of the challenges we face when communicating with or on behalf of our clients during a crisis is how to leverage the skills of both elements of our role to guide them through the process.

Control Your Emotions

In most human interactions, you get what you give. If you project negativity or defensiveness, that's what you get in return. If you project calm and openness, you're more likely to experience the same from the other person. Your own calm demeanor makes it hard for the other person to continue to be combative. Calm is not the same as passive or disengaged. It means you manage your body language, facial expressions, and tone of voice to project involvement, interest, and commitment. Consider the following:

Breathe

If you are about to face the cameras at a news conference or meet with a reporter inquiring about a client's behavior, take a moment beforehand to take a few deep breaths. This will help you center yourself and calm your nerves. Especially if you don't consider yourself to be an anxious person, you may not realize the higher levels of adrenaline running through your body before you go in front of the cameras or speak to the press. You'll be surprised how you can feel your heart rate slow down and your nerves abate if you just take a moment to relax your breathing. Try what's called "square breathing." Breath in for four seconds. Hold your breath for four seconds. Exhale slowly for four seconds. Wait four seconds before inhaling again. Two or three rounds of this breathing method before you enter a conference room, walk on stage, or meet with a client on the verge of a meltdown will help you maintain your composure and remain the calm voice in the room. When I met with clients or parents in crisis, my ability to stay calm helped the other person to eventually do the same.

Manage Your Body Language and Tone

Avoid any body language that can be perceived as controlling or closed off. Relax your arms by your side and keep your hands open rather than clenched. If you put your hands in your pockets, you can appear to be too relaxed or disengaged. If you fold them across your chest, you might be misperceived as remaining closed off from other ideas.

Equally important (if not more important) than the actual words you speak is your tone. These cues will affect how others interpret what you say. You can come across as self-assured and assertive or as tentative and uneasy. Many people have adopted a habit referred to as "upspeak" where their voice inflects up at the end of a sentence, suggesting they are asking a question rather than making a statement. It's a manner of speaking that is more prevalent among younger generations and is often intended to make the speaker sound more conciliatory and less forceful. Unfortunately, it can also come across as less confident or poised, which can undermine your message.

The easiest way to minimize upspeak is to use crisp gestures when speaking. Your gestures don't need to be large or over the top. They merely need to be definitive.

The vocabulary equivalent of upspeak is "qualifying language." Qualifying language is any phrase that qualifies the integrity of the content we are sharing. The most common examples are:

"Kind of"
"Sort of"
"Basically"
"Essentially"

If I say "It's *basically* X," I'm telling you "it's not X. It's near X, or in the vicinity of X, but it's not X." If I say that to the press during a crisis, the first thing a competent journalist would ask is: "What's the gap between X and where we are?"

There are so many times when we as lawyers must qualify our statements. We'll never tell a client "You will win the case." We can't guarantee it. As a result, we often adopt a more qualified tone and approach in general. However, that doesn't serve us well in a crisis. It's not helpful to tell a client in crisis "We probably need to do X?" with our voice inflecting up at the end as if it's a question. If we're speaking to the press, it isn't helpful to say "We're sort of upset with the court's decision? We're going to appeal?" You can't advocate with questions, and you aren't leading unless you sound sure of yourself.

Maintain Your Eye Contact

Looking down at your notes when someone is asking a question or challenging an idea can make you seem dismissive. Look at your notes when you need to while you are speaking, but look at individuals when you are both delivering your content and listening to their questions.

The best way to manage your eye contact and settle your nerves simultaneously is to speak to one person at a time for a full thought. When you're talking to that one person, he or she is the only person on the planet at that moment. If you scan the room, you will notice all the activity around you. You'll either get distracted or become overwhelmed. If you talk to one person, you're much more likely to adopt a confident, conversational tone and appear more comfortable with yourself and your surroundings. If you look comfortable with yourself in front of the camera, you'll be more convincing.

If you are speaking to the media, focus on and talk to that individual reporter, not her ultimate readers or listeners. If you are giving a statement on camera, envision a single individual listening to you on the other side of the lens, not the mass audience you might be reaching. It's not in the normal human experience to speak to thousands or tens of thousands of people. There's no way to do that and sound natural. Instead, just talk to one person at a time, or envision one—ideally friendly—face. You'll bring a stronger, more confident voice to that conversation.

Be Conscious of "Personal Space"

If you move too close to someone when they are in crisis, you can come across as threatening. If you move away from someone who has asked a tough question, you can be perceived as evasive. Find a comfortable distance from the other person and maintain that distance during the discussion.

Stay Focused in the Face of Distractions

In a crisis, focus on the most important elements to be addressed. The Hollywood films *The Right Stuff* and *The Martian*—both about NASA scientists dealing with crises in outer space—provide great lessons on how to act during a crisis. One line used in both movies is "Work the problem." Space is only somewhat less forgiving than the press can be, and the dangers of a vacuum are as tangible whether you are in orbit or are facing a microphone and can't think of what to say next.

You "work the problem" differently if you are helping your client through the crisis or addressing the press on behalf of your client.

When dealing with your client, your job is to constantly remind the client of the real issue at hand. You are likely to see that problem more clearly than the client because he or she is in crisis and you are not. As side issues arise, you must have a very clear sense of what's important, so you can decide in the moment if that's something to address or to table until later. If you know yourself well enough to realize that you can sometimes allow your attention to wander, or unwisely try to deal with multiple issues at the same time, you'll serve yourself and your client better by resisting such impulses. Warren Buffett once said, "Make two priority lists. List A contains your top priorities. Your goal should be to never deal with List B." The instinct for some of us is to try to manage everything at once. Bad idea. How do you know what's most important? Listen to your client. If you've done a good job listening up front, asked the right questions, confirmed your understanding of what's important, and checked in again occasionally, you'll know where to put your energy. Once you and the client agree on what's most important, you can make an informed decision about what *not* to address.

In the case of communicating with the press in a crisis, you "work the problem" first by controlling the message by defining the problem. You can change the audience's view of the crisis by characterizing your response to it. Politicians are masters of this, as are the panels of commentators on the evening news. Each side frames the issue presented in a way that supports its position.

Second, you "work the problem" by ignoring the tangential issues. If you're giving a press conference and the press is trying to get helpful, accurate information to the public, you'll listen carefully to their questions and respond as succinctly as possible. In that setting, their questions aren't side issues; they are the main reason for your briefing. If you're dealing with a hostile press, their questions are intended to derail you or to reframe the issue in their own preferred language. In that case, simply repeat your message so that you continue to control the dialogue.

Earlier in this chapter, I discussed ways to respond to tough questions. Keep in mind that questions that begin with "Wouldn't you agree that . . ." or "Don't you think that. . . ." aren't questions at all. They are statements by the interviewer thinly disguised as questions. The interviewer wants you to commit to a statement worded in a way that gives the interviewer the exact sound bite they are seeking. When you hear a question that asks you to confirm language you didn't use, be very leery of agreeing. Instead, reaffirm your main message.

Conclusion

During a crisis, everything is heightened—awareness of timing constraints, the importance of snap decisions, your adrenaline. You'll perform better in the moment if you've honed a clear and simple message, stick to that message and repeat it often, address the inherent emotion in the situation, manage your own emotions by staying calm, and avoid getting sidetracked.[5]

NOTES

1 N.Y. Executive Law §532.

2 For Kahneman's discussion of framing, see, DANIEL KAHNEMAN, THINKING, FAST AND SLOW 334–76 (2011).

3 The U.S. Supreme Court has echoed these sentiments:

A syllogism is not a story, and a naked proposition in a courtroom may be no match for the robust evidence that would be used to prove it. People who hear a story interrupted by gaps of abstraction may be puzzled at the missing chapters, and jurors asked to rest a momentous decision on the story's truth can feel put upon at being asked to take responsibility knowing that more could be said than they have heard. A convincing tale can be told with economy, but when economy becomes a break in the natural sequence of narrative evidence, an assurance that the missing link is really there is never more than second best.

Old Chief v. United States, 519 U.S. 172, 189 (1997).

4 Jennifer K. Robbennolt, *Apologies and Medical Error*, 467 CLIN. ORTHOP & RELAT. RES. 376 (2009).

5 The author acknowledges the assistance of Allison Barrett of Exec|Comm, LLC, in the preparation of this chapter.

Conclusion

RAY BRESCIA AND ERIC K. STERN

Whether it is dealing with hostage negotiations, climate change, critical incidents at sea or on land, police violence, pandemics, or human rights violations, lawyers are, more and more, thrust into situations of crisis. Sometimes they are asked to utilize their understanding of the law to provide crisis-response services; sometimes they are asked to bring law and the rule of law to situations of crisis; sometimes they must look outside the law to address such crises. Regardless, their legal training, experience, and the ability to take a clear-eyed measure of a situation—assessing both immediate and long-term ramifications of action and inaction—can serve to provide effective ethical guard rails, useful leadership skills, and good judgment in crisis situations. However, it is also important to recognize that other lawyerly "virtues" and professional cultural traits such as risk aversion, rule-following and enforcement, perfectionism, and inaccessible professional jargon can create obstacles to crisis problem-solving and make lawyers unwelcome, marginalized, and isolated in crisis teams and organizations. In order to understand the ways in which crisis lawyering is different from traditional lawyering, we wish to examine a series of questions that we believe help to illuminate these differences. These questions, and their implications, follow:

How Do Lawyers Define a Crisis Situation in Their Work and Does This Vary Depending on the Context?

The first concept to emerge from the contributions to this volume is that crisis lawyering, though similar in some respects to traditional lawyering, does have unique features that differentiate it from what most lawyers do in their day-to-day work. For most individuals and organizations, in many instances in which a lawyer is enlisted to help address a problem, that problem may seem like a crisis to that individual or entity. The individual is being charged with a crime and faces the prospect of a prison sentence. The organization is the subject of an investigation by a government agency that could result in a large fine or an order to cease doing business. Two inventors fight over the origins and ownership over a patent. To these individuals and the employees or share-holders of the companies, these situations might seem like crisis situations. For lawyers, it is their stock-in-trade. For many lawyers, these types of situations are those for which their legal training prepares them. Their problem-solving skills and judgment are put to use to resolve the disputes, hopefully bringing them to a successful resolution for the lawyer's client. In the traditional context in which lawyers find themselves, they generally enjoy a high degree of dis-tinctly relevant experience, salient training, and sufficient time and resources to help resolve the problem utilizing a range of skills, from the formal legal skills of legal analysis, oral advocacy, negotiation, and persuasive writing to softer skills like exhibiting emotional intelligence and maintaining one's poise under some degree of pressure. Even when the stakes may be high, and a client may face the prospect of conviction and a significant sentence, or a company may face bankruptcy in the event of an adverse ruling on a matter of intellec-tual property or in a dispute over its business practices, the lawyers' training, expertise, judgment, and the experience he or she brings to the conflict all prepare the lawyer for handling the matter, regardless of the outcome.

In the crisis situation, by contrast, the stakes may be just as high as in the traditional context (and they are always high), but there are a range of vari-ables that differentiate the crisis situation from the traditional problem the lawyer is asked to solve. First and foremost, the crisis situation tends to unfold *on a much more compressed or accelerated time frame* than the traditional legal problem space. When combined with the high stakes, this tends to accentuate and amplify atypical pressures on the lawyer to make critical judgments and render advice without the luxury of reflection and some degree of profes-sional and critical distance from the problem. The crisis time frame demands rapid analysis and decision-making. This time frame, when coupled with the high stakes, makes for a particularly volatile combination of forces bearing down on the lawyer and those with whom he or she is working to resolve the crisis situation. Another feature of the crisis problem is that the state of the law is often unsettled. A death penalty case is, by all measures, a serious context in which to practice law (the most serious, perhaps), but the law and practice of death penalty defense—relating to the criminal charges faced, the evidence that the lawyer must gather and review, the trial practice maneu-vers—is all fairly well settled. Indeed, even in such situations where there is a degree of novelty to the problem the lawyer is asked to address, there is a ten-dency toward path dependency in the lawyer's approach to them. The lawyer has developed mental models and a practical approach to problem-solving in the context that he or she may alter in response to changed facts and cir-cumstances, but the general approach is mostly well-honed and time-tested, giving the lawyer a set of tactics and strategies from which to chart a course toward resolution of the problem before him or her.

In contrast, a critical component of crisis lawyers is the unsettled and uncertain nature of the facts, risks, client interests, laws, and policies that may come into play during a crisis situation. Given the unsettled nature of the crisis situations that crisis lawyering must resolve, there may be little guidance or training that helps a lawyer maneuver within and through them. Each crisis is, in a way, unique, presenting novel challenges and threats. And yet, as these pages suggest, there is a repertoire of crisis lawyering skills that lawyers who work on crises—from such radically different practice areas as serving as counsel to governments and media outlets to representing immigrants in detention and homeless people living on the streets—that appears to emerge from a case- or career-retrospective review of the work such crisis lawyers do on a day-to-day basis. This exploration of the contexts and conditions under which lawyers work in crisis mode helps us to understand better—and contribute to specifying—the practice of crisis lawyering itself.

Who Is the Client in Crisis Lawyering?

In traditional lawyering, the client is often easy to identify. An individual or organization comes to the lawyer with a discrete problem that the client wants solved. Perhaps the lawyer works with the client on an ongoing basis, as in-house counsel, or is simply on retainer. The lawyer makes him- or herself available to the client in service of that client's current needs. Once the dust settles and the problem is solved or resolved, the lawyer may sit down with the client and try to plan to avoid the problem recurring. In most instances, while the lawyer and client should consider the likely consequences of a client's course of action on third parties, the concerns tend to center around making decisions in light of the best interests of the client. While the potential ramifications of a particular course of conduct on third parties, and whether those third parties might have recourse against the client if their rights and interests are affected, the lawyer's client is always at the center of the calculus, and the lawyer will focus mostly on the client's interests over those of third parties. This focus on client interests, whatever the problem or the solution, presupposes the fact that the traditional lawyer typically knows who he or she is serving and where the primary duty of professional care resides. Furthermore, the lawyer strives to develop clear lines of communication with the client so that the lawyer knows just what the client wants and when she wants it: at the outset of the representation, as that representation moves forward, and when it concludes.

Few of these conditions reliably hold in crisis lawyering. First of all, the lawyer in the crisis lawyering context may not always know who the client really is in a given crisis. When Richard Pinner worked as an advocate in New York City during the mid-1980s in efforts to stem the rising tide of homelessness, he worked with the Coalition for the Homeless to bring class-action litigation against the city to try to establish a right to shelter in that jurisdiction. Finding actual clients among the street homeless was fairly difficult. The homeless population is by nature transient and prone to displacement. Pinner was representing the homeless per se, but he was also pressing the perspective of his organization while simultaneously pursuing the interests of the residents of New York City, many of whom cared about the plight of the homeless on a humanitarian level, and also those residents who were likely concerned about the public safety and public health ramifications of street homelessness. Similarly, Eleanor Stein served as an administrative law judge in New York State, managing a process by which the state sought to overhaul the manner in which it regulates the consumption of energy in that jurisdiction to reduce the impact of greenhouse gasses on the environment. As one of the largest economies in the world, New York's energy consumption makes an impact on the global climate. Who was Judge Stein's client in that situation? Can a judge have clients? When Christy Lopez, a lawyer with the US Department of Justice, worked on analyzing conflict situations involving local police and communities of color in Ferguson, Missouri, her client was technically the US government, but she had to balance the needs of that client, the interests of the community, and the relationship among federal, state, and local public safety officials. The explicit goals of her work were to investigate the facts of police interactions with members of communities of color that resulted in violence, in addition to helping rebuild trust and develop strategies for improving police-community relations. Who is the client in these situations? It is sometimes hard for the crisis lawyer to know.

Similarly, lawyers embedded in crisis field teams, such as the leadership team of the Federal Emergency Management Agency (FEMA) Joint Field Office, are charged with supporting the Federal Coordinating Officer in charge but also report to the Office of Chief Counsel and face unique professional duties to ensure compliance with regulations, policy, the law, and ultimately the Constitution. When FEMA leaders "push the envelope" and test the boundaries of their authorities in responding to acute humanitarian needs—or attempt to cut red tape or other administrative corners in the interest of crisis expediency—lawyers may experience turbulent crosscurrents and dilemmas of divided loyalties. Furthermore, lawyers may observe breaches of ethics or other forms of wrongdoing and face conflicts between collegiality and professional obligation to "blow the whistle." Note that these issues also arose in parallel fashion for the Swedish government lawyers (described in chapter 13) engaging in crisis lawyering, despite differences in the substantive legal framework, organizational structures, and political-administrative culture.

Are the Ethical Rules Governing Lawyer Conduct and Standards of Care (Diligence) Relaxed in Crisis Situations?

Given that crisis lawyering often involves high-stakes matters that must be resolved in a compressed time frame under conditions of uncertainty, does and should crisis lawyering occur within a different ethical framework than traditional lawyering? The touchstone of professionalism for the lawyer is that he or she is expected to provide, at a minimum, competent services and must have adequate training and supervision to provide services that meet that baseline ethical standard. The crisis lawyer, by contrast, must operate in contexts in which it might be impossible for the lawyer to practice and prepare for such situations; indeed, even the best training or supervision may not prepare the lawyer to navigate novel situations of extreme uncertainty and high risk that emerge along a rapid, condensed time frame. The rules governing lawyer conduct generally appear to lower the level of training and supervision that are required in routine settings where the stakes are low. In such low-risk settings, the degree of experience and oversight is relaxed where a lawyer can develop the competence to handle the matter with some ease.[1] There, we still expect the lawyer to perform at a basic level of competence, but we recognize that, when the stakes are low, the matter is not complex, and the lawyer can understand what is expected of him or her with little effort, then it is fairly easy for the lawyer to satisfy his or her ethical obligations to provide competent services in such settings.

At the same time, when a lawyer finds him- or herself in a crisis situation, is it appropriate to relax the requirement of competence, just as we would in a low-stakes setting where one can easily provide a basic level of care? Paradoxically, it might be that a higher standard of care might be expected when the stakes are high, as in crisis situations. But given the time frame within which a lawyer must act, and the unsettled nature of the legal issues that the lawyers must confront in crisis situations, is it appropriate to lower expectations and provide crisis lawyers with some leeway to make reasonable decisions given the situation—with all of its intendent pressures—and thereby create a new standard of competence appropriate for such situations?[2] Whether one is negotiating for the release of a kidnapped journalist, as contributor David McCraw does with surprising regularity in his work on behalf of the *New York Times*, or obtain freedom for an immigrant child being held in detention without access to a parent, as Sarah Rogerson does in her day-to-day crisis lawyering work, is it appropriate to raise our expectations, and the duty of care, for such lawyers? Or is it more aligned with the spirit of the rules governing ethical conduct to relax such requirements in such settings?

Some guidance regarding this issue may be found in the world of operational (e.g., military, police, and emergency management) law. Where operations take place at a rapid pace, legal advice must keep up with that pace lest the crucial decisions be made anyway—and without the benefit of even the most basic legal guidance. To the extent that issues are foreseeable and recurring, drawing upon well-developed and established opinions can help to speed up the process and enable well-prepared lawyers to keep up even in very high tempo operations. When problems are urgent, novel in important respects, and presenting in an organization or jurisdiction for the first time (which are all too common phenomena in crisis situations as we have defined them), lawyers face a common dilemma: provide advice that is "quick and dirty," or be sidelined and provide no advice at all. In such situations, there is reason to believe that lawyers (and those who evaluate them and hold them accountable) may need to rethink their views of professional quality to take crisis operational tempo and working conditions into account. Note that the medical profession has made provision for this, introducing notions such as crisis standards of care, triage, and wilderness medicine. All of these reflect the idea that excellent professional performance may look very different at a mass casualty site or a remote field location as opposed to a planned procedure at a top-notch medical facility.[3]

What Are the Potential Value Conflicts and Conflicts of Interest That Emerge in Crisis Lawyering That May Not Arise in Traditional Lawyering Settings?

Crisis lawyering can create unforeseen and novel conflicts that the traditional lawyer rarely faces. One of the main reasons for this is that crises are rarely discrete, such as the problem a client may bring to a lawyer in the traditional lawyer-client relationship. The crisis lawyer must wrestle with the impact that a given crisis situation has on clients, for sure, but given the nature of crises and their cascading impacts in contexts characterized by complex interdependencies, there are often third parties who are deeply affected by a client's actions or inaction. These broader ramifications can sometimes place the crisis lawyer in a bind. As noted above, the traditional lawyer in private practice owes a duty of loyalty to his or her client, yet the crisis lawyer sometimes faces conflicting duties, duties that are imposed on him or her based on the professional role the lawyer fills. But the crisis lawyer might also feel the moral weight of decisions he or she must make in situations where there is a high risk of harm to the broader community from a client's actions. This can sometimes create conflicts between the crisis lawyer's professional role and, quite simply, his or her humanity. In a traditional professional setting, the lawyer may (and sometimes must) consider the ramifications of his or her actions, in addition to those of the client, on third parties. Sometimes the consequences of the lawyer's actions on third parties can be profound: A prosecutor may work to confine a criminal defendant for the rest of his or her life; a bankruptcy filing on behalf of a client could wipe out the holdings of a fund that invests in the company that could represent the pensions of former employees. In the crisis situation, given what is at stake and the potential consequences of client action or inaction in a given setting, the potential impact of the crisis lawyer's decision on third parties is almost always significant, which is another of the hallmarks of crisis lawyering. Given that crisis lawyering typically involves the risk that third parties will face significant consequences from a lawyer's decision regarding his or her client's current and future course of conduct, the crisis lawyer might feel an undertow from the conflicts that arise in such settings; this real likelihood of third-party harm in the crisis situation means the crisis lawyer will likely take into account that harm when counseling a client. In the traditional lawyering setting, the advocate may consider the prospect of third-party harm in order to minimize the risk his or her client will be held to account for such harm. In the crisis lawyering setting, the gravity of the potential harm to third parties justifies the lawyer taking that harm into account directly and conscientiously. These consequences are to be avoided in their own right, not merely because of the potential second-order effects on the lawyer's own client.

What is more, in movement lawyering crises, where the law is unfair and civil disobedience may be justified, this creates a potential conflict between the lawyer's duty to uphold the law and ethical imperatives to the client(s) to work to change the law, including counseling the client to violate the law. Sometimes the lawyer feels compelled to violate the law him- or herself. Another classic dilemma—one that often arises for government lawyers—has to do with the situation where the law (or lesser rules and policies) have been set up with a different situation in mind and the law/rules become an obstacle to solving the problem. For example, should a lawyer demand that a client follow normal purchasing rules and competitive bidding procurement processes in dire, time-sensitive situations (e.g., humanitarian disasters such as Hurricanes Katrina and Maria) where materials are needed for saving lives? What about cases where security concerns may come into conflict with individual rights and liberties? What is more, Baher Azmy and hundreds of colleagues defending Guantánamo detainees often found themselves on the other sides of such decisions, often fought against their consequences, and had to take dramatic actions—and risks—to resolve the tragic dilemmas that had been created.

How Do Lawyers Ensure Effective Lines of Communication in Crisis Situations?

Crisis situations, by their nature, are situations of high risk that must be resolved within an extremely accelerated time frame. Crisis lawyers must develop situational awareness, take into account the actual and potential risks to clients and third parties, make decisions with incomplete information, and make those decisions quickly. Because he or she is still a lawyer, the crisis lawyer must strive to develop meaningful lines of communications with clients so as to understand those clients' interests and needs and obtain any guidance they might offer the lawyer as to the course of action that he or she should take. But what if the crisis lawyer cannot speak to his or her client? Muneer Ahmad and Michael Wishnie recount their efforts to bring litigation to oppose the application of the travel ban imposed by the Donald Trump administration during its first days in office when their clients were cordoned off and held incommunicado in a facility at John F. Kennedy International Airport. Similarly, Baher Azmy and the lawyers who represented detainees held at Guantánamo Bay had to commence litigation even to identify and speak with their clients. What these and other contributors show is that developing effective lines of communication with clients in crisis lawyering situations is not only imperative given the stakes and the time pressure of representation in such situations; it is often difficult if not impossible. Note that in the high-pressure and high-tempo environments typical of operational law—such as the military, law enforcement, and emergency management—and given the many demands on the time and attention of the leaders that lawyers are tasked to serve, lawyers may also find it difficult to gain access to the leaders they are supposed to advise and/or get a seat at the table where critical decisions are being made. This may be particularly difficult where stereotypes of lawyers as naysayers who erect obstacles to swift and decisive action prevail. This was a recurring challenge in both the US and Swedish contexts explored in chapter 13 by Eric K. Stern, Brad Kieserman, and their coauthors.

In addition to communication with clients, as spelled out by Jay Sullivan in chapter 16, lawyers in many settings (government and corporate) will need to work with communications professionals regarding internal and external messaging. The FEMA and Swedish Legal Advice in Crisis projects described

in chapter 13 found that mutual understanding and close collaboration between lawyers and communicators is helpful in making sure that communication is not only legally correct and sustainable but also effective in reaching
a variety of nonlawyer target groups as well as protecting the "brand" and
legitimacy of the organization. As Sullivan points out, taking responsibility
for organizational mistakes or negligence and doing what is required to maintain viability in the court of public and media opinion may require publicly
assuming responsibility and maintaining degrees of transparency that likely
increase legal (and possibly financial) exposure in court.

What Expertise Must a Crisis Lawyer Possess in a Given Crisis Situation?

Carrie Bettinger-López's client faced a situation many lawyers face: it seemed
like she was out of options. While only a handful of clients see their cases
resolved by the United States Supreme Court, Bettinger-López's client had
sustained her fight to the nation's highest court, but she lost there, finding
any road to formal, domestic recourse foreclosed. But being out of domestic
options did not mean it was the end of the proverbial road. Bettinger-López
brought her client's case before an international tribunal and saw the practices
that were at the center of her client's lawsuit declared a violation of international law. Sarah Rogerson's clients—immigrants in detention—seemed to
have few options as well, but such limitations forced Rogerson and her colleagues to generate more creative solutions to address their clients' needs.
What is more, Lee Wang and the lawyers who fought to make the courthouses
safe spaces for their clients ultimately had to engage in acts of civil disobedience because they had pressed their clients' interests to the limits of the law
and beyond. Traditional lawyers typically find their clients in situations the
lawyers have seen before, and those lawyers have time-honored strategies for
helping their clients address those situations. Crisis lawyers, in contrast, often
find their clients in situations where the path forward may be uncharted.
Given the nature of the work, crisis lawyers face novel situations of extreme
complexity and must react to them within a limited time horizon. They must
often develop expertise in a given subject-matter area implicated in the crisis
quickly. They might turn to experts in the given field (if any exist) for guidance. They often have to assimilate knowledge from other professionals, as in
the natural disaster setting, or they might have to create knowledge that did
not exist before, sometimes creating a new field of law as the crisis unfolds, as
was the case with the work of the Guantánamo Bay Bar Association.

How Do Crisis Lawyers Interact with Leaders and Other Constituencies in Crisis Situations, Including Other Professionals and Individuals from Other Disciplines?

The results of the case studies in this volume suggest that these issues tend to be intertwined, so we will discuss them together in this section. The high stakes involved in crisis lawyering and the truncated time frame within which decisions must be made require effective communication between the lawyer, constituents, leaders, third parties, and anyone who can help the lawyer gather information and respond to it effectively. In very different settings, John Travis Marshall (disaster recovery) and David Turetsky (election day lawyering) show how important functioning lines of communication are in crisis situations: across disciplines, with advocates and adversaries. While the traditional lawyer certainly needs effective lines of communication with critical constituencies, the nature of crisis lawyering casts in high relief the importance of efficient and effective lines of communication to bring information to the lawyer about the nature of the crisis and its risks, as well as to communicate information to critical constituencies about the tactics and strategies that will be used to carry out the lawyer's legal guidance.

Facilitating coordinated approaches to complex, multidimensional, multiagency problem-solving of the kind described in chapter 12 by Brian Johnson and Nora Wilson on Maritime Operational Threat Response requires lawyers to work under crisis or quasi-crisis conditions with a broad range of generalists, experts on sometimes arcane subject-matter areas, professions, and domestic and international legal specialties. These will vary considerably across issues such as modern piracy, human trafficking, migration, maritime cyberattacks, outbreaks of infectious disease at sea, major narcotics or fisheries violations, and others. These lawyers are engaged in a time-sensitive effort not only to interpret the law but also to deploy it as one dimension of a broader effort to promote interagency information-sharing and enhanced situational awareness. They seek to identify and weigh agency priorities and national interests while seeking to forge a consensus regarding courses of action and the division of responsibility among agencies with regard to the implementation of policy. Parallel issues emerge for FEMA lawyers working in Joint Field Offices comprising a broad range of federal agency representatives grouped into various emergency support functions under the National Incident Management framework, state government officials, and other societal actors involved in response and recovery efforts with regard to natural disasters as noted in chapter 13 by Stern and Kieserman and their coauthors.

John Travis Marshall in chapter 7 and Eleanor Stein in chapter 8 describe efforts to address climate change and its impacts, which is a complex problem requiring complex solutions; lawyers may find themselves out of their depth when it comes to climate science. In such crisis settings and many others, lawyers must rely on expertise from other disciplines, and this can often become a hallmark of crisis lawyering itself: the crisis lawyer must often work and learn to communicate with other professionals (communications professionals, engineers, medical doctors, scientists, public health officials, military officers, law enforcement, fire and rescue services, etc.) in order to develop a complete understanding of the risks inherent in the crisis situation and to craft solutions to address and minimize those risks in an effective and holistic way. In crisis situations, legal solutions are rarely the only solutions that will address the problem. This often means that the crisis lawyer must come to the crisis situation with a degree of professional humility—to recognize his or her own limitation when it comes to understanding the crisis, as well as the solutions that might emerge that could potentially respond to it. The crisis lawyer must also identify and develop a familiarity with, and even the vocabulary of, the disciplines that might aid in his or her work in resolving any given crisis. One of the critical elements of legal practice generally is for the lawyer to "know what she does not know." In the crisis lawyering setting, it is imperative for the lawyer to recognize that the depth of his or her knowledge about crisis situations and potential solutions to address the risks of such settings runs deep and that the real limitations on the lawyer's knowledge mean that he or she must not only communicate with but also rely on the expertise of other professionals.

Are There Common Guiding Principles for Crisis Lawyering That Emerge from These Contributions?

Scott Westfahl in chapter 15 and this concluding chapter help to define some of the contours of crisis lawyering as a field of practice. Crisis lawyering is a product of the nature of the situation the lawyer finds him- or herself in, given the stakes, the risks, the time pressures, and the consequences of action and inaction. Given these components of crisis lawyering, a picture of the field emerges from the narratives and images portrayed in these pages. Crisis lawyering requires a lucid situational awareness; a problem-solving orientation; a critical knowledge base of the legal and practical ramifications of the client's conduct and options for future decision-making; well-developed ethical judgment; an appreciation for the real and potential risks inherent in the situation; clear lines of communication both within an organization and the broader community that enable the free flow of information and tactical direction; a willingness to enlist guidance from disciplines outside the law; and the humility to take into account the perspectives and expertise of those other disciplines.

Can One Plan and Train for Crisis Lawyering?

If crisis lawyering is a new field of practice, is there specific education and training that a lawyer can undertake to plan to work in this field? Muneer Ahmad and Michael Wishnie, Scott Westfahl, Brian Wilson and Nora Johnson, and Eric Stern and his coauthors help to identify some approaches that have proven effective when it comes to training law students and lawyers to engage in crisis lawyering. There is no substitute for experience in crisis lawyering, and a crisis lawyer gains experience by engaging in the field of crisis management, as the contributions to this work demonstrate. Yet as the questions set forth in this conclusion seem to indicate, and even though every crisis has its unique features, crisis lawyering involves a set of practices and generic approaches to crisis situations that tend to be helpful across a broad range of crises.

Because crises present extraordinary challenges to lawyers and it is critical to "get it right the first time" in complex, dynamic, high-stakes processes and events, it seems prudent to leverage actual experience with virtual experience through dedicated education, training, and exercises—all of which are relatively underdeveloped in today's legal community, and not just in the United States. The results of the FEMA and Swedish Legal Advice in Crisis projects described in chapter 13 suggest that in-service training and exercise methods largely developed for crisis preparedness writ large (as well as for other educational purposes) can be helpful. Lawyers can further develop their understanding and ability to work with other professions under crisis conditions through tailored role-plays, teaching cases, simulations, red-teaming, and other similar techniques. These enable lawyers to practice and develop crisis skills and role empathy and to hone the ability to interact heedfully with teammates from other professions in high-tempo and high-pressure situations.

For example, the Maritime Operational Threat Response functions described by Wilson and Johnson in chapter 12 have benefited from regular "war games," including not only sharing lessons learned from previous cases but also scenario exercises in which lawyers have the opportunity to work with other professionals to rehearse and practice interagency problem-solving skills relevant to crisis management.

Returning to the literature on crisis leadership described in the introduction to this volume, crisis lawyering also faces the following challenges: preparing, sense-making, decision-making, meaning-making, ending and accounting, and learning. As we have seen throughout this volume, the authors describe the many ways they have grappled with these challenges in their work.

Preparing involves having systems in place to respond to crises as well as a disposition toward effective crisis management; understanding the role that leaders and lawyers play in such management; and a commitment to addressing the crisis in a meaningful, effective, ethical, and legitimate way. The experiences described by our authors take place in a variety of contexts, ranging from ad hoc to highly organized, planned, trained, and rehearsed, although the old adage that "no plan survives contact with the enemy" demonstrably applies to highly prepared contexts as well when it comes to crisis lawyering. Many of the chapters throughout this work address questions related to the authors' varying degrees of preparedness for crisis, as noted in the immediately preceding discussion of planning and training.

Experience and anticipation are also key elements of preparedness for crisis situations. In some lawyering contexts, one may know that the crisis is coming. In fact, the lawyer might know the season in which certain types of disasters are more likely to occur and /or receive a few days' warning regarding heightened risk. She might know more or less when a hurricane is going to hit and might have a good sense of its strength and projected trajectory, and she can try to prepare and plan accordingly. If she practices in an area like election law, such as David Turetsky, she may know the exact day on which election law issues will require an emergency response. Even when a lawyer who may deal with crisis situations may not always know the exact day on which a crisis will occur, the nature of the lawyer's work—whether it is David McCraw's efforts on behalf of the *New York Times* or Baher Azmy's advocacy as a human rights lawyer—may mean that he or she is thrust into crisis situations with some regularity. And though the nature of the crisis may change, maintaining one's composure in the face of such crises is critical to effective crisis management. Given the nature of the work, the knowledge that such crises are likely to occur is perhaps the best preparation for crisis situations. At the same time, however, the crisis may be completely unforeseen, in which case the nature of the crisis requires creativity and commitment to the lawyer's core values and dedication to pursuing the client's best interests in uncertain settings and against long odds, as reflected in the experiences of Sarah Rogerson, Lee Wang, and Muneer Ahmad and Michael Wishnie. Similarly, other forms of natural disasters such as earthquakes and tsunamis as well as crises sparked by human adversaries or other forms of adversity may manifest with little or no notice and may require lawyers to ramp up their efforts very abruptly.

The second challenge is that of *sense-making*. When facing this challenge, lawyers may be involved in responding to warning signals and/or warning others regarding impending/escalating crises; clarifying the core values and identifying stakeholders relevant to the case; identifying and critically evaluating historical analogies/precedents; and identifying alternative scenarios (e.g., worst-case, most likely, best-case). In this regard, lawyers can play a key role with regard to sense-making as demonstrated by Brian Wilson and Nora Johnson's chapter regarding interagency coordination of maritime threat response. Lawyers can help determine which agencies, missions, statutes, and national interests are relevant to the problem at hand. Lawyers in that space play a key role in developing institutional memory and serving as repositories of precedent that can help to clarify and guide crisis policy-making. Similarly, such precedents can serve as historical analogies helping to clarify alternative options and scenario trajectories for the case. Similarly, in the election law context, David Turetsky emphasizes the need for lawyers to maintain situational awareness at individual polling stations and to contribute to statewide situational awareness by their reporting. This role includes monitoring warning signs of irregularities or inefficiencies that might influence voting. Turetsky's findings, like those of Stern and Kieserman and their coauthors in the Advice in Crisis project, emphasize the importance of proximity and centrality; it is critical to get in early and seek a seat at the table in order to be able to keep track of the information flow and detect problems as soon as possible to maximize one's potential to influence the course of events in positive ways. Similarly, the FEMA lawyers and their counterparts in Sweden as described by those same authors play a critical role in developing situational awareness and clarifying stakeholders and core values in disaster/crisis response and recovery. Furthermore (and this is relevant to both sense- and decision-making), lawyers play an indispensable role in clarifying the range (and boundaries) of permissible action by identifying authorities, prohibitions, and ethical imperatives that enable and constrain government action in crisis.

The next challenge lawyers in crisis situations face is *decision-making*, which entails developing technical expertise in bodies of law relevant to the situation; serving as a wise counselor who engages in problem-solving; engaging in risk assessment; serving as a mediator and consensus-builder; overseeing effective processes; and sometimes managing operations. Christy Lopez, in her work at the US Department of Justice confronting a crisis in police-community relations, helped to play a critical role in moving communities toward decisive action to overcome systemic and chronic injustices. Eleanor Stein, in her work as a judge facilitating an administrative process involving many stakeholders with diverse interests, helped to move the parties toward consensus on how to address the critical issue of climate change, which involved process monitoring, mediation, management, and decision-making throughout the process. In terms of natural disaster management and response, John Travis Marshall described his work to create a long-term recovery response to a crisis that entailed many instances of critical decision-making.

Lawyers in crisis situations often play a critical role in *meaning-making* and *messaging*, which often involve issue-framing as well as shaping strategic narratives. This can also entail advising and participating in symbolic actions and behaviors that arise in crisis situations, like mourning, commemoration, mobilization, and apology. Lawyers often play a part in these rituals, particularly from a legal perspective. The chapters contributed by Jay Sullivan and Muneer Ahmad and Michael Wishnie describe effective communications strategies in crisis situations that help reframe the context in ways that are beneficial to the client, may help defuse the situation, or may (conversely) heighten tensions to create space for change and effective interventions. Stern and Kieserman and their coauthors elaborate on the ways in which lawyers can participate in such practices to ensure they reflect and incorporate appropriate understandings of the legal perspective on the crisis, while recognizing that effective crisis management is likely to require balancing legal and other political or reputational concerns. Similarly, Caroline Bettinger-López, Baher Azmy, and Lee Wang in their contributed chapters describe the efforts of lawyers in different crisis situations to bring attention to those situations through both traditional and unconventional advocacy strategies, helping to highlight injustice while shaping a narrative of empowerment surrounding their advocacy. Christy Lopez faced challenges of communicating the proper role for the Department of Justice in interjecting itself into a local crisis situation that had national ramifications. Carmen Huertas-Noble and her coauthors similarly reframed crises of health disparities as embodiments of racial and economic inequality and have developed effective legal crisis-management responses to the injustices their client-communities face.

Lawyers in crisis situations also must confront the challenge of *ending* and *accounting*. As some of the examples in this volume reveal, identifying the "end" of the crisis can itself be a challenge. Baher Azmy was able to secure freedom for his client, but there are still detainees held at Guantánamo. Muneer Ahmad and Michael Wishnie's team had to decide when it was time to pass along the crisis-intervention work with respect to the acute crisis it faced to other teams. Caroline Bettinger-López followed her client's lead on when the crisis had *not* ended, even though most lawyers would likely accept that she had come to the proverbial end of the road—that is, when the client lost her case before the Supreme Court. And sometimes a crisis is not over, even though the lawyer's role in addressing it for the time being may come to an end, as reflected in the work of Eleanor Stein. She continues to work on climate-crisis response efforts in her work, but the specific case on which she worked as an administrative law judge has come to its conclusion. Similarly, Richard Pinner's work advocating on behalf of the homeless in New York City continues through the work of many others, even though the initial efforts reached some obvious milestones—like victories before New York State's highest court in which the fundamental right to shelter under the state constitution was established.

Finally, although lawyers in crisis situations typically do face a degree of novelty in each crisis situation, effective crisis lawyering involves *learning* from the crisis and developing systems to respond to similar crises in the future (which would bring the lawyer back to the "preparing" challenge). Scott Westfahl, John Travis Marshall, and Muneer Ahmad and Michael Wishnie all are explicit about their efforts to "train for crisis," which is also reflected in the chapters by Stern and Kieserman and their coauthors. What is more, the entire effort of this volume has been to draw lessons from the different crisis lawyering contexts described here so that we may learn from them and be better prepared—as lawyers and leaders—to respond to crisis situations.

But crisis lawyering, as the experiences recounted here indicate, is really an approach, one that requires a particular set of skills more than a body of knowledge. That approach is one that manifests itself in professional humility; a willingness and an ability to gather and assimilate information rapidly and in an open-minded way; a commitment to communication with clients, constituents, community leaders and representatives, and affected third parties; and, above all, an understanding of the lawyer's role in crisis situations—both its capacities and its limitations. The contributions to this work paint a vivid picture of what this crisis lawyering approach entails so that lawyers, and the individuals, entities, and communities they serve, will understand the critical role lawyers can and must play in addressing and resolving crises. In the wake of COVID-19 and ongoing and pervasive threats to the rule of law, the need to cope with crises looms ever larger as a challenge and imperative for contemporary society in general and lawyers in particular. We hope that this work has made it clear that lawyers have had and will continue to have a crucial part to play in this effort and must be prepared for action, effective in their service, courageous in defending values, comprehensive in their approach, and wise in their judgment even when facing issues shrouded in the fog of crisis.

NOTES

1 *See* AMERICAN BAR ASSOCIATION, MODEL RULES OF PROFESSIONAL CONDUCT, Rule 1.1, Comments 1 & 2 (Aug. 2018) (describing level of legal skill and training required in a given situation depends on what is at stake and the complexity of the matter).

2 For example, under the FEDERAL RULES OF CIVIL PROCEDURE, a lawyer and party can be sanctioned if their conduct lacks merit or a good faith basis after an inquiry "reasonable under the circumstances," thus recognizing that these rules require a level of attention and thoroughness that varies with "the circumstances." FED. R. CIV. PROC. 11 (2017).

3 For a discussion of standards of care for medical professionals in crisis situations, *see, e.g.,* Lawrence O. Gostin & Dan Hanfling, *National Preparedness for a Catastrophic Emergency: Crisis Standards of Care,* 302 J. OF AM. MED. ASS'N 2365 (2009).

ACKNOWLEDGMENTS

Ray Brescia and Eric Stern wish to thank, primarily, the contributors to this volume as well as the University at Albany and Albany Law's Affiliation Committee, particularly Ann Marie Murray and Connie Mayer. They are also grateful to the research assistants who worked tirelessly on bringing the project to fruition: Alex-Marie Baez, Claire Burke, Jake Eislano, Hannah Hage, Lauren McCluskey, Francis Pellicciaro, Victoria Soracco, and Lauren Wilt.

The work was made possible in part from a grant from the University at Albany and Albany Law School Innovation Fund, for which the editors are grateful.

Ray would like to thank the many mentors and friends, some of whom contributed to this volume, but also Harold Hongju Koh, Robert Solomon, and Doug Lasdon, who taught him how to lawyer through crisis. He is also grateful to his colleague Sherri Meyer for her tireless support, as well as the assistance of the staff at the Albany Law School library and its Information Technology Services department.

Eric also wishes to thank the outstanding University at Albany CEHC Research Faculty and Staff, Swedish Defense University, Swedish Civil Contingencies Agency, Brad Kieserman, and FEMA OCC (for getting him interested in this topic in the first place), as well as Per-Åke Mårtensson, Torkel Schlegel, the Swedish Crisis Lawyers network, and the contributors to this volume for helping to sustain and renew his interest in studying and teaching crisis lawyering. Eric would also like to acknowledge the contributions of Dr. Gregory Saathoff of the University of Virginia and Patrick Walsh (formerly of the University of Virginia) to the original FEMA Advice in Crisis Project, a precursor to this work.

The editors and contributors would especially like to thank Clara Platter and the team at New York University Press who were willing to support the vision for this work and see it through to publication.

ABOUT THE EDITORS

RAY BRESCIA is the Hon. Harold R. Tyler Chair in Law & Technology and a Professor of Law at Albany Law School. He practiced law in New York City and New Haven at the Legal Aid Society of New York, where he was awarded the prestigious Skadden Fellowship; New Haven Legal Assistance; and the Urban Justice Center, where he was the Associate Director. He also clerked for civil rights icon Constance Baker Motley, a federal judge in Manhattan. He is a graduate of Yale Law School and Fordham University. His scholarship covers social change, technology, and social justice. He is the author of *The Future of Change: How Technology Shapes Social Revolutions* (Cornell University Press, 2020) and the coeditor, with John Travis Marshall, of *How Cities Will Save the World: Urban Innovation in the Face of Population Flows, Climate Change, and Economic Inequality* (Routledge, 2016). His legal scholarship has appeared in such law reviews as *Oregon Law Review, Georgia State Law Review*, and *Kentucky Law Journal*. His opinion pieces have been published by the *Washington Post, National Law Journal, Huffington Post*, and *Slate*.

ERIC K. STERN is Professor of Political Science at the College of Emergency Preparedness, Homeland Security and Cybersecurity at the University at Albany (SUNY). Dr. Stern holds a PhD from Stockholm University and a BA from Dartmouth College. He has published extensively in the fields of crisis and emergency management, crisis communication, resilience, security studies, executive leadership, foreign policy analysis, and political psychology. He is also affiliated with Swedish Defense University, where he served as Director of the National Center for Crisis Management Research and Training (CRISMART) from 2004 to 2011. Stern served as a Principal Investigator for the FEMA Office of Chief Counsel [Legal] *Advice in Crisis Project* (2010–2012) and has provided intensive crisis management training to hundreds of government lawyers in the United States and Sweden. His book *The Politics of Crisis Management: Public Leadership Under Pressure* (Cambridge University Press, [2005] 2017) is a winner of the American Political Science Association's Herbert A. Simon Award. Other key areas of interest and expertise include social media and crisis preparedness, postcrisis

397

evaluation and learning, interactive education and instructional design, and case research/teaching methodologies. In addition to his scholarly work, Professor Stern has collaborated closely with a number of international organizations as well as European, Asian, and US government agencies on a wide range of applied research and educational—including training and exercise development—projects.

ABOUT THE CONTRIBUTORS

CHRISTOPHER ADAMS is a Supervising Attorney in the Community & Economic Development Clinic at the CUNY School of Law, where he provides transactional legal services and technical assistance to cooperatives, not-for-profit organizations, and associations that intend to pursue equitable economic development. christopher.adams@law.cuny.edu

MUNEER I. AHMAD is Deputy Dean for Experiential Education, Sol Goldman Clinical Professor of Law, and the Director of the Jerome N. Frank Legal Services Organization at Yale Law School. Muneer.ahmad@yale.edu

BAHER AZMY is the Legal Director of the Center for Constitutional Rights, a national litigation, advocacy, and educational institution dedicated to the use of law to promote progressive legal change. bazmy@ccrjustice.org

CAROLINE BETTINGER-LÓPEZ is a Professor of Law and Director of the Human Rights Clinic at the University of Miami School of Law. clopez@law.miami.edu

ELLA CARLBERG is an attorney at he Swedish Civil Contingencies Agency and currently seconded by the Swedish Civil Contingencies Agency to the Swedish Embassy in Washington, DC. Ella.Carlberg@msb.se

CARMEN HUERTAS-NOBLE is a Tenured Professor of Law and the Founding Director of the Community & Economic Development Clinic at CUNY School of Law. carmen.huertas@law.cuny.edu

NORA JOHNSON is the Director, Office of Incident Management, at Transport Canada. nora.johnson@tc.gc.ca

BRAD KIESERMAN has been the Vice President for Disaster Operations and Logistics at the American Red Cross since June 2015. He previously served as Chief Counsel of the Federal Emergency Management Agency (FEMA), among other leadership and operational legal roles at the Department of Homeland Security, FEMA, and the United States Coast Guard. brad.kieserman@redcross.org

CHRISTY E. LOPEZ is a Professor at Georgetown Law Center since 2017, after seven years serving in the Civil Rights Division of the United States Department of Justice. cel105@georgetown.edu

JOHN TRAVIS MARSHALL is an Associate Professor at Georgia State University College of Law, where he teaches Environmental Law, Land Use Law, and Property Law. John is coauthor of *Market Demand-Based Planning and Permitting* (with Arthur C. Nelson, Julian Juergensmeyer, and James Nicholas) (ABA Press, 2017) and coeditor (with Ray Brescia) of *How Cities Will Save the World* (Routledge, 2016). jmarshall32@gsu.edu

PER-ÅKE MÅRTENSSON is a veteran Swedish Police Commander with nearly thirty years' experience including SWAT and Counterterrorism duty. He played a key role in developing the Swedish Crisis Legal Advisors Training Course at the Swedish Defense University. PerAke.Martensson@fhs.se

DAVID E. McCRAW is Senior Vice President and Deputy General Counsel of The New York Times Company, where he is the lead lawyer for newsroom affairs and heads up the company's international crisis response. He is an adjunct professor at New York University Law School and a visiting lecturer at Harvard Law School. He is the author of the book *Truth in Our Times: Inside the Fight for Press Freedom in an Age of Alternative Facts (St. Martin's/ All Points Books, 2019)* a first-person account of the legal fights behind some of the *Times*'s biggest stories. mccrad@nytimes.com

RICHARD PINNER is the Associate General Counsel at the Local Initiatives Support Corporation, the nation's largest non-profit community development financial institution. He worked on homeless rights litigation, focusing on the rights of homeless mentally ill individuals, while at the Coalition for the Homeless and in private practice between June 1987 and September 1990. rpinner@aol.com

MISSY RISSER-LOVINGS is a Visiting Professor of Law and Supervising Attorney in CUNY Law School's Community & Economic Development Clinic, where she provides legal and policy support to community-led organizations that redress structural inequities faced by marginalized populations. missy.risser@law.cuny.edu

SARAH ROGERSON is the Director of the Justice Center at Albany Law School, where she is also a Professor of Law and runs the Immigration Law Clinic. sroge@albanylaw.edu

TORKEL SCHLEGEL is Senior Legal Adviser at the Swedish Civil Contingencies Agency and served for many years as the head of the agency legal division.

ELEANOR STEIN has taught Law of Climate Change: Domestic & Transnational, and Climate Change in the Courts, at Albany Law School and the State University of New York at Albany since 2005. eleanorstein16@gmail.com

JAY SULLIVAN is the Managing Partner at ExeclComm, LLC, and leads the firm's Law Firm Group. He is the author of the book *Simply Said: Communicating Better at Work and Beyond* (John Wiley & Sons, 2016). jsullivan@exec-comm.com

DAVID S. TURETSKY is Professor of Practice at the University at Albany's College of Emergency Preparedness, Homeland Security and Cybersecurity and an affiliated faculty member at Albany Law School. He has held senior roles in government, business, and law practice. dturetsky@albany.edu

LEE WANG is the Director of Strategic Initiatives at the Immigrant Defense Project and founding member of the ICE Out of Courts Coalition in New York State. lwang@brooklynbailfund.org

SCOTT WESTFAHL, is a Professor of Practice and the Director of Harvard Law School Executive Education. He is the author of *You Get What You Measure: Lawyer Development Frameworks and Effective Performance Evaluations* (NALP, 2008). Professor Westfahl earned his JD from Harvard Law School in 1988 and graduated summa cum laude from Dartmouth College in 1985. swestfahl@law.harvard.edu

BRIAN WILSON is the Deputy Director, Global Maritime Operational Threat Response Coordination Center, US Coast Guard/US Department of Homeland Security, a Visiting Professor at the United States Naval Academy, and a Nonresident Fellow at the Stockton Center for International Law at the US Naval War College. brianstwilson@gmail.com

MICHAEL J. WISHNIE is William O. Douglas Clinical Professor of Law and Counselor to the Dean at Yale Law School. Professor Wishnie's teaching, scholarship, and law practice have focused on immigration, labor and employment, habeas corpus, civil rights, government transparency, and veterans law. michael.wishnie@yale.edu

INDEX

ABA (American Bar Association), 134, 188n41, 314–15

Abolish ICE movement, 154

Abolish Prisons movement, 161

"abolish the police" demands, 74

ABPCo (Association of Pro Bono Counsel), 156

Abraham, Steven, 60n59

Abu Ghraib, 40

accounting and terminating, 5, 393

ACLU. *See* American Civil Liberties Union

ACT UP! movement, 215

acute policing crises, 75, 79–85, 101

Adams, Christopher, 7, 229, 399

Addario, Lindsay, 119–21

Advice in Crisis (AIC) Project, FEMA/Swedish Legal Advice in Crisis, 286–87, 290–94, 304–7, 341, 392

Afghanistan, 44, 50, 56n13, 59n47, 109–18, 160

African Americans: Black Lives Matter movement, 366; in Chesterfield Co., Virginia, 2008 presidential primary, 258, 261; mass incarceration of, 36, 247n7; "personal responsibility" argument aimed at, 86, 101; policing crises and police reform, 71, 73–74, 76, 77, 366, 371–72; worker cooperatives and, 229, 234, 236, 239. *See also* Ferguson, DOJ and policing crisis in

Ahmad, Muneer I., 7, 36, 52, 53, 311, 386, 390, 391, 393, 394, 399

AIC (Advice in Crisis) Project, FEMA/Swedish Legal Advice in Crisis, 286–87, 290–94, 304–7, 341, 392

AIDS/HIV and homelessness, 211, 214–17

Akuno, Kali, 247n7

al Dosari, Jumah, 45

Al Jazeera, 112

Al Odah v. United States (2009), 40

al-Assad, Bashar, 123

Albany, State University of New York at: College of Emergency Preparedness, Homeland Security and Cybersecurity, SUNY Albany, 269–70, 286n6; relationship between Albany Law School and County Sheriff's Office, de-

velopment of, 149, 150–52. *See also* Detention Outreach Project

Alberts, David S., 5

al-Qaeda, 42, 43, 45, 50, 58n24, 59n46, 61n72, 61n77

Alshawi, Haider Sameer Abdulkhaleq, 311, 320, 321

"alternative facts," 361

Amazon (company), 247n9

American Bar Association (ABA), 134, 188n41, 314–15

American Civil Liberties Union (ACLU): on Ferguson policing crisis, 66, 67, 68, 97; on Guantánamo detainees, 46, 58n42; immigrants and IRP (Immigrants' Rights Project), 149, 311, 319, 320, 333, 338n4; John Adams Project, 58n42; on voter protections, 255; WPR (Women's Rights Project) and domestic violence, 17, 20, 21

American Declaration on the Rights and Duties of Man, 21–22

Amnesty International, 46, 66

Amsterdam, Anthony, 37, 41

anchor institution strategy for worker cooperatives, 235, 246

AniBioThreat (European Union U 7th Framework Program), 303

Anthony, Susan B., 261

Anthropocene, 194, 203n18

ArchCity Defenders, 67, 72, 88, 93, 97, 104n37

Arendt, Hannah, 51

arrests and crime rates, lack of correlation between, 91, 106n58

ASAP (Asylum Seeker Advocacy Project), 327, 339n8

Associated Press, 108

Association of Pro Bono Counsel (APBCo), 156

Asylum Seeker Advocacy Project (ASAP), 327, 339n8

Australia, 38, 46, 121, 201, 271, 273

azidothymidine (AZT), 217

Azmy, Baher, 6, 32, 385–86, 393, 399

Gandhi, Priya, 155
Garner, Eric, 71
Gelernt, Lee, 322
General Motors ignition switch recall, 353
Geneva Conventions, 35, 46
Georgia (country), 271
Germany, 32, 38, 42, 46–47, 55, 59n46
Gilbert, Elizabeth, 259
Ginsburg, Ruth Bader, 18
Goldberg v. Kelly (1970), 209, 227n36
Goldsmith, Jack, 51
Gonzales, Jessica. *See* domestic violence
  restraining orders
Good Morning America (TV show), 17
Gore, Al, 250
government exception doctrine to class actions,
  in New York State, 224n11, 227n37
government lawyers in Sweden and US, crisis
  training for, 7, 290–307, 390; AIC (Advice in
  Crisis) Project, 286–87, 290–94, 304–7, 341,
  392; clients, identifying, 382–83; communica-
  tions challenges, 386–87; GAIN good practice
  model, FEMA, 293–94, 295–97, 305; PREP
  good practice model, FEMA, 293, 294–95, 305;
  SALT performance standard, 292–93, 306, 351;
  skills needed from lawyers by FEMA, 291–94;
  SOAP good practice model, FEMA, 293, 297–
  303, 305; Swedish initiative, 303–6
Grant v. Cuomo (1987), 225n18
Gray, Freddie, 73
Great Barrier Reef, Australia, 201
Great Depression, 207, 208, 230
Great Recession (2008), 230, 365
Greater New Orleans Community Data Center,
  182
Green, Joyce Hens, 42, 43
Greyhound Therapy, 226n22
Guantánamo Bay Bar Association, 43, 54, 387
Guantánamo detainees, 6, 32–55; access to
  clients, 41–42, 386; CCR (Center for Constitutional Rights) and, 33, 34, 37–48, 51, 54,
  57n20; habeas corpus petitions, 34, 38–48,
  56n7; Haitian refugees, 57n18, 337; history
  and background, 33–35; hunger strikes,
  50–51; interrogation/torture programs and,
  33, 35–36, 40, 45, 51, 56n8; Murat Kurnaz
  case, 32–33, 42, 45, 46–47, 54–55, 58–59n46;
  Adnan Latif case, 49, 50; lawyer conflicts
  of interest/values and, 385–86; legal lessons
  learned from, 34–35, 51–55; logic for holding
  as enemy combatants, 35–37, 40–41, 43, 55n5,
  58n34; monsters, cast as, 33, 36, 45; Supreme

Court decisions regarding, 33, 34, 40–41, 47–
  51, 60n59, 61n79; victory and legal/political
  retrenchment on, 34, 47–51; wholesale and
  retail lawyering processes in, 43–48
Guantánamo Review Task Force, 48, 50
Guatemala, 325, 326–27
Gutierrex, Gita, 44

habeas corpus petitions: defined, 319; for
  Guantánamo detainees, 34, 38–48, 56n7; for
  immigrant detainees, 314, 316, 319–21, 334
Haiti, 278–80, 288n38, 299
Haitian refugees interned at Guantánamo,
  57n18, 337
Halifax Disaster (1917), 3
Hamdan v. Rumsfeld (2006), 59n55
Hamilton, Alexander, 40
Hansen, James, 193
Hansford, Justin, 97
Harrison, John, 117
Harvard Business Review, 230
Harvard Law School Executive Education lead-
  ership programs, 341, 346, 353, 355n25
Harvard School of Public Health, 340
Hayes, Richard E., 5
Hayes, Robert, 208, 209, 228n43
hazard mitigation planning, 172
health. *See* medicine and health
Health Bucks, 233
Healthy Savings Program, 233
Heard v. Cuomo (1987), 213, 217, 219, 220
heat wave, NYC (2006), 195–96
Heifetz, Ron, 350
Heisig, Eric, 105n41
Heller, Becca, 318, 338n1
Her Justice, 131
Hicks, David, 46
Hispanic/Latinx community, 14, 82, 137, 151, 367
HIV/AIDs and homelessness, 211, 214–17
Holder, Eric, 64, 66, 67–68, 70
Homan, Thomas, 129
HOME TRUTH (film), 26, 27, 28
Homeland Security. *See* Department of Home-
  land Security
homelessness, 7, 207–23; *Callahan* consent
  decree, terms of, 210, 224–25n15; character-
  ization of legal agenda, 217–18; children and
  youth, runaway and homeless, 356–58, 371;
  defined, 223n2; effectiveness of litigation
  strategy, 220–21; elections and voting rights,
  222; "end" of crisis, determining, 222–23; factors to be considered in litigating, 218–19;

Maduro, Nicolás, 123

Magna Carta, 37, 38, 53

major disasters. *See* disasters and disaster recovery

Malaysia, 122

managing up and managing across, 345

Manning, Stephen, 152, 158

Margulies, Joe, 36, 37, 40, 41, 42, 55–56n6

Margulies, Peter, 9n2

Marines, leadership training for, 352–53

Maritime Event Response Protocol (MERP), Canada, 271–73, 281

Maritime Operational Threat Response Plan (MOTR), United States, 271–73, 288n43, 390

maritime response networks, 270–72, 388, 390, 391–92. *See also* multiagency crisis coordination

Marks, Lawrence, 136, 139

Marshall, John Travis, 7, 166, 388–89, 392, 394, 400

Marshall, Thurgood, 250

Martensson, Per-Åke, 7, 290, 303, 305, 400

The Martian (film), 376

Martin, Emily, 20

Matos, Kica, 325

McCain, John, 48, 108

McCain v. Koch (1987), 211, 216, 225n18

McCraw, David, 6, 108, 116, 383, 400

McCulloch, Robert P., 71

McKesson, DeRay, 97

McKibben, Bill, *The End of Nature,* 193

McNally, Terrence, 228n46

meaning-making, 5, 392–93

media lawyering and protection of journalists, 6, 108–24; deaths, injuries, and detentions, 118–19; decline of newspaper industry, 108, 124–25n2; disappearance/detention of 4 journalists in Libya, 118–21; Farrell/Munadi kidnapping, in Afghanistan, 116–18, 126n15; Foley/Sotloff hostage-taking and execution, in Syria, 108, 115, 121; hybrid legal and operational role of lawyer, 112–15; lessons learned from, 124; news organizations compared to other corporations, 113–14; presidential anti-media rhetoric and, 122–23; ransom payments, 112, 114–15, 117–18, 125n9, 125nn6–7; rise of social media, 109; Rohde kidnapping and recovery, in Afghanistan, 109–18; security protocols, establishing, 121–22; skills required for, 109–16

media relations in crisis situations, 363

media scrutiny of postdisaster lawyering, 173–77

medicine and health: health inequalities, 231–33, 236–37; malpractice claims, 370–71; medical crisis standards, 384; SDOH (social determinants of health), 231, 237

Mennonite Disaster Service, 298

mental illness: deinstitutionalization movement, 226n23, 226n26; homelessness and, 208, 211–14, 219, 220, 225–26nn20–23; involuntary hospitalization for, 226–27n28; youth and children, runaway and homeless, 356

Merkel, Angela, 46

MERP (Maritime Event Response Protocol), Canada, 271–73, 281

MERP/MOTR Strategic Protocol, Canada/US, 272–73

meta-leadership model, 340–41, 344–45, 349

#MeToo movement, 14, 366

Mexico, 319

Military Commissions Act, 44, 47

mind-set shifting, 351

Mixon v. Grinker (1995), 215–17, 219, 221

Mori, Dan, 46

MOTR (Maritime Operational Threat Response Plan), United States, 271–73, 288n43, 390

Movement for Black Lives, 239

Mowat, Farley, 280

Moynihan, Daniel Patrick, 193

MSNBC, 373

Mukherjee, Elora, 339n5

Mukunda, Gautum, 230

multiagency crisis coordination, 7, 269–85; CSAV *RIO Pueblo* biological threat, 276–78, 280; definition of coordination, 286n9; education and training in, 269–70, 281–82; *FARLEY MOWAT* environmental conservation ship, 280–81; FEMA and, 388; Hurricane Katrina, 287n25, 287n29; maritime response networks, 270–72, 388, 390, 391–92; *M/V NORDIC* drug trafficking case, 278–80; "Rules for Crisis Lawyering in a Multi-Agency Environment," 270, 281–84; *SUN-SEA* migrant ship, 274–76, 280; terminology developed for, 270; Tianjin (China) explosion, 272–73, 276; validating and sharing information, problems with, 275–76, 277–78, 279–80

Munadi, Sultan, 116–18, 126n15

Muslim travel ban, 1, 7, 152–53, 311–12, 318–24, 331, 332, 334–35, 338

M/V NORDIC drug trafficking case, 278–80

Myanmar, 123

Nadler, Jerry, 27

Nagin, C. Ray, 176

Nancy Grace (TV show), 17

Nangwaya, Ajamu, 247n7

www.ingramcontent.com/pod-product-compliance
Lightning Source LLC
Chambersburg PA
CBHW030449210326
41597CB00013B/602